Time Out London

LONDON'S BEST SHOPS

timeout.com

Time Out London

Printer St Ives, Roche, Cornwall PL26 8LX.

Time Out Group uses paper products that are environmentally friendly, from well managed forests and mills that use certified (PEFC) Chain of Custody pulp in their production.

ISBN 978-1-905-04248-7
ISSN 1752-6167

Distribution by Comag Specialist (01895 433 800).
For further distribution details, see www.timeout.com.

While every effort and care has been made to ensure the accuracy of the information contained in this publication, the publisher cannot accept responsibility for any errors it may contain. All rights reserved. No part of this publication may be reproduced, stored in a retrieval system, or transmitted in any form or by any means, electronic, mechanical, photocopying, recording or otherwise, without prior permission of Time Out Group Ltd.

© Copyright Time Out Group Ltd 2010

LINES storage furniture. Design: Peter Maly. **ligne roset**
www.ligne-roset-westend.co.uk

Live beautifully.

Ligne Roset Westend | 020 7323 1248
23/25 Mortimer St, London W1T 3JE

Published by
Time Out Guides Limited
Universal House
251 Tottenham Court Road
London W1T 7AB
Tel +44 (0)20 7813 3000
Fax +44 (0)20 7813 6001
email guides@timeout.com
www.timeout.com

Editorial
Editor Anna Norman
Deputy Editor Jan Fuscoe
Copy Editor Edoardo Albert
Listings Editors William Crow, Gemma Pritchard
Proofreader Patrick Mulkern
Indexer William Crow

Managing Director Peter Fiennes
Editorial Director Sarah Guy
Series Editor Cath Phillips
Business Manager Daniel Allen
Editorial Manager Holly Pick
Assistant Management Accountant Ija Krasnikova

Design
Art Director Scott Moore
Art Editor Pinelope Kourmouzoglou
Senior Designer Kei Ishimaru
Guides Commercial Designer Jodi Sher

Picture Desk
Picture Editor Jael Marschner
Picture Desk Assistant/Researcher Ben Rowe

Advertising
New Business & Commercial Director Mark Phillips
Magazine & UK Guides Commercial Director St John Betteridge
Account Managers Jessica Baldwin, Michelle Daburn, Ben Holt
Production Controller Chris Pastfield
Copy Controller Alison Bourke

Marketing
Sales & Marketing Director, North America & Latin America Lisa Levinson
Group Commercial Art Director Anthony Huggins
Circulation & Distribution Manager Dan Collins
Marketing Co-ordinator Alana Benton

Production
Group Production Director Mark Lamond
Production Manager Brendan McKeown
Production Controller Damian Bennett
Production Assistant Katie Mulhern

Time Out Group
Director & Founder Tony Elliott
Chief Executive Officer David King
Group Financial Director Paul Rakkar
Group General Manager/Director Nichola Coulthard
Time Out Communications Ltd MD David Pepper
Time Out International Ltd MD Cathy Runciman
Time Out Magazine Ltd Publisher/MD Mark Elliott
Group Commercial Director Graeme Tottle
Group IT Director Simon Chappell

Sections in this guide were written by
Trading Places Dan Jones. **A suit to behold** Jeff Kuntz. **Shop talk interviews** Edwina Attlee. **Streetwise features** Edwina Attlee (Cecil Court), Katie Cordell (Columbia Road), Jeff Kuntz (Denmark Street), Anna Norman (Broadway Market), Daniel Smith (Camden Passage, Mount Street).
New shops reviews by Edoardo Albert, Jan Fuscoe, Dan Jones, Daniela Morosini, Anna Norman.

The Editor would like to thank Edwina Attlee, Jeff Kuntz, Dan Jones, Daniela Morosini, Elizabeth Winding, and all previous contributors to the Time Out Shops & Services guide (edition 14), whose work forms the basis for parts of this book.

Maps London Underground map supplied by Transport for London. London Overview map by JS Graphics (john@jsgraphics.co.uk).

Cover photography Jonathan Knowles
Products Leica X1 digital camera courtesy of Leica www.leica-storemayfair.co.uk; Noah Sandals courtesy of Georgina Goodman, www.georginagoodman.com; Ringstead Patchwork Cushion courtesy of Aubin & Wills, www.aubinandwills.com; selection of shower gels courtesy of Ortigia, www.ortigia-srl.com; Tea Service Cookie Stand courtesy of Anthropologie, www.anthropologie.eu; cupcake courtesy of Peyton & Byrne, www.peytonandbyrne.co.uk; mini cupcake courtesy of the Hummingbird Bakery, www.hummingbirdbakery.com.

Contents photography Pages 13, 14 (left), 15 (top), 35, 36, 49, 50, 51, 52, 72, 196 Ed Marshall; pages 14 (right), 15 (bottom), 27, 42, 67, 96, 112 (bottom left), 138 (centre), 147, 180, 229, 230, 234 Rob Greig; pages 21 (left), 25, 33, 44, 47, 54 (right), 68, 80, 81, 102, 105, 108, 110, 114, 123 (bottom), 129, 132, 133, 135, 136, 151, 160, 162, 171, 189 (centre), 190, 202, 215, 218, 243 (centre), 220, 226, 240, 252, 253, 262 (right), 268 Britta Jaschinski; pages 21 (centre), 26, 40, 54 (left), 64, 77, 90, 91, 93, 112, 115, 122, 139, 150, 154, 191, 195, 198, 204, 210, 217, 236, 245, 254, 257 Michelle Grant; page 21 (right) Katy Peters; pages 22, 104, 138 (right), 153, 159, 177, 179, 183, 185, 189 (left), 194, 222, 260, 264 Gemma Day; pages 224, 231 Anna Norman; page 24 (top left) Jonathan Perugia; page 24 (top left) Scott Wishart; page 24 (bottom left) Olivia Rutherford; page 24 (bottom right) Oliver Knight; page 97 Jonas Rodin; page 123 (top) Iove K Breitstein; pages 28, 30, 71, 75, 94, 95, 106, 111, 127, 165, 173, 193, 203, 235, 239, 259 Ben Rowe; page 29 Susannah Stone; pages 37, 57, 59, 60, 61, 70, 73, 99, 119, 159 (left), 161, 166, 169, 170, 172, 186, 189 (right), 197, 206, 207, 209, 211, 212, 214, 219, 228, 233, 238 Ming Tang-Evans; page 48 Katie Peters; page 124 courtesy of Sanderson & Nina Saunders, photos by Uli Schade; pages 138 (left), 144, 145, 243 (left), 244, 248 Alys Tomlinson; page 184 Susie Rea; pages 215, 243 (right), 249, 250, 258, 262, 266, 267 Heloise Bergman; page 216 Sean Gallagher; page 223 Marzena Zoladz; page 246 Magnus Andersson; page 251 www.jasonalden.com; page 255 Jitka Hynkova.

The following images were provided by the featured establishments/artists: pages 17, 34, 38, 39, 43, 54 (centre), 74, 76, 79, 82, 84, 85, 86, 87, 88, 107, 117, 118, 126, 148, 149, 199, 163.

© Copyright Time Out Group Ltd 2010

Introduction

With its grand department stores, avant-garde boutiques, vibrant markets, glamorous designer flagships and classic book, record and accessories shops, London will always be one of the world's most exciting cities for shopping. Its size and diversity can, however, make it an overwhelming – not to mention exhausting – place in which to flex the plastic. To save you pounding the busy streets in search of the often quite hidden gems, our knowledgeable team of shopping experts has narrowed the huge number of London shops down to around 500 of the very best – places that aren't just marketplaces, but which engage customers through lovely interiors, exemplary service, original products and a personal atmosphere.

Independent shops exemplify this experience-led spirit better than the large chain stores (the best of which aren't far behind, however), which is why we've chosen to include so many of them in this guide. From traditional old faves such as Soho's Lina Stores, to newcomers like Smug on Camden Passage, London's indie shops are getting better and better, despite some sad recession-induced closures. Our **Shop talk** interviews illuminate what it's like to own an independent shop in London, and show that, despite unstable economic conditions, things are looking fairly positive for the city's dedicated shopkeepers. Opening a small business is always going to pose a degree of financial risk, but the fact that so many enterprising folk are still prepared to take that risk is testament to their faith that a sizeable number of city dwellers and visitors will be there to support them. And, as Dan Jones shows in his feature on page 13, this support appears to be increasing, with the growth of an experience-fused shopping scene led by the capital's concept stores and pop-up shops. Our **Streetwise** features flag up shopping streets containing a high number of these places, and which are therefore some of the most enjoyable places in which to shop. They also highlight the chasm that has formed between the high street and the indie boutiques.

London has long been associated with cutting-edge fashion and design, but these scenes have become especially active of late, spawning a plethora of avant-garde boutiques, as well as making the city's host of art and design bookshops – such as Artwords, which recently opened a branch on Hackney's Broadway Market – increasingly bustling spots. Like the food industry, the clothing sector has been under the eco spotlight over the past few years, and, consequently, a more eco-minded brand of consumerism has been developing. The number of shops led by ethical and green principles is still in a minority, but the opening of the achingly trendy yet sustainably driven 123 Boutique (*see p42*) in 2010 gives us reason to remain hopeful. Our list of green shops on pages 144 and 145 flags up other contenders for the prize of most eco-conscious London store.

One good way to shop more ethically, of course, is to buy second-hand, and London's vintage and thrift shops are looking stronger than ever; Merchant Archive opened in Queen's Park in 2010, selling a range of well-edited pieces, while the east's Beyond Retro continues to inspire new vintage openings on and around Brick Lane.

There may have been a tightening of belts over the past few years due to the economic doom and gloom, but, partly as a consequence of this, many of us have become more discerning about where we shop. This guide will help you get to the heart of the city's exciting consumer culture and discover its myriad of lovely stores. Happy shopping!

Anna Norman, Editor

FILLING THE TOWN WITH ARTISTS

£4.95 LETRASET PROMARKER SET OF 5 RRP £10.45

PREMIER PORTFOLIO BLACK FITTINGS
A1 RRP £76.10 CASS £49.95
A2 RRP £54.65 CASS £32.50
A3 RRP £38.80 CASS £22.50
A4 RRP £28.55 CASS £19.95

£8.95 WINSOR & NEWTON WINTON OIL 200ML TITANIUM WHITE DOUBLE PACK RRP £22

£39.95 DALER ROWNEY COTSWOLD EASEL RRP £130.10

£6.95 FABER CASTELL 9000 8B-2H 12 DRAWING PENCILS RRP £13.75

£6.95 SEAWHITE A5 CONCERTINA SKETCHBOOK 70 PAGES 140GSM

£49.95 WINSOR & NEWTON THAMES RADIAL EASEL RRP £162

£12.95 CASS ART HOG BRUSH PACK SET OF 6 RRP £21.20

£4.35 DALER-ROWNEY SYSTEM 3 ACRYLIC 250ML POT ALL COLOURS RRP £8.75

£10.50 WINSOR & NEWTON HENRY & WILLIAM COLLECTION INK SET OF 8X14ML RRP £22

£10.50 CASS ART SYNTHETIC BRUSH PACK SET OF 6 RRP £28.50

£10.50 CASS ART SABLE BRUSH PACK SET OF 5 RRP £28.50

£24 LIQUITEX ACRYLIC BASICS SET 48 x 22ML SET RRP £49.95

WINSOR & NEWTON ARTIST ACRYLIC 60ML
SERIES 1 RRP £5.99 CASS £3.95
SERIES 2 RRP £8.50 CASS £4.50
SERIES 3 RRP £11.95 CASS £5.95
SERIES 4 RRP £12.75 CASS £8.50
SERIES 5 RRP £12.75 CASS £8.85

£39.95 DALER-ROWNEY SCREEN PRINTING KIT RRP £79.85

£3.95 DALER-ROWNEY OIL PASTEL SET OF 24 RRP £10.45

CASS PROMISE – CREATIVITY AT THE LOWEST PRICES. WE'RE CONFIDENT OUR PRICES CAN'T BE BEATEN

PHTHALO TURQUOISE | QUINACRIDONE MAGENTA | VIRIDIAN | SCARLET LAKE

SPEND OVER £30 AND GET ONE OF OUR FOUR FREE BAGS

FLAGSHIP STORE: 66-67 COLEBROOKE ROW ISLINGTON N1 020 7354 2999

ALSO AT: 13 CHARING CROSS RD WC2 (NEXT TO THE NATIONAL GALLERY), 24 BERWICK ST W1, 220 KENSINGTON HIGH ST W8 AND 58-62 HEATH STREET NW3, HAMPSTEAD STORE OPENING IN SEPTEMBER 2010. ALL STORES OPEN 7 DAYS WWW.CASSART.CO.UK

CASS ART LONDON

PRICE SUBJECT TO CHANGE AND AVAILABILITY. PRICES VALID AT 01/06/10.

About the Guide

This guide to London's shops isn't meant to be completely comprehensive; instead, we have tried to select what we believe are the very best of the capital's shops. If you feel we've missed somewhere exceptional, or included a place that's gone downhill, please email us at guides@timeout.com.

Opening hours
Although many of the shops, companies and individuals listed in this guide keep regular store hours, others are small concerns run from private addresses or workshops that have erratic opening hours, or are open by appointment only. In such cases, the times given are a guide as to when to phone, not when to visit.

The opening times were correct at the time of going to press, but if you're going out of your way to visit a particular shop, always phone first to check (especially as stores are constantly launching and closing down in London). Many outlets extend their opening times in summer to benefit from tourist traffic and in the run-up to Christmas. Some are closed on bank holidays or have reduced opening times.

Credit cards and abbreviations
Most shops featured in this book accept all of the major credit cards; if they don't accept plastic, we have indicated this in the listings. Some larger shops and department stores accept euros as well as sterling. For shops in this guide that sell clothes and/or fashion accessories, we have indicated whether they sell menswear and/or womenswear with the letters **M** and **W**, respectively. Childrenswear is represented by a **C**.

Prices
Any prices listed in this guide were accurate at the time of writing, but are subject to change.

Mail order & online
Many of the shops listed have online ordering services; visit their websites for details.

Branches
We have included details for shops' London branches after the listings and in the A-Z Index. For shops with branches throughout the city, please see the phone directory or the shop's website for the location of your nearest. Note that branches may have different opening hours from the reviewed shop, so it is advisable to call to check times before visiting.

Hot 50
While all of the shops listed are recommended – by virtue of their inclusion in a guide to London's best shops – we have selected 50 that are especially interesting or appealing to us at the moment. These are highlighted by a HOT 50 symbol. See page 10 for the full list.

Contents

One-Stop

Department Stores	**21**
Shopping Centres & Arcades	**28**
Concept Stores & Lifestyle Boutiques	**35**
Markets	**46**

Fashion

Indie Boutiques	**56**
High Street	**76**
Designer Chains	**85**
Tailoring & Bespoke	**95**
Vintage & Second-hand	**98**
Lingerie, Swimwear & Erotica	**107**
Weddings	**115**
Maternity & Unusual Sizes	**117**
Shoes	**119**
Jewellery & Accessories	**128**

Health & Beauty

Skincare & Cosmetics	**138**
Perfumeries & Herbalists	**146**
Eyewear	**153**

Home

Furniture & Homewares	**159**
Vintage Furniture & Homewares	**175**
Gardens & Flowers	**183**

Leisure

Books	**189**
CDs & Records	**201**
Electronics & Photography	**208**
Crafts, Hobbies & Parties	**214**
Musical Instruments	**225**
Sport & Fitness	**232**
Pets	**240**

Food & Drink

Food	243
Drink	256

Babies & Children

Babies & Children	262

Indexes & Maps

A-Z Index	270
London Underground Map	287
Central London Overview Map	288

Features

Trading Places: London's Shopping Scene	**13**
Streetwise features:	
Ledbury Road	75
Mount Street	94
Camden Passage	106
Columbia Road	173
Cecil Court	199
Broadway Market	224
Denmark Street	231
Lamb's Conduit Street	239
Shop talk interviews:	
Lizzie Evans (Smug)	43
Francesca Forcolini (Labour of Love)	71
Charles Boyd-Bowman (Alexander Boyd)	95
Astrid Blake (Alice & Astrid)	111
Richard Ward (Wawa)	165
Ben Hillwood-Harris (Artwords)	193
Simon Singleton (Pure Groove)	203
Rob Sargent (Sargent & Co)	235
Catherine Conway (Unpackaged)	251
Jamie Hutchinson (The Samper)	259

Time Out's Hot 50

We've selected 50 shops that offer some of the most interesting consumer experiences in London right now. They are not necessarily better than other shops featured in this book, but each one has tapped into the consumer zeitgeist – whether consciously, as with some of the avant-garde concept stores, or accidently, through being old independents that we've fallen in love with again. Each shop review is marked with a **HOT 50** symbol in the relevant chapter of the guide.

Aesop
Skincare & Cosmetics p138.
The no-nonsense skincare brand is a hit for its quality products and divine scents.

Algerian Coffee Stores
Drink p258.
A latte at this much-loved Soho old-timer is only £1.10!

Ally Capellino
Jewellery & Accessories p128.
London's favourite bag designer celebrated her 30th anniversary in 2010.

Anthropologie
Concept Stores & Lifestyle Boutiques p35.
This US import is a must-visit for its shop displays, cute homewares and feminine garb.

Apartment C
Lingerie, Swimwear & Erotica p107.
London's most stylish lingerie shop has made Marylebone its home.

Apple Store
Electronics & Photography p208.
iPads, iPods, iPhones galore.

Aria
Furniture & Homewares p160.
Über-modern furniture and accessories in a stylish space.

Artwords
Books p192.
This contemporary art bookshop now has a larger branch on Broadway Market.

Aubin & Wills
Concept Stores & Lifestyle Boutiques p35.
Redchurch Street has changed forever with the opening of this Brit concept store.

B store
Indie Boutiques p56.
A showcase of London's most innovative fashion labels.

Beyond Retro
Vintage & Second-hand p98.
The city's top spot for second-hand garb.

Black Truffle
Shoes p119.
Gorgeous shoes, bags, tights, hats and jewellery.

Bobbin Bicycles
Sport & Fitness p232.
The shop to visit for classic sit-up-and-beg style rides.

Browns/Browns Focus
Indie Boutiques p56.
At the forefront of fashion for decades, Browns is still going strong.

Caravan
Furniture & Homewares p167.
Emily Chambers' vintage home accessories shop is a joy to browse.

Coco de Mer
Lingerie, Swimwear & Erotica p110.
London's most glamorous erotic emporium.

Darkroom
Concept Stores & Lifestyle Boutiques p39.
One of the latest concept stores to dazzle us with cool products and an arty interior.

Daunt Books
Books p190.
One of the best bookshops in town, with top travel, literary and children's sections.

Diverse
Indie Boutiques p56.
This N1 boutique has a top selection of stylish labels.

Dover Street Market
Concept Stores & Lifestyle Boutiques p39.
The Comme des Garçons shop that led the way for the concept store phenomenon.

Duke of Uke
Musical Instruments p227.
The ukelele trend continues.

Fortnum & Mason
Department Stores p21.
This legendary department store marries tradition and innovation perfectly.

Foyles
Books p190.
Hugely comprehensive, Foyles is a must for those who like a good old browse.

Goodhood
Indie Boutiques p59.
East London's fave clothes boutique for on-trend garb.

Honest Jon's
CDs & Records p206.
An old and beloved record store that's still going strong.

Hurwundeki
Indie Boutiques p61.
Directional fashion at affordable prices.

John Sandoe
Books p191.
Local bookshops like this are sadly a dying breed.

Kabiri
Jewellery & Accessories p134.
The cream of jewellery design.

KJ's Laundry
Indie Boutiques p70.
A lovely Marylebone boutique.

Kokon to Zai
Indie Boutiques p63.
Wierd and wonderful fashion.

L Cornelissen & Son
Crafts, Hobbies & Partics p215.
This quaint art supplies shop resembles an old apothecary.

Labour of Love
Indie Boutiques p73.
A true independent that promotes style over trends.

Le Labo
Perfumeries & Herbalists p146.
This US perfumerie sells personalised, top-quality scents from a slick space.

Liberty
Department Stores p25.
This much-loved department store is a symbol of London.

Lomography shop
Electronics & Photography p213.
Join the backlash against too-perfect digital photos.

Loop
Crafts, Hobbies & Parties p220.
Spearheaded our new-found crush on crafts and nostalgia.

Louis Vuitton Maison
Designer Chains p88.
The LV flagship is as much an experience as a shop.

Merchant Archive
Vintage & Second-hand p101.
The best vintagewear in town.

123 Boutique
Concept Stores & Lifestyle Boutiques p42.
The east's Dover Street Market, but with an eco slant.

Pure Groove
CDs & Records p206.
A pioneer (with Rough Trade) of the in-store gigs trend.

Rough Trade East
CDs & Records p201.
London's best record shop, for its stock and its vibe.

Sasti
Babies & Children p267.
Stylish clothes for children at non-ridiculous prices.

Selfridges
Department Stores p27.
London's most fashion-forward department store.

The Sampler
Drink p256.
Sample as you shop at this Islington wine store.

Tokyo Fixed
Sport & Fitness p234.
The latest hotspot for fixed-gear bike obsessives.

Topshop
High Street p81.
Still queen of the high street.

Tracey Neuls
Shoes p126.
Timeless yet trendy footwear.

Twentytwentyone
Furniture & Homewares p164.
Vintage originals, design classics and modern styles.

Unpackaged
Food p251.
Produce without packaging.

Urban Outfitters
High Street p82.
UO's boutique floors hold all the best fashion labels.

OXO

BE INSPIRED
BE UNIQUE
BE DIFFERENT

INNOVATIVE DESIGN
DESTINATION DINING

New Wedding by design gift list service

30 independent design shops
accessories, art & design, ceramics, fashion, furniture, gifts, interiors, jewellery, lighting, products & textiles

Open Tues–Sun 11am–6pm
Free exhibitions open daily
Cafes, restaurants & bars open daily till late

Find us on the riverside walkway between the Southbank Centre & Tate Modern. A few minutes from Waterloo or Southwark tubes

Oxo Tower Wharf, Bargehouse Street,
South Bank, London SE1 9PH
24 hour information line 020 7021 1686

www.coinstreet.org/shopeatdrink

Coat by Lauren Shanley
Pantone bag by W2 Whitbread & Wilkinson
Stem vase by Innermost
Rings by Alan Vallis

Oxo Tower Wharf is owned and managed by

Coin Street community builders

14 Hinde Street
London W1U 3BG

36 New Bond Street
London W1S 2RP

othercriteria
.com

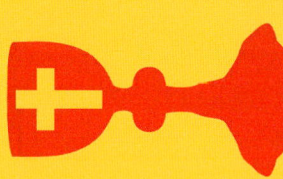

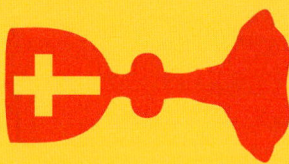

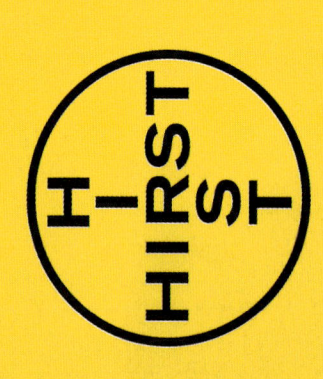

HIRST

Other Criteria

Trading Places: London's Shopping Scene

Has the recession altered London's shopping landscape for the better? **Dan Jones**, *Time Out London*'s Shopping & Style editor, looks at the impact of the financial crisis on the city's consumer culture.

London shoppers are a tenacious bunch. We'll brave Topshop on a Saturday afternoon, storm Selfridges for the latest beauty launch, queue up in the rain outside sample sales at the Truman Brewery, rummage through bin bags at retro jumble sales, and even cause a riot for cheap leggings outside an American Apparel sale on Brick Lane.

But in the depths of recession, it was hard to gauge how our shopping habits might change, and what the long-term effects might be. One thing is certain: London's shopping landscape has changed. Not only has the recession snuffed out a host of independents (including Koh Samui, A Butcher of Distinction, Murder One bookshop and Uptown Records), but it also felled high street behemoths Zavvi and Borders, leaving gaping holes on our favourite shopping streets. The financial freefall saw us collectively baulk at the idea of luxury – we'd hide our Swarovski-encrusted BlackBerries and cancel invites to degustation dinners, and those £2,000 Gucci it-bags suddenly seemed, well, a bit gauche when you could hang an unbleached cotton tote from your shoulder. At London Fashion Week, meanwhile, designers created appropriately boring-but-worthy clothes and cancelled parties in deference to the crisis, or alternatively offered hyper-colourful collections to distract us from the fact that we could no longer afford them.

Dr Marten's pop-up shop, Spitalfields

But even before the recession we had begun to eschew mass-produced products, developing a crush on crafts and nostalgia, heritage and ethical brands. Home-made bunting was hoisted, tea was sipped from vintage teacups across the city and sites like www.etsy.com became our ever more popular gateway to handmade goods. The financial crisis only exaggerated this trend. Sustainability was no longer a dirty word, and we became adept at hunting out pop-up shops, supper clubs and the Hidden Tea Room. We promised that from now on we would take a packed lunch to work, recycle our potato peelings and crochet our own undies, guilt-free. Shops such as Unpackaged (*see p250* and *p251* **Shop talk**), the lovely Islington food shop that eschews all packaging, have led the way in this area. And new green initiatives continue to open, the lastest being the achingly avant-garde and eco-friendly 123 Boutique (*see p42*) concept store at the top of east London's Brick Lane.

For all our good intentions, though, we haven't quite matched up to our ideals, and we're coming out of the financial gloom a little befuddled. We just can't relinquish our love for hardcore, plastic-swiping shopping. And, although we continue to express our love of independent shops, we're also back on the high street, tempted by cleverer and more irresistible deals, sharpening our elbows for the usual summer and winter sales stampedes. What we want, it seems, is something to bridge the gap between art and commerce. We want ethical, affordable and meaningful products, and the sugar-rush of shopping in the world's most exciting city.

Undoubtedly the most important post-recession, indie retail phenomenon of late is the pop-up shop. At any given time, the city is now peppered with temporary shops that have taken advantage of the burgeoning number of empty units, paying nominal rent and burning brightly for a brief period before packing up and moving on. Many are projects of leftfield hipster groups like Swanfield (www.myspace.com/swanfieldinn) – a reoccurring pop-up that has appeared in both east London and Soho – that offer specialist, artisan stock; then there's Idea Books (www.idea-books.com), the excellent vintage style and fashion book and magazine seller that has held residencies in Covent Garden's St Martin's Lane hotel; and Jeanette's (www.jeanettesshop.blogspot.com), once east London's most avant-garde boutique, hidden in a garage on Redchurch Street, near Brick Lane, now a temporary project appearing at Somerset House during London Fashion Week and most recently within Hoxton boutique Start.

Other pop-ups are marketing stunts masterminded by creative agencies attempting to add a little hipster kudos to well-known brands. Nike's 1948 (*see p127*) pop-up shop

123 Boutique

Trading Places: London's Shopping Scene

Anthropologie

123 Boutique

has been such a success that it's looking to remain a feature of Shoreditch for the foreseeable future. Either way, it's made for a creative and interesting shopping landscape that's always changing, and it's the focus on a shopping 'experience' that resounds with the city's consumers. Uptight boutiques that make you feel like you're in *Pretty Woman* are slipping out of fashion, with shopping in London increasingly focused on the shopper's whole encounter, rather than a quick buy.

Anthropologie (*see p35*), a Brit reworking of an American chain, understands this perfectly. Since its launch on Regent Street in October 2009, and its second opening on the King's Road in March 2010, it has battled London cynicism with ruffles, bows and cute home accessories. Its crafty approach to its stock means that almost everything feels artisanal and handmade, from the necklaces adorned with puppies to the lobster motif short shorts – only on a jaw-dropping scale, in London's most breathtaking shop interior (the Regent Street store, for example, has a 1,500 square foot 'living wall' of plants). It's a brand that thinks big and small at the same time.

Liberty, London's most beloved mock-Tudor masterpiece, also battled the recession in a rather inspired way. Its revamp, or 'renaissance' as they liked to call it, was masterminded in part by creative consultant and unofficial store muse

London Captured

Stunning photography through the ages.

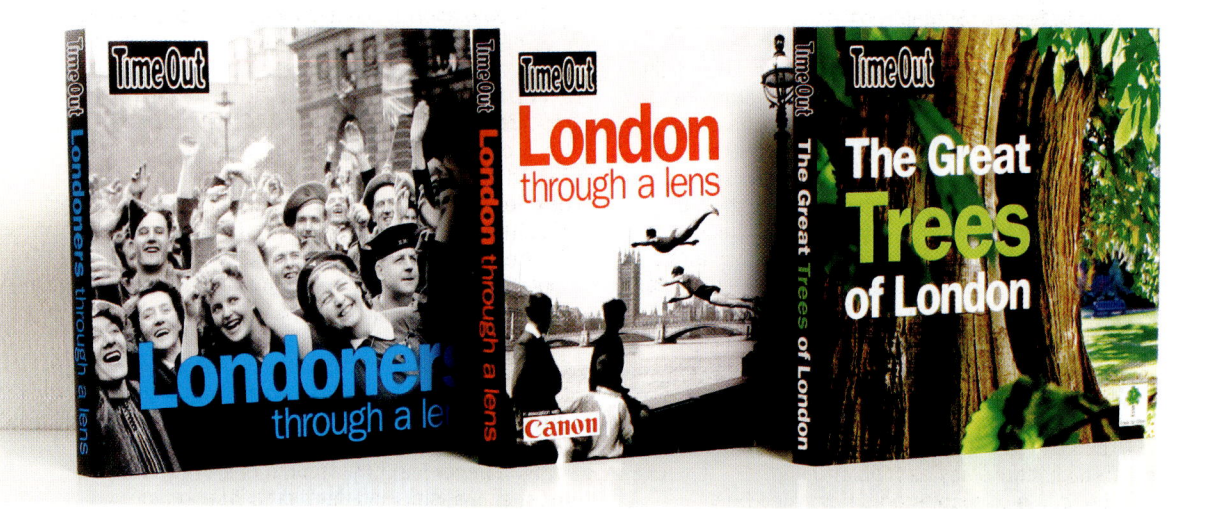

**TIME OUT GUIDES
WRITTEN BY
LOCAL EXPERTS**
visit timeout.com/shop

Time Out Guides

Trading Places: London's Shopping Scene

Nike's 1948 pop-up shop

Yasmin Sewell. She not only negotiated any number of hipster labels and exclusives back into the store, but also underlined its personality. It's now packed with idiosyncratic whatnots and collaborations, which have garnered it a new floral-obsessed fan base across the globe.

But one department store seemed to weather the recession better than any other. With the opening of 3rd Central, a huge new fashion concept on the third floor, Selfridges saw a raft of must-have labels hit the store, from Alexander Wang to Chloë Sevigny for Opening Ceremony and Christopher Kane. It sidestepped luxury and focused on the ultra-hip (even if the prices are the same). Inspired events underpinned this move – and the iconic store used appearances from fashion bloggers and TheSelby.com's creator Todd Selby as hipster bait.

London's concept stores have also been successful in weathering the economic storm, becoming a successful new strand of shop that is now identifiable by the average London shopper. From independent accessories boutique Darkroom (*see p39*) on independents-heavy Lamb's Conduit Street (which displays its stock as though it's art), to continually changing concessions in the Shop at Bluebird (*see p45*) and Dover Street Market (*see p39*) – Comme des Garçons' epicentre of leftfield fashion – concept stores have redefined the shopping experience and raised Londoners' expectations when it comes to spending our hard-earned pennies. The latter store, in particular, is less a market and more a hushed gallery of fashion – the rarity of its stock, its artful projects and sprawling interior mark it out as utterly unique. In London's concept stores, the shopping 'experience' is a marketable commodity.

Limited edition and designer collaborations have swamped high street stores, and we continue to buy celeb-branded fashion lines. As Topshop, Evans and even Wallis collaborate with portly singers and it-models, stores like Debenhams (www.debenhams.com), which has a flagship on Oxford Street, take the collaboration idea to the next level. With concessions by Henry Holland, Matthew Williamson and lingerie by Sadie Frost, it's the *Heat* magazine of department stores.

We have also fallen back in love with London's best markets, haggling over anything from wonky organic carrots to vintage jumpsuits, splashing cash at Portobello Market and Brick Lane and trying to ignore the freshly opened high street brands (trying to muscle in on the action) on our favourite market streets. Broadway Market (*see p224* **Streetwise**) has become one of London's most successful models of gentrification: a textbook 'how to' in reviving the forgotten corners of the city. Local residents reopened the market in 2004 and it is now swollen with gourmet foods and vintage clothing, alongside the more traditional fare of fruit and veg. On Saturdays, the street's pubs burst at the seams, queues snake out of cafés and neighbouring park London Fields is littered with skinny trendoids eyeing each other up.

Even after its financial battering, London remains the epicentre of international retail – trends are set here, rules are broken and new shops are still opening with hyper-creative concepts, sweetly idiosyncratic stock, or a nod to British heritage. Perhaps the age of the clinical, luxury boutique is over, with a more meaningful, inventive way of shopping soon to spring up in its place? Either way, our retail tenacity remains. See you at the checkout.

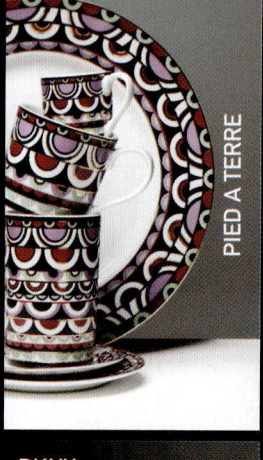

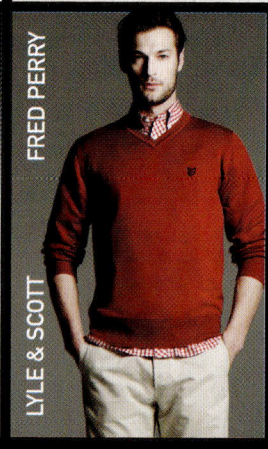

HOUSE OF FRASER

OXFORD STREET LONDON W1C 1HF   TEL 0844 800 3752
VICTORIA STREET LONDON SW1E 6QX   TEL 0844 800 3762
WESTFIELD SHOPPING CENTRE LONDON W12 7GA   TEL 0844 800 3765
KING WILLIAM STREET LONDON EC4N 7HR   TEL 0844 800 3718

houseoffraser.co.uk

One-Stop

Department Stores	**21**
Shopping Centres & Arcades	**28**
Concept Stores & Lifestyle Boutiques	**35**
Markets	**46**

harrods.com +44 (0)20 7730 1234

ENTER A DIFFERENT WORLD

Harrods

One-Stop

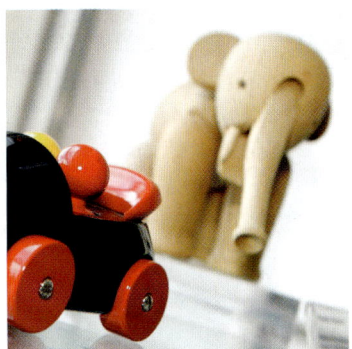

These days, department stores aren't just rather dull places to buy all your essentials under one roof: those listed here contain top-notch eateries, indulgent spas and an entire market town's worth of mini-shop concessions. While London has always been famous for its department stores, we didn't know just how much better they could be until **Selfridges** (*see p27*) upped the ante by bringing in niche labels and exciting interior design. And the store continues to innovate. Even the more classic stalwarts, **John Lewis** (*see p23*) and **Fortnum & Mason** (*see p21*), have submitted to the winds of change, with major nip and tucks that have ushered in swanky food halls and beauty counters.

The city's markets have enjoyed revived popularity in recent times – as evidenced by the continual crowds at **Borough**, and **Broadway Market**'s (*see p49*) evolution into the place to be seen on a sunny Saturday. Markets are an asset to any local economy as they draw consumers to the shops that surround them.

Mayfair's royal arcades are often overlooked by residents, but they have more to offer than the quaint looks the tourists love. These genteel proto-shopping centres have been back in the spotlight since the daddy of them all, **Burlington Arcade** (*see p32*), was restored to its Regency glory.

Shopping centres, meanwhile, are getting bigger and bigger, and are symbolic of the chasm that has developed within London's shopping scene; at the opposite end of the scale to the mall shoppers are those who are embracing London's increasingly experience-led shopping culture, frequenting the increasingly popular concept stores (such as **Dover Street Market** and **Darkroom**; *see p39*) and lifestyle boutiques, which offer a range of covetable products under one, normally very stylish, roof.

Department Stores

Fortnum & Mason [HOT 50]
181 Piccadilly, W1A 1ER (7734 8040, www.fortnumandmason.com). Green Park or Piccadilly Circus tube. **Open** *10am-8pm Mon-Sat; noon-6pm Sun.*
The results of F&M's recent £24 million, two-year revamp (revealed in 2007, 300 years after its opening in 1707) are stunning: the store retains all that was marvellous about its Georgian past while changing just enough to position itself as a 21st-century shopping experience. A sweeping spiral staircase soars through the four-storey building, while light floods down from a central glass dome. The iconic F&M eau de nil blue and gold colour scheme with flashes of rose pink abounds on both the store design and the packaging of the fabulous ground-floor treats, like the chocolates, biscuits, teas and preserves. The

Fortnum & Mason. See p21.

first floor is for homewares: china- and glassware as well as finishing touches such as silver scoops for stilton, eau de nil linen and cashmere hot water bottles; there are regular cooking sessions too. The second floor is home to beauty rooms, fashion accessories, jewellery and a perfumery, while the third floor has menswear, luggage and writing accessories, along with an excellent wrapping service. The five restaurants, all redesigned by David Collins (of Wolseley fame), are equally impressive, with the ice-cream parlour a welcome addition. A new food hall in the basement has a huge range of fresh and dried produce, as well as top-notch wines from all over the world, meaning that Fortnum & Mason is no longer just a place for a picnic hamper, biscuits or an eye-catching jar of pickle. Look out too for craft exhibitions, literary lunches as well as gallery collaborations. Fortnum & Mason is fabulously redolent of a time when luxury meant the highest degree of comfort rather than ostentation and remains a treat for all who venture through its oak doors.

Harrods

87-135 Brompton Road, SW1X 7XL (7730 1234, www.harrods.com). Knightsbridge tube. **Open** 10am-8pm Mon-Sat; noon-6pm Sun (browsing from 11.30am).

Harrods' distinctive terracotta façade with dark-green awnings stirs up mixed emotions. For every tourist who yearns for a Harrods teddy, there's a Londoner who sniffs at its vulgarity. But for all the marble and glitz, the store that boasts of selling everything is working hard to inject its image with ever more style: always strong on fashion, Harrods offers women a 10,000sq ft Designer Studio with a host of British designer launches, as well as swimwear, Designer Plus (for the larger lady), a wedding dress boutique, a Denim Lounge with coveted jeans lines (Vintage 1, Citizens of Humanity) and a refurbished lingerie boutique stocking exquisite designs from Alberta Ferretti, Agent Provocateur, Elle Macpherson and Roberto Cavalli. Menswear on the ground floor provides a gentlemen's club atmosphere where tailoring, fragrance and a cigar shop are joined by directional tailoring from Bespoken. Also on ground are the legendary food hall, 13 restaurants and cafés and the Beauty Concierge service offering advice across all Harrods' treatments, services and products – essential for navigating the 250 or so brands on offer. The excellent sports section, with equipment and clothing for a vast range of sporting occasions, now also has dedicated Nike and Adidas areas. Harrods' extravagance is much in evidence in the bakery in the pet department, which can sell you pet-friendly profiteroles, while the Pet Concierge service can source a rare breed from a reputable breeder.

Harvey Nichols

109-125 Knightsbridge, SW1X 7RJ (7235 5000, www.harveynichols.com). Knightsbridge tube. **Open** *Store* 10am-8pm Mon-Sat; noon-6pm Sun (browsing from 11.30am). *Café* 8am-11pm Mon-Sat; 11.30am-6pm Sun. *Restaurant* noon-3pm, 6-11pm Mon-Thur; noon-4pm, 6-11pm Fri, Sat; noon-4pm Sun.

Compared to some of the incredible refurbs that rival emporia have indulged in, Harvey Nics feels like it's coasting a little. That said, you'll still find a worthy clutch of unique brands over its eight floors of beauty, fashion, food and home. In beauty, there's skin-firming Rodial, La Prairie Platinum and Bed of Nails pillows and mats, with slick Gentlemen's Tonic for men, as well as beauty services that include Beyond MediSpa, with a team of doctors and medical 'aestheticians', and the Daniel Hersheson hair salon. Fashion on Four showcases emerging British talent (Peter Pilotto, Mary Katrantzou), new designers (Meadham Kirchoff, Brian Reyes) and favourites Donna Karan and Marc Jacobs. A Sneaker Wall displays hi-tops and plimsolls by Christian Louboutin and Alejandro Ingelmo, and then there's the denim phenomenon… everyone from Lanvin to D&G. Rick Owens has joined Balenciaga and Marc Jacobs in Menswear, alongside Prada, Armani, D&G and a host of brands such as Aussie Bum, King Baby and U Boat. The fine Foodmarket on the fifth floor boasts over 600 exclusive products in Harvey Nichols' smart black and silver livery, along with accessories and kitchen products such as the wonderfully whimsical Blaue Blume china. Those with a taste for luxury can adjourn to the bar, which even has a private vodka tasting room. Hunger pangs can be sated by Wagamama, Yo! Sushi or the fab Fifth Floor restaurant, bar and café.

John Lewis

300 Oxford Street, W1A 1EX (7629 7711, www.johnlewis.co.uk). Bond Street or Oxford Circus tube. **Open** 9.30am-8pm Mon-Wed, Fri; 9.30am-9pm Thur; 9.30am-7pm Sat; noon-6pm Sun (browsing from 11.30am).

With a sensible ratio of quality to price for all its products, John Lewis retains its rightful crown as the retail world's safe pair of hands. Arguably the strongest

Best for…

Designer garb
Harrods (*see p22*), **Harvey Nichols** (*see left*) and **Selfridges** (*see p27*).

Sports equipment
Harrods (*see p22*) and **Selfridges** (*see p27*).

Luggage
Harrods (*see p22*), **John Lewis** (*see left*), **Selfridges** (*see p27*).

Directional fashion
Liberty (*see p25*) and **Selfridges** (*see p27*).

Kitchen- and homewares
John Lewis (*see left*).

Packaging and gifts
Fortnum & Mason (*see p21*) and **Liberty** (*see p25*).

Foodhalls
All the stores listed here.

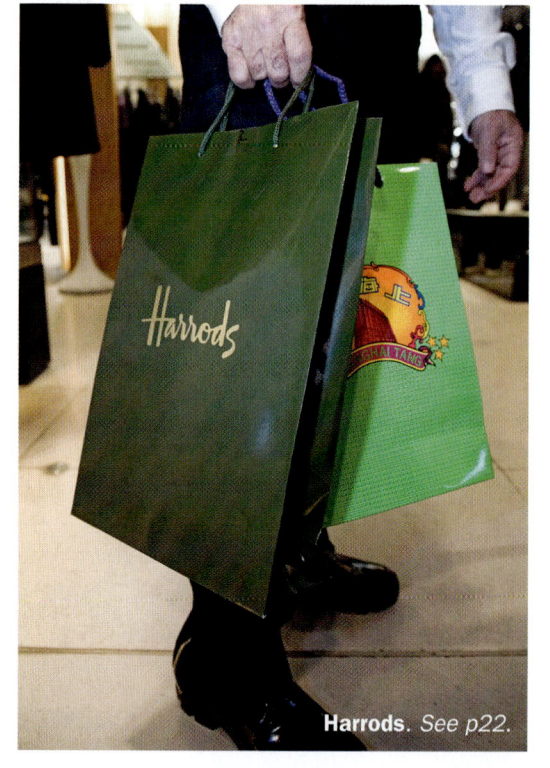

ONE-STOP

Harrods. *See p22.*

24 Time Out London's Best Shops

selling point is the lower ground-floor cookware and white goods section, where an excellent range of kitchen staples is backed up by exemplary customer service. Well-informed staff will guide you to the right product for your purse, delivery is usually smooth and the after-care service, should you need it, admirable. The new(ish) food hall from Waitrose has speciality food galore, a walk-in cheese room and the plethora of check-out staff to keep the queues moving swiftly. Although the much-touted redesign of the ground-floor beauty hall didn't quite transform the store into the emporium of style the directors were hoping for, niche lines such as This Works and Bliss, alongside stalwarts like Benefit, MAC and Clarins, have upped the beauty ante. There's also an Elemis spa pod for express facials. Under the auspices of the Director of Buying, Peter Ruis, fashion at John Lewis is fast becoming more directional, with hipper labels like Day Birger et Mikkelsen and BCBG Max Azria being added. The clutch of respectable classics is also still strong with Coast, Jaeger and Fenn Wright Manson among them. Other strengths include technology, schoolwear and home furnishings and the website is equally straightforward to use.

Branches Wood Street, Kingston upon Thames, Surrey KT1 1TE (8547 3000); Brent Cross Shopping Centre, NW4 3FL (8202 6535); (Peter Jones) Sloane Square, SW1W 8EL (7730 3434).

Liberty HOT 50
Regent Street, W1B 5AH (7734 1234, www.liberty.co.uk). Oxford Circus tube.
Open 10am-9pm Mon-Sat; noon-6pm Sun.

Shopping at Liberty is an experience to savour; artful and arresting window displays, exciting new collections, fabulous exclusives and luxe labels help to create a very special atmosphere. The wood-panelled interior provides the perfect backdrop for such fashion labels as Gareth Pugh, Spencer Hart and PPQ. The shoe bar on the second floor includes exclusives from Nicholas Kirkwood, Rupert Sanderson, Giuseppe Zanotti and Stella McCartney. It's also strong on bags, with names like Marc Jacobs, Mulberry and Chloé. The array of beautiful and original jewellery includes newcomer Lucy Hutchins's delicate and unusual necklaces and Stephen Dweck's dramatic pieces. The Rosa Clara Bridal Boutique consists of own-label styles and those by Karl Lagerfeld and Christian Lacroix. And despite being fashion forward, Liberty still respects its dressmaking heritage with an extensive range of cottons in the third-floor haberdashery department. Stationery also pays court to the traditional, with beautiful Liberty of London notebooks, address books, photo albums and diaries embossed with the art nouveau 'Ianthe' print. Interiors are equally impressive with regular exhibitions showcasing new and classic furniture designs on the

Harvey Nichols. *See p23.*

Liberty. *See p25.*

ONE-STOP

Department Stores

fourth floor, alongside a dazzling permanent collection of 20th-century classics like Charles and Ray Eames's famous armchair and Le Corbusier's chaise. Meanwhile, a well-edited collection of homeware includes ethereal and romantic Astier de Villatte ceramics and beautiful silk and Egyptian cotton bedlinen. There's also a made-to-measure curtain service. New arrivals in the beauty department include Le Labo (*see p146*) fragrances, mixed by hand, and fresh and modern scents from Eau d'Italie. Beauty lines include botanical extracts Malin & Goetz, with Zirh for men. With the launch of an online shop, Liberty shows no sign of slowing down.

Selfridges HOT 50
400 Oxford Street, W1A 1AB (0800 123 400, www.selfridges.com). Bond Street or Marble Arch tube. **Open** 9.30am-8pm Mon-Wed, Fri, Sat; 9.30am-9pm Thur; noon-6pm (browsing from 11.30am) Sun. Selfridges – one of *Time Out*'s favourite department stores – celebrated its centenary in 2009. With its concession boutiques, store-wide themed events and collections from the hottest new brands, it's a first port-of-call for stylish one-stop shopping, while useful floor plans make navigating the store easy-peasy. The basement is chock-full of hip home accessories and stylish but practical kitchen equipment (think Alessi, Le Creuset and Marco Pierre White for Russell Hobbs),while on the ground floor the Wonder Room – 19,000sq ft of luxury brands – goes from strength to strength. There are plenty of concessions worthy of note: Cycle Surgery on the first floor is a knowledgeable pitstop for two-wheelers, while Beautiful Blooms on the ground floor specialises in cut, scented English and French garden roses. Too many shoppers bypass these delights as they make a beeline for Selfridges's excellent fashion floors. With a winning combination of new talent, hip and edgy labels, smarter high street labels and mid and high end brands, the store stays ahead of the pack. Kingston graduate and Student of the Year Sophie Hulme joined the hallowed second-floor womenswear halls with her dramatic first collection of luxury streetwear along with Alexis Mabille's beautiful collection of androgynous tailoring inspired by Jane Birkin. Elsewhere, Simon Miller Jeans joins the already phenomenal jeans stable, while the new Halston boutique in Superbrands shows that Selfridges is not neglecting its big labels either. Menswear is also superb, with concepts like the b store pop-up shop continuing to excite customers. The store's recent 3rd Central initiative – located, funnily enough, in the centre of the third floor – is where you'll find the hippest brands of the day, with an ever-evolving mix of contemporary labels such as Ashish, Preen Line and jewellery brand Zoe & Morgan. There's plenty of new draws in the food hall, too, with great deli produce from London-based Baker & Spice and the appropriately named Australian raw food company Raw.

ONE-STOP

Shopping Centres & Arcades

Shopping centres

The next two years will see increasing competition among London's shopping centres, with **One New Change**, a Jean-Nouvel designed mall, due to open in October 2010 near St Paul's and, in late 2011, the huge **Westfield Stratford City**.

Brunswick
Hunter Street, Bernard Street & Marchmont Street, WC1N 1BS (7833 6066, www.brunswick.co.uk). Russell Square tube or King's Cross tube/rail. **Open** *varies; see website for info on individual shops.*
Conceived as an experimental retail and social housing complex in the 1960s, the Brunswick was neglected throughout the 1980s and '90s. In 2006, however, the Grade II-listed centre was given a much-needed £24 million facelift by an architectural partnership that included the building's original designer, Patrick Hodgkinson. The concrete-heavy complex has retained its 1960s character but it is now brighter, whiter and considerably more popular. The retail outlets are largely of the high street chain variety (there's French Connection, Benetton, Joy, Space NK, Hobbs, Oasis), but on a summer evening the central walkway buzzes with shoppers and diners (at Apostrophe, Carluccio's, Yo! Sushi and Strada, among other eateries) creating a lively continental vibe. And the crowning glory is still here – the arthouse Renoir cinema.

Cardinal Place
Victoria Street, SW1E 5JH (www.cardinalplace.co.uk). Victoria tube/rail or 11, 24, 148, 211, 507 bus. **Open** *see website for opening hours of individual shops.*
This slickly impressive glass and metal building on the corner of Victoria Street and Bressenden Place opened in 2004, bringing a much needed burst of new life to what was a rather bleak part of Westminster as far as shopping was concerned. You'll find Topshop, L'Occitane, Zara, North Face and Hawes & Curtis, and there's a good range of eateries. The space also houses the sleekly designed 3,000sq ft SW1 Gallery (www.sw1gallery.co.uk). And if you want to exercise – or exorcise – your soul after an excess of consumption, cross the road and duck into the darkly mysterious interior of Westminster Cathedral.

Covent Garden Market
Between King Street & Henrietta Street, WC2E 8RF (0870 780 5001, www.coventgardenmarket.co.uk). Covent Garden or Embankment tube, or Charing Cross tube/rail. **Open** 10am-7pm Mon-Sat; 11am-6pm Sun.

Brunswick

Shopping Centres & Arcades

Covent Garden Market

Although something of a London institution, Covent Garden Market is too commercial and generally too crowded to provide a particularly characterful retail experience. However, the colonnaded 19th-century building is impressive, and occasionally some of the performers and entertainers can even be worth watching. And while the market itself has mainly succumbed to chain stores and shops catering to the tourist trade, there are some worthwhile independent shops still holding their ground, such as Eric Snook's Toyshop, Benjamin Pollock's, which specialises in traditional toy theatres made of card or wood (*see also p267*), and the specialist tobacconist and cigar shop Segar & Snuff Parlour.

Kingly Court
Carnaby Street, opposite Broadwick Street, W1B 5PW (7333 8118, www.carnaby.co.uk). Oxford Circus tube. **Open** 11am-7pm Mon-Sat; noon-6pm Sun.
Kingly Court has helped London's Carnaby Street to reclaim its 1960s reputation as the heart of swinging London (well, at least a vein of it, anyway). The three-tiered complex boasts a funky mix of established chains, independents, vintage and gift shops. The café-filled courtyard generates the most bustle, attracting custom to ground-level shops such as Marshmallow Mountain, which has a good selection of vintage shoes, clothes and bags, Lazy Oaf (trendy menswear), Henri Lloyd, Vans and Mnini (vintage-style gifts). There's more vintage clothing from Stromboli's Circus (formerly Twinkled), which goes the whole hog with vintage homewares as well as clothes. Also check out the women's boutique BirdCage. Crafts get a look in on the second floor at Buffy's Beads (*see p216*) and All the Fun of the Fair (knitting supplies). There are also outposts of Triyoga and Walk-In Backrub, and decent beauty treatments (manicures, waxing, facials) can be had at the Beauty Lounge (no.1, 7734 6161, www.thebeautylounge.co.uk).

Westfield London
Westfield London, W12 7SL (3371 2300, www.westfield.com/london). Shepherd's Bush tube. **Open** 10am-9pm Mon-Wed; 10am-10pm Thur, Fri; 9am-9pm Sat; noon-6pm Sun; see website for details of opening hours of individual shops.
Occupying 46 acres and covering nine different postcodes, Westfield London took the crown of Europe's largest shopping centre when it opened in autumn 2008. The impressive site, which was where the 1908 Olympics were held, cost around £1.6 billion to build, and houses some 265 shops. Popular labels that have never had stand-alone stores in the UK, such as Hollister, have shops here; you'll also find luxury fashion houses, including Louis Vuitton and Burberry. Highlights from the boutique-like labels include Sienna Miller's

Finally a rest for the Wicked!

Make sure you get the best seat this summer with the new WickedWedge inflatable lounger. The sueded groundsheet, with its triangular, inflatable back support adds a level of superb comfort when chilling in the sun.

Available in five funky colours, the WickedWedge is waterproof and comfortable, even in the heat. It inflates effortlessly and quickly by mouth or with by pump. When not in use it takes up next-to-no space, folding away into a small, lightweight package that is easy to store or carry in a backpack.

Cost of comfort? £14.95 + p&p

Available online at www.wickedwedge.co.uk or selected retail outlets

---

To advertise in the next edition of…

Email: guidesadvertising@timeout.com   Call: 020 7813 6020

Shopping Centres & Arcades

Kingly Court. See p29.

FIVE More shopping centres

Brent Cross Shopping Centre
Prince Charles Drive, NW4 3FP (8457 3997, www.brentcross.co.uk). Brent Cross tube then 210 bus or Hendon Central tube then 143, 326, 186 bus.
The UK's first enclosed shopping centre has a number of high-quality chains, including Kate Kuba and an Apple Store.

Canary Wharf Shopping Centres
Canada Place, Cabot Place & Jubilee Place, E14 5EW (7477 1477, www.mycanary wharf.com). Canary Wharf tube/DLR.
A clutch of upper-end high street stores (Church's, Myla, Reiss, Bang & Olufsen et al) fill this centre's three main malls.

Duke of York Square
King's Road, between Sloane Square & Cheltenham Terrace, SW3 4LY. Sloane Square tube.
This made-over military barracks houses upper-end high street and designer shops (Kate Kuba, Agnès B, Myla, Liz Earle skincare), plus a Patisserie Valerie and slick hairdresser Richard Ward.

N1 Islington
21 Parkfield Street, N1 0PS (7359 2674, www.n1islington.com). Angel tube.
High street fashion names dominate in this unremarkable but practical complex.

Thomas Neal Centre
29-41 Earlham Street, WC2H 9LD (7240 4741). Covent Garden tube.
Small complex with a skate/surfwear slant.

The Arcades Project

A taste of 19th-century London, with a modern twist.

The capital's royal arcades are a throwback to the gentility of the 19th century shopping experience, with many of the shops holding royal warrants for decades. By way of contrast Portobello Green gives retail space to emerging designers and quirky one-offs.

Built in 1819 by Lord Cavendish, to provide 'industrious females' with employment, and to stop people throwing oyster shells into the garden of Burlington House, **Burlington Arcade** is the grandest in London (Mayfair, 7630 1411, www.burlington-arcade.co.uk). With its 'whale mouth' entrance and soft globe lights, you can dive from the flurry of Piccadilly into a far more genteel shopping experience. Decorum is guarded by the ever-present Beadles who to this day prevent shoppers from whistling, running, and 'making merry loudly'; you've been warned.

Step into Ladurée's golden grotto for one of their rainbow hued macaroons before idling past the arcade's sparkling row of jewellers. The strands of pearls hanging in Milleperle caught our eye, as did the antique jewellery in Matthew Foster. Luxury goods abound in the form of watches from David Duggan, pens from Pen Friend and custom made gloves from Sermoneta Gloves.

Make sure you step into the quintessentially English fragrance house, Penhaligon's, for old fashion scents like Bluebell, Violetta, and the rather bracing Extract of Limes. Burlington Arcade also houses a proper shoe-shine boy working with waxes and creams for just £3.50. Suits you guv'nor!

Just across the road, running from Piccadilly to Jermyn Street, you will find **Piccadilly Arcade** (www.piccadilly-arcade.com). Smaller than Burlington but with just as impressive a lineage, this arcade is well worth a visit. Squeezed into the cusp of the arcade is the beautiful mirrored space of Santa Maria Novella. Established by Dominican monks in Florence in 1612, this perfumery is sacred in perfume circles and new to the arcade last year. Try 'Opoponax' which was created as a preventative from witchcraft! Further reverence is required in Iconastas, the hallowed home to Russian fine art and antiques, specialising in orthodox icons. For militaria and royal memorabilia stop off at the Armoury of St James where you will find model soldiers, orders of chivalry and antiques. We spotted a signed royal wedding photograph too. Gents, if wedding season is upon you then why not swagger through the nuptial proceedings in one of Favourbrook's sumptuous waistcoats and bow ties. It's worth checking out the shoes in Jeffrey West who, with their skull-bedecked shop and gothic influences, are something of a renegade presence in the otherwise austere arcade. Shop for shirts at Budd, Beson & Clegg and Neal & Palmer.

Continue down the road to the smallest of London's arcades. Nestled between Fortnum and Mason on one side and Isaac Newton's house on the other, **Princes Arcade** (38 Jermyn Street) does not shy away from its historic credentials. This is the place that a gentleman's gentleman might be dispatched, as it conveniently houses everything the well-heeled chap might desire. For sir's toilette, first stop would be Czech & Speake, the luxury bathroom shop where Edwardian bathroom fixtures and fittings elegantly hold traditional shaving tools and their signature fragrance: the 88 cologne. Spiffing shoes can be found at Barkers (we are told that debonair Londoner Bill Nighy regularly does his window-shopping here.) Then it's off to Hilditch & Key or Andy & Tuly for top hats, tail coats and silk bow ties. The ladies could wish for no better than the chocolates from Prestat. The shop itself is dazzling and the chocolates come with recommendations from Roald Dahl and the Queen.

The passage with the most curious collection of shops has to be the **Royal Opera Arcade** (between Charles II Street & Pall Mall, 7839 2440, www.royaloperaarcade.com). Designed by John Nash (who went on to make the Brighton Pavilion), it is the oldest arcade in London and has survived fire and the Blitz. It's an eclectic collection of odds and ends: shoppers can get politically schooled at Ducketts political bookstore before stopping off for some acupuncture at the Chinese Medical Centre; Pall Mall Printers and Stationers have a wide range of cards, and you will find beautiful arrangements at Vivella Rose Florist; old tribal artefacts are bought and sold in the dusty D Barrett which looks like somewhere Indiana Jones might be found browsing; old men doze outside the Sandwich Centre where waiters in bow ties serve off-duty thespians and homesick New Zealanders head for Kiwi Fruits, which this year won an Artisan Award, selling books, food and jewellery. The Stephen Wiltshire Gallery features work from the autistic artist of cityscapes.

Shopping Centres & Arcades

Burlington Arcade

The **Royal Arcade** (28 Old Bond Street, www.mayfair.org.uk/shopping/royal-arcade) retains its old fashioned charm while ringing the changes with the presence of some more contemporary names. You are far less likely to find your average tourist here so the pace is relaxed and you can meander at your leisure. Enjoy mouthwatering chocolates at Charbonnel et Walker (chocolatier to the Queen) and peruse rare lithographs in the William Western Gallery. Get your fashion fix at the Paul Smith accessory shop and visit visionary shoe shop Camper. The arcade also holds opticians EB Meyorwitz whose very hip glasses were featured in the Gieves & Hawkes catwalk shows this fashion week. How's that for London style?

Our fashionable arcade pick has to be **Portobello Green Arcade** (281 Portobello Road, www.portobellodesigners.com). Here new and established designers are showcased minutes away from the rowdy markets of Portobello Road. Loved by John Galliano and Jerry Hall, Zarvis London is a mix of witch's parlour and homeopathic pampering shop. Using only natural ingredients, Zarvis offers pure and simple products that are especially suitable for sensitive skins. Check out Preen, which features collections from Thornton and Bregazzi, and boasts Kate Moss, Chloë Sevigny and Samantha Morton among its followers. Step into Baby Ceylon, a beautifully presented boutique, and grab some cutting edge clobber for toddlers from Sasti. Make like a pre-war pin-up and slip into something more slinky with help from What Katie Did. With a beautiful selection of faux-vintage lingerie and hosiery that evokes the golden age of Hollywood, WKD offers screen-inspired seduction at very reasonable prices (Agent Provocateur, eat your heart out!)

Westfield London. *See p29.*

Twenty8Twelve, Tabio, Myla lingerie and Cos. Michelin-starred chefs Pascal Aussignac and Vincent Labeyrie can soothe away any shopping-induced stress with their gastronomic creations at Croque Gascon. If they don't manage to tempt your tastebuds, then one of the other 50 eateries (including Balans, Square Pie and Wahaca) surely will. And in late 2011, in time for the Olympics, Westfield Stratford City is due to open, bringing a similar mix of shopping and eating to east London.

Whiteleys

151 Queensway, W2 4YN (7229 8844, www.whiteleys. com). Bayswater or Queenswayy tube. **Open** *10am-8pm Mon-Sat; noon-6pm Sun; see website for details of opening hours of individual shops.*
Shop until you drop at London's first official department store, considered the height of luxury when it was opened in 1911 (the original Whiteleys department store in Westbourne Grove burned down in 1897). Today's largely mainstream tenants are at odds with the refined Edwardian structure – its marble floors, huge glass atrium and impressive La Scala staircase mean the place sometimes gets used in film shoots (it features in both *Love Actually* and *Closer*). The mainly mid-range high street shops include Zara, Dune, Muji and E&A Moda, and there's also an eight-screen Odeon cinema and a branch of the upmarket bowling chain All Star Lanes.

Concept Stores & Lifestyle Boutiques

The term 'concept store' has now infiltrated the collective consciousness of London shoppers; defined as shops selling a range of items from desirable brands aimed at discerning and aspirational shoppers, they provide a shopping 'experience' rather than just a marketplace.

The lines between a concept store, a lifestyle boutique and a good gift shop are thin, and sometimes just a question of self-labelling by the shop. What all of the places listed below have in common is their covetable items for sale that span a wide range of categories – from cult homewares and retro stationery to original jewellery and stylish clothes; they all make excellent browsing grounds for gifts.

Anthropologie HOT 50
158 Regent Street, W1B 5SW (7529 9800, www.anthropologie.co.uk). Piccadilly Circus tube. **Open** 10am-7pm Mon-Wed; 10am-8pm Thur; 10am-7pm Fri, Sat; noon-6pm Sun. **Sells** W.

Anthropologie, the romantically inclined elder sister to Urban Outfitters, opened the doors of its first European store in autumn 2009, so those who stocked up during New York shopping sprees can now access the US brand's signature classics closer to home. The store's signature large-scale window displays and installations, and a light-filled atrium with a jaw-dropping 1,500 square foot living wall of 11,000 plants, help to challenge London gloominess, while stock is of a feminine bent, with delicate necklaces adorned with puppies and birds, soft knit cardies, craft-edged homewares and blouses with ruffles and bows. London designers, such as Eley Kishimoto and Beyond the Valley, have collaborated with the label to produce exclusive pieces for the store; but it's the vintage-inspired range of homewares that has really filled a hole in the London market. A second store in the old Antiquarius building on the King's Road opened in spring 2010.

Aubin & Wills HOT 50
64-66 Redchurch Street, E2 7DP (3487 0066, www.aubinandwills.com). Shoreditch High Street rail. **Open** 10am-7pm Mon-Sat; 11am-5pm Sun. **Sells** M, W.
Brit brand Aubin & Wills opened this ambitious and rambling boutique, 45-seat cinema and gallery in a hipster apartment block on Redchurch Street in June 2010. The 7,500 square foot space houses its mens, womens and

ONE-STOP

Anthropologie. *See p35.*

Concept Stores & Lifestyle Boutiques

homeware lines in a sort of grown-up collegiate style reminiscent of Aubin's teen labelmate Jack Wills. Upstairs is Brit artist and curator Stuart Semple's Aubin Gallery, and down in the basement is the Aubin Cinema – a collaboration with neighbour Shoreditch House. Of all the recent openings on Redchurch Street, it's by far the most high-reaching, but that rough, hipster edge the area is known for could be under threat from Aubin's arsenal of blankets, biscuit tins, candles and stylish clothes.

Bermondsey 167

167 Bermondsey Street, SE1 3UW (7407 3137, www.bermondsey167.com). London Bridge tube/rail. **Open** 11am-7pm Tue-Sat; noon-4pm Sun. **Sells** M, W.

Former Burberry designer Michael McGrath has poured his heart into Bermondsey 167, an intriguing, slick boutique that opened in 2007. The shop's own-label (M2cG) shirts (made in Northern Ireland), fine merino wool sweaters (made in Italy), ties and scarves, and swimwear (from £48) are the main draw, but the unique, commission-only furniture, home accessories, jewellery and coconut-leaf lights are intriguing too; all are sourced from artists and artisans around the world, and particularly in South America. There's also a great range of trendy perspex Toy watches, beloved of celebs and fashionistas, and a tiny collection of womenswear items.

Beyond the Valley

2 Newburgh Street, W1F 7RD (7437 7338, www.beyondthevalley.com). Oxford Circus tube. **Open** 11am-7pm Mon-Sat; 12.30-6pm Sun. **Sells** M, W.

Set up in 2004 by three Central Saint Martins graduates, this concept boutique is a showcase for creations by hot new names. There's a casual-urban feel to the trendy offerings, with own-label T-shirts and sweaters plus choice pieces by cutting-edge designers. The range of affordable jewellery, in a glass wall cabinet, is a strong point, and the collection has grown steadily over the past few years. The small room to the right as you enter acts as an impromptu event space showcasing the work of new artists and collaborations. On the lower-ground floor you'll find a range of stylish and often exclusive interiors items, including wallpaper, lighting, furniture, fine art, as well as design books. The witty accessories, such as colourful umbrellas, ruffled 'neck-warmers' and wooden bird coathangers, are also worth a peak.

Cath Kidston

28-32 Shelton Street, WC2H 9JE (7836 4803, www.cathkidston.co.uk). Covent Garden tube. **Open** 10am-7pm Mon-Wed, Fri, Sat; 10am-8pm Thur; noon-6pm Sun.

There are numerous ways to embrace the nostalgic Cath Kidston lifestyle, with her retro floral/cherry/stripey/dotty prints covering everything from washbags to tableware, via plimsoles, laptop cases, key rings,

Beyond the Valley

ONE-STOP

Concept Stores & Lifestyle Boutiques

coats, scarves and more. The Covent Garden store is always bustling with shoppers in search of gift items and traditional English accessories. Oilcloth accessories are in abundance, used for glasses and phones cases, ticket holders, and the well-designed cosmetics cases and washbags, which come in a wide variety of sizes. Bedspreads, cushions, blankets and eiderdowns, umbrellas, chinaware and a wide range of bags and luggage are also for sale, and there's a range of kidswear and accessories to boot, including kids' lunchboxes, bath sets, teddybears and cute babygrows.
Branches throughout the city.

Couverture & the Garbstore
188 Kensington Park Road, W11 2ES (7229 2178, www.couverture.co.uk, www.garbstore.com). Ladbroke Grove tube. **Open** 10am-6pm Mon-Sat; (Dec only) noon-5pm Sun.
Husband and wife team Emily Dyson and Ian Paley opened their new venture Couverture & the Garbstore in March 2008; Emily's Couverture shop was previously housed in Chelsea, while the Garbstore was a wholesale operation with a cult international fanbase. Couverture, upstairs, stocks clothes, accessories and jewellery, a large selection of choice kids' items, homewares, furniture and the odd vintage knick-knack. Both shops stock exclusive label collaborations, such as the backpacks produced with Battle Lake in 2008. Garbstore, on the lower level, is the first stand-alone shop stocking Paley's vintage-inspired label for men; every item is made using old-school techniques from the 1940s and '50s (some of the garments, for instance, feature three-hole buttons that have to be hand-sewn on to the item). The shop also stocks footwear from Pointer, womenswear from Humanoid, T-shirts and sweatshirts from Australia's Rittenhouse, and is the UK stockist of Japan's Bedwin & the Heartbreakers label.

Darkroom HOT 50
52 Lamb's Conduit Street, WC1N 3LL (7831 7244, www.darkroomlondon.com). Holborn tube. **Open** 11am-7pm Mon-Fri; 11am-7pm Sat.
Darkroom is not somewhere you go to develop 35mm film. It is in fact a new concept store, which opened at the start of 2010, adding further credence to Lamb's Conduit Street's claim to being one of London's most intriguing shopping destinations. The shop is quite literally dark (the walls and lampshades black), creating a blank canvas for the carefully chosen selection of unisex fashion, accessories and interiors items on sale. Designer items include Borba Margo bags, DMK glassware and Solomia ceramics. The space doubles up as a gallery, with displays (such as etchings by artist Marcus James) intermingling with a range of sculptural jewellery by Florian, Scott Wilson and Maria Francesca Pepe. Each piece begs the question – do I wear it or hang it on the wall?

Dover Street Market HOT 50
17-18 Dover Street, W1S 4LT (7518 0680, www.doverstreetmarket.com). Green Park tube. **Open** 11am-6pm Mon-Wed; 11am-7pm Thur-Sat. **Sells** M, W. Comme des Garçons designer Rei Kawakubo's ground-breaking six-storey space combines the edgy energy of London's indoor markets – concrete floors, tills housed

Exit through the gift shop

Many of the city's museums and galleries have gift shops that are destination-visits in their own right. Profits generally go straight back into the museums themselves so you can support the arts while you shop.

First up for style fiends is the **Design Museum** (28 Shad Thames, SE1 2YD, 7940 8753, www.designmuseumshop.com), which stocks slick gifts ranging from modern design classics, such as the mini wooden radios, to innovative pieces; we particularly like the eco Sun Jar light and the retro-style timepieces. Not far from here is the **Fashion & Textile Museum** (83 Bermondsey Street, SE1 3XF, 7407 8664, www.ftmlondon.org); committed to supporting young design talent, this is the place to visit for pieces by up-and-coming fashion, textiles and jewellery designers.

Children and nostagic adults alike love the shop at the **V&A Museum of Childhood** (Cambridge Heath Road, E2 9PA, 8983 5229, www.museumofchildhood.org.uk), which stocks retro-inspired toys, games and posters, while the shop at the main Kensington branch of the **Victoria & Albert Museum** (Cromwell Road, SW7 2RL, 7942 2000, www.vam.ac.uk) is as eclectic as the museum's collection, with kooky curios as well as merchandise inspired by exhibitions. The V&A print series, featuring 6,500 images, is also a big draw, with prices starting at just £5. Nearby, the **Science Museum** (Exhibition Road, SW7 2DD, 7942 4499, www.sciencemuseum.org.uk) sells gizmos aimed mainly at kids – from the useful (wind-up torches) to the fun (space ice-cream).

London's art galleries are also well worth a look. The gift shop at **Tate Modern** (Bankside, SE1 9TG, 7401 5167, www.tate.org.uk/shop) has a huge range of books, gadgets, prints, homewares and accessories; if you can't afford the art on the walls, then this is your chance to get your hands on some art-inspired products. The Designers for Tate range sells stylish products made especially for the Tate – check out the bags by Ally Capellino (*see p128*), Mimi (*see p131*) and Orla Kiely, and exclusive jewellery lines from Tatty Devine (*see p136*), among others.

The bookshops at the **Serpentine Gallery** (Kensington Gardens, W2 3XA, 7402 6075, www.serpentinegallery.org) and the **Photographers' Gallery** (5 & 8 Great Newport Street, WC2H 7HY, 7831 1772, www.photonet. org.uk) are good places to pick up coffee-table art books as well as hard-to-find magazine imports; the latter is also excellent on novelty gadgets. Two smaller galleries with fantastic bookshops are the **Whitechapel Gallery** (77-82 Whitechapel High Street, E2 7QX, www.whitechapelgallery.org) and the **ICA** (The Mall, SW1Y 5AH, 7930 0493, www.ica.org.uk), while the **National Portrait Gallery** (2 St Martin's Place, WC2H 0HE, 7306 0055, www.npg.org.uk) also has a good selection of books and posters, many relating to current shows.

If this all sounds rather high brow, then head to the **Museum of London** (150 London Wall, EC2Y 5HN, 7814 5600, www.museumoflondon.org.uk) for a fluffy 'plague rat' toy, a cockney rhyming slang teapot and Olympic pin badges. It also has a selection of tube map paraphernalia, though the shop at the **London Transport Museum** (39 Wellington Street, WC2E 7BB, 7379 6344) has the best range of iconic London Underground goods.

in corrugated-iron shacks, Portaloo dressing rooms – with rarefied labels. All 14 of the Comme collections are here, alongside exclusive lines such as Lanvin, Givenchy and Azzedine Alaïa. Dover Street's biannual 'Tachiagari' event sees the store close while designers make changes to their concessions, ensuring the space is constantly evolving. There's a Hussein Chalayan area with exclusive pieces, and an area devoted to designer du jour Henry Holland. New jewellery areas include Tom Binns Couture on the first floor, and Solange Azagury-Partridge on the ground floor. Once you've taken it all in, have a sit-down in the Rose Bakery on the top floor.

Family Tree
53 Exmouth Market, EC1R 4QL (7278 1084, www.familytreeshop.co.uk). Angel tube/Farringdon tube/rail/19, 38, 341 bus. **Open** 11am-6pm Mon-Sat.
A little gem on hip Exmouth Market, Family Tree offers a carefully chosen selection of designer-made gifts, homeware and accessories sourced from all around the globe. Owner Takako Copeland makes sure the shop's wares have an eco slant, with plenty of Fairtrade and organic cotton represented in the stock; but the main draw is her delicate lamps, made from Japanese rice paper. A diminutive version costs around £20; £65 will get you the tallest shade plus the base. A few pretty pieces point to Copeland's past as a jeweller – like the rice paper patterns of birds and butterflies encased in resin.

Ganesha
3-4 Gabriel's Wharf, 56 Upper Ground, SE1 9PP (7928 3444, www.ganesha.co.uk). Waterloo tube/rail. **Open** 11.30am-6pm Tue-Fri; noon-6pm Sat, Sun.
Jo Lawbuary and Purnendu Roy source goods from local co-operatives and small-scale producers in India, Bangladesh and beyond, to ensure every item in their store is fairly traded. There's a good selection of Fairtrade and recycled homewares (organic bedlinen; embroidered cushions from Bangladesh; lamps and colanders made from recycled tin; disposable leaf plates made from sali leaves from forests in India), as well as wallhangings and clothes and accessories, including attractive silk scarves, camel-wool hats, baby alpaca gloves, and a range of bags much from cotton, leather, and recycled rice sacks. Ganesha also offers a wedding list service. There's now a branch in Covent Garden.
Branch 38 King Street, WC2E 8JT (7240 8068).

Grace & Favour
35 North Cross Road, SE22 9ET (8693 4400). East Dulwich rail/176, 185 bus. **Open** 10am-6pm Mon-Sat; 11am-5pm Sun.
One of East Dulwich's most established and best-loved retail haunts, Rose Ratcliffe's lovely shop is the first port-of-call for clueless gift buyers. The space is jam-packed with covetable stuff for the home, garden and body, including designer stationery from cool brand Rosehip, Illumens fragrant candles and room sprays, locally made cushions, ceramic mugs, handmade French soaps and bigger home accessories such as a range of striking, crackle-glaze vases in contrasting shades of shocking yellow, olive-green and stone. There's also a sizeable selection of ornate mirrors, as well as several choice items of vintage clothing.

Lucas Bond
45 Bedford Hill, SW12 9EY (8675 9300, www.lucasbond.com). Balham tube/rail. **Open** 10am-6pm Mon-Sat; noon-5pm Sun.
Combining elegance with prettiness and chucking in a dollop of individuality for good measure, Lucas Bond has become something of an institution on Bedford Hill. Ceramics and British-designed treasures are the strong points: Andrew Tanner's simple white plates with the shapes of birds and butterflies cut out look charming displayed high on the wall; meanwhile, Snowden Flood's mugs capture stylised views of London from the Thames. The vintage tiered cake stands are perfect for a retro tea party. There's also a good range of stationery, including cute notebooks and rubber stamps, trendy dog-shaped plastic lamps, silver jewellery, passport holders and sweet gifts for new-borns and new mums.

Luna & Curious
198 Brick Lane, E1 6SA (7033 4411, www.lunaandcurious.com). Aldgate East tube or Shoreditch High Street rail. **Open** noon-6pm daily. **Sells** W, M.
The stock here is put together by a collective of young artisans. Look out for the quintessentially English teacups and ceramics from Polly George and welovekaoru, as well as 'illustrated porcelain' by Grace Wilson and jewellery by Rheanna Lingham, who uses ceramics, feathers and old embroidery from military jackets to make necklaces, earrings and headbands. Also adorning the walls are intricate masks by Natasha Law, while the unique Paperself patterned paper eyelashes, based on Chinese papercut designs, have been selling thick and fast. Every month, the shop offers up space to a team of emerging designers to display their work, while themed events create a fresh and inspiring vibe. Prices are surprisingly reasonable for products so lovingly put together.

Muji
37-78 Long Acre, WC2E 9JT (7379 0820, www.muji.co.uk). Covent Garden tube. **Open** 10am-8pm Mon-Sat; 11.30am-6pm Sun. **Sells** M, W.
The Japanese concept store has long been a favourite of style-conscious Londoners when it comes to practical, affordable and aesthetically pleasing goods for the office, home or wardrobe. Stock runs the gamut from useful gadgets (umbrellas, alarm clocks) and stationery (a huge range of pens, notebooks, photo albums) to pleasingly plain bedroom furniture, storage units and furnishings. While you can't help feeling that some of the plastic

storage drawers are a little steep, the collection of vanity cases, hair grips and travel pots for creams and lotions is unbeatable in terms of usefulness. Bedlinen – in understated colours – is reasonably priced, as are the durable laptop bags. The kitchenware range is of good quality and particularly strong on glasses and tableware, while the clothing range is worth a look if you're not after anything wildly exciting.
Branches throughout the city.

Oliver Bonas
137 Northcote Road, SW11 6PX (7223 5223, www.oliverbonas.com). Clapham Junction rail.
Open *10am-6.30pm Mon-Fri; 10am-6pm Sat; 11am-5pm Sun.*
With branches in Battersea, Islington, Richmond, Dulwich, Hampstead and Fulham, as well as its original location of Clapham, Oliver Bonas's target clientele is crystal clear; twenty- and thirtysomething yummy mummies flock here for safely trendy clothing from the likes of Ichi, Emily & Fin and Vero Moda, funky and affordable jewellery, bodycare products of the Korres and Ortigia ilk, as well as a good range of gifty type items such as cookbooks, Moleskin notebooks, arty birthday cards and cutesy kitchenware (think 'Keep Calm and Carry On' mugs and Cath Kidston-esque teapots). The chain is also an unsurprisingly good bet for 'new baby' presents.
Branches throughout the city.

123 Boutique HOT 50
123 Bethnal Green Road, E2 7DG (www.123 bethnalgreenroad.co.uk). Shoreditch High Street rail.
Open noon-7pm Tue, Wed, Fri, Sat; noon-8pm Thur; 11am-6pm Sun.
This avant-garde, four-storey mini department store opened in 2010 in a Grade II-listed warehouse on the corner of Brick Lane and Bethnal Green Road. The Dover Street Market of the East End isn't packed with big brands or accessories, however, but – whisper it – recycled clothing. The former secret HQ of a firm that used to sell dodgy shooters to London's underworld is now a rambling bazaar, with accessories and books spread out over antique furniture and fittings. Wonky wooden stairs lead to other floors. Indie designer JJ Hudson's NHS label takes over the light-filled top floor, his rag-tag ripped T-shirts painstakingly reworked into leftfield designs. The second floor house's 123's core project, a self-titled fashion label that just happens to be completely sustainable.

Potassium
2 Seymour Place, W1H 7NA (7723 7800, www.potassiumstore.co.uk). Marble Arch tube.
Open 11am-7pm Mon-Thur; 11am-6pm Fri, Sat.
Sells M, W.
It's stylish, modern and – its USP – all of its unique products are ethically sourced and environmentally friendly. There's a collection of clothes for men and women, accessories, such as the vegan-friendly leather-

123 Boutique

Concept Stores & Lifestyle Boutiques

Shop talk
Lizzie Evans, owner of Smug

Tell us about your shop
'The shop opened in the middle of 2009, but we bought the building a long time before.
 I didn't want a 'design supermarket'; I wanted it to feel more like a home. So at Smug we have proper rooms; in our kitchen, there's a sink, mixing bowls and bits to make a pie, so that you can look at something and think "That's how that will look in my house."
 'I grew up near here too, so it feels like home. And my father runs an art business on the top floor, and my mother helps out in the shop.'

What gave you the idea?
'The idea behind the name Smug is the feeling that people will get when they find something they love, when they feel like they've been let into a secret, that they've found a great little boutique to buy their presents from. Lots of people think it must be me the one who's smug but it's not, it's the customer!'

Who shops here?
'I've been really surprised and pleased at the diversity of people who shop here. I never thought I'd get young girls, but they get really excited about the Pixie make-up that we stock. And we get a lot of over 60s too. Our biggest margin is the twenty- to thirtysomethings market; it's people who love great design but don't go in for 'design icons' like Philippe Starck; they want something a little more quirky and one-off – for example, our hand-knitted farm animals in vintage jumpers that come from a lady called Marcy in New Hampshire. We're the only place in the world that stock them, apart from when Marcy goes to country fairs.
 'I thought long and hard about how not to overlap with all the great design stores on Upper Street, so we're a little more quirky.'

Have you noticed changes in the London shopping scene over the past few years?
'I'm very aware of the changes in Camden Passage. When we first acquired the building, my brother, who's an estate agent, was a little sceptical, but I had a good feeling about the Passage; it wasn't ready for us then but it's changed and is now a great spot for shopping.
 'It wasn't ideal opening a business in the recession, but at the same time it's been great to really have to be a lean machine. Had we been open before the crunch I might have found I was having to let people go; as it is we've started with only the very basics and are building ourselves up. In terms of customers, just recently it feels like people have had enough of being overly cautious, and want to be a little indulgent again. It's great!'

What is the most enjoyable aspect of owning a shop?
'I love being able to work in a space that I designed myself and then filled with beautiful things that I've chosen. It's a great place to work; familiar faces are always stopping by. It beats working in an office.'

What are your favourite shops in London?
'I am obsessed with Liberty's (*see p25*) underwear section. I also love Pixie on Fouberts Place for make-up and the Peanut Vendor in Newington Green (*see p182*).'

Any plans for the future?
'Well, I'd love to have all three floors of the shop open, and to expand into our yard. I want to sell garden furniture there and get my [other] brother, who's a pâtisserie chef, to come and do some cooking.
 'I think when other people expand they tend to let others run things for them but I'll always be here, sourcing and displaying my finds.'

▶ For **Smug**, see p45.
▶ For more on **Camden Passage**, see p106.

ONE-STOP

Shelf

look bags and wallets from Canadian brand Mat & Nat, candles (including own-brand soy candles made in Canada as part of a return-to-work programme), glass- and kitchenware, bathroom objects, and more. Owner Karim Ladak – who earned his stripes working for Habitat and Ralph Lauren – is friendly and informed, making shopping here a memorable experience. Also look out for classic and sustainable womenswear by designers such as Bitte Kai Rand – know for its natural fibres such as merino wool – and Frank & Faith, with a stylish and affordable range of dresses made from bamboo. Menswear includes the covetable Original Penguin polo tops, while unisex Dutch line Kuyichi has proved a big hit because of its stylish, fairly traded denim.

Shelf
40 Cheshire Street, E2 6EH (7739 9444, www.helpyourshelf.co.uk). Shoreditch High Street rail. **Open** noon-6pm Fri, Sat; 11am-6pm Sun.
Owners Jane Petrie and Katy Hackney set up this cute shop on Cheshire Street some ten years ago, and it's become a key destination when searching for a unique gift. The well-edited range of items for sale are intensely covetable, making it difficult to leave emptyhanded. Stylish notebooks and stationery, innovative ceramics – such as the adorable range from Berlin-based designer Frerk Muller, and storage jars and mugs from the Moomin Valley Collection – glassware from Japanese brand Shinzi Katoh, Rob Ryan-esque prints, beautiful wooden toys, including a set of 'naked' Russian dolls, are all sourced from designers and artists worldwide. A box in the corner is full of typesetting letters from silent movies that Petrie once picked up in Los Angeles.

Shop at Bluebird
350 King's Road, SW3 5UU (7351 3873, www.theshopatbluebird.com). Sloane Square tube. **Open** 10am-7pm Mon-Sat; noon-6pm Sun. **Sells** M, W, C.
In an airy art deco garage on the King's Road you'll find this chic lifestyle boutique. Owners John and Belle Robinson (the people behind womenswear chain Jigsaw) may cite European concept stores such as Colette in Paris as inspiration, but there's none of the froideur associated with such temples to avant-garde design. On display in the 10,000sq ft space is a broad selection of designer clothing, shoes, accessories, books, music (both CDs and vinyl) and the odd piece of furniture. The shop also boasts a spa offering shoppers the chance to unwind with a variety of treatments. There's also a slew of hard-to-find niche skincare brands, including New York's Bigelow, Ole Henriksen, DCL and Kaeline. Fashion is wide-ranging; London-based designers Emma Cook and Peter Jensen are to be found here, as are US faves Alexander Wang and Marc by Marc Jacobs and Japanese heavyweights Junya Watanabe and Comme des Garçons. Look out for lesser-known labels as well, such as the rock-inspired Rika and Isabel Marant, and vintage-inspired eyewear from hip label Prism. Cool denim brands also feature heavily, and there's a trendy range of prints, coffee-table books and CDs.

Smug
13 Camden Passage, N1 8EA (7354 0253, www.ifeelsmug.com). Holborn or Russell Square tube. **Open** 11am-6pm Wed, Fri, Sat; noon-7pm Thur; noon-5pm Sun.
Graphic designer Lizzie Evans has decked out this new lifestyle boutique with all her favourite things; the result is a space that's a labour of love as well as a canny commercial move. With its rainbow kitchen accessories, Lisa Stickley wash bags, vintage-inspired soft toys and 1950s and '60s furniture (of the Formica and Maid Server ilk), you can see why she might be proud of it. Pixie make-up, retro brooches, old-fashioned notebooks, stylish alarm clocks, colourful cushions and a cute range of aprons and tea towels are further draws. The old-skool Casio watches for men and women, displayed in the glass-top counter, are particularly popular purchases. *See also p43* **Shop talk**.

Something…
58 Lamb's Conduit Street, WC1N 3LW (7430 1516, www.something-shop.com). Holborn or Russell Square tube. **Open** 10.30am-6pm Mon-Fri; 11am-5pm Sat.
Toni Horton's bright shop is crammed full of keepsakes and accessories. Stock is of a feminine and romantic – yet mature – bent: think sophisticated, bead-encrusted evening bags, embroided scarves, girly toiletries bags, slipper socks, Cath Kidston-esque mugs and cake stands and heart-shaped mirrors. Books with titles such as *Things to Do with Mum* and *Love Letters of Great Women* continue the theme, ensuring that this place is a first-port-of-call for Mothers' Day shopping. The jewellery, meanwhile, has a more youthful feel, featuring bead bracelets, heart charms and gobstopper-sized cocktail rings. High-end beauty and bath goodies include solid bars of fine Provençal soap. In the summer, head to the back garden for a pots and furniture.

Space EC1
25 Exmouth Market, EC1R 4QL (7837 1344). Angel tube or Farringdon tube/rail or 19, 38, 341 bus. **Open** 10.30am-6pm Mon-Fri; 11am-5pm Sat.
This kitsch independent gift shop does novelty with humour and class, and is a good bet for quick-fix presents with heart. You'll find a cache of top-notch cards, quirk and gifty items, such as origami kits, Celia Bertwell gardening tools and gloves, Moleskin notebooks, tea cosies, knitted hot-water bottle covers, and Joseph Joseph kitchenware. Items by cult designers are high on the agenda here, with bags from Lisa Stickley, homewares and placemats from Ella Doran, as well as the cute baby fashion range by Organics for Kids. Tasteful wrapping paper rounds off Space EC1's well-chosen selection.

Markets

London's neighbourhood markets remain the lifeblood of London shopping, but relatively few remain the domain of salt-of-the-earth Cockney costermongers. Instead, you'll find fashion kids showing off their new vintage sunglasses over a soy latte and a bag of heirloom tomatoes – something that is particularly the case with the now hyped to the max **Broadway Market**.

London's most famous markets are also still going strong: despite ongoing major redevelopment, **Camden Market**, **Borough Market** and **Portobello Road Market** remain key tourist attractions – so only visit if you can stomach the crowds or get there as early as possible and move on when others move in.

For antiques markets and arcades, *see p178*.

Central

Borough Market
Southwark Street, SE1 1TL (7407 1002, www.boroughmarket.org.uk). London Bridge tube/rail. **Open** 11am-5pm Thur; noon-6pm Fri; 8am-5pm Sat.
London's oldest market – dating back to the 13th century – is also the busiest, and most popular for gourmet goodies. Here, traders satisfy the city's insatiable appetite for beautifully displayed organic fruit and veg, cakes, bread, olive oil, fish, meat and booze. Our favourite stalls include Northfield Farm for rare-breed meat, Furness for fish and game, Elsey & Bent for fruit and veg and Flour Power City Bakery for artisan loaves. Enjoy free samples and be prepared for lengthy queues for Brindisa's barbecued chorizo and rocket rolls. Seasonal tasting days and festivals run throughout the year and opening hours extend in the run-up to Christmas.

Cabbages & Frocks
St Marylebone Parish Church Grounds, Marylebone High Street, W1 (7794 1636, www.cabbagesandfrocks.co.uk). Baker Street tube. **Open** 11am-5pm Sat.
Held in the attractive cobbled yard of St Marylebone parish church, this market was started by food-loving fashionista Angela Cash. The Saturday crowd is drawn to a host of fashion retailers as well as mouthwatering grub. Stalls satisfy even the most demanding taste buds, with stuffed organic chicken, hog roast, Jamaican rum cakes, flavoured olives and shortbreads. You can choose to take your goods home or eat them on the spot. There's a range of retro and vintage clothing plus work from independent designers and craftspeople. Look out for special events (dog day, children's workshops) that are held throughout the year.

Camden Markets
Camden Market *192-200 Camden High Street, junction with Buck Street, NW1 (7267 3417, www.camdenmarkets.org). Camden Town tube.* **Open** 9.30am-5.30pm daily.
Camden Lock Market *Camden Lock Place, off Chalk Farm Road, NW1 (7485 7963, www.camdenlockmarket.com). Camden Town tube.* **Open** 10am-6pm Mon-Thur, Sun; 10am-6.30pm Fri, Sat.
Electric Ballroom *184 Camden High Street, NW1 (7485 9006, www.electricballroom.co.uk). Camden Town tube.* **Open** 10am-5pm Sat, Sun.
Stables Market *off Chalk Farm Road, opposite junction with Hartland Road, NW1 (7485 5511, www.stablesmarket.com). Camden Town tube.* **Open** 10am-6pm daily.
Camden's collection of markets offers a smörgåsbord of street culture. It's quieter during the week but weekends are better for variety and atmosphere – pass loitering goths and scowling punks to join crowds of tourists, locals and random celebs bustling around 700 shops and stalls. The multi-million-pound development of the Stables area sees a combination of fashion and food focused around the art and exhibition space. Find stalls selling antiques and bric-a-brac at the Horse Tunnel Market. Camden Lock sells everything from corsets and childrenswear to Japanese tableware and delicious food stalls. Head to Camden (Buck Street) Market for cheapo jeans, T-shirts and accessories.

Portobello Road Market
Portobello Road, W10 & W11 (www.portobello road.co.uk). Ladbroke Grove, Notting Hill Gate or Westbourne Park tube. **Open** *General* 8am-6pm Mon-Wed; 9am-1pm Thur; 7am-7pm Fri, Sat. *Antiques* 4am-4pm Sat.
Portobello is actually several markets stretched out up one long strip of road: antiques start at the Notting Hill Gate end; further up are food stalls; and emerging designer and vintage clothes are found under the Westway flyover and along the walkway to Ladbroke Grove. A visit here is as much about soaking up the vibe as it is about shopping. Saturdays are manically busy so head out early, especially if you're serious about buying antiques. Friday is less hectic and one of the best days for sourcing clothes from up-and-coming fashion designers. Best of all are the fantastic shops lining the surrounding streets; escape the crowds with a browse round Ledbury Road's boutiques.

Spitalfields Market
Commercial Street, between Lamb Street & Brushfield Street, E1 (7247 8556, www.visitspitalfields.com). Liverpool Street tube/rail or Shoreditch High Street rail. **Open** *General* 10am-4pm Mon-Fri; 9am-5pm Sun. *Antiques*

Markets

Borough Market

ONE-STOP

Time Out London's Best Shops 47

ONE-STOP

FIVE More central markets

Berwick Street Market
Berwick Street, Rupert Street, W1. Oxford Circus tube.
Open 9am-6pm Mon-Sat.
This buzzy street market, in a sometimes sleazy area, is one of London's oldest.

Leather Lane
Leather Lane, between Greville Street & Clerkenwell Road, EC4 (www.leatherlane market.co.uk). Chancery Lane tube.
Open 10am-2.30pm Mon-Fri.
Lunchtime market selling cut-price clothing, cheap towels, plus flowers, fruit and veg.

Lower Marsh
Lower Marsh, from Westminster Bridge Road to Baylis Road, SE1 (7926 2530, www.lower-marsh.co.uk). Lambeth North tube. **Open** 8am-6pm Mon, Tue, Thur, Sat; 10am 3pm Wed; 8am-7pm Fri.
A street market since Victorian times; there's some quality veg, women's clothes, decent jewellery and vintage shops.

Petticoat Lane Market
Middlesex Street, Goulston Street, New Goulston Street, Toynbee Street, Wentworth Street, Bell Lane, Cobb Street, Leyden Street, Strype Street, E1 (7364 1717). Aldgate or Aldgate East tube.
Open 8am-4pm Mon-Fri (Goulston Street, Toynbee Street & Wentworth Street only); 9am-2pm Sun.
Mainly tat, but good for the odd bargain.

Whitecross Street Food Market
Whitecross Weekly Food Market, Whitecross Street, EC1 (7378 0422, www.whitecrossstreet.co.uk). Barbican tube/rail. **Open** 11am-5pm Thur, Fri.
Now a twice-weekly affair; the Latin American street food stalls are excellent.

Sunday (Up)Market

9am-4pm Thur. *Food* 10am-5pm Wed, Fri, Sun. *Fashion* 10am-4pm Fri. *Records & books* 10am-4pm 1st & 3rd Fri of mth.

Redevelopment has seen this East End stalwart combine the refurbished 1887 covered market with a modern shopping precinct. Around the edge, enthusiastic stallholders sell grub from just about every corner of the world. Sunday is busiest; browsing options include creations by up-and-coming designers, vintage clobber, crafts, jewellery, books and sheepskin rugs. There's a new fine food market held three times a week in Crispin Place with over 20 traders, many of whom can also be found at Borough Market. A record market is held twice a month. Note that Spitalfields is not open on Saturdays.

Sunday (Up)Market

91 Brick Lane, The Old Truman Brewery (entrances on Brick Lane & Hanbury Street), E1 6QL (7770 6028, www.sundayupmarket.co.uk). Shoreditch High Street rail. **Open** 10am-5pm Sun.

Another good reason to head out east on Sundays (and very easily combined with a trip to nearby Spitalfields (*see p46*) or Brick Lane (*see below*), the Old Truman Brewery's buzzy (Up)Market boasts some 140 stalls toting edgy fashion from young designers (many fresh from fashion college), vintage gear, gifts, art and crafts and well-priced jewellery. Food stalls offer everything from dainty, pastel-coloured cupcakes to rich Ethiopian coffee, Japanese yakisoba, tapas and dim sum (a few of the vendors have lounging areas for customers too). There's a more relaxed vibe here than at Spitalfields and prices tend to be lower.

Local

Brick Lane Market

Brick Lane (north of railway bridge), Cygnet Street, Sclater Street, E1; Bacon Street, Cheshire Street, E2 (7364 1717). Aldgate East tube or Shoreditch High Street rail. **Open** 8am-3pm Sun.

Tools, household goods and fruit and veg sold by the bowl are among the offerings at this busy East End market. Also worth a look are the fascinating makeshift stalls set up on blankets at the side of the road – dodgy old videos, broken dolls, CD players and dubiously acquired bicycles abound. After you've browsed the Sunday (Up)Market (see above), nip into the Backyard Market (on the right just past Dray Walk) for more than 100 stalls selling vintage clothes, accessories, jewellery, antiques, collectibles, innumerable food stalls, and a certain amount of bric-a-brac.

Broadway Market

Broadway Market, E8 4PH (www.broadway market.co.uk). London Fields rail or 236, 394 bus. **Open** 8.30am-4.30pm Sat.

ONE-STOP

Columbia Road Market

If it's Saturday, then it must be Hackney's Broadway Market, at least as far as east London's fashionably attired food-lovers are concerned. Many of the congregate on the market, picking up well-priced fresh fruit and veg, artisan cheeses, rare-breed meat, luscious cakes and indulging in top-notch snacking options from an array of hot food stalls (the Ghanaian food from Spinach & Agushi is particularly worth making a beeline for). It also has stalls selling vintage and new designer threads, old *Vogue* patterns, buttons, Ladybird books, flowers and hand-knits. The shops, restaurants and pubs that line the street are worth browsing through as well – in particular Black Truffle, Fabrications, the Broadway Bookshop and Artwords; for further information on all of these shops and the street in general, *see p137* **Streetwise**.

Columbia Road Market

Columbia Road, E2 (7364 1717). Hoxton or Shoreditch High Street rail. **Open** *8am-2pm Sun.*
One of London's most visually appealing markets, Columbia Road overflows with buckets full of beautiful flowers. There are bulbs, herbs, shrubs and bedding plants too. Alongside the market you'll find a host of independent galleries and shops selling pottery, perfume, vintage clothes, hats (two shops), children's clothes and the like. Turn up as things start to wind down at around 2pm for the best bargains, or as early as humanly possible if you want to guarantee yourself the pick of the crop. There are also a number of decent places to have coffee and cake or a full blown Sunday lunch.

Greenwich Market

Off College Approach, SE10 (8269 5096, www.greenwichmarket.net). Greenwich rail or Cutty Sark DLR. **Open** *Antiques & collectibles* 10am-5.30pm Thur, Fri. *Village Market Stockwell Street,* 10am-5.30pm Wed-Sun. *Arts & crafts* 9.30am-5.30pm Thur-Sun.
There are plenty of stalls selling bric-a-brac, second-hand clothes, ethnic ornaments, CDs, crafts and jewellery galore at Greenwich Market on the weekends. We love Sophia & Matt's bags (washbags, make-up bags, handbags) and accessories made in funky laminated fabrics. On Thursdays and Fridays, the market takes a different turn with an excellent antiques and collectibles market. Thursday is best time for unearthing unusual finds and provides a selection of stalls dealing in antique jewellery, vintage clothes, old books, music and

Markets

ONE-STOP

Columbia Road Market. See p50.

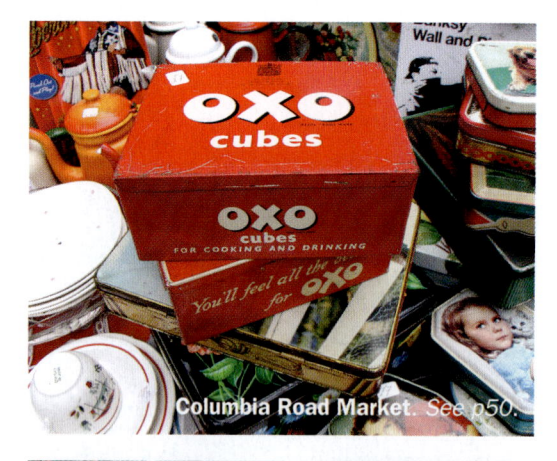

collectibles – the Calneva Vintage stall with its cool 1950s and '60s homewares, ceramics, lamps, handbags and compacts is just one such example.

Shepherd's Bush Market
East side of railway viaduct, between Uxbridge Road & Goldhawk Road, W12 (8749 3042, www.shepherdsbushmarket.co.uk). Goldhawk Road or Shepherd's Bush tube. **Open** 10.30am-6.30pm Mon-Sat.

While Shepherd's Bush Market is just a hop and a skip away from Europe's largest urban shopping centre at Westfield, it's a world apart in every other sense. At this gritty, multicultural market you'll find a fantastic range of ethnic foodstuffs (Indian, Caribbean, African and Polish). Stalls selling fragrant spices, yams, coconuts, cassava, okra, falafel, mangoes and some of the freshest fish in the capital line the strip between Uxbridge and Goldhawk Roads. You'll also see vivid print fabrics, goatskin rugs, saris, home furnishings, electronic equipment, CDs and DVDs. Visit the nearby branch of TRAID (154 Uxbridge Road, 8811 2400, www.traid.org.uk) for its 'remade' items: second-hand goods transformed into fashionable gear.

FIVE More local markets

Brixton Market
Electric Avenue, Pope's Road, Brixton Station Road, SW9 (7926 2530, www.brixtonmarket.net). Brixton tube/rail. **Open** 8am-6pm Mon, Tue, Thur-Sat; 8am-3pm Wed.
Head here for exotic fruit and veg, halal meats, fish, fabrics, household goods, reggae music, and wigs.

Northcote Road Market
Northcote Road, SW11. Clapham Junction tube/rail. **Open** 10am-6pm Mon-Sat. *Antiques* 10am-6pm Mon-Sat; noon-5pm Sun.
Decent fruit and veg, flowers, ceramics, vintage clothes, plus the Antiques Market (no.155A, 7228 6850) and some excellent independent shops.

Ridley Road Market
Ridley Road, off Kingsland High Street, E8 (www.ridleyroad.co.uk). Dalston Kingsland tube. **Open** 9am-5pm Mon-Fri; 9am-5.30pm Sat.
Everything from domestic and exotic fruit and veg, fish and meat to cheap clothes, bric-a-brac and fabrics from Africa and India.

Southall Market
The Cattle Market, High Street, opposite North Road, Southall, Middx UB1 3DG. Southall rail. **Open** *General* 9am-3pm Sat. *Furniture* 4am-1pm Fri.
A cross between a traditional market and a visit to India: fresh produce, spices and sari fabrics.

Walthamstow Market
Walthamstow High Street, E17 (8496 3000). Walthamstow Queen's Road tube. **Open** 8am-5pm Tue-Sat.
The longest market in Europe, with loads of fruit and veg stalls, a good selection of Asian and Caribbean products, fabric, flowers and more.

Fashion

Indie Boutiques	**56**
High Street	**76**
Designer Chains	**85**
Tailoring & Bespoke	**95**
Vintage & Second-hand	**98**
Lingerie, Swimwear & Erotica	**107**
Weddings	**115**
Maternity & Unusual Sizes	**117**
Shoes	**119**
Jewellery & Accessories	**128**

Fashion

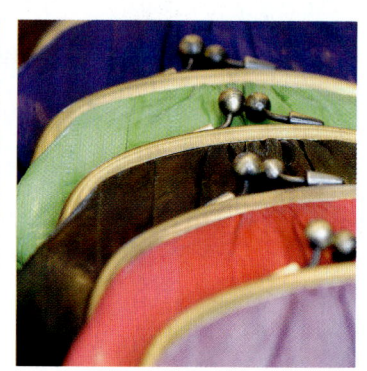

London remains one of the world's top destinations for clothes shopping, catering for all styles and budgets; designer fiends, directional fashionistas, as well as those with more traditional sartorial tastes, all have a host of top-notch independents in which to flex the plastic, on top of the excellent fashion sections of London's department stores. For, despite the nationwide homogenisation of the high street over the past decade or so, London's independent fashion shops are flourishing, with boutique-dominated shopping streets – such as **Lamb's Conduit** and **Ledbury Road** – well-trodden destinations for style-conscious consumers who want a more relaxed and personal shopping experience.

This experience-led trend has been propelled by the city's concept stores and pop-up shops – places that are particularly strong in the realm of fashion. As shopping has become a form of entertainment, stores such as **Dover Street Market** (see p39) have become hip hangouts for the city's fashionistas. There has been an increasing number of shops catering for menswear in recent years too; boutiques such as **Hurwundeki** (see p61), **Goodhood** (see p59) and **Hub** (see p60) are as well versed in current menswear styles and labels as they are women's.

Those with wallets thick enough to buy them a designer wardrobe also have much to celebrate; the opening of the fabulous **Louis Vuitton Maison** (see p88) in summer 2010 means yet another high-profile designer flagship in the city. Many used designer pieces can also be picked up from the city's superb vintage shops. **Merchant Archive** (see p101), an excellent west London newcomer, has great pickings; or, for cheaper, flea-market-style garb, head to east London's huge **Beyond Retro** (see p98), a fun destination that also puts on regular events for the local hipsters.

For a traditional London experience, head to the capital's excellent accessories boutiques; shops such as umbrella specialist **James Smith & Sons** (see p128) and **Bates the Hatter** (see p131) have been features of the city's shopping scene for well over a century, and are complemented by excellent comparative newcomers such as **Mimi** (see p131) and **Ally Capellino** (see p128) – both firm faves with the city's creatives.

In London, high street shops still have much to compete with, meaning that the chains are forced to stay on their toes; the flagships of **Urban Outfitters** (see p83) and **Topshop** (see p81) are much more than your average high street shops, stocking a huge range of directional international labels to compliment their own stylish lines. And although the lure of £3 Primark T-shirts is evidently still irresistible to many, the wave of more eco-conscious fashion shops continues to edge forwards, with shops such as **Equa** (see p69) and new concept store **123 Boutique** (see p42) leading the way.

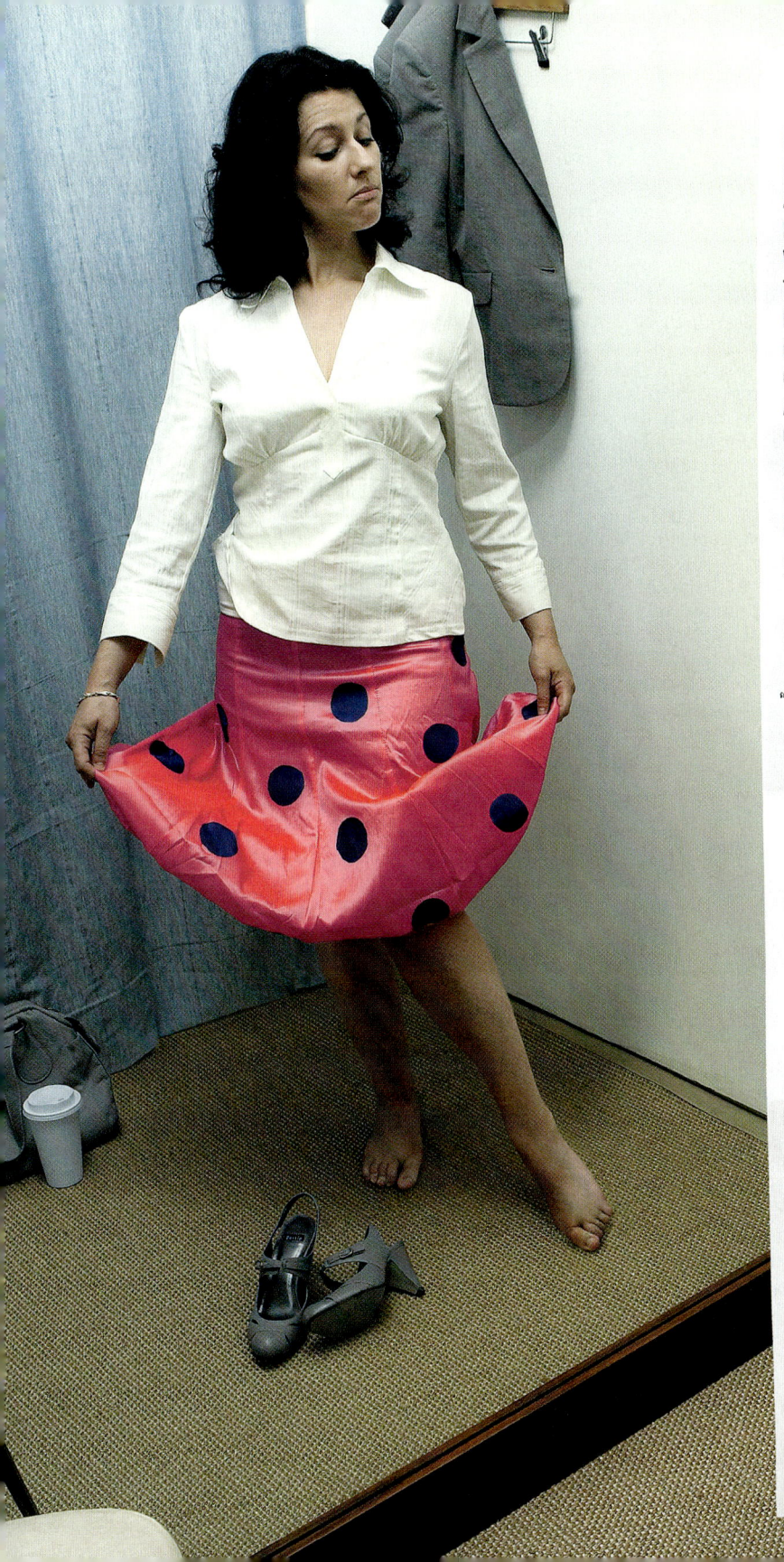

POLKADOT SKIRT, BOUGHT THE MORNING AFTER THE STAFF PARTY WHEN I WASN'T FEELING TOO WITH IT. I'D ONLY POPPED OUT TO GET A COFFEE WHEN ALL THE MEMORIES OF THE NIGHT BEFORE CAME FLOODING BACK - SQUEEKY JOANNE WITH THAT NEW BOY IN FINANCE. SHE GETS ALL THE ATTENTION. "IT'S THOSE OUTRAGEOUS OUTFITS," I SAID TO MYSELF. THE NEXT THING I KNEW, I WAS IN A DRESSING ROOM TRYING ON THIS SKIRT.

WELL, SOMEONE'S GOTTA GIVE JOANNE A RUN FOR HER MONEY: £95

KEEPING THE RECEIPT: PRICELESS®

MasterCard

There are some things money can't buy.
For everything else there's MasterCard.

Indie Boutiques

Men & women

b Store [HOT 50]
24A Savile Row, W1S 3PR (7734 6846, www.bstorelondon.com). Oxford Circus tube. **Open** 10.30am-6.30pm Mon-Fri; 10am-6pm Sat.
One of London's trendiest clothes shops, b store's reputation as a stockist of innovative fashion labels remains unimpeachable – where else can you pick up clothes designed by this year's Saint Martin's graduates? Choose from both emerging and more established designers, including Ian Batten, Opening Ceremony and Peter Jensen. The in-house b Store label goes from strength to strength, with stylish but wearable clothing for both men and (since 2009) women. The look manages to be simultaneously avant-garde and classic, with simple cuts, muted tones and a unisex aesthetic composed of simple blazers, striped T-shirts and linen shirts; created originally as a shoe brand, the label's large collection of footwear remains equally cutting-edge. The store itself often houses installations by artists, and also stocks a range of trendy fashion and photography coffee-table books.

Bread & Honey
205 Whitecross Street, EC1Y 8QP (7253 4455, www.backin10minutes.com). Old Street tube/rail. **Open** 10am-6.30pm Mon-Wed, Fri; 10am-7pm Thur; 11am-6pm Sat.
Given its petite size and off-centre location, this French-owned men and women's boutique does surprisingly well. The reason being that the selection of goods – the interesting but not ostentatious end of streetwear – is well selected and the staff friendly and frank. On our last visit we were given a definite 'no' verdict on a T-shirt, surely not something that happens all too often. Menswear is particularly strong – look out for pieces by Baracuta, fine-knit sweaters by Modern Amusement and Pointer footwear. Women are catered for with pieces by Marimekko, Sessùn, Ben Sherman Women and Laura Lees. Bready & Honey's sister store, the Store Rooms (43 Pitfield Street, N1 6DA, 7608 105, www.thestorerooms.com) is a timely idea: a crisply styled sale shop where all items are discounted 35-70%, all the time. The stock changes constantly, but past finds have included Penfield gilets or Sibin Linnebjerg's 1960s-inspired cardigans.

Browns [HOT 50]
23-27 South Molton Street, W1K 5RD (7514 0000, www.brownsfashion.com). Bond Street tube. **Open** 10am-6.30pm Mon-Wed, Fri, Sat; 10am-7pm Thur.
For the ultimate fashion fix look no further than Joan Burstein's venerable store, which celebrated its 40th anniversary in 2010. Among the 100-odd designers jostling for attention at its five interconnecting shops are fashion heavyweights Chloé, Dries Van Noten, Balenciaga and Christian Dior. Burstein (aka 'Mrs B') has always championed the next-big-things from the fashion elite, so you'll also find designs from rising stars like Christopher Kane, Marios Schwab and Todd Lynn, and shop exclusives are common. The women's shoe salon, meanwhile, showcases fabulous footwear from Alaïa, Alexander McQueen and Christian Louboutin. The two-floor menswear section brings together an unrivalled collection of high-end designer gear, from Dior Homme to Miu Miu. Across the road, Browns Focus caters for a younger crowd, with more accessibly priced labels, such as 3.1 Phillip Lim, Alexander Wang and Ann-Sofie Back, as well as shoes by Charlotte Olympia and denim from Superfine and J Brand. Up at no.50, the sale shop, Browns Labels for Less (*see p89* **Sales & events**), is loaded with leftovers from the previous season.
Branches Browns Focus, 38-39 South Molton Street, W1K 5RD (7514 0000); Browns Labels for Less, 50 South Molton Street, W1K 5RD (7514 0000); Browns Bride, 11-12 Hinde Street, W1U 3BE (7514 0056); 6C Sloane Street, SW1X 9LE (7514 0040); Browns Shoes, 59 Brook Street, W1K 4HS (7514 0000).

Cinch
5 Newburgh Street, W1F 7RB (7287 4941, www.eu.levi.com). Oxford Circus tube. **Open** 11am-6.30pm Mon-Sat; 1-5pm Sun.
Levi's Cinch store is the geeky-cool little brother of the flagship round the corner on Regent's Street, stocking anything that's too exclusive or expensive for its mainstream sibling. Denim enthusiasts come here for Levi's conceptual RED line as well as its vintage collection that harks back to the label's 1873 origins, or maybe just back to 1994 and that Stiltskin advert of lore. Think classic white T-shirts in cuts that correspond to the decade they came out in and USA-made vintage dry jeans. The latter are justifiably popular, though some pairs come in ridiculously baggy cuts. You might prefer to play it safe with the 1947 501s classic fit.

Diverse [HOT 50]
294 Upper Street, N1 2TU (7359 8877, www.diverseclothing.com). Angel tube. **Open** 10.30am-6.30pm Mon-Wed, Fri, Sat; 10.30am-7.30pm Thur; noon-5.30pm Sun.
Islington stalwart Diverse does a fine job of keeping N1's style queens in fashion-forward mode. Despite the cool clobber, chic layout and striking window displays, this is the sort of place where you can rock up in jeans and scuzzy Converse and not feel uncomfortable trying on next season's See by Chloé. And while you're there,

Diverse

Clerkenwell Vintage Fashion Fair
★★★★★

Check website for dates

Heirlooms not Landfill!

45 Stalls, 1800s-1980s,
Menswear & Womenswear,
Tea Room, Alterations,
Special guests

The Urdang, The Old Finsbury Town Hall,
Rosebery Avenue, EC1

www.clerkenwellvintagefashionfair.co.uk

Frock Me!

the essential vintage fashion event
CHELSEA
www.frockmevintagefashion.com

Laird London

caps • hats • accessories
020 7240 4240
23 NEW ROW, COVENT GARDEN, LONDON, WC2N 4LA
128 COLUMBIA ROAD, SHOREDITCH, LONDON, E2 7RG

www.lairdlondon.co.uk

you might as well give that Marc by Marc Jacobs dress a try, and maybe a little something by Vanessa Bruno, and those Repetto ballet slippers are looking good, come to think of it. You get the picture. This is a well-edited collection of incredibly desirable garments, plus some original jewellery, accessories and shoes thrown in for good measure. There's plenty for the more feminine or classic dresser too, such as Diana von Furstenberg and tasteful Parisian label Isabel Marant. Dutch label Humanoid is also represented, as well as Sonia Rykiel, APC and APC Madras and Future Classics. There are also Open Ceremony shoes, Elliot jeans and gorgeous cashmere from CASH CA. The menswear labels that used to be stocked in the branch at no.286 (Marc by Marc Jacobs, Trovata, Universal Works and Unconditional among them) were being moved into this branch as this guide went to press.

Folk

49 Lamb's Conduit Street, WC1N 3NG (7404 6458, www.folkclothing.com). Holborn tube.
Open 11am-7pm Mon-Sat; noon-5pm Sun.
Folk was born in 2001 and is the label of choice for guys who once dressed like skaters, then progressed to labels like Silas and are now after more quality, more respectability and less branding. The silhouette and the fabrics are comfortable but hip and slightly dishevelled – in a tasteful rather than grungey way (think stripes, quality knits and casual jackets in bold colours). Sister brand Shofolk offers stylish but comfortable shoes for men and women that have a hand-crafted feel (the moccasin-inspired styles dominate the collection). This is the place to head to for stylish womenswear labels Humanoid and Sessùn, and women are also catered for with a well-edited selection of jeans (from brands such as Lee) and accessories. Keep a look out for the shop's excellent sample sales. A second standalone store opened in east London's Old Truman Brewery in December 2009, while the also brand has concessions in Shop at Bluebird (*see p45*) and Selfridges (*see p27*).
Branch 11 Dray Walk, E1 6QL (7375 2844).

Goodhood HOT 50

41 Coronet Street, N1 6HD (7729 3600, www.goodhood.co.uk). Old Street tube/rail.
Open 11am-7pm Mon-Fri; 11am-6.30pm Sat.
Stock for this boutique-like store is selected by streetwear obsessives/owners Kyle and Jo with items weighted towards Japanese independent labels. Knits and T-shirts from Australia's Rittenhouse are particularly strong, while other hot picks from the well-edited selection include shirts and tops for men from Norse Projects, womenswear from APC Madras, and supremely covetable pieces for both men and women from Peter Jensen and Wood Wood. A cabinet full of reasonably priced watches, sunglasses and jewellery makes this a great place for pressies for hard-to-please hipster boyfriends and girlfriends, while the limited-edition Vans will have trainer nerds frothing at the mouth.

Folk

howies

42 Carnaby Street, W1F 7DY (7287 2345, www.howies.co.uk). Oxford Circus tube.
Open 10am-7pm Mon-Wed, Fri, Sat; 10am-8pm Thur; 11am-5pm Sun.

Ethical UK brand howies started off as a small-scale T-shirt business, and has evolved to become a core label for youthful outdoorsy types, with a strong following among mountain bikers, surfers and skaters. Its merino wool thermals are wardrobe staples. This Carnaby Street store currently remains the only standalone shop in London – but watch this space, as more are likely to follow. Products are made to last (with the 'hand-me-down' line of jackets and bags guaranteed for a minimum of ten years) and are designed with a mix of the functional and stylish in mind. For instance, the brand's trendy wet weather jeans are made with rainproof Epic cotton; T-shirts – often with witty slogans – are made with organic cotton; while women's underwear is made using Modal fibre, which is softer and longer-lasting than cotton. Beyond the bestselling jackets, sweaters and other outdoorsy gear is a range of straightforward but stylish skirts, dresses, trousers, polos, shirts and kidswear, with stripes, checks and summery shades in abundance; while additional non-clothing items include Green Oil bike cleaner and Ras Label knitted iPod cases. What's more, the company continues to have a conscience, despite its continued growth, with 1% of the company's turnover pledged to environmental and social projects. Children's clothes are also stocked.

Hub

49 & 88 Stoke Newington Church Street, N16 0AR (7254 4494, www.hubshop.co.uk). Bus 73, 393, 476. **Open** 10.30am-6.30pm Mon-Sat; 11am-5pm Sun.

Hub stocks a well-edited selection of covetable mid-range designer labels, with See by Chloé and Sonia by Sonia Rykiel much in evidence. Spot a brace of trendy-looking yummy mummies in a Stokey café and chances are they'll have picked up their Acne skinny jeans or Cacharel blouses here. No.49 houses the womenswear; as well as the labels mentioned above, there are pieces by Thomas Burberry and Hoss Intropia, jeans by Lee, Won Hundred, coats from Mackintosh, lingerie from Princesse Tam Tam, Peter Jenson T-shirts and sweatshirts, Ally Capellino and Mimi bags, affordable jewellery from the likes of Comfort Station, plus everyday knits, stylish tops and dresses with a quirky edge by co-owner Beth Graham. It's also a good bet for a choice selection of shoes (by the likes of F-Troupe) and scarves. Over the road at no.88, Hub Men stocks many of the same labels, as well as knits by John Smedley and a selection of items from Folk, Fred Perry, Barbour and more. An excellent neighbourhood boutique.

Indie Boutiques

Hurwundeki HOT 50
98 Commercial Street, E1 6LZ (7734 1050, www.hurwundeki.com). Liverpool Street tube/rail. **Open** 11am-7.30pm Mon-Fri; 10am-7.30pm Sat, Sun.

The first Hurwundeki store – a mix of vintage boutique and trendy hair salon – was established in Spitalfields in 2004. Six years later and the East End unit now houses cherry-picked vintage alongside the successful Hurwundeki own-label – a wearable and well-priced collection of mens- and womenswear, designed in east London, which mixes British and Far Eastern heritage, with an arty east London twist. Meanwhile, the salon has moved around the corner to Puma Court, a West End outpost has opened, just off the perennially modish Carnaby Street, and a café and retro homewares branch has now been set-up under the railway arches on Hackney's Cambridge Heath Road. The original store's idiosyncratic interior (think exposed brick walls, stripped floorboards and an assortment of curios and antiques acting as props and display cabinets) complements the label's garments perfectly – tartan and checks are often in evidence, while cuts of the shirts, shift dresses and chino-style trousers are of a unisex bent; the brand is particularly strong on winter coats, rain jackets, dresses and accessories, which include a fabulous array of bags, scarves, hats, braces and bow-ties for the modern dandy.

Branch Unit G4, Kingly Court, W1B 5PW (7734 1050).

Imperious Rex!
75 Roman Road, E2 0QN (8981 3392, www.imperiousrex.com). Bethnal Green tube/rail. **Open** noon-7pm Mon-Fri; 10am-6pm Sat; noon-5pm Sun.

True, this hyper-trendy T-shirt boutique is a little out of the way, and it's also one of the smallest shops in the capital – if tried to swing a cat in here you'd knock all the stock off the walls. But a schlep here is rewarded with the crème de la crème of independent, mainly US streetwear brands, with Tees, hoodies and tops from Rocksmith, Mishka, Sixpack France and DIM MAC keeping the place busy since early 2008. Staff, or rather the other guy in the room with you, is the knowledgeable, chirpy TC, the owner, who'll be happy to talk you through what's hot in LA, New York or Paris. Girls can choose from an expanding selection of tops from the likes of Darkhouse and Coup De Grace but will often end up leaving with an oversized boys Tee. Best of all, you'll be hard pressed to find anything over £25. A gem.

JW Beeton
48-50 Ledbury Road, W11 2AJ (7229 8874). Notting Hill Gate tube. **Open** 10.30am-6pm Mon-Sat; noon-5pm Sun.

Now in its 14th year, JW Beeton is one of the longest serving boutiques in this now crowded patch of west London. Keen to cater for all sorts of budgets, owner Debbie Potts buys small quantities of European and

Hub

FASHION

Hub. *See p60.*

international labels (for men, women and children) and sells them at non-extravagant prices. Recent labels stocked include Diab'Less from Paris, Rützou from Denmark and funky knits from Brazilian label Cecilia Prado. A selection of bags, belts and shoes by the Jacksons are also on display, as well as pieces from Stella Forest, Hartford, Michael Stars, European Culture, Olive & Orange, and Odd Molly.

Kokon To Zai HOT 50
86 Golborne Road, W10 5PS (8960 3736, www.kokontozai.co.uk). Ladbroke Grove or Westbourne Park tube. **Open** 10am-6pm Mon-Sat.
Kokon To Zai specialises in avant-garde, weird and wonderful fashion. The buyers are adept at picking up young designers from the nearby London College of Fashion and Central Saint Martins, so you'll often see new names here first. The selection is constantly changing, but labels the shop continues to stock include darling of the nu-rave scene Cassette Playa, Bernhard Wilhelm and Vivienne Westwood. Ever present, however, is Marjan Pejoski, who made Björk's famous swan dress. Look out for his line of jewellery too; quirky silver and diamond pieces start at £250. For offbeat streetwear look no further than the house label KTZ, which excels in T-shirts and sweats with wacky prints (from £40).
Branch 57 Greek Street, W1D 3DX (7434 1316).

Lewis Leathers
3-5 Whitfield Street, W1T 2SA (7636 4314, www.lewisleathers.com). Goodge Street tube. **Open** 11am-6pm Mon-Sat.
With Kate Moss parading around in its tough-ass boots and every rocker worth their salt (The Clash, The Sex Pistols, Ramones, Iggy Pop) having worn its biker jackets, Lewis Leathers is a true Brit heritage brand. Reopening in January 2010 a stone's throw away from its old Great Portland Street site, which stood from 1892 until 1993 (and still using the same phone number it had in the 1930s), this icon of bikerwear cool is back with a fashion vengeance. Despite its cult Tokyo following and recent collaboration with Comme des Garçons, Lewis has left high-tech wizardry at the door at this made-to-measure shop selling 15 classic vintage designs from the '60s and '70s. It's not cheap – the top selling Roadmaster jacket is £700 – but if it ain't broke…

Machine-A
60 Berwick Street, W1F 8SU (7998 3385, www.machine-a.com). Oxford Circus tube. **Open** 11am-7pm Mon-Sat; noon-5pm Sun.
Having switched its name from Digitaria, this store-gallery (previously a 1950s tailor) in the heart of Soho continues to showcase hotly tipped young names, showcasing an eclectic but complementing range of styles. Its voluminous, old-fashioned shop windows, bisected by a narrow walkway to the door, are infamous in the neighbourhood. Packed with graduate collections, one-off pieces and artwork by Kate Moss's stylist, Johnny Blue Eyes, the place is a first port-of-call for stylists and fashion students. The shop's leftfield stock includes items from guest designers such as I Dream of Wires, Fanny & Jessy, Belle Sauvage and Gabriella Marina Gonzalez.

Matches
60-64 Ledbury Road, W11 2AJ (7221 0255, www.matchesfashion.com). Notting Hill Gate tube. **Open** 10am-6pm Mon-Sat; noon-6pm Sun.
The pick of the crop of assorted international designers are on show at this well-established west London boutique. Get yourself kitted out in high-end labels, the likes of Bottega Veneta, Burberry, Stella McCartney, Chloé, D&G, Lanvil, Balenciaga, Alexander McQueen, Prada, John Varvatos and Marc Jacobs. Across the road at Matches Spy there's more casual gear to be had, such as Acne Jeans, Heidi Klein and Theory. The dedicated Diane von Furstenberg store at no.83 is also part of the Matches empire. A good bet for fashion exclusives, the shop is aimed at monied women and men who have an eye for luxury.
Branches (Matches Spy) 85 Ledbury Road, W11 2AJ (7221 7334); Diane von Furstenberg, 83 Ledbury Road, W11 2AJ (7221 1120).

no-one
1 Kingsland Road, E2 8AA (7613 5314, www.no-one.co.uk). Old Street tube/rail. **Open** 11am-7pm Mon-Sat; noon-6pm Sun.
On the style-setting axis between Old Street and Kingsland Road, and entered via the adjoining coffee-shop, this cutting-edge store is a favourite of Shoreditch locals and noncomformist style icons. The store's buyers are brilliant at spotting cool new labels, and were the first to champion Swedish denim label Cheap Monday in Britain, which it continues to sell alongside denim by Lee. The stock ranges from the latest Ryan Noon womenswear, Via Snella and Trainspotter garb for men, reasonably priced feminine frocks by Mine (from £70), and kooky clothing by Henrik Vibskov. Shoes are catered for by Opening Ceremony, Swedish Hasbeens and b Store. The shop has counters brimming over with vintage sunglasses, knitted accessories, badges, jewellery, wittily branded toiletries and cult magazines and books.

Preen
5 Portobello Green, 281 Portobello Road, W10 5TZ (8968 1542, www.preen.eu). Ladbroke Grove tube. **Open** 11am-6pm Thur, Fri; 10am-6pm Sat.

FASHION

Hurwundeki. *See p61.*

Tucked quite literally under the Westway overpass, Preen – the hip British label from Justin Thornton and Thea Bregazzi – brings imaginative takes to traditional silhouettes; it's all about not trying too hard. Collections are characterised by urban, minimalist shapes and tame colour palettes cut with splashes of bombastic colour, such as cobalt blue, to stunning effect. Other highlights include typical Preen cocoon-shaped jackets, billowy shirt-dresses, skirts with belts, slouchy trousers and hoodie knitwear. It was one of the first labels to produce a capsule collection for Topshop. Look out for a great range of bags and shoes, plus an accessories range, launched in spring 2009. Other London stockists include Selfridges (*see p27*), Harrods (*see p22*) and Browns (*see p56*).

Sefton
271 Upper Street, N1 2UQ (7226 9822, www.seftonfashion.com). Highbury & Islington tube/rail. **Open** 10am-6.30pm Mon-Wed, Sat; 10am-7pm Thur, Fri; noon-6pm Sun.
At Sefton, another of Upper Street's stylish boutiques, high-end international designers sit alongside emerging labels. The ladies' branch at no.271 is brimming with reliably stylish names like Acne Jeans, the Miller sisters' Twenty8Twelve, Vivienne Westwood, YMC, Theory, Helmut Lang, Carven, J Brand, Marcus Lupfer, Epice and Jonathan Saunders. Sefton is also an excellent bet for affordable gold-plated jewellery of the Alex Monroe ilk. Further up Upper Street, on the other side of the road (at no.196), is the menwear store. Check out the Comme des Garçons KAWS wallets and polka-dot undies; quality pieces by the likes of John Smedley, Marni, Edwin, YMC, Marc Jacobs and Alexander McQueen swing from Sefton's rails.
Branch (menswear) 196 Upper Street, N1 1RQ (7226 7076)

Start
42-44 Rivington Street, EC2A 3BN (7729 3334, www.start-london.com). Old Street tube/rail. **Open** 10.30am-6.30pm Mon-Fri; 11am-6pm Sat; 1-5pm Sun.
Philip Start (founder of Woodhouse) and his wife Brix (former guitarist for punk rock band the Fall, and style expert on *Gok's Fashion Fix*) own these his 'n' hers boutiques. In the women's store you'll find well-known brands such as Sonia by Sonia Rykiel and Vanessa Bruno alongside up-and-coming labels like Richard Nicoll, David Szeto and Jean Pierre Braganza. There's also a hugely covetable range of accessories such as sunglasses by Cutler & Gross, an expanding shoe section and jewellery by Lucy Hutchings. Across the road at the men's store enjoy browsing rails of Neil Barrett, Martin Margiela, McQ, Moncler, ACNE, City Company and Comme des Garçon, who fragrances are also stocked. A recently opened third store on Rivington Street houses the Mr Start label including suits, ties, shirts and a made-to-measure service (prices for the latter start at £750), as well as Mulberry bags and a selection of cashmere.
Branches (menswear) 59 Rivington Street, EC2A 3QQ (7739 3636); **(Mr Start)** 40 Rivington Street EC2A 3LX (7729 6272).

Three Threads
47-49 Charlotte Road, EC2A 3QT (7749 0503, www.thethreethreads.com). Old Street tube/rail. **Open** 11am-7pm Mon-Sat; noon-5pm Sun.
Despite its trendy location in the heart of the Shoreditch Triangle, the Three Threads manages to be both laid-back and friendly. Decent background tunes, sofas and chatty, down-to-earth staff collude to create an experience more akin to lounging than shopping. The well-stocked shop is particularly good for shoes, stocking a carefully edited range that takes in Loakes, for an unpretentious British brogue, Clarks Originals and the largest range of Pointers in town. There's a good choice of T-shirts too, with many of the labels – Tonite, Suburban Bliss or Alakazam – run by mates of the store. Ultra-practical raincoats from Sweden's Fjall Raven, shirts from Denmark's Won Hundred and Garbstore; Libertine Libertine, Levis Vintage, Edwin Jeans are further draws. For women, there are tops, dresses and skirts from boho French label Sessùn, YMC, hip Oz brand Something Else, hip Swedish label WhyRed and bags by local fave Mimi. Commendably, much of the stock is from labels that take pride in manufacturing their clothing nationally – brands such as Post NY (made in New Jersey) and New Balance (from Cumbria). The a small but covetable range of jewellery and sunglasses (of the Wayfarers ilk).

YMC
11 Poland Street, W1F 8QA (7494 1619, www.youmustcreate.com). Oxford Circus tube. **Open** 11am-7pm Mon-Sat.
The flagship of the London label that made us go weak at the wallets for impeccably designed staples. YMC (You Must Create) is the place to head for simple vest top, stylish macs and duffle coats, tasteful knits and on-trend chino-style trousers for women, and a larger range of casual jackets, shirts and T-shirts in pleasing tones, chinos, nicely fitting jeans, shorts and shoes for men and women. And the brand has now also gone back to basics, finally taking heed of the whole diffusion line trend by launching a collection of budget menswear. Unlike some flog-it-cheap endeavours, however, this one's totally worth the hype. There are raglan shirts, Oxford stripe shorts, and – the most expensive item – a waxed cotton mac, a snip at £117. With not an ounce of fit or detail compromised throughout the collection, it's a rare chance to nab something designer at high-street prices.

Men

Albam
Old Spitalfields Market, 111A Commercial Street, E1 6BG. (7247 6254, www.albamclothing.com). Liverpool Street tube/rail. **Open** 11am-7pm Mon-Sat; 11am-6pm Sun.
Late in 2007, Alastair Rae and James Shaw's excellent menswear line, Albam, jumped off the internet and into its first store on Beak Street. The label's refined yet rather manly aesthetic soon won it a loyal fanbase, dressing well-heeled gents, fashion editors and regular guys who appreciate no-nonsense style. With a focus on classic, high-quality design with a subtle retro edge (Steve McQueen has been cited as inspiration), the store is the label's unofficial clubhouse: airy and minimal, but unselfconsciously warm and friendly. Bestsellers such as the Classic T-shirt (£25) and chinos (£85). periodically sell out, having popped up in style mags and Saturday supplements the week before.
Branches 23 Beak Street, W1F 9RS (3157 7000); 286 Upper Street, N1 2TZ (7288 0835).

Hideout
7 Upper James Street, W1F 9DH (7437 4929, www.hideoutstore.com). Piccadilly Circus or Oxford Circus tube. **Open** 11am-7pm Mon-Fri; 11am-6.30pm Sat; noon-5pm Sun.
This small but central streetwear store has a New York feel to it – unsurprising as much of the stock, such as Supreme, comes from the Big Apple and Japan. There are also cool labels from London and further afield popular with the city's skater contingent– such as Norse Projects, W Taps, Neighbourhood, NBHD denim and Original Fake. All the streetwear staples are in attendance – hoodies, polos, sneakers and caps – and the quality and design of the garments are a definite cut above. Labels like Pharell, William's Ice Cream or Billionaire Boys Club justify their slightly above-average pricing. One of those into exclusives and rare releases.

Interstate
17 Endell Street, WC2H 9BJ (7836 0421). Covent Garden tube. **Open** 11am-6.45pm Mon-Fri; 11am-6.30pm Sat; noon-6pm Sun.
Interstate was a central London staple for denim, polos and overcoats long before the likes of Urban Outfitters muscled in on the scene and it's still as popular as ever. Denim and workwear are the focus, and it's packed with a decent range of sizes and well-chosen brands. There's a stack of Tees and polos but its real appeal lies in its selection of jackets and parkas from the likes of Spiewak, Woolrich and Penfield, or as a place to pick up a sturdy pair of jeans from Japan's Edwin or Sweden's Nudie. Staff are helpful, if a little hawk-eyed, but overall the place is laid-back and unpretentious compared with some of its Covent Garden competitors.

Wholesome
47 Rivington Street, EC2A 3QB (7729 2899, www.wholesomelondon.com). Old Street tube/rail. **Open** 10am-7pm Mon-Sat; noon-6pm Sun.
No longer a spooky Shoreditch back-alley, Rivington Street has become a buzz destination for shoppers keen to avoid the ubiquity of high street London. With its exposed brick and well-edited streetwear collection, Wholesome fits right into the Rivington scene – but it's inimitably more affordable. Opened by Kyle Miller and Kyle Hougham – both former fashion buyers – young London labels like AIT and Trapstar hang next to cult US brands, such as Crooks & Castles, Mishka and Diamond. T-shirts start at a friendly £30, and the sleek selection of Supra trainers is set to expand into a few Puma styles (one brand increasingly keen to be seen away from the high street). If this is the route back-road stores are headed, we're in for a good time ahead.

Women

Aimé
32 Ledbury Road, W11 2AB (7221 7070, www.aimelondon.com). Notting Hill Gate tube. **Open** 10am-6.30pm Mon-Sat.
Shoppers searching for a touch of Gallic chic on London's streets should make Aimé – the offspring of French-Cambodian sisters Val and Vanda Heng-Vong – their first port-of-call. Inside you'll find the crème de la crème of French designers, with labels like APC, APC Madras, Isabel Marant and Forte Forte. Also check out the Sarti range of tasteful scarves. Biker jackets and boots are big news again as are all items inspired by the 1970s Jane Birkin look. Bath products and seductive home accessories, including Aimé's range of scented candles, are equally attractive. Next door, Petit Aimé stocks an adorable range of clothes for babies and children.
Branch (Petit Aimé) 34 Ledbury Road, W11 2AB (7221 3123).

Austique
330 King's Road, SW3 5UR (7376 4555, www.austique.co.uk). Sloane Square tube then 11, 22 bus. **Open** 10.30am-7pm Mon-Sat; noon-5pm Sun.
Opened by sisters Katie Cancin and Lindy Lopes, Austique displays a super-feminine collection of clothes, lingerie and accessories in a light, two-floor space. Unsurprisingly, given the name, there's a strong Antipodean influence, with designs from the likes of Thurley and Camilla & Marc. The shop also stocks its own label, Austique, offering an assortment of silk dresses, pyjamas and pretty ballet shoes. There's a lovely selection of jewellery from the likes of Alex Monroe, Missoma and Zara Simon, and clutches from

Indie Boutiques

Kokon To Zai. See p63.

TEN Top boutique labels

APC Madras
APC's more affordable line is a London boutique staple, and a good bet for summer garb. Stocked at Aimé (see p66), Diverse (see p56), Iris (see p70), Press (see p74) and Urban Outfitters (see p82).

Future Classics
High-end, directional womenswear. Diverse (see p56), Dover Street Market (see p39), and Selfridges (see p27) are the shops to visit.

Karen Walker
Casual but stylish Kiwi label inspired by Amelia Earhart. Head to Diverse (see p56), Hub (see p60), Matches (see p63), Goodhood (see p59), Start (see p65) and Urban Outfitters (see p82).

Opening Ceremony
Cult US label known for its footwear, for men and women. Buy into the hype at Goodhood (see p59), No-one (see p63) and Selfridges (see p27).

Rittenhouse
This high-end casual label from Sydney is a fave of Goodhood (see p59); the cool mens' and women's threads are also stocked by the Garbstore (p39).

Three Threads. *See p65*.

Wilbur & Gussie – all in keeping with the girly feel of the clothes. Upstairs you'll find everything for the boudoir including a great range of knickers, negligees and camisoles. Essie nail polish is also stocked. Children's pieces are also stocked.

Cochinechine
74 Heath Street, NW3 1DN (7435 9377, www.cochinechine.com). Hampstead tube.
Open 10am-6pm Mon-Sat; noon-6pm Sun.
Eftychia Georgilis's airy and feminine boutique brings an interesting selection of designer labels to Hampstead. Spread over two floors are hip, wearable clothes from boutique favourites 3.1 Phillip Lim, Vanessa Bruno, McQ, Sonia Rykiel, ACNE and Peter Jensen, as well as lesser-known but equally interesting names from around the world. Turkish knitwear label Eternal Child is stocked, specialising in gorgeous shrugs and skirts from £100. Accessories include vibrant bags and clutches by Philip Roucou, Jennifer Behr headbands, an extensive range of Comme des Garçons perfumes, candles and wallets, and shoes from Disaya. Customer service and a welcoming vibe are high priorities here.

Equa
28 Camden Passage, N1 8ED (7359 0955, www.equaclothing.com). Angel tube. **Open** 10am-6pm Mon; 10am-6.30pm Tue-Sat; noon-5pm Sun.
Since it opened in 2005, this airy and calm 'ethical boutique' on atmospheric Camden Passage has become an Islington favourite thanks to its Fairtrade and organic fashion collections. The rails are packed with feel-good clothing brands, including established green clothing labels Annie Greenabelle, People Tree, Bibico, Outsider, and Danish brand Jackpot. Shoes, arranged attractively on a central block, come from Veja Volley (trainers), Terra Plana and Beyond Skin; skinny jeans come courtesy of Monkee Genes. There are also vegan wallets and brands from Canadian brand Mat & Nat, toiletries from Timothy Han, beauty products from Ila, and jewellery from Made. Children's clothes are also for sale.

House of Weardowney
11 Porchester Place, W2 2EU (7402 8892, www.weardowney.com). Marble Arch tube.
Open 10am-6pm Mon-Sat.
Get stitched up at House of Weardowney, a mecca to all things woolly. Former models Amy Wear and Gail Downey – one-time knitwear designer for John Galliano – launched their label in 2004, and it's helped put handcrafted knit couture on runways and in wardrobes all over. As well as supplying knitting needles, patterns and yarns, its 'getUp boutique' reveals the brand's flirty designer knitwear featuring vintage-inspired frocks (their Racerback dress is £137), pashminas and hotpants, and, for men, oversized stripy wool boxers.

See by Chloé
A long-established staple of feminine boutiques, such as Hub (*see p60*) and Diverse (*see p56*).

Sessùn
French hippy-chic womenswear label stocked by Folk (*see p59*) Urban Outfitters (*see p82*), Three Threads (*see p65*) and Whistles (*see p82*).

Something Else
This cult Aussie label designed by Natalie Wood can be found at Harvey Nichols (*see p23*), Three Threads (*see p65*) and Urban Outfitters (*see p82*).

Swedish Hasbeens
These high-heeled clogs – based on models from the 1970s – have been spotted on fashionista feet around town of late. Stocked by Ally Capellino (*see p128*), No-one (*see p63*) and Urban Outfitters (*see p82*).

WhyRed
Swedish label WhyRed has been creeping into the city's most stylish boutiques. Check out the beautifully cut womenswear at Three Threads (*p65*), Urban Outfitters (*see p82*) and Whistles (*p82*).

Look out for the ever-expanding collection of modern and antique books on the craft. The shop also now stocks collections from other designers, including Anthony Price, Boudicca, Acne, Richard Sorger, as well as a select range of vintage items.

Hoxton Boutique

2 Hoxton Street, N1 6NG (7684 2083, www.hoxtonboutique.co.uk). Old Street tube/rail. **Open** 11am-7pm Mon-Fri; 11am-6pm Sat; noon-5pm Sun.

This gallery-like store has been a favourite with crooked-fringed locals since it opened in 2000; and although it may not have the kudos it once held, it's still a good bet for affordable designerwear. The reason for its continued success is a host of niche labels; the owners make an effort to source interesting and emerging brands from around the world, with choice garments from the likes of Isabel Marant, Nümph, Sugar Hill, Once Upon a Time and Gat Rimon, as well as hard-to-get DR Denim and the shop's own +HOBO+ label. There's also a cabinet full of costume jewellery, plus pieces from British jewellery designer Jennifer Corker – a store exclusive.

Iris

97 Northcote Road, SW11 6PL (7924 1836, www.irisfashion.co.uk). Clapham Junction tube/rail. **Open** 10am-6pm Mon-Sat; 11am-5pm Sun.

The first Iris – the ultimate yummy mummy's neighbourhood boutique – opened in 2005 in Queen's Park; since then, owners Annie Pollet and Sarah Claassen have opened two more stores – this one on Battersea's Northcote Road, and another one more recently on Chiswick High Road – turning the brand into a mini-chain of feminine frocks. As well as stylish womenswear from a good mix of classic boutique labels, such as APC, Orla Kiely, Vanessa Bruno, Humanoid, Isabel Marant, Antik Batik and J Brand, the shop stocks pretty lingerie, Paul & Joe make-up, Cowshed beauty products, Zoe & Morgan jewellery, and a range of cute kidswear. The customer base is stylish young mums, and Pollet and Claassen's thoughtful and friendly approach (there are toy boxes provided to keep the tots occupied, for instance) helps to create a stress-free shopping experience.
Branches 73 Salisbury Road, NW6 6NJ (7372 1777); 129 Chiswick High Road, W4 2ED (8742 3811).

KJ's Laundry HOT 50

74 Marylebone Lane, W1U 2PW (7486 7855, www.kjslaundry.com). Bond Street tube. **Open** 10am-7pm Mon-Wed, Fri, Sat; 10am-8pm Thur; 11am-5pm Sun.

Owners Jane Ellis and Kate Allden stock a mix of lesser-known designers in their super-chic and spacious Marylebone store, including Sydney's Ginger & Smart,

Albam. See p66.

Shop talk
Francesca Forcolini, owner of Labour of Love

Tell us about your shop
'We've been open for nearly six years and we see ourselves as one of the only truly independent shops out there. We sell independent labels that aren't readily available and try to differentiate ourselves as much as we can from department stores. We've been selling Peter Jensen for five years and have other great brands like Eley Kishimoto and MighT. We only buy one of each size for the shop and try to keep to small numbers across a wide range of styles. We love that we can offer an exclusive product to our customers.'

Who shops here?
'Because we're not trend-led, we tend to have creative types, people with a truly individual sense of style. We have a wide range of ages as well, from 16 to 50, which is great because our clothes focus on character. We have a nice mix of bikers, musicians and comedians; eclectic creatives!'

What else do you do?
'I design our own brand, which includes one of our bestsellers, our range of jazz shoes, which we constantly reinvent in different colours and leathers. We are part of an online portal for independent shops [www.far-fetch.com] and I also source the books, jewellery, ceramics and cards for the shop. At the moment we're tending towards fairytales. It's very Tim Burton-esque.'

Have you noticed changes in the London shopping scene over the past few years?
'Definitely. I've noticed the homogenisation of the high street. It's very hard for independent shops when London becomes just another version of any other capital city. Areas that used to epitomise London style, like Carnaby Street or the King's Road, are just the same as any high street now, all selling the same thing. And it's shortsighted because tourists who come to London want to find something different here.

'Unfortunately, it's a very expensive business, and although there are loads of people out there doing their own thing and being really creative, there just aren't the outlets and space for them. Big brands are safe bets, because the marketing is already done for you.'

What is the best thing about owning a shop?
'Interacting with the client base. Our customers are so varied and interesting and it's like a mutual exchange. As a designer I get such a buzz from seeing someone in my clothes, and then seeing them come back again. It's just brilliant.'

What are your favourite shops in London?
'I love Palette (*see p103*) on Canonbury Lane; it sells high-end vintage alongside really modern pieces. I go to Relik (*see p104*) for inspiration, and I love Daunt Books (*see p190*). I also love this really old Florentine brand of body products called Santa Maria Novella; their shop (*see p160*) is beautiful; the brand was originally set up by monks.'

Any plans for the future?
'We're hoping to grow our internet sales and one day I'd love another shop. At the moment we're launching a children's area.'

▶ For **Labour of Love**, see *p73*.

Wholesome. *See p66.*

S Sung from New York, Swedish brand Filippa K, Kiwi designer Rebecca Taylor, and Suzannah from the UK. Hidden behind the over-hyped high street this attitude-free boutique has lines you won't see all over town (as well as a few established names such as YMC and American Retro), and by manning the shop floor themselves, they can adapt their buying according to demand. There are also leathers and separates by Mike & Chris (around £600), an interesting range of jewellery of the Alex Monroe ilk, and easy-wear pieces by East by East West (from £50) – the 1940s-influenced dresses and coats have an oriental simplicity.

Labour of Love HOT 50

193 Upper Street, N1 1RQ (7354 9333, www.labour-of-love.co.uk). Highbury & Islington tube/rail. **Open** 11am-6.30pm Mon-Sat; noon-5.30pm Sun.

This Islington gem stocks a delightful range of colourful clothing for those who want something a little bit different. The shop stocks individual pieces by the likes of Manoush, Peter Jensen (renowned for his witty prints), Erotokritos (for wearable dressy jersey pieces) and Eley Kishimoto (for stylish footwear), all hand-picked by owner Francesca Forcolini. Forcolini's own Labour of Love label goes from strength to strength. Expect to find playful yet wearable clothes at reasonable prices for the level of quality: key pieces include trenches, ruffle-detail blouses, and leather and suede gloves, as well as the label's popular jazz shoes in six new patent colours. It's also a great place to browse for gifts; look out for Tatty Devine giant plastic knit zip necklaces and earrings, original jewellery by Gemma Lister, and hats from Eugenia Kim. The place to go for pieces that combine high style with longevity. *See also p71* **Shop talk**.

Laden Showroom

103 Brick Lane, E1 6SE (7247 2431, www.laden.co.uk). Shoreditch High Street rail. **Open** 11am-6.30pm Mon-Fri; 11am-7pm Sat; 10.30am-6pm Sun.

The Laden Showroom's range of cutting-edge but very affordable designer clothing from the hottest independent talent on the scene is second to none. There are some 55 designers to choose from, including Emily & Fin, for great cotton tops, skirts and dresses, Dahlia, for retro styles, and Charles of London, for rock-inspired pieces. Peruse the shoes section for cheap ballet pumps and Brazilian trainers. Some pieces are more trend than style-led, but ideal for that just off to art college look. It's a great place to put together an interesting look on a shoestring budget, and its range of accessories (lace and patterned tights, cheap and trendy sunglasses, kitsch bags and jewellery, and vintage-style belts) means that the place is brimming with style-hungry teens and twentysomethings at weekends.

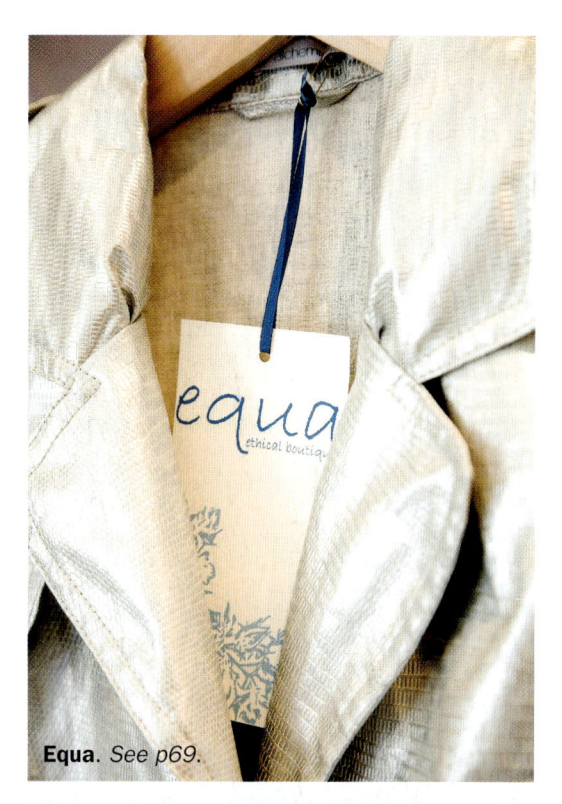

Equa. *See p69.*

Press

3 Erskine Road, NW3 3AJ (7449 0081, www.pressprimrosehill.com). Chalk Farm tube.
Open 9.45am-6.15pm Mon-Sat; noon-6pm Sun.
Before opening her boutique in 2004, Melanie Press had solid retail credentials as former creative director of Whistles. The ultimate Primrose Hill chick's closet, Press sells a good mix of trendy designer labels from its shabby chic space, such as APC and diffusion line APC Madras, Current Elliot, Pringle, Made in Heaven, and Jasmine Di Milo, alongside a select range of vintage pieces. Another addition are Golden Goose boots, made from 100% leather and already worn in for you (they've already garnered a long waiting list). The shop also stocks an impressive range of denim including cult jeans label J Brand and Wrangler.

Relax Garden

40 Kingsland Road, E2 8DA (7033 1881, www.relaxgarden.com). Old Street tube/rail. **Open** noon-7pm Mon-Wed; noon-8pm Thur, Fri; noon-6pm Sat, Sun.
This small Kingsland Road boutique aims to bring lesser-known independent labels from abroad to the UK and is a good bet for original garb at affordable prices. Look out for LA-based GLAM, jersey knitwear by Italian label Northland and a wide selection of Japanese labels. The shop's own label, Relax Garden, designed by owner Eriko Nagata offers reasonably priced, simple, feminine designs in silk and jersey. There's also a good selection of well-priced accessories and shoes, and pretty jewellery by London-based label Mille & Me. The shop is a good stop off for cute hair clips, hairbands, vintage-style plastic earrings and patterned tights.
Branch Unit 18, Portobello Green Arcade, WT 5TZ (8968 0496).

Sixty 6

4 Blenheim Terrace, NW8 0EB (7372 6100). St John's Wood or Maida Vale tube. **Open** noon-6.30pm Tue-Sat.
The owner of this lovely St John's Wood boutique, former antiques dealer Jane Collins, has a knack for choosing clothes that are eye-catching and feminine without being showy; many items are distinguished by interesting trimmings or embellishments. A tempting mix of designers is in evidence, including Vivienne Westwood, Anne Louise Roswald, David Meister and Betty Jackson, and there's a mid-range line-up too, with Malene Birger and Just In Case pieces displayed in combinations you might not have thought of putting together yourself. The shop also has the widest range of tops and dresses by Velvet we've seen in the capital, including unusual styles. Look out also for the large variety of cashmere, knitwear and scarves by Magaschoni, Crumpet and more, plus accessories by Lara Bohinc, famed for her art deco-inspired pieces. The original, and much smaller, Marylebone branch has now closed.

Iris. *See p70.*

Streetwise Ledbury Road, W11

Boho vibes combine with high fashion style on this smart but laid-back West London street.

As fantasy high streets go, swankily bohemian Ledbury Road is up there with the best of them. Even for Notting Hill's most pampered, spoilt and well-heeled residents, shopping here is an unalloyed indulgence. With an impressive choice of high-end independents and a smart yet laid-back vibe, the street is made for unhurried browsing. Accessorise with a cappuccino, a cherubic child and someone else's credit card, and you'll fit right in.

Passing elegantly refined residences and starting from the Westbourne Park end of the road, make **Matches** (nos.60-64; see p63) your first stop for assorted luxe labels by Chloé, Balenciaga and Lanvin. Or, for sharply dressed guys, **Matches Menswear** has a host of brands including Marc Jacobs, Miu Miu, Paul Smith and Prada.

Matches Spy, across the road, is also worth a browse for a more casual collection.

A bit further along, classy kids (or, rather, their mums) will be happy at chic **Caramel** (no.77; see p265) and classic **Petit Bateau** (no.73; 7243 6331); the former also has its own range of shoes and accessories and a hair salon in the basement.

Next up, on the other side of the road, is the quirky and undefinable **JW Beeton** (nos.48-50, 7229 8874), one of the longest-serving boutiques in this now-crowded patch of town. Owner Debbie Potts buys up small quantities of international labels and sells them on at non-extravagant (for these parts) prices. Recent hits include Diablesse from Paris, Rützou from Denmark and funky knits from Brazilian Cecilia Prado.

Ottolenghi (7727 1121, www.ottolenghi.co.uk) is next, at no.63; a quick glance at the window display and you can see why it's a winner when it comes to interior deli design. There's a selection of colourful Mediterranean, Middle Eastern and oriental dishes on offer alongside tempting pastries and salads. If you're not ravenous (and not calorie-counting), at least sample one of the meringues or muffins. The designs next door come by way of **Anya Hindmarch** (no.63A; 7792 4427, www.anyahindmarch.com) and her hip bags, while opposite, on the corner of Westbourne Grove, is the shop of swimwear designer **Melissa Odabash** (no.48B; see p109); her bikinis and one-piece swimsuits don't come cheap, but you may decide that it's worth the splurge for amazingly flattering cuts in gorgeous materials.

The road is also host to a clutch of top Gallic boutiques – shops that make dressing like a Parisienne easy. **Aimé** (no.32; see p66), founded by French-Cambodian sisters, has simple cardies from the étoile range by Isabel Marant, cute smock dresses by Antik Batik and Bardot-style ballet shoes by Repetto. Bath products, scented candles and quality home accessories are also a hit, while next door, at **Petit Aimé** (no.34), you'll find equally desirable children's garb.

For a one-stop shop for gorgeous shoes, head to **Joseph** (no.61, 7229 1870). The Milan-based boutique houses so many top designers – among them Chloé, John Galliano, Marc Jacobs, Victor & Rolf and Paul Smith, to name but a choice few – that you should find something that matches your newly purchased Ledbury Road designer outfit.

Next door at no.59, the indulgence continues at **Melt** (7727 5030, www.meltchocolates.com). Assailed by the enticing aroma of cocoa, you'll be hard pressed to avoid the temptation of taking a break from all the shopping frenzy to sample some mouth-watering chocolates, all lovingly handcrafted on the premises.

On the other side of the road at **Bodas** (no.38B; see p107) you'll find a simple and sexy underwear line, all made with high-quality fabrics.

Where once antique shops lorded it over the road, nowadays you'll have to walk further up the block to see them; don't miss art deco specialist **B&T Antiques** (no.47, 7229 7001, www.bntantiques.co.uk), which has a near cult following.

High Street

Abercrombie & Fitch
7 Burlington Gardens, W1S 3ES (0844 412 5750, www.uk.abercrombie.com). Oxford Circus or Piccadilly Circus tube. **Open** 10am-7pm Mon-Sat; noon-6pm Sun. **Sells** M, W.
This is a case of having to be seen to be believed. The US clothing brand's 2007 arrival horrified the neighbours. The way not to impress the Savile Row set that it's now geographically a part of: with banging tunes and a topless male model standing in the doorway at all times. Indeed, with its dimmed lighting and weird scent, the place feels more like a bizarre, posh club than a shop. Despite this, or maybe because of it, A&F's logo-heavy sweaters, jeans and polos (to be worn with collars turned up, of course) are mighty popular with the Sloane Square set. Oddly, you may have to queue to get in.

All Saints
57-59 Long Acre, WC2E 9JL (7836 0801, www.allsaints.co.uk). Covent Garden tube. **Open** 9.30am-8pm Mon-Sat; 11am-5pm. **Sells** M, W.
With its distressed denim, leather and glitzy sequinned asymmetric dresses, All Saints provides edgy glamour with a dose of knowingly trashy bling. Inside the store, the exposed brickwork and pumping music create a warehouse-like feel that has made it a hit with the twentysomethings market. On offer is a blend of check shirts, ranch boots and embellished vest tops and dresses. The selection of jeans is probably the brand's high point, along with the statement shoes and edgy women's accessories. Boys are well looked after with a good selection of slim-fitting shirts, skinny jeans and offbeat T-shirts.
Branches throughout the city.

American Apparel
3-4 Carnaby Street, W1F 9PB (7734 4477, www.americanapparel.net). Oxford Circus tube. **Open** 10am-8pm Mon-Sat; noon-6pm Sun. **Sells** M, W, C.
Since it opened its first shop in London some five years ago, ethically minded US-import American Apparel has expanded at breakneck speed. The colourful, vaguely kinky, 1980s-inspired garb (leggings, figure-hugging jersey dresses, spandex leotards, skinny jeans, tracksuit bottoms, cheerleader-style knee-highs, gold headbands and a large range of tops) seemed to capture the spirit of recent times – at least as far as twentysomethings were concerned – with simple cuts, comfortable materials and affordable prices. The company first conquered with well-fitting cotton tees, then the nigh-on-perfect hoody that became the uniform of the East End trendy, and, more recently – in spite of their tendency to sag – with its nudge nudge, wink wink retro briefs.
Branches throughout the city.

Banana Republic
224 Regent Street, W1B 3BR (7758 3550, www.bananarepublic.eu). Oxford Circus tube. **Open** 10am-8pm Mon-Wed, Fri; 10am-9pm Thur; 9am-8pm Sat; noon-6pm Sun. **Sells** M, W.
The 17,000sq ft store on Regent Street covers two vast floors and feels like a posh hotel lobby, with its chandeliers, spiral staircases and plush chairs. The stock is equally elegant, encompassing a selection of refined clothes and accessories. For women, there is a good selection of wardrobe staples and workwear, as well as chic eveningwear in the form of ruffled shirts and fitted shift dresses. The ground-floor collection has more than a nod to Burberry with its creamy trenches and gathered blouses, while upstairs are more youthful numbers, like silk printed smock dresses, nautical tees and embellished tops. Pieces are often highly tactile, with lots of cashmere and satin. The modern city gent will also feel at home here, with a choice of casual chinos, V-neck sweaters and smart shirts in the basement. Back on the ground, the impressive array of moderately priced jewellery is well worth a gander, as is the collection of shoes. Styles here may not be hot-off-the-runway, but it's a good bet for timeless style.
Branches Brent Cross Shopping Centre, Hendon, NW4 3FP (8203 1397); 132 Long Acre, WC2E 9AA (7836 9567).

COS

222 Regent Street, W1B 5BD (7478 0400, www.cosstores.com). Oxford Circus tube. **Open** 10am-8pm Mon-Wed, Fri, Sat; 10am-9pm Thur; noon-6pm Sun. **Sells** M, W.

H&M created a buzz when it opened this flagship store in 2007, and the brand has gone from strength to strength. Catering for those who have grown tired of fighting their way through a frenzy of teenagers at the sale rails, COS (which stands for Collection of Style) is the antithesis to H&M's throwaway trend-led fashion. But what was supposed to be a grown-up sister of H&M actually looks more like Gap's posh sibling. The slick, well laid-out store houses an impressive range of simple, classic separates and coats, jackets and eveningwear in good-quality fabrics and both neutral and vibrant colours. Recent collections have focused on simple shift dresses, classic narrow leg suits for men, and unfussy boxy tops and skirts for women, with soft leather jackets, fine suede coat dresses and split-shoulder eyelet-embellished blazers thrown in for good measure. Prices start at around £50 for a dress and £80 for jackets; men's suits average between £200 and £250. The store also boasts some cute retro underwear, sweet baby gear and hip accessories (such as studded belts). There's a concession in Selfridges.
Branches 124-126 Kensington High Street, W8 7RL (7361 1050); 130-131 Long Acre, WC2E 9AA (7632 4190); Westfield London, W12 7GB (8600 3310).

French Connection

396 Oxford Street, W1C 1JX (7629 7766, www.frenchconnection.com). Bond Street tube.
Open 10am-8pm Mon-Wed, Fri; 10am-9pm Thur; 10am-7pm Sat; noon-6pm Sun. **Sells** M, W.

Now considered an old-timer on the list of high street brands, French Connection has worked hard over the past couple of years to free itself from the shackles of its FCUK identity – and it appears to have succeeded. Designs are a mix of mature and on-trend, with unfussy separates and outerwear in a range of good-quality fabrics and in bright but rarely garish colours and patterns; the look manages to be very distinctively 'French Connection', even though it's not that obviously different from the rest of the high street. Dresses and eveningwear in sequinned and glittery fabrics, and simple cotton shift dresses are among the most popular offerings for women. The classic T-shirts and knitwear remain firm favourites, and its good selection of denim jeans and cotton workwear trousers complement every wardrobe. The new French Connection Denim boutique is at 11 James Street in Covent Garden.
Branches throughout the city.

H&M

261-271 Regent Street, W1B 2ES (7493 4004, www.hm.com). Oxford Circus tube. **Open** 9am-9pm Mon-Sat; noon-6pm Sun. **Sells** M, W.

STYLIST

TOPMAN STYLIST.
NO HASSLE. NO CHARGE.

SERVICE AVAILABLE AT
TOPMAN OXFORD CIRCUS 2ND FLOOR.

APPOINTMENTS. 020 7927 0155
WWW.TOPMAN.COM/STYLIST

TOPMAN

High Street

H&M, for those who have been living under a rock, has been one of the high-street forerunners for catwalk-inspired, affordable (but low quality) clothing. The low-priced retailer that opened its first store in Västerås, Sweden back in 1947 is now a multinational with over 2,000 stores worldwide. The brand partly made its name through attracting superdesigners such as Karl Lagerfeld and Viktor & Rolf – as well as, um, Madonna and Kylie – to create in-house diffusion lines. Recent innovations have included an organic, affordable skincare range as well as a nice lingerie line, with designs by Sonia Rykiel, who also produced a knitwear collection for the company in 2010. The shop is a good bet for on-trend jackets and T-shirts, stylish accessories, and attractive beachwear.
Branches throughout the city.

Jigsaw
21 Long Acre, WC2E 9LD (7240 3855, www.jigsaw-online.com). Covent Garden or Leicester Square tube or Charing Cross tube/rail. **Open** 10am-8pm Mon-Fri; 10am-7pm Sat; noon-6pm Sun. **Sells** W, C.
With its classic lines, simply cut separates and luxurious fabrics, Jigsaw feels every inch the grown-up of high street fashion; and after keeping something of a low profile in the early noughties, it's now back on the radars of the capital's style-conscious thirtysomethings. While designs seem to vary little from season to season, there's the occasional on-trend surprise, with jackets and dresses a strong point. But Jigsaw is really more about the quality of the materials rather than the edginess of the cuts – with tweed, merino wool, cashmere and silky cottons often appearing, in earthy, tasteful tones. Accessories are a highlight, with a good range of sunglasses, belts, scarves and soft leather bags, shoes and boots.
Branches throughout the city.

Oasis
12-14 Argyll Street, W1F 7NT (7434 1799, www.oasis-stores.com). Oxford Circus tube. **Open** 10am-8pm Mon-Wed, Fri; 10am-9pm Thur; 10am-7pm Sat; noon-6pm Sun. **Sells** W.
Well-made, often vintage-inspired clothes for young women. Over the past few seasons, Oasis has been particularly strong on shift and tea-style summer dresses, pretty blouses, leather biker jackets, khaki parkas and playsuits. Its aesthetics could broadly be defined as 'trend-led but feminine', with polka-dots, stripes and floral prints in abundance. As well as being a good bet for glamorous eveningwear for fashion-conscious twentysomethings, Oasis also does a good line in cheap spangly jewellery, patterned tights, silky lingerie, leather bags, printed neckscarves, and other accessories. It's also worth checking out its affordable workwear, such as suit jackets, tube skirts and court shoes.
Branches throughout the city.

COS. *See p77.*

Primark

499-517 Oxford Street, W1K 7DA (7495 0420, www.primark.co.uk). Marble Arch tube.
Open 8.30am-9pm Mon-Fri; 8.30am-8pm Sat; noon-6pm Sun. **Sells** M, W, B, C.

London's (now-fading?) obsession with Primark began with the hallowed opening of its 70,000sq ft Oxford Street store in April 2007. The shopping experience itself is somewhat chequered (with changing-room queues so long customers often strip off on the shop floor), but it's the fashionable cheap-as-chips clothes you go for, not the genteel ambience. The clothing, accessories and footwear (for women, men and children) are definitely trend-led, and cover a range of brands, including Atmosphere, the Secret Possessions lingerie line, and Backswing, for sports clothing. Butlerandwebb, meanwhile, is the line for formal menswear. Primark also does a line in products for the home.
Branches throughout the city.

Reiss

Kent House, 14-17 Market Place, W1H 7AJ (7637 9112, www.reiss.co.uk). Oxford Circus tube.
Open 10am-7pm Mon, Tue, Sat; 10am-8pm Wed-Fri; 11.30am-6pm Sun. **Sells** M, W.

Bridging a cavernous gap between high street and high-end fashion, Reiss is the place to shop if you like your clothing well made and safely trendy. With its mix of tailored suits and separates and glamorous after-dark and special-occasion dresses, it's not hard to figure out why this shop is popular. The layout of the shop is clean, uncluttered and well organised, with staff readily available to offer advice. The look is smart, classy and trendy with menswear offering heavyweight dark denim, crisp shirts with epaulettes and chunky knits in neutral colours. For ladies, there are flirty shift dresses with exquisite details and ruching in the finest of fabrics. The brand's 1971 Reiss collection is a highlight, while its no-refunds policy is a definite low point.
Branches throughout the city.

Topman

214 Oxford Street, W1W 8LG (0844 848 7487, www.topman.com). Oxford Circus tube. **Open** 9am-9pm Mon-Sat; 11.30am-6pm Sun. **Sells** M.

Topman is as on-trend as the high street gets for guys. And while it's true that on a Saturday this flagship resembles something of a teenage Hades – blaring music and endless queues – everyone here knows that they're on to a good thing. Well-cut jeans for all shapes and sizes are cheap and always popular. Other offerings range from brightly coloured print T-shirts and arty trenchcoats to knitted polos, faux leather jackets and a wide range of patterned pyjamas. September 2008 saw the launch of twice-yearly capsule collections by young designers; Lens offers clothing by the likes of Dexter

High Street

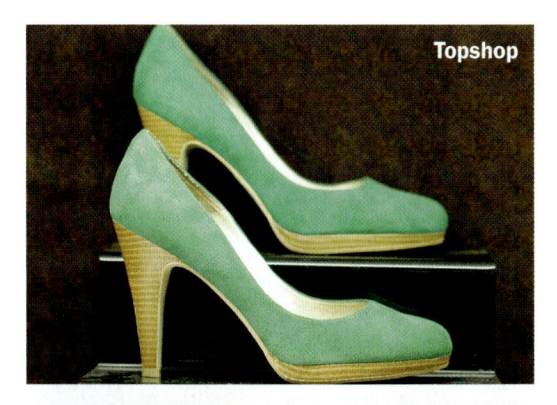

Wong, Christopher Shannon and Carolyn Massey, released in February and September. The Topshop Design collection, meanwhile, fuses sharp tailoring with technical sportswear: think collarless shirts, scoop neck jumpers, salopettes and wayfarer-style sunglasses. **Branches** throughout the city.

Topshop HOT 50
214 Oxford Street, W1W 8LG (0844 848 7487, www.topshop.com). Oxford Circus tube. **Open** 9am-9pm Mon-Sat; 11.30am-6pm Sun. **Sells** W. London's teenage girls (and their parents) are no stranger to Topshop. The biggest, bossiest, pushiest member of Philip Green's Arcadia group, the brand has been the queen of the British high street for the past decade, and walking into the busy Oxford Street flagship, it's easy to see why. A simple, stark layout, but with every surface crammed full of gear, the place is buzzing with fashion-forward teens and twentysomethings. Spanning three floors, the store boasts accessories collections from Mikey, Marc B and Orelia, and has in-house concessions for Office and Miss Selfridge. Keen to reinforce its hipster credentials with links to London Fashion Weekend, Topshop also champions the cause of the young British designer – the lower floors are filled with pieces from the likes of Ann Sofie Back, Jonathan Saunders and Richard Nicoll, as well as the teen-friendly party dress lines Lipsy and

Best for…

On-trend womenswear
H&M (*see p77*); **Topshop** (*see p81*); **Urban Outfitters** (*see p82*); **Whistles** (*see p82*).

Styles with longevity
Banana Republic (*see p76*); **Jigsaw** (*see p79*); **Reiss** (*see p80*).

Menswear
American Apparel (*see p76*); **Topman** (*see p80*)

Wardrobe staples
American Apparel (*see p76*); **Banana Republic** (*see p76*); **COS** (*see p77*)

Throwaway fashion
H&M (*see p77*); **Primark** (*see p80*).

Online shopping services
French Connection (*see p77*); **Topshop** (*see p81*); **Urban Outfitters** (*see p82*).

Blue Velvet

Blue Velvet experts in luxury Italian footwear specialising in Ballerinas and Moccasins from £39.

Always one step ahead, they have established themselves on their quality and first rate service.

Visit them at 174 Kings road, Chelsea, SW3 4UP
or call 02073767442
www.bluevelvetshoes.com

Galleria Conti
about.fashion

Established in 2007 and now one of Clapham and Battersea's best kept secret, Galleria Conti has quickly gained a reputation among the fashion savvy women of SW11 and beyond for offering a beautiful and friendly atmosphere in which to shop. The buying is so creative that you will find pieces from labels like Maxmara, Nicole Miller, Alberta Ferretti, Bernshaw, Nicole Farhi, alongside Moschino Cheap'n'Chic, BCBG

Twenty 8 Twelve, Pyrus, Designers Remix, Serfontaine and many more....so whatever your style, you are bound to find something individual to maintain and build upon your existing wardrobe

22 Battersea Rise, London SW11 1EE
Tel: 0207 228 4077
web: www.continista.com
Mon-Sat: 10-18, Sun: 12-17

Cath Kidston®

VINTAGE INSPIRED
FASHION • HOME • KIDSWEAR

BATTERSEA 142 Northcote Road, SW11 6RD Tel: 020 7228 6571
CHELSEA 12 Cale Street, SW3 3QV Tel: 020 7584 3232
CHISWICK 125 Chiswick High Road, W4 2ED Tel: 020 8995 8052
COVENT GARDEN 28-32 Shelton Street, WC2H 9JE Tel: 020 7836 4803
FULHAM 668 Fulham Road, SW6 6RX Tel: 020 7731 6531
KING'S ROAD 322 King's Road, SW3 5UH Tel: 020 7351 7335
MARYLEBONE 51 Marylebone High Street, W1U 5HW Tel: 020 7935 6555
NOTTING HILL 158 Portobello Road, W11 2EB Tel: 020 7727 5278
SELFRIDGES 400 Oxford Street, W1A 1AB Tel: 020 7318 3312
WIMBLEDON VILLAGE 3 High Street, SW19 5DX Tel: 020 8944 1001

WWW.CATHKIDSTON.COM

Rare. The huge range on offer covers a multitude of styles, with often poor-quality fabrics the flipside of the brand's on-trend styles. The flagship also has personal shoppers, a blow dry bar, Nails Inc manicures, brow threading, a café and a sweet shop. A fun, if frenzied, shopping experience. If you lack the stamina to fight your way through the throng, then try the less stressful Brompton Road 'boutique branch', which opened in summer 2010; or, better still, use Topshop To Go, where a selection of clothing is brought to your home or office.
Branches throughout the city.

Uniqlo
311 Oxford Street, W1C 2HP (7290 7701, www.uniqlo.co.uk). Oxford Circus tube. **Open** 10am-8pm Mon-Wed; 10am-9pm Thur-Sat; noon-6pm Sun. **Sells** M, W.
Uniqlo ferociously attempted to rebrand in 2007, with celeb envoys like Chloë Sevigny, a Terry Richardson advertising campaign and the opening of two new stores on Oxford Street. However, whether Uniqlo is more than simply a Japanese Gap is a case for debate; useful staples – such as the HEATTECH thermal underwear for men and women, the well-cut jeans, graphic T-shirts, and cut-price cashmere and merino wool jumpers and cardigans – are the brand's strong point. However, look beyond these items, and it becomes apparent that many of the styles here are rather unremarkable, although the occasional vintage-inspired top or well-cut mac may surprise.
Branches throughout the city.

Urban Outfitters HOT 50
200 Oxford Street, W1D 1NU (7907 0815, www.urbanoutfitters.co.uk). Oxford Circus tube. **Open** 10am-8pm Mon-Wed, Fri, Sat; 10am-9pm Thur; 11.30am-6pm Sun. **Sells** M, W.
One for the hipsters, Urban Outfitters is vintage shopping for people who don't like vintage shopping; the brand may hail from America but its London stores have strong traces of Cool Britannia. You'll find homewares, accessories and clothes for every occasion; step into the Oxford Street store and be greeted by an overwhelming mix of casualwear and kitschy pieces for gifts, such as floral picture frames, retro lip balm, coffee-table books and plastic cameras from Lomography and Holga. Menswear is in the basement, with the first and second floors dedicated to womenswear, covering a wide range of styles, from vintage and bohemian to classic, and with lots of pieces from in-house concessions Kimchi Blue and Silence + Noise. There's also a good selection of jeans and denim (including popular Swedish brand Cheap Monday). Prices climb as you go upstairs to the second floor, where ultra-stylish labels such as Something Else, Whyred, APC Madras, Sessùn, Vanessa Bruno and Vivienne Westwood are all stocked – making the place a veritable goldmine for fashionistas.

Reiss. See p80.

If prices are above your budget, keep an eye out for the sales periods when real bargains can be had.
Branches 42-56 Earlham Street, WC2H 9LJ (7759 6390). 36-38 Kensington High Street, W8 4PF (7761 1001).

Whistles
12 St Christopher's Place, W1U 1NH (7487 4484, www.whistles.co.uk). Bond Street tube. **Open** 10am-7pm Mon-Fri; 10am-6pm Sat; noon-5pm Sun. **Sells** W.
All eyes are on Whistles now that Jane Shepherdson is at the helm. The shop has traditionally had a loyal following among well-heeled women looking for feminine, practical styles. With its floaty fabrics and eclectic mix of separates, the overall feel is a sort of suburban Bohemia. Prices are higher than the usual high street outlet but, with an emphasis on quality and finishing, these well-made pieces should last a lifetime. Staple items include blouses in soft fabrics, loose knits, drop-waist gathered skirts and pencil skirts. As well as its own label, this impressive flagship stocks others such as Antik Batik, Michael Stars, Odd Molly, Pink Soda and Diablesse. Prices start from around £60 for knitwear, £100 for dresses and £195 for coats.
Branches throughout the city.

FASHION

Designer Chains

Old Bond Street, **New Bond Street** and **Sloane Street** are key streets to familiarise yourself with if you're a fan of high-end designer garb.

Men & women

Alexander McQueen
4-5 Old Bond Street, W1S 4PD (7355 0088, www.alexandermcqueen.com). Green Park tube.
Open 10am-6pm Mon-Wed, Fri, Sat; 10am-7pm Thur. **Sells** M, W.
The late Alexander McQueen's only UK store is a groovy, contemporary space with curved lines and soft lighting. The ground floor is dedicated to womenswear and accessories, which spill into the lower-ground floor, where you'll also find some wickedly sharp men's tailoring, outrageously dapper footwear and manbags. The bags for women are equally delectable. The last collections from the famously confrontational McQueen seemed more wearable than ever; the business is continuing without its Creative Director, but in what direction remains to be seen. Fans of the label on a tighter budget should seek out the diffusion line, McQ, which packs a gutsy McQueen punch at pocket-friendly prices.

Aquascutum
100 Regent Street, W1B 5SR (7675 8200, www.aquascutum.co.uk). Piccadilly Circus tube.
Open 10am-6.30pm Mon-Wed, Fri, Sat; 10am-7pm Thur; noon-5pm Sun. **Sells** M, W.
Balancing heritage alongside fashion is always a tricky business, but it's one that Aquascutum, now in British hands again, having been bought from its previous Japanese owners by Harold Tillman and Belinda Earl, knows all about. Aquascutum, now part of the Jaeger group, is rightly proud of its 157-year history and of the fact that it still makes some of its core pieces in Corby, Northamptonshire. But it also knows that heritage and tradition are no substitute for fashion when it comes to attracting new customers, and that's why models such as Gisele have appeared in recent ad campaigns, and why the brand has sought to develop its fashionable, mod-influenced Aquascutum LTD. range for men in recent seasons. More classic pieces are designed by Graeme Fidler. The brand has also now added women's tailoring to its men's made-to-measure service.

Burberry
21-23 New Bond Street, W1S 2RE (3367 3000, www.burberry.com). Bond Street tube. **Open** 10am-7pm Mon-Sat; noon-6pm Sun. **Sells** M, W, C.
Burberry, established back in 1856, continues to place great emphasis on its Britishness. The fashion house's

John Smedley. *See p87.*

Louis Vuitton Maison. See p88.

iconic macs, still made in Birmingham, remain investment pieces that will justify the heavy price tag (£700 plus), but the brand is also known for its simple polo tops, knits and narrow menswear lines, its fragrance range, and its accessories, such as scarves, bags and umbrellas in the distinctive and much-copied tan, black and red Burberry Check tartan. Sharp tailoring can be found in the Burberry Prorsum line, designed by Creative Director Christopher Bailey, while the Burberry Brit and Burberry London ranges are more casual and youthful. For the factory shop in Hackney, *see p89* **Sales & events**.
Branches 157-167 Regent Street, W1B 4PH (3367 3000); 2 Brompton Road, SW1 X7PB (3367 3000); 199 Westbourne Grove, W11 2SB (3367 3000); Westfield London, W12 7GB (3367 3000).

Jaeger
200-206 Regent Street, W1R 6BN (7979 1100, www.jaeger.co.uk). Oxford Circus tube. **Open** 10am-7pm Mon-Wed, Fri, Sat; 10am-8pm Thur; noon-6pm Sun. **Sells** M, W.
Founded over 125 years ago, Jaeger was once synonymous with middle England; today it's a byword for classic British chic, and Jaeger's womenswear, menswear and accessories lines are highly covetable once again. Coats, tailoring and luxurious knitwear in classic fabrics, such as herringbone, tweed and plaid, are central to the brand's collections, while most of the clothes have a chic but serious look, with black, ivory and navy dominating over bright colours. The hipper Jaeger London diffusion label has given the brand a boost in recent years, broadening its customer base by appealing to younger shoppers who still want to buy into a luxury heritage brand. One of Jaeger's printed silk neckscarves could be a good place to start.
Branches throughout the city.

John Smedley
24 Brook Street, W1K 5DG (7495 2222, www.johnsmedley.com). Bond Street tube.
Open 10am-6pm Mon-Wed, Fri, Sat; 10am-7pm Thur; noon-5pm Sun. **Sells** M, W.
This cult British knitwear label has been around in some form or other since 1784 – and the brand still manufactures its high-quality garments in its original Lea Mills factory in Derbyshire. Initially an underwear specialist, John Smedley is now a brand associated with fine-knit merino wool sweaters and tops for both men and women; and despite its proud heritage, the label manages to retain a contemporary look with colourful yet muted hues and flattering cuts. The relaxed and stylish flagship shop has been open since 2000, receiving a redesign in 2009 to reflect the company's Derbyshire roots with limestone flooring and green tones. As well as ethically sourced New Zealand merino wool, extra-fine jersey is now used for some garments.

Marc by Marc Jacobs

Louis Vuitton Maison HOT 50
17-20 New Bond Street, W1S 2UE (7399 3856, www.louisvuitton.com). Bond Street tube. **Open** 10am-7pm Mon-Sat; noon-6pm Sun. **Sells** M, W.
Move over Kanye West the (self-proclaimed) 'Louis Vuitton don'. The soothsayer of monogram chic has its eyes on a bigger prize: London. After securing (35,000 sq ft (3,260 square metres) of prime Bond Street real estate, the city is to be blessed with – drum roll please – the most luxurious Louis Vuitton store in the world. Designed by New York City's Peter Marino, the Maison (which is LV lingo for megastore) is similar to flagships in New York, Paris and Hong Kong, but stocked with the most rare and exclusive of Louis Vuitton finds. Complete with a Men's Club Area, huge changing rooms and a 'Librairie', which will sell a selection of contemporary British art books, it's a new branded universe. Dog bags priced at £1,000 are just the beginning.

Marc by Marc Jacobs
56 South Audley Street, W1K 2RR (7408 7050, www.marcjacobs.com). Bond Street or Green Park tube. **Open** 11am-7pm Mon-Sat; noon-6pm Sun. **Sells** M, W, C.
So cheap are the branded trinkets prominently displayed as you walk into London's first Marc by Marc Jacobs store that you could be tempted to walk straight out again, mistaking the goods for dodgy knock-offs. Lipstick-shaped pens, key loops and bangles are all less than a fiver. But take a closer look at the rails of fun clothing, rows of Jacobs's signature Wellington boots and the cul-de-sac filled with the perfumes and sunglasses, and you know you're in the right place. Head downstairs into 'The Vault' (the building used to be a bank) to find shoes and bags. And keep 'em peeled for nude photos of a number of the shop's staff on the walls and ceilings. They're very well hung…
Branch (Marc Jacobs) 24-25 Mount Street, W1K 2RR (7399 1690).

Margaret Howell
34 Wigmore Street, W1U 2RS (7009 9009, www.margarethowell.co.uk). Bond Street tube.
Open 10am-6pm Mon-Wed, Fri, Sat; 10am-7pm Thur; noon-5pm Sun. **Sells** M, W.
The thing that makes Howell's wonderfully wearable clothes so contemporary is her old-fashioned attitude to quality. She believes in making things well, in the UK and with the finest of fabrics (Harris tweed, Irish linen). These principles combine with her elegant designs to make for the best 'simple' clothes for sale in London. Her pared-down approach means prices can seem steep, but unlike cheap, throwaway fashion these are clothes to cherish, and which will seem to improve with time. Her shops are also worth a visit for anyone interested in 20th-century British design – she now offers both vintage and reissued homeware classics by Ercol, Anglepoise, Robert Welch and others. As well as the branches listed below, there is a Margaret Howell concession within Selfridges (*see p27*).
Branches 111 Fulham Road, SW3 6RL (7591 2255); 1 The Green, Richmond, TW9 1LZ (8948 5005).

Designer Chains

Mulberry
41-42 New Bond Street, W1S 2RY (7491 3900, www.mulberry.com). Bond Street tube. **Open** 10am-6pm Mon-Wed, Fri, Sat; 10am-7pm Thur. **Sells** M, W.
Having established its credentials as a bona fide fashion brand in recent years – in particular for its leather 'it' bags – Mulberry is working to maintain the momentum. Creative Director Emma Hill's first collection featured Bayswater clutches, soft leather canvas Taylor totes for men, and leather biker jackets. A range of shoes designed by Hill is one of a series of in-store collaborations. Meanwhile, classic handbags like the Bayswater, Elkington and Roxanne are reinvented in new finishes, colours and materials. The latest must-have bag, the Alexa, is named after British fashion icon Alexa Chung, who's long been a fan of the brand.
Branches throughout the city.

Paul Smith
Westbourne House, 120 & 122 Kensington Park Road, W11 2EP (7727 3553, www.paulsmith.co.uk). Notting Hill Gate tube. **Open** 10am-6pm Mon-Fri; 10am-6.30pm Sat. **Sells** M, W, C.
Paul Smith's Notting Hill shop is branded a 'shop in a house'; customers step through its doors into a world of eccentricity. There are clothes for men, women and children, plus accessories, homewares and the odd piece of furniture, spread over four floors. The place is dotted with Sir Paul's collection of art and other objects, giving insight into the vision behind his quirky-classic tailoring. Womenswear is characterised by silhouette-enhancing garments cut from top quality textile (with abundant use of silk and jersey) and eye-catching, but very wearable, prints. Masculine jackets are cut in traditional Prince of Wales checks, pinstripes and flannels. Menswear is a rich

Sales & events

Designer sample sales and discount shops for every savvy shopper's diary and address book.

Browns Labels For Less
50 South Molton Street, W1K 5RD (7514 0052). Bond Street tube. **Open** 10am-6.30pm Mon-Wed, Fri, Sat; 10am-7pm Thur.
The outlet store for renowned fashion boutique Browns. Prices are permanently discounted, for men and women.

Burberry Factory Shop
29-53 Chatham Place, E9 6LP (8328 4287). Hackney Central rail. **Open** 10am-6pm Mon-Sat; 11am-5pm Sun.
A vast range of excess stock at up to 70% off. Classic men's macs can be had for around £199.

Designer Sales UK
01273 858 464, www.designersales.co.uk. Venues vary.
Bringing you the best of Bond Street at rock-bottom prices, DSUK has been holding sample sales for more than 30 years. Reductions of up to 90% on everything from Yohyi Yamamoto to Biba for men and women.

Designer Warehouse Sale
Thane Works, 5-6 Islington Studios, Thane Villas, N7 7NU (7697 9888, www.dws london.co.uk). Arsenal or Finsbury Park tube.
Holding events throughout the year, with separate sales for men and women, DWS is one of the most exclusive sales out there. Designers include Sophphia Kokosalaki and Christian Dior.

London Accessory Sale
www.londonaccessorysale.co.uk. Venues vary.
Chloë, Marc Jacobs, Peter Werth and Burberry are just a few of the designers whose accessories are slashed in this huge sale. Register online to become a member.

London Fashion Weekend
www.londonfashionweekend.co.uk. Venues vary. Feb, Sept.
Twice a year designers set city tongues wagging and everyone gets a little more chic. At these sales – held in conjunction with the catwalk shows – you'll find a host of familiar names at very unfamiliar prices.

Paul Smith Sale Shop
23 Avery Row, W1X 9HB (7493 1287, www.paulsmith.co.uk). Bond Street tube. **Open** 10.30am-6.30pm Mon-Wed, Fri, Sat; 10.30am-7pm Thur; 1pm-5.30pm Sun.
Mostly end of season stock from this classic British designer. Reductions are between 30 and 50% on everything from tees to suits. Note: it's strictly menswear.

Secret Sample Sale
www.secretsamplesale.co.uk. Venues vary.
Samples and clearance stock from hundreds of London's designers, agents and retailers, all with up to 80% off. Find everything from silk lingerie to Savile Row suits. Register online for details of dates and venues.

FASHION

collection of tartans, checks and colourful stripes with contrast detailing, satin lapels and velvet trims. The brand is strong on accessories, with a standalone Paul Smith Accessories store on Marylebone High Street. **Branches** throughout the city.

Vivienne Westwood
44 Conduit Street, W1S 2YL (7439 1109, www.viviennewestwood.com). Oxford Circus tube. **Open** 10am-6pm Mon-Wed, Fri, Sat; 10am-7pm Thur; noon-5pm Sun. **Sells** M, W.
Vivienne Westwood is part of British fashion history, with over 30 years in the business and a damehood to her credit. Perhaps still best known for pioneering the punk look, she's since become one of Britain's most revered designers. Her pieces are recognisable for their voluminous quantities of fabric (frequently in her trademark tartan), and of course those signature corsets. The Conduit Street flagship houses the women's Gold Label main line, two diffusion ranges – Red Label and the more casual Anglomania – and menswear and accessories. The original World's End premises carries a smaller selection of clothing and the full range of accessories, as well as special-edition pieces, which are exclusive to the store. The small Davies Street salon stocks only the Gold Label and accessories, and provides a couture and bridal service. There are also concessions within Harrods, Liberty, Harvey Nichols and Selfridges (for all, *see pp21-27*).
Branches 6 Davies Street, W1Y 1LJ (7629 3757); World's End, 430 King's Road, SW10 0JL (7352 6551).

Men

Nigel Hall
18 Floral Street, WC2H 9DS (7379 3600, www.nigelhallmenswear.co.uk). Covent Garden or Leicester Square tube. **Open** 10.30am-7pm Mon-Sat; 11am-5pm Sun. **Sells** M.
Nigel Hall, with its no-nonsense sense of style, is fast becoming a staple. Clean, simple garments have a Riviera elegance, but Hall also gives them a fashionable edge. Knitwear is modern, straightforward and wearable, in a range of unfussy pastel hues. Trousers and jackets are gently fitted and appeal to those of a retro-preppy persuasion. But the clincher is the winning combination of affordable prices and high quality; the details are particularly impressive – stitching, hems and collars are every bit as sophisticated as grander brands that cost three times as much. The clothes are arranged by colour in the airy store and the staff are smart and obliging.
Branches 15 Floral Street, WC2E 9DH (7836 7922); 106A Upper Street, N1 1QN (7704 3173); 75-77 Brushfield Street, E1 6AA (7377 0317); 42-44 Broadwick Street, W1F 7AE (7494 1999).

Women

Hoss Intropia
213 Regent Street, W1B 4NF (7287 3569, www.hossintropia.com). Oxford Circus tube. **Open** 10am-8pm Mon-Sat; noon-6pm Sun. **Sells** W.

Margaret Howell. *See p88.*

TEN
Designer flagships

Agnès b
35-36 Floral Street, WC2E 9DJ (7379 1992, www.agnesb.com). Covent Garden tube. **Open** 10.30am-6.30pm Mon-Wed, Fri; 10.30am-7pm Thur, Sat; noon-6pm Sun. **Sells** M, W.

Chanel
167-170 Sloane Street, SW1X 9QF (7235 6631, www.chanel.com). Knightsbridge tube. **Open** 10am-6pm Mon-Sat; 1-5pm Sun. **Sells** W.

Chloé
152-153 Sloane Street, SW1X 9BX (7823 5348, www.chloe.com). Sloane Square tube. **Open** 10am-6pm Mon, Tue, Thur-Sat; 10am-7pm Wed. **Sells** W, C.

Diane von Furstenberg
25 Bruton Street, W1J 6QH (7499 0886, www.dvf.com). Bond Street tube. **Open** 10am-6pm Mon-Wed, Fri, Sat; 10am-7pm Thur; noon-6pm Sun. **Sells** W.

Gucci
18 Sloane Street, SW1X 9NE (7235 6707, www.gucci.com). Knightsbridge tube. **Open** 10am-6pm Mon, Tue, Thur-Sat; 10am-7pm Wed. **Sells** M, W.

Hoss Intropia's Regent Street flagship proved so successful that the Spanish label opened a second shop in Sloane Square in autumn 2007, and a third in Covent Garden in spring 2010. It seems London can't get enough of the brand's individual, wearable designs. Expect clothing characterised by unusual fabrics, contrasting prints and vibrant colours. As well as useful basics, collections boast fantastic dresses: look out for short and sassy sequined mini-dresses, full-length silk gowns, smocks and knitted dresses. Other recent highlights have included elegant black, beaded, pleated funnel-neck coats. Attention to detail is paramount, hence the use of hand embroidery, sequins, stones and beading. Prices vary considerably – a simple dress or trousers can be had for as little as £60 to £70, but more elaborate pieces are over £300. The accessories range has expanded significantly, with shoes, bags, watches and jewellery.
Branches 27A Sloane Square, SW1W 8AB (7259 9072); 124 Long Acre, WC2E 9PE (7240 4900).

Orla Kiely
31-33 Monmouth Street, WC2H 9DD (7240 4022, www.orlakiely.com). Covent Garden tube. **Open** 10am-6.30pm Mon-Sat; noon-5pm Sun. **Sells** W.
Orla Kiely's individual mismatching colour combos made her a name in the fashion world, and graphic prints and layered textures adorn the Covent Garden flagship. The Dublin-born designer has been called a 'quiet force' in the industry but her designs speak loud and clear, from original laminate totes and purses to leather bags. It may have been accessories that shot Kiely to fame, but her womenswear is attracting an increasing following. Stripy jackets, tops and flowery dresses are inspired by the 1960s and '70s. The quality of the fabrics is top notch and garments are temptingly tactile, but they're not cheap. This flagship store also stocks a selection of the label's increasingly established homewares line.

Paul & Joe
134 Sloane Street, SW1X 9AX (7243 5510, www.paulandjoe.com). Notting Hill Gate tube. **Open** 10am-6.30pm Mon-Sat. **Sells** W.
French designer Sophie Albou's Paul & Joe is a seductive space with interiors that resemble a princess's boudoir and match the romantic, elegant and forward-thinking collections. Think classic French tailoring with a contemporary edge: structured jackets, wide-leg trousers, fringe and lace detailing, alongside impressive party dresses, all in flamboyant prints and feminine fabrics. And there's a make-up range to match. Albou named her brand after her two sons and aimed to introduce variety on to the menswear market (gents should visit the Floral Street branch). This is prêt-à-porter at its best, so invest to possess timeless pieces. Also worth a peek is Paul & Joe Sister, a more casual range featuring mini-dresses and often stocked in

Designer Chains

boutiques. Paul & Joe has concessions in Harrods (*see p22*), Harvey Nichols (*see p23*) and Selfridges (*see p27*). **Branch (Paul & Joe Homme)** 33 Floral Street, WC2 E9DJ (7836 3388).

Stella McCartney
30 Bruton Street, W1J 6QR (7518 3100, www.stella mccartney.com). Bond Street or Green Park tube. **Open** 10am-6pm Mon-Wed, Fri, Sat; 10am-7pm Thur. **Sells** W.

It's been more than six years since Stella McCartney launched her label, and, with every collection stronger than the last, even her original doubters have become converts. Her easy-to-wear, luxe but sporty look has enduring appeal and is a hit with young Hollywood, off-duty supermodels and fashionistas with cash to flash. Sweater dresses, swing coats, poetic blouses, broderie anglaise dresses and platform boots have all featured heavily in collections, and are destined to work their way into many fashion-conscious wardrobes. Joining the main line, fragrance, skincare and sportswear collaboration with Adidas, is an expanded accessories line, as well as a lingerie line. McCartney's views on animal rights are well known, so her bags, belts and shoes are made in cruelty-free fabrics such as satin, velvet, nylon and canvas. Stella McCartney is also available from Harvey Nichols (*see p23*) and Selfridges (*see p27*).

Miu Miu
123 New Bond Street, W1S 1EJ (7409 0900, www.miumiu.com). Bond Street or Oxford Circus tube. **Open** 10am-6pm Mon-Wed, Fri, Sat; 10am-7pm Thur. **Sells** W.

Nicole Farhi
158 New Bond Street, W1S 2UB (7499 8368, www.nicolefarhi.com). Green Park tube. **Open** 10am-6pm Mon-Wed, Fri; 10am-7pm Thur; 10am-6.30pm Sat; noon-6pm Sun. **Sells** M, W.

Prada
16-18 Old Bond Street, W1X 3DA (7647 5000, www.prada.com). Green Park tube. **Open** 10am-6pm Mon-Wed, Fri, Sat; 10am-7pm Thur; noon-5pm Sun. **Sells** M, W.

Sonia Rykiel
27-29 Brook Street, W1K 4HE (7493 5255, www.soniarykiel.com). Bond Street tube. **Open** 10am-6.30pm Mon-Wed, Fri, Sat; 10am-7pm Thur. **Sells** W, C.

Temperley London
6-10 Colville Mews, Lonsdale Road, W11 2DA (7229 7957, www.temperley london.com). Notting Hill Gate tube. **Open** 10am-6pm Mon-Wed, Fri; 10am-7pm Thur; 11am-6pm Sat. **Sells** W.

Streetwise **Mount Street, W1**

This traditional Mayfair enclave has become a byword for upmarket but hip brands.

Significant swathes of W1 have always been known for their rather stuffy atmosphere. Doormen – that is, men who open doors for a living – are prone to sneer at potential customers who might rank below viscount. Mount Street, with its dignified Victorian terracotta façades and by-appointment-only art galleries, still harbours a superior Mayfair elite; consider, for example, traditional vendors such as master butcher **Allens of Mayfair** (no.117, *see p244*), cigar shop **Sautter** (no.106, 7499 4866), with its dusty collection of antique crocodile skin cigar cases, and **Purdey** (7499 1801), the traditional gunsmith that has stood aloof at 57 South Audley Street since 1882.

But Mount Street is now home to a raft of top-notch shops that have given the area's traditional luxury aesthetic a youthful, less exclusive twist – but without compromising on quality.

first of the superbrands to appear. A stand-alone **Marc by Marc Jacobs** store opened at no.44 in spring 2009. Another of the red-hot names is revered shoe designer **Christian Louboutin** (no.17, *see p121*), whose eye-catching storefront displays are often the talk of the street. Parisian perfumer **Annick Goutal** has opened shop at no.109, and contemporary jeweller **Fiona Knapp** is next door. You'll also find niche Australian skincare brand **Aesop** (no.91; *see p138*) and the best highlights in London at **Jo Hansford** (no.19, 7495 7774).

High-end fashion brands may have opened up on this previously sleepy stretch, then, but it's the deliberate absence of brash, ultra-luxe fashion houses like Louis Vuitton and Gucci that has given Mount Street its real cachet. The idea behind the renaissance was to source the best of everything – and not necessarily the most expensive or best known. Some of the biggest brands are conspicuous

Towards the east end of the street, near the Connaught Hotel, sits the **Balenciaga** flagship (no.12, 7317 4400), its super-chic clothing set against a glowing sci-fi interior. Next door, you can splurge on a Moser wristwatch at Asprey offshoot **William & Son** (no.10, 7493 8385) – or buy a rifle at their branch at no.14.

Across the road, gentlemen's tailor **Rubinacci** (no.96, 7499 2299) sits near the **Mount Street Galleries** (no.94, 7493 1613), one of several fine art dealers in the area. Antiques dealers, perhaps unsurprisingly, also feature, including **Kenneth Neame** (no.27, 7629 0445) just up the street. Indeed, just round the corner on South Audley Street is **Adrian Alan** (nos.66-67, 7495 2324), selling extremely impressive items. It holds court with **Thomas Goode & Co** (no.19, 7499 2823); and **Spa Illuminata** (no.63, 7499 7777) day spa.

But it's back on Mount Street where the new lease of life is most in evidence, with **Marc Jacobs'** first UK boutique (nos.24-25; *see p88*), one of the

by their absence. So there's no chance of this becoming another Bond Street – at least for now.

Other shops on or around the street include a **Lanvin** store (no.128, 7491 1839), a branch of bridal and cocktail dress shop **Jenny Packham** (3A Carlos Place; *see p115*), men's shoe store **Harry's of London** (59 South Audley Street, 7409 7988), and **Wunderkind** (no.16, 7493 4312), a youthful diffusion line from German label Joop!

When the luxury gets too much for you, take some time out in **Mount Street Gardens**, which snakes behind the south side of the street. You can sit and watch long-term residents of this history-loaded area puzzle over its new-found popularity with fashionable young upstarts.

Local dining options include afternoon tea at the Connaught Hotel's **Gallery at the Connaught** or a drink at its opulent **Coburg Bar**. There's also long-running, recently refurbished fish restaurant **Scott's** (no.20). Or sneak down the road to the **Audley** pub (no.41) for a pint of Young's.

Shop talk Charles Boyd-Bowman, Managing Director of Alexander Boyd

Tell us about your shop
'We have been in this shop for five and a half years. We are bespoke shirtmakers and we offer bespoke tailoring in the shop, so if you come in we can measure you up and make the shirt to order.

'We make 80 per cent of what we sell ourselves, and everything we do is made in England. We have two factories – one in Kent and one in Suffolk – where we make shirts for ourselves and for others.'

Who shops here?
'Quite a wide variety of people. We get the hedge-fund managers down from the West End, the men from the City, and the more fashionable crowd who shop near Brick Lane and Spitalfields. We've also launched a website, and that's bringing more people to the shop.'

Is it harder to run an independent shop than it used to be?
'No, because what we offer is unique, and what we offer in the time we can offer it is unique too.

'We are very fortunate because we actually make the product ourselves – we don't have to go anywhere else or rely on anyone else to do so, which enables us to be flexible. For example, a man came in at three o'clock one day in desperate need of a bespoke shirt for that evening, and we had two made for him by 5pm. It was an unusual situation, but it goes to show what you can do!'

What are your favourite shops in London?
'Well, near here is the Albion café (2-4 Boundary Street, E2 7DD, 7729 1051, www.albioncaff.co.uk), where we go for food and bits and bobs; we actually made the uniforms for the staff there, so it's a reciprocal relationship.

'There is also a great new cheese shop in Spitalfields Market (*see p46*), and I have picked up quite a few things from the nearby [vintage] furniture store Elemental (67 Brushfield Street, E1 6AA, 7247 7588, www.elemental.uk.com).

'I don't have to go anywhere else for clothes because everything I need is here.'

What is the most enjoyable aspect of owning a shop?
'Well, we're a family business in the way we are run and in the way we treat our customers; we like to think of them as our family too and to treat them as such.'

Any plans for the future?
'We are looking to bring other products into the shop – outerwear and knitwear will be next – but we will always look to our core values when expanding and make very key choices about what we bring in.'

▶For more on **Alexander Boyd**, *see p97*.

A suit to behold

London has long been the centre of the universe when it comes to bespoke suits and expert tailoring.

Mayfair's **Savile Row** is famous the world over, having been synonymous with bespoke tailoring since the 1800s. However, what the term 'bespoke' actually means has been the subject of controversy in recent years, with many of the street's old-school tailors arguing that newcomers have been using the term to offer tailoring services that were not actually bespoke, but simply 'made-to-measure'.

Determined to preserve their centuries-old technique, the high houses of Mayfair tailoring formed the **Savile Row Bespoke Association** (www.savilerowbespoke.com) in 2004, drawing up a list of standards by which to distinguish themselves as the real deal. Their 'pure bespoke' standards included: measuring the customer's body by at least 21 individual points; creating and keeping an original paper pattern for each customer; advising and consulting on all aspects of the suit's fit and fabric; and, perhaps most importantly, performing virtually all needlework by hand.

Four years later, though, the Advertising Standards Authority created considerable wiggle room for UK tailors by allowing businesses to label themselves 'bespoke' even if they measured, framed and cut by hand, but sewed by machine.

In the end, going 'pure bespoke' is a question of intimacy with your clothing. Initial outgoings for made-to-measure will always be cheaper. However, if you're after a suit that will exactly fit your proportions and physique, which will last for decades, be easily adjustable with age (if you gain weight, for instance), and which will be a real expression of your tastes and personality, then you might choose to enlist the services of an expert bespoke tailor, such as those mentioned below, who train for years before they're let loose on the luxurious fabrics of your choosing. The level of craftmanship employed is unbeatable.

The following Savile Row shops are all members of the Savile Row Bespoke Association.

Henry Poole & Co (15 Savile Row, W1S 3PJ, 7734 5985, www.henrypoole.com) was established in 1806, and founded Savile Row. Since then, it has served royalty and historical notables, from Napoleon III and Emperor Haile Selassie to 'Buffalo' Bill Cody, Winston Churchill, and the livery of Queen Elizabeth II. History buffs can examine King George II's household livery on display in the store. All suits here are 'pure bespoke', with two-piece suits from £2,646 and three-pieces from £2,828 (prices exclude VAT).

Dege & Skinner (10 Savile Row, W1S 3PF, 7287 2941, www.dege-skinner.co.uk), a few doors down, has built a formidable reputation as a bespoke tailor and highland dressmaker, but also commands great respect for its military uniforms and shirt-making services. With three royal warrants to its name, it's a sure bet for top-notch service, and, according to owner William Skinner, it makes 'the best uniforms in London.' Prices for a Dege & Skinner bespoke suit start at £3,000, with shirts from £195 (prices include VAT); master shirt-maker Robert Whitaker cuts with a skill that's hard to match, even on Savile Row. Equally impressive are Dege & Skinner's selection of dressing gowns.

John Lobb

Tailoring & Bespoke

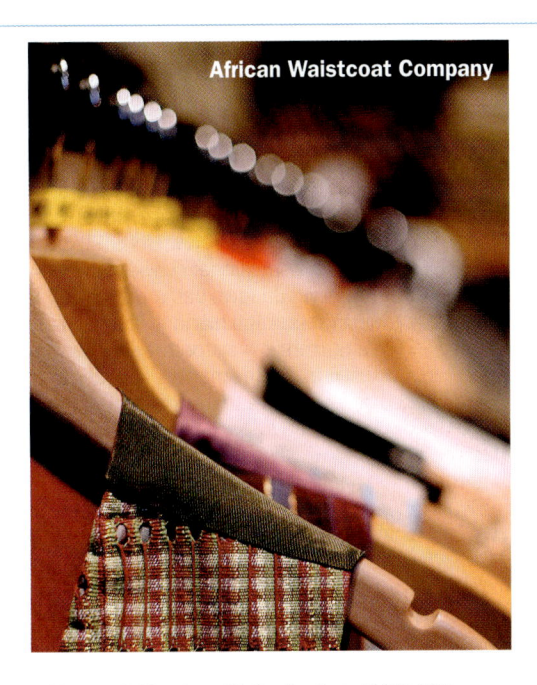

Gieves & Hawkes (1 Savile Row, W1S 3JR, 7434 2001, www.gievesandhawkes.com) isn't just about fine tailoring; it's also a history lesson for anyone interested in the development of men's clothes. Despite having held royal warrants without interruption for 200 years (the Queen, the Duke of Edinburgh and Prince Charles are all customers), the company continues to innovate.

It offers three services: the beautiful ready-to-wear collection starts at £595, while its made-to-measure service starts a little higher, at £895; handmade bespoke is the premier service – it's a long procedure (we're talking months), but you'll eventually take home a luxury handmade garment made to your exact measurements and requirements.

While the majority of the finest suit-makers are still on Savile Row, there is one London tailor who offers Mayfair sophistication on a Soho budget: **Chris Kerr** (52 Berwick Street, W1F 8SL, 7437 3727, www.chriskerr.com) – who learnt the trade from his father, legendary 1960s tailor Eddie Kerr.

Located in the heart of Soho, the purple façade of his shop is a stylish stand-out amid a row of curry houses, hair salons and bustling sidewalk cafés. Inside, the vibe is more artist's studio than shop, and everyone from Johnny Depp to James Bond (in his Daniel Craig incarnation) has stepped inside; Nick Cave is a regular (ten suits in the last ten months, apparently). But despite the star-studded clientele, Eddie tells us that the shop's mission remains simple: to make pure bespoke suits for the man on the street. '£1,200 is expensive enough,' he says. It's thus the ideal place to commission your first bespoke suit.

However, if you're still baulking at this price, and aren't yet ready to invest in a bespoke suit, then quality ready-to-wear and tailored suits are available at Dutch-owned **SuitSupply** (9 Vigo Street, W1S 3HH, 7851 2961, www.suitsupply.com), which opened in 2010, around the corner from Savile Row. You won't get the personal attention of a truly bespoke tailor, but the company's tailoring session is still comprehensive – customers are measured by a 35-point system, and then details are sent to Italy, where a tailor creates your suit in 100% Italian fabric, posting it back to the UK in six to eight weeks. Alterations can then be made in store, if necessary. And with prices starting at just £349, it's a fraction of the price of a Savile Row number.

Whether you go for fully bespoke, off-the-peg, or somewhere in between, you'll need a decent shirt and a pair of shoes to complete the look. As well as offering expert tailoring (master cutter Clive Phythian trained at Gieves & Hawkes), **Alexander Boyd** (54 Artillery Lane, E1 7LS, 7377 8755, www.alexanderboyd.co.uk; see also p95 **Shop talk**), over in Spitalfields, can measure you up and make you a beautiful handmade tailored shirt to order (prices start at £175). Even the shop's off-the-peg shirts are made in the finest cotton in a factory in Kent, as are its ties, handmade from silk woven in Suffolk. For bespoke shoes, meanwhile, head to **John Lobb** (see p126), where, for a price (around £2,000), you'll get a handmade pair that will last a lifetime. And for a snazzy contrast to a classic English look, head to Camden Passage (see p106 **Streetwise**) to check out the colourful garments made by the **African Waistcoat Company** (33 Islington Green, N1 8DU, 7704 9698, www.africanwaistcoatcompany.com). Here, old Etonian Calum Robertson marries African and Savile Row traditions and craftsmanship, producing dazzling waistcoats made from West African cottons and silks.

Vintage & Secondhand

Absolute Vintage
15 Hanbury Street, E1 6QR (7247 3883, www.absolutevintage.co.uk). Shoreditch High Street rail. **Open** 11am-7pm daily. **Sells** M, W.
The range here will make you giddy: there are over 1,000 pairs of shoes, arranged in size, colour and era, from 1940s suede courts, through to 1980s white high-heels. Men can find brown country brogues or lizard-skin pimp numbers. Stock is priced to sell and you can kit yourself out for £50. There are day dresses, of mixed vintage and arranged by colour, cotton maxis, slinky '70s disco dresses and '80s posh frocks. A matching clutch bag won't be a problem; they are stacked in their hundreds. Around the corner, sister store Blondie (Unit 2, 114-118 Commercial Street, 7247 0050) has a more boutiquey atmosphere and an edited selection, ideal for those who don't want to trawl through the rails.

Annie's Vintage Clothes
12 Camden Passage, N1 8ED (7359 0796). Angel tube. **Open** 11am-6pm Mon, Tue, Thur, Fri; 9am-6pm Wed, Sat; 11am-3pm Sun. **Sells** W, C.
Annie Moss's shop was the obvious choice for providing dresses for the 1980s *Brideshead Revisited* TV series. Knockout flapper dresses are the speciality. Everything is sheer, floaty and ethereal. The paler dresses are currently popular with brides, and are good value compared to modern off-the-peg frocks. For a more traditional choice, there's a rail of wedding dresses from the Victorian period and slinkier bias cut numbers from the 1930s. Most day dresses date from the 1930s and '40s, but you'll also find later vintage too, such as 1950s appliqué skirts. There is a good selection of accessories – delicate fans, parasols, chic hats, 1920s shoes, swimwear and even baby clothes.

Bang Bang
21 Goodge Street, W1T 2PJ (7631 4191). Goodge Street tube. **Open** 10am-6.30pm Mon-Fri; 11am-6pm Sat. **Sells** W.
It's all down to luck and timing at this lunch-break browser's fave. More dress agency than vintage shop, top-end labels such as Dries Van Noten and Moschino hang alongside mediocre high street pieces. Sharp eyes are rewarded: in the past a well-priced Ossie Clark gown has been spotted in the mix. Nearly new shoes sport labels such as Gina, Costume National and Miu Miu, and there are usually plenty for larger feet too. The turnover of stock is fast, so it's worth popping in regularly. There's also a sister store on Berwick Street (no.9), with similar vintage womenswear on the ground floor and menswear in the basement.
Branch 9 Berwick Street, W1F 0PJ (7494 2042).

Beyond Retro HOT 50
110-112 Cheshire Street, E2 6EJ (7729 9001, www.beyondretro.com). Shoreditch High Street rail. **Open** 10am-7pm daily. **Sells** M, W.
This East End institution has a loyal following of fancy dress-seekers, hard-up students and offbeat musicians. The vast former warehouse is crammed with around 10,000 items of stock, helpfully arranged by colour and, if you have the time and patience, you can literally dress yourself from top to toe: vintage corsets and suspender belts, silk slips and net petticoats, Polynesian-print maxi dresses, frou-frou prom dresses, vintage kimonos, lace and satin wedding dresses and lots more. For men, there are sharp '70s suits, trilbies, waistcoats and a vast array of T-shirts and denim. Not everything is in great nick, but it's priced accordingly and ideal if you're after an instant wear-once look.
Branch 58-59 Great Marlborough Street, W1F 7JY (7434 1406).

Butler & Wilson
189 Fulham Road, SW3 6JN (7352 8255, www.butlerandwilson.co.uk). South Kensington tube. **Open** 10am-6pm Mon, Tue, Thur-Sat; 10am-7pm Wed; noon-6pm Sun. **Sells** W.
The costume jewellery range, for which the brand is famous, is at ground level, along with original pieces by Stanley Hugler. But to the left of the jewellery showroom, a gated stairway leads to vintage heaven. Up here, rails of beaded dresses that once shimmied to the charleston are ready to party once more. You'll also find ultra-feminine Edwardian white lace dresses, bought by brides-to-be. And if you've ever fancied delivering the line 'I'll just change into something more comfortable', then one of the exotic silk kimonos should do the job. There are later vintage surprises here too. Collectable 1950s novelty bags – such as raffia animals – are another Butler & Wilson strength.
Branch 20 South Molton Street, W1K 5QY (7409 2955).

Cloud Cuckoo Land
6 Charlton Place, Camden Passage, N1 8AJ (7354 3141). Angel tube. **Open** 11am-5.30pm Tue-Sat. **Sells** W.
This fun little shop has a great selection of very wearable dresses from the 1930s to 1970s. Stock is feminine and quirky: elegant 1930s full-length silk slips, '40s crêpe cocktail gowns and '50s circle skirts. There are often some good '70s labels here too, such as John Varon, Bus Stop and Janice Wainwright or perhaps a superb 1960s Susan Small black satin duster coat, beautifully lined. At the back of the shop you'll find accessories, coats and jackets, plus a good selection of wraps, scarves, shawls and '50s novelty bags. The cheerful owner is happy to make suggestions if you're after a particular vintage look.

Vintage & Secondhand

Annie's Vintage Clothes

London Beatles Store

231 BAKER STREET LONDON NW1 6XE
TEL : 020 7935 4464 / FAX : 020 7935 9347
OPEN DAILY 10AM - 6:30PM
www.beatlesstorelondon.co.uk

We stock a large range of merchandise including T-shirts & clothing, wallets, bags, accessories, mugs, posters, collectibles, photographs, records, DVDs plus original memorabilia including film and promo posters, autographs and much more !
You can also find out about tours, Beatles sites and purchase guide books and maps.

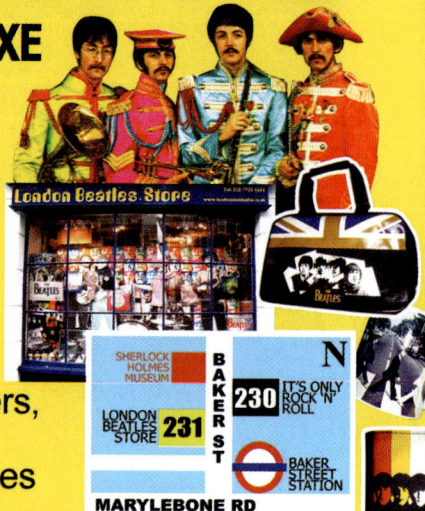

IT'S ONLY ROCK 'N' ROLL

230 BAKER STREET LONDON NW1 5RT
Tel: 020 7224 0277
OPEN DAILY 10AM - 6:30PM
www.itsonlyrocknrolllondon.co.uk

LONDON'S ONLY ROCK 'N' ROLL MEMORABILIA STORE

If you love The Rolling Stones, AC/DC, The Who, Led Zeppelin, Queen, Pink Floyd, Ramones, Jimi Hendrix, Iron Maiden, David Bowie, Sex Pistols, Metallica, The Doors, etc. this is the place for you! We sell T-shirts & other clothing, mugs, posters, badges, bags, wallets and accessories, photographs plus original memorabilia and autographs.

Dolly Diamond

51 Pembridge Road, W11 3HG (7792 2479, www.dollydiamond.com). Notting Hill Gate tube. **Open** 10.30am-6.30pm Mon-Fri; 9.30am-6.30pm Sat; noon-6pm Sun. **Sells** M ,W.

One minute you're in the 21st century, then you step through the door into the 1940s. The shop has a delightfully old-fashioned feel, with its neat displays and vintage bra mannequins. It's also popular with classic car enthusiasts who dress in post-war fashions for the glamorous Vintage at Goodwood weekend. The stock doesn't disappoint, whether it's a glam 1940s grosgrain gown or a cute burlesque hat. There are men's clothes too, with 1940s dinner jackets and shirts. At the back of the store you'll find a rail of vintage bridalwear, which takes in accessories and headdresses, and offers a custom alteration service on all its exquisite vintage gowns.

East End Thrift Store

Unit 1A, Watermans Building, Assembly Passage, E1 4UT (7423 9700, www.theeastendthrift store.com). Stepney Green tube. **Open** 11am-6pm Mon-Wed, Sun; 11am-7pm Thur-Sat. **Sells** M, W.

The clue's in the name – 'thrift' rather than 'vintage', which means you get essentially all the fab gear of yesteryear at prices that would get Del Boy all a-quiver. Most of the stock is around the £7-£10 mark, but if you splash £15 you could get the one-of-a-kind turquoise evening dress with marabou trim on its hem (spotted on a previous excursion), or a Gloria Vanderbilt bomber jacket. It might not be as pretty as some of the other vintage shops, but the stripped warehouse space has a certain functional charm all of its own.

Branch (Brick Lane Thrift Store) 68 Sclater Street, E1 6HR (7739 0242).

The Girl Can't Help It

Alfie's Antique Market, 13-25 Church Street, NW8 8DT (7724 8984, www.thegirlcanthelpit. com). Edgware Road tube or Marylebone tube/ rail. **Open** 10am-6pm Tue-Sat. **Sells** M, W.

Named after the Jayne Mansfield film, the Girl Can't Help It is classic Hollywood territory, personified by co-owner Sparkle Moore, an exuberant platinum maned New Yorker who, with partner, Cad Van Swankster, sources most of her stock from the US. Always in stock are classic 1940s suits and 1950s circle skirts, decorated with everything from kitsch kittens to Mexican-style patterns. You can achieve the total look here, right down to the lingerie and glam accessories. Van Swankster presides over the suave menswear – Hawaiian shirts, gabardine jackets, slick 1940s and '50s suits, pin-up ties and camp accessories, such as tiki-themed bar glasses.

Also at Alfie's (*see p178*), on the 2nd floor, you'll find Gwyneth Trefor-Jones's shop with its ever-changing stock (and no strict adherence to a particular period) and the guarantee of a bargain. Trimmings are Trefor-Jones's real passion – beads, buttons, sequins and the like – and there are drawers full of goodies, divided up into £3 bags.

Lost 'n' Found Vintage Clothing

25 Stables Market, Chalk Farm Road, NW1 8AH (7482 2848). Camden Town tube. **Open** 11am-6.30pm Mon-Fri; 10.30am-6.30pm Sat, Sun. **Sells** M, W.

Set out over two levels, this fun vintage shop is perfect rummaging territory. It's well organised and stock is competitively priced, making it an ideal source for one-off party gear and cheap vintage clobber to wear every day. There are no big labels here, but patience may unearth worthwhile pieces – perhaps a 1960s Samuel Sherman wool dress or a floral Marion Donaldson day dress. There are cotton maxi dresses and 1950s cocktail dresses. Find elegant '60s handbags and '70s tooled leather shoulder bags too. Men will be happy here as well, with shirts, biker jackets and denims. On a previous visit it even had proper pipe band kilts.

Merchant Archive Boutique HOT 50

320 Kilburn Lane, W9 3EF (8969 6470, www.merchantarchive.com). Queen's Park tube/rail. **Open** 10am-7pm Tue-Fri; 10am-6pm Sat; 11am-5pm Sun. **Sells** W.

Among a nondescript parade of shops on a rather scuzzy bit of Kilburn Lane stands Merchant Archive, an artfully crumbling old Lipton general store that's been reworked into a stylish emporium with striking art and sporadic taxidermy. The shop emanates an atmosphere of specialness as soon as you enter, and as a destination shop for both vintage and contemporary clothing, it takes pride of place in the address books of many a stylist, fashion designer and celebrity. Owner Sophie Merchant's discerning eye is evident in the well-edited selection of beautiful one-off antique pieces for sale, with vintage numbers from Lanvin, jumpsuits from the 1920s, antique velvet jackets, a good range of elegant dresses and some very special jewellery all waiting to be snapped up.

Old Hat

66 Fulham High Street, SW6 3LQ (7610 6558). Putney Bridge tube. **Open** 10.30am-6.30pm Mon-Sat. **Sells** M.

David Saxby's menswear emporium is perfect for those with lord of the manor pretensions but without the trust fund to match. It's worth persevering when perusing the rails of tightly packed suits, as Savile Row suits can be had for under £100 (and originals can cost upwards of £3,000). All the gentlemanly requisites are here: top hats, tailcoats, silk scarves, overcoats and moleskin trousers, and the shop is a favourite with those off to retro events such as the Goodwood Festival of Speed. Saxby also has a branch in Tokyo, and his own-label menswear shop down the road (no.62), selling traditional tweed suits, silk waistcoats, overcoats and cords for off-duty gents.

Beyond Retro. *See p98.*

Vintage & Secondhand

Sales & events

Loved, lost or just last season. Hunt for something special at one of the capital's vintage happenings.

Angels
1 Garrick Road, NW9 6AA (8202 2244, www.angels.uk.com). Leicester Square tube. Venues vary.
With a huge stock of film, television and theatre costumes, Angels sales of vintage fashions and original uniforms from the 1950s to the 1990s, have become infamous. Thanks to their hysteria-inducing 'fill a bag' method, you need to come with elbows at the ready.

Anita's Vintage Fashion Fairs
Battersea Arts Centre, Lavender Hill, SW11 5TN (8325 5789, www.vintagefashionfairs.com). Clapham Junction rail.
Attended by fashion editors and designers, these fairs are a great place to pick up vintage designer clothes from the likes of Ozzie Clarke, Prada, Eley Kishimoto, Chanel and YSL. See website for dates.

Christie's South Kensington
85 Old Brompton Road, SW7 3LD (7930 6074, www.christies.com). South Kensington tube. See website for dates.
Costume, textiles and fans sales take place about four time a year, with collectors items like bonnets, knickerbockers and 18th-century clothing to be had. There are also biannual sales of 1940s to '80s clothes by leading designers.

Frock Me!
www.frockmevintagefashion.com. Venues vary.
A complete cross-section of vintage clothing and accessories, from the 1890s right up to the 1980s. Loved by designers, students and models alike, these sales keep on getting better.

Kerry Taylor Auctions
Unit C27, Parkhall Road Trading Estate, 40 Martell Road, SE21 8EN (8676 4600, www.kerrytaylorauctions.com). East Dulwich rail.
The leading specialist auction house for antique vintage fashion and textiles. Notable past sales include the Givenchy haute couture black chantilly lace cocktail dress worn by Audrey Hepburn in How to Steal a Million; the dress went for £60,000.

London Vintage Fashion, Textiles & Accessories Fair
Hammersmith Town Hall, King Street, W6 (www.pa-antiques.co.uk). Hammersmith tube.
A huge sale with over 100 dealers offering wares dating from 1800 to 1980. Rifle through piles of handbags, linen, lace, dresses, gloves, boas, compacts and combs. Everything is competitively priced.

London Vintage Wedding Fair
20th Century Theatre, 291 Westbourne Grove, W11 2QA (www.londonvintageweddingfair.co.uk). Notting Hill Gate tube.
Everything for the contemporary bride who loves vintage fashion – but along the lines of Grace Kelly rather than Miss Haversham. Vintage make-up and hairdressing is on offer as well as gowns and accessories.

Primrose Hill Vintage Fair
Cecil Sharp House, Primrose Hill, NW1 7AY (www.vintagefashionlondon.co.uk). Chalk Farm tube.
Set in lovely surroundings with an old-fashioned tea room, this fair is a browser's delight. Clothes and accessories from a bygone age are sold.

One of a Kind
259 Portobello Road, W11 1LR (7792 5853, www.1kind.com). Ladbroke Grove tube.
Open 10am-6pm daily. **Sells** M, W, C.
Lindsay Lohan reportedly shelled out £10,000 in one visit here, selecting dresses and accessories sporting labels such as Chanel, Dior and YSL. No wonder owner Jeff Ihenacho plans to open a shop in LA. There are photographs of Jeff posing with various celebs in the window, and you certainly need an A-lister's wallet to shop here. Fashionistas are fans too – Alice Temperley has been spotted here. Rare pieces are kept in a 'secret' room in the back, to be viewed by appointment. During a previous visit, Jeff revealed sequinned Pucci harem pants and an early '70s YSL lace gown. One of a kind, without a doubt.

Palette London
21 Canonbury Lane, N1 2AS (7288 7428, www.palette-london.com). Highbury & Islington tube/rail. **Open** 11am-6.30pm Mon-Sat; noon-5.30pm Sun. **Sells** W.
Owner Mark Ellis knows what flatters certain body shapes, and he's a great stylist too – for example, using a wide 1980s belt to cinch in a gorgeous '30s dress, completing the look with a great pair of heels. The

boutique has a 50/50 mix of vintage and contemporary designers, selected to complement each other. Look out for Viennese designer Anna Aichinger, who trained with Viktor & Rolf and creates wonderful 1940s-inspired dresses and pencil skirts. Vintage glamour comes courtesy of legendary labels such as Pucci and Courrèges, US designers like Pauline Trigère and Norma Kamali and home-grown talents Ossie Clark, Biba and Janice Wainwright. Prices are mid to high end, but the quality is superb.

Rellik
8 Golborne Road, W10 5NW (8962 0089, www.rellikklondon.co.uk). Westbourne Park tube. **Open** 10am-6pm Tue-Sat. **Sells** W.
Rellik (the Trellick Tower is opposite) is often cited as a favourite among the Kates and Siennas of the celebrity world, but neither the shop nor its price tags are intimidating. It's big enough for a lingering browse and small enough to get advice should you need it. The shop is run by three former Portobello market stallholders – Fiona Stuart, Claire Stansfield and Steven Philip – and their different tastes mean there's a good mix of pieces by the likes of Lanvin, Halston, Bill Gibb, Christian Dior and Ossie Clark. Philip's particular passion is the 1980s (Westwood, Alaïa) and he's popular with stylists (Kylie wore Rellik vintage in her Showgirl tour). There are earlier pieces too and one wall of the shop is dedicated to glam accessories, such as enormous Hermès sunglasses.

Rokit
42 Shelton Street, WC2 9HZ (7836 6547, www.rokit.co.uk). Covent Garden tube. **Open** 10am-7pm Mon-Sat; 11am-6pm Sun. **Sells** M, W.
As Rokit's flagship store – there's also one in Camden and two in Brick Lane – this branch stocks the most comprehensive selection of second-hand items, from tutus and military gear right through to cowboy boots and sunglasses. You won't find many well-known labels here, but it's still worth a rummage; on previous visits a Gunne Sax prairie dress and a Marimekko day dress were unearthed, and they were an absolute steal. There are also scarves, belts and hats galore. For men there are Doherty-style trilbies, waistcoats and shirts, as well as the usual male Americana. The shop at 107 Brick Lane is more boutiquey.
Branches 101 Brick Lane, E1 6SE (7375 3864); 107 Brick Lane, E1 6SE (7247 3777); 225 High Street, NW1 7BU (7267 3046).

Old Hat. *See p101.*

Vintage & Secondhand

Palette London. *See p103.*

Streetwise Camden Passage, N1

Angel's pedestrianised crooked alley mixes 19th-century charm with some seriously stylish boutiques.

One of the attractions of antiques and boutique shopping is that very special thrill of a unique or unusual find, and visitors to Islington's Camden Passage are unlikely to be disappointed on that score: expect to stumble across anything from Marmite-flavoured chocolates and Nigerian waistcoats to Regency candle snuffers. The alleyway, running between Islington High Street (near Angel tube) and the tip of Essex Road, is a glorious throwback to 19th-century London, with Victorian lamp-posts, wonky paving, traditional shopfronts and a time-warp pub, the **Camden Head**.

Antiques dealers, active throughout the week but especially energetic on Saturdays, hawk their curiosities from shops around **Pierrepont Arcade** (*see p178*), or from stalls set back in nooks and crannies. There are lots on the corner of Charlton Place and opposite the Camden Head.

Coming from Angel tube, you'll first pass some lovely gems on connecting Islington High Street, among them cute but pricey shoe boutique **Laura J** (*see p122*), which stocks strappy heels and stylish pumps from the likes of the Jackson Twins, as well as the in-house label. On Camden Passage proper, your first stops might include **Christina's Boxes** (no.8; 07780 961663), purveyor of tasteful lacquered antique boxes, and **Esme** (no.6; 07810 382565), for unique antique jewellery. The nearby **Japanese Gallery** (7226 3347) at no.23 sells and displays 18th- and 19th-century oriental prints.

Keep ambling north to find **Kirt Holmes** (no.16; *see p134*); his chain mail-style jewellery is perennially popular, and his smart monochrome shop is a chic standout.

On the other side, at no.13, is newcomer **Smug** (*see p45*), a lifestyle boutique selling a covetable range of products handpicked by owner Lizzie Evans (*see p43* **Shop talk**); Lisa Stickley bags, vintage furniture, retro Casio watches and adorable stationery fill the cute premises. Next door is yarn shop **Loop** (*see p220*), a four-storey knitter's paradise that recently relocated from Cross Street.

The ladies' collection at **Annie's Vintage Clothes** (no.12; *see p98*), a little further along on the other side, is particularly strong on wedding dresses from the Victorian era to the 1950s, and she's got a fab stock of pretty 1930s tea dresses; Kate Moss is said to be a fan. Which brings us nicely on to **Frost French**, the first standalone boutique of Kate's pal, Sadie (no.22-26, 7354 0053); despite past financial troubles, the brand has kept its place here on the passage; it makes an appropriate neighbour to two similarly stylish clothes shops: **Susy Harper** (no.35; 7704 0688), selling upmarket, structured-yet-floaty linen womenswear, and ethical boutique **Equa** (no.28; *see p69*).

Check out the life-size suit of armour outside the **Furniture Vault** (no.50; 8366 5959), before moving on to a profoundly more modern gentleman's outfitters, the **African Waistcoat Company** (no.33; 7704 9698, www.africanwaistcoatcompany.com). Here, traditional, bright and eye-catching fabrics hand-woven by Nigeria's Yoruba weavers are perfectly tailored to fit around any waist by the Old Etonian owner Calum Robertson.

For some gastronomic respite, your eating and drinking options along Camden Passage include the **Elk in the Woods** (no.39), for a hearty main or a sandwich or snack and a decent pint; **Macondo** (no.20), for Latin American snacks; and, if you get here early – which you'll need to do if you want to make the most of the antiques – the **Breakfast Club** (no.31). Make sure you reserve some of your daily calories for **Paul A Young Fine Chocolates** (no.33; *see p247*), however. This chocolatier has frequent themed ranges, with some adventurous flavour combinations.

▶ www.camdenpassageislington.co.uk

Lingerie, Swimwear & Erotica

Lingerie

The lingerie sections of many of London's department stores (*see pp21-27*) make great browsing grounds for underwear and bikinis. Our faves are **Liberty** and **Selfridges**.

Agent Provocateur
6 Broadwick Street, W1F 8HL (7439 0229, www.agent provocateur.com). Oxford Circus or Tottenham Court Road tube. **Open** 11am-7pm Mon-Wed, Fri, Sat; 11am-8pm Thur; noon-5pm Sun. **Sells** W.
First port of call for the glamorous, decadent and fashion-forward lingerie fan, Agent Provocateur designs some of the most desirable bras, briefs and babydolls around. The first AP opened in Soho way back in 1994, and the brand now boasts an international reputation. Slip into the seductively lit shop, complete with saucy pink-uniformed staff, and lose a happy hour flipping through rails of wispy tulle and luxurious silk. It's a fine place to stock up on honeymoon fripperies (note for men: you cannot go wrong with a gift from this place); there's also a brilliant bridal range. Designs of the bras, briefs and thongs often feature sheer materials with bows and side ties. Nipple tassels, slips, waspies, suspenders and corsets are also all on the menu.
Branches throughout the city.

Alice & Astrid
30 Artesian Road, W2 5DD (7985 0888, www.aliceandastrid.com). Notting Hill Gate tube.
Open varies, phone for details. **Sells** W.
This bright and breezy boutique exudes a carefree summery vibe. Rails are lined with simple and beautiful lingerie (camis, soft-cup bras and french knickers), night- and loungewear, beachwear and ready-to-wear separates in soft cotton, delicate silk chiffon and amazingly soft baby alpaca. Alice & Astrid's exclusive, subtle prints (sweet birds, flowers and delicate stripes) are showcased to perfection in a palette of fresh pinks, blues, greens and white. The Trousseau collection of knicks and nightwear is particularly strong, drawing on archive shapes and bestsellers, recreated in creamy satins and vintage lace for brides. Also on offer are Lilly Lewis Hair Accessories. *See also p111* **Shop talk***.*

Apartment C HOT 50
70 Marylebone High Street, W1U 5JL (7935 1854, www.apartment-c.com). Regent's Park tube. **Open** 10am-6pm Mon-Sat; noon-5pm Sun. **Sells** W.
A fantasy bachelorette pad, Kenya Cretegny's Marylebone lingerie emporium is a unique concept perfectly rendered. It's all about 'hanging out in your knickers, drinking gin out of a teacup and reading *The Last Tango in Paris* out loud'. From the boudoir-like fitting rooms and flock of stuffed pigeons to its independent gallery hidden in the basement, it's London's most stylish place to buy your smalls. The list of designers is long – Afterwear and Aloe to Lounge Lover and Paperself – and the range of styles impressive; bras, briefs, bodies, suspenders and corsets are displayed alongside loungewear, swimwear, books, candles and exclusive perfumes with names such as Hotel Slut and Jasmine & Cigarettes. Something for everyone, then.

Bodas
38B Ledbury Road, W11 2AB (7229 4464, www.bodas.co.uk). Notting Hill Gate tube.
Open 10am-6pm Mon-Sat. **Sells** W.
There's a time and a place for seductive peepholes, tie-side knickers and marabou mules – and we urge you to embrace it. The rest of the time, boutiques such as Bodas are a real godsend. Head here for simple, well-cut and super-flattering bras and knickers. There are smooth padded bras in invisible 'maquillage' (a dark pink that works much better than nudes) for the perfect line under a flimsy frock, and sheer white soft-cup bras for stylish comfort. Matching knickers start at around £10 (in sheer,

Agent Provocateur. See p107.

Tactel and cotton) and the lovely nightwear encompasses chic white pyjamas, nightdresses and kimonos. Great for cut-above essentials and wardrobe basics.
Branch 43 Brushfield Street, E1 6AA (7655 0958).

Myla
74 Duke of York Square, King's Road, SW3 4LY (7730 0700, www.myla.com). Sloane Square tube.
Open 10am-6.30pm Mon-Sat; noon-5pm Sun. **Sells** W. Since it was founded in 1999, the luxury lingerie brand Myla has acquired a devoted following (its lace and freshwater pearl g-string acquired particular infamy after being featured in a classic Samantha *Sex and the City* scene). There are now five London stores and various concessions around town, which makes getting one's hands on the label's stylish, high-quality bras, knickers, toys and accessories a breeze. Seasonally updated collections always include fashion-forward colours and designs, though classics such as the signature silk and lace couture range are always in stock. There's a lovely swimwear range, elegant nightwear (like classic silk satin pyjamas) and accessories such as candles, silk-bow nipple tassels and blindfolds. The brand is also known for its elegant and subtle sex toys (such as the Myla Spot vibrator).
Branches throughout the city.

Lingerie, Swimwear & Erotica

Rigby & Peller
22A Conduit Street, W1S 2XT (7491 2200, www.rigbyandpeller.com). Oxford Circus tube.
Open 9.30am-6pm Mon-Wed, Fri, Sat; 9am-7pm Thur. **Sells** W.
Unquestionably the Rolls-Royce of the bra-fitting world, Rigby & Peller – corsetière to the Queen, no less – offers a professional, service-oriented experience in its Mayfair boutique. Once you've seen the difference these properly fitting undergarments make, there'll be no returning to the grab-and-go guesswork and the greying rejects from the back of the drawer. Either arrive early or make an appointment if you want to be measured (it takes 45 minutes), and come prepared to splash some cash. Not because it's outrageously expensive – prices are, in fact, pleasingly affordable – but because you'll be dying to get your hands on the array of fabulous items. Brands include Spanx, Speedo, Marlies Deckers, Eda, Aubade and Fantasie as well as own-brand designs (a R&P swimwear range launched in 2009). Sports, mastectomy and maternity bras are available too. There are branches in Knightsbridge, Chelsea and Westfield London.
Branches throughout the city.

What Katie Did
26 Portobello Green, 281 Portobello Road, W10 5TZ (0845 430 8943, www.whatkatiedid.com). Ladbroke Grove tube. **Open** 10am-6pm Mon-Sat; noon-6pm Sun. **Sells** W.
If you want to recreate Gemma Arterton's Bond girl look, get fitted/kitted out in WKD's Harlow Bullet Bra (not so much a push-up as a push-out). Even Gwynnie hasn't been able to resist the look (also snapped in Maitresse knickers by Mario Testino, no less, for *Vogue*). Vintage glamour is the USP here – think sexy corsets inspired by music hall and cabaret, seductive silks and satins (as well as velvet and leather, cotton and lace), and seamed stockings 'to bring out the showgirl in you'. Along with fabulous collections from the UK's top retro lingerie designers, WKD is now stocking the complete range of Besame cosmetics in gorgeous retro-vintage packaging, so that you can complete the look.

Swimwear

Biondi
55B Old Church Street, SW3 5BS (7349 1111, www.biondicouture.com). Sloane Square tube.
Open 10.30am-6.30pm Mon-Sat. **Sells** W, C.
For the ultimate indulgence, and buckets of beach confidence, this luxury bikini boutique offers a fantastic bespoke service. Check out the array of shapes, styles, patterns and colours with the online 'bikini designer', then pop in and let the team make your dream one- or two-piece a reality. Obviously, this all comes at a price, but slightly less extravagant is the made-to-measure option (from £250), where staff produce tailored items from existing shapes and materials. There's also a great ready-to-wear selection of swimwear and beachwear from the likes of Vix, Fisico and Delfina, as well as hats, sunglasses and other beach accessories.

Heidi Klein
174 Westbourne Grove, W11 2RW (7243 5665, www.heidiklein.com). Notting Hill Gate tube. **Open** 10am-6pm Mon-Sat; noon-5pm Sun. **Sells** M, W.
The divine aroma of own-brand coconut candles (£32) at this glam beachwear store is enough to transport you to a world where stress-free grooming (there's an on-site beauty salon offering waxing, tanning, facials and manicures), sampling beauty products (including the fabulous St Barth's range) and choosing the latest Missoni bikini are numbers 1, 2 and 3 on your to-do list. Own-brand bikinis start at £135 and come in classic black and white, with a choice of fashion-forward colours (turquoise, coffee, striped) too. Also on offer are bikinis by Lenny, Missoni, Helen Kaninski, and Vix and Eres, men's togs by Orlebar Brown and Vilebrequin, and Tom Ford and Tod's eyewear, as well as a host of own-brand kaftans, sandals and cover-ups. Robes and flip flops in every dressing room add to the VIP feel. A finer place to buy a bikini we can't imagine.
Branch 257 Pavillion Road, SW1 0PB (7259 9418).

Odabash
48B Ledbury Road, W11 2AJ (7229 4299, www.odabash.com). Notting Hill Gate tube. **Open** 10am-6pm Mon-Sat; noon-5pm Sun. **Sells** M, W, C.
Slink into ultra-glam Odabash (unbelievably white, white carpets, driftwood lamps) and even if the best you can hope for this summer is a week in a caravan in Wales, you'll feel like there's a yacht with your name on it somewhere. Frankly, nothing less would do justice to the kaftans, amazingly flattering bikinis (£130-£175), sparkly flip flops and beachy-glam jewellery. Recent collections have featured palettes of white, sky and silver, and yellow, khaki, brown and metallic gold that'll guarantee you stand out on the beach. A range of Odabash flip flops are also available, while children get their own range of swimsuits, bikinis and kaftans. The shop's late summer sale is a fantastic way to stock up on high-quality swimwear on the cheap.

Pistol Panties
75 Westbourne Park Road, W2 5QH (7229 5286, www.pistolpanties.com). Westbourne Park tube.
Open noon-6pm Tue-Sat; 1-5pm Sun. **Sells** W.
If the eye-catching window displays don't draw you in, the flattering cuts certainly will. Started up by British/Columbian designer Deborah Fleming, Pistol Panties proved an instant success (her entire first collection was snapped up by Selfridges), attracting a loyal following for its fresh take on swimwear classics.

FASHION

Time Out London's Best Shops **109**

Retro-style designs with polka dots, houndstooth patterns, paint-splashes and frills create some of the most eye-catching, original and flattering designs available, while the perfectly formed can brave the stares in the cool cutaway swimsuits. Bright, oversized beach bags, attractive cover-ups (such as asymmetric dresses), flip flops and beachy jewellery are also on offer, as are candles. Friendly and refreshingly honest staff will steer you in the direction of the perfect beachwear for you.

Erotica & fetishwear

Forget the stiff upper lip and British prudery; if it's latex, bondage and fetish gear you're after, London is the place to unleash your wildest fantasies. Visit the monthly **London Fetish Fair** (www.londonfetishfair.co.uk) for the last word in fetish fashion, or celebrate your sexual freedom at the **London Alternative Market** (www.londonalternativemarket.com). Fetish fashionistas never miss the annual **Erotica** (www.eroticauk.com), an exhibition that attracts around 80,000 visitors; and the high-end lingerie brand **Agent Provocateur** (see p107) also has a continually expanding range of accessories (crystal whips, nipple tassels, metal cuffs) for sale in store and online.

Breathless
131 King's Cross Road, WC1X 9BJ (7278 1666, www.breathless.uk.com). King's Cross tube/rail.
Open 11am-7pm Mon-Sat.
Owner and designer Dolenta and her team continue to expand the house label and explore beyond fetishwear essentials. The ranges lie somewhere between glam street and vintage-inspired couture – and there's plenty to choose from with around ten new designs emerging each year and a made-to-measure service. Women's lines nod to London's obsession with burlesque shapes (black and lilac mini-dresses with contrasting flared red petticoats and bow belts, and black and white striped Cruella DeVil-esque tailored jackets that look divine with the Vogue range of latex miniature top hats). Classics include the 1930s-style baby doll dresses with latex rose detail and the bestselling straight and flared-leg catsuits in a cornucopia of colours. For men, the white latex zoot suit and floor-length 'Hellraiser' skirt remain the most striking outfits. It also stocks leather products from Flap.

Coco de Mer HOT 50
23 Monmouth Street, WC2H 9DD (7836 8882, www.coco-de-mer.co.uk). Covent Garden tube.
Open 11am-7pm Mon-Wed, Fri, Sat; 11am-8pm Thur; noon-6pm Sun.
This erotic emporium is London's most glamorous introduction to kink. The boudoir aesthetic creates an

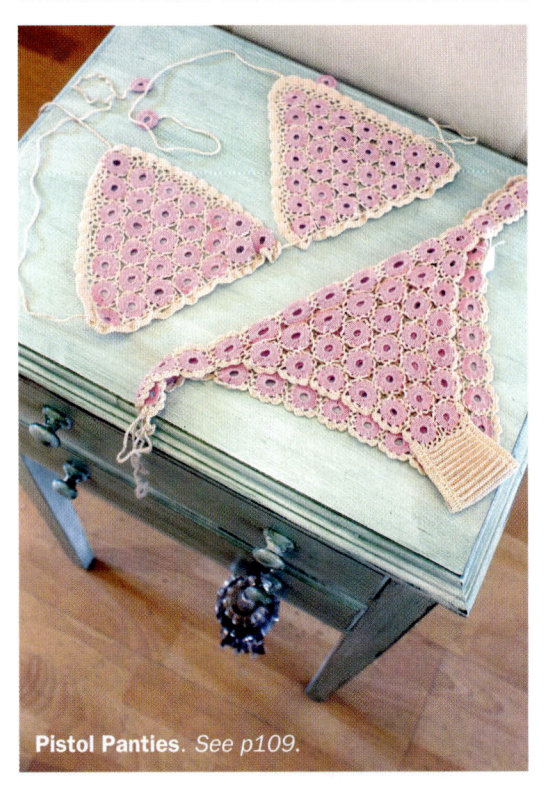

Pistol Panties. See p109.

Lingerie, Swimwear & Erotica

Shop talk
Astrid Blake, owner of Alice & Astrid

fans of the Alice & Astrid style and live in the neighbourhood. And, very excitingly, further afield, Nicolette Sheridan was spotted wearing Alice & Astrid's classic Babydoll nightie in *Desperate Housewives*!

'We sell to people who are looking for luxurious loungewear but also those looking for cosy cotton winter pyjamas.'

Have you noticed any changes in the London shopping scene over the past few years?
'I think that the middle market is the one that seems to have suffered; it's either cheaper mass-produced brands like Primark that people are still buying or expensive hand-crafted quality individual products that are in demand. We are lucky enough to sell individual products to individuals.'

Has it become harder to be an independent shop?
'Yes and no. By being small you can keep your overheads down and move swiftly and adapt to shifting circumstances.
'I think if you're individual and you are well positioned and in a niche market then you're home and dry.'

What's the most enjoyable aspect of owning a shop?
'It gives us the opportunity to showcase the collections in an environment that we have designed – that reflects the feel at the heart of Alice & Astrid, as a kind of mixture of Nordic influence and a touch of nostalgic British.
'And I love the area of London we are in. I am finding it hard to work in the shop at the moment, though, as I have just had a little boy, called Konrad.'

Tell us about the shop
'We sell luxury lingerie, loungewear and nightwear designed by me. We opened in 2004 when I was looking for an office and ended up with a shop! My sisters in law have a shop on Portobello Road and I was encouraged by them to open in the area.'

Who shops here?
'We sell to mainly locals. The stylist Martha Ward and the fashion writer Plum Sykes are

What are your favourite shops in London?
'Melt (59 Ledbury Road, W11 2AA, 7727 5030, www.meltchocolates.com) because I love chocolate; Gray's Antiques Market (*see p100*) for vintage clothes and jewellery, and Scarlet & Violet (*see p186*) for flowers. And of course [vintage and classic clothing specialist] Jessie Western on Portobello Road (no.82B, W11 2QD, 7229 2544, www.jessiewestern.com).'

▶ For **Alice & Astrid**, *see p107.*

Coco de Mer. *See p110.*

unmistakable vibe of refined naughtiness, and trying items on is a particular highlight, what with the peepshow-style velvet changing rooms that allow your lover to watch you undress from a 'confession box' next door. Stock has an ethical, artisan-led twist; you can be sure your dildo is made from WWF-endorsed wood (owner Sam Roddick clearly inherited her mother Anita's green credentials). The jewelled nipple clips, jade cock rings and rose-decorated ceramic butt plugs and dildos are among the list of intriguing pieces. There's a deliciously large lingerie selection including Mimi Holiday, Lascivious, Aloe, Bordelle and Coco de Mer's own range as well as an array of leather masks, locking gauntlets and corseted belts by Paul Seville and Ilya Fleet. The female-oriented book range now includes an exclusive rare vintage selection, where you can find 1920s pornography and fiction originals, like *Lolita*.
Branch 108 Draycott Avenue, SW3 3AE (7584 7615).

Expectations
75 Great Eastern Street, EC2A 3RY (7739 0292, www.expectations.co.uk). Old Street tube/rail. **Open** 11am-7pm Mon-Fri; 11am-8pm Sat; noon-5pm Sun.
This leather, rubber and fetish store has an industrial, boiler-house setting that evokes a club-like vibe. Pass the cage at the bottom of the stairs, where you may find 'players' locked up during late-night shopping sessions, and you'll find plenty to wear to the ball. Premium jock straps, vivid rubber wrestling suits and cycling shorts, kilts and army surplus togs (such as combat pants) all make a statement, as do the sleek black rubber Adonis pouches and the rubber jeans and streetwear from Nasty Pig. For private play, there are over 100 electro-stimulation accessories, ranging from butt plugs to cock rings, in stainless steel and conductive plastic, and masked men can choose from a multiplicity of hoods in breath control, executioner or Hannibal styles, to name just a few. Other hardware includes restraints, collars, slings, harnesses, hogties, a quality metalwork series from Fuck Pig Dungeons, and the new in-house range of stimulation aromas and herbal sex aids.

Fettered Pleasures
90 Holloway Road, N7 8JG (7619 9333, www.fettered pleasures.com). Holloway Road tube or Highbury & Islington tube/rail. **Open** 11am-7pm Mon-Sat.
There are few kinks that this friendly fetish monolith doesn't cater for, but for bondage enthusiasts it's deviant paradise: chain and rope by the metre; whips, canes, floggers and paddles; and a vast playground of high-quality restraints and contraptions to ensure your dungeon is the best equipped in town. The impressive menswear collection incorporates a large selection of 'playing sportswear', surplus army gear, including East German tank and flight suits, camouflage trousers as well as a variety of respiratory masks. Womenswear flails in comparison but there is a good number of latex uniforms and some decent corsets. The vast shop is still rich in niche lines, with a large display of electrics, dildos, horse-hair butt plugs, worship pants, puppy masks, hoods in over 80 styles, mitts and cages – and staff will try their utmost to source specific items. Although they share the same address, FP is not connected to the House of Harlot company (*see below*).

Honour
86 Lower Marsh, SE1 7AB (7401 8219, www.honour.co.uk). Waterloo tube/rail. **Open** 10.30am-7pm Mon-Fri; 11.30am-5pm Sat.
Honour's wide-ranging stock has something to suit all budgets. The ground level is home to a wealth of PVC and latex fashion, from tops, skirts and catsuits to classic uniforms such as nuns and maids to the 'high school honey' and 'flirty wench' look. Much of this is available up to size 26 and there's also a range of plus-size PVC and rubber. The latex menswear line includes a metallic red and blue fireman's costume and new olive-green military suit. Fetish magazine *Skin Two*'s sartorial offshoot, the popular, good-value rubber and PVC clothing range, is also available in store – fantastic for mistresses in the making. High, high heels, other shoes and boots are stocked up to size 11, and to complete the look you'll also find lingerie, wigs, eyelashes and long gloves. Hardcore guys and girls should venture upstairs to the 'bondage attic', where there's a no-nonsense display of toys, cuffs and collars, restraints and clamps.

House of Harlot
90 Holloway Road, N7 8JG (7700 1441, www.house ofharlot.com). Holloway Road tube or Highbury & Islington tube/rail. **Open** 10am-6pm Mon-Fri; noon-6pm Sat.
Don't let this tiny boutique deceive you – the displays only represent a fraction of the sartorial wonders that this leading hydra-headed latex monster can produce. Corset queen Miss Katie shows her wares alongside Prong Jewellery and Lacing Lilit. Eye-catching accessories include kinky cobbler Natacha Marro's six-inch thigh-high boots and Prong's latex boa. Other garments range from basic T-shirts and trousers to handmade stockings (£70), rubber corsets to catsuits (starting at £280), and rubberised uniforms – with themes like military muscle or kinky air hostess. Torture Garden's range is stocked, but the shop's own new lines have a more hardcore and retro-oriented feel, giving seasoned fetishists the extreme clothing they crave. Prices may be commensurate with workmanship involved, but service is friendly and professional. Clothing can be cut to measure at no extra cost, or created from scratch in around three to four weeks.

Liberation
49 Shelton Street, WC2H 9HE (7836 5894, www.libidex.com). Covent Garden tube.
Open 11am-7pm Mon-Sat; also by appointment.

Liberation. See p113.

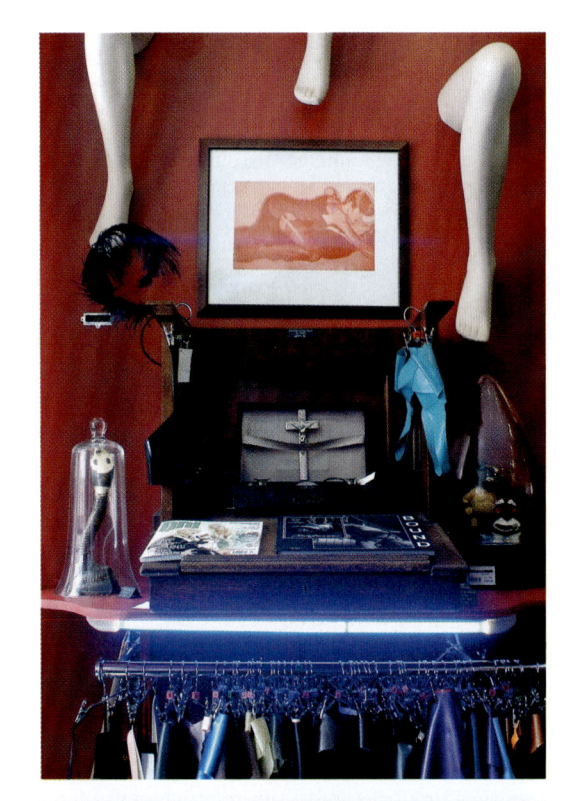

The flagship store for latex couturiers Libidex has considerably extended its range of glossy clothing delights, but you can still find intriguing accessories, all in Little Shop of Horrors-like surrounds. Pick up a hand-carved wooden cane (£35-£75), antique ivory dildos (£650) or a World War I operating table with original straps (and blood stains!). Downstairs you'll find clothing, accessories and hardware lines from Radical Rubber, Bondinage, hot new designer Bordello, Scarlet Diva, Prong, Beautiful & Damned and a range covering classic fetish staples and 1940s Hollywood glamour puss and army-inspired couture. For men, ponytailed Leigh Bowery-esque hoods, extreme catsuits and shirts with vintage pin-up and intricate Japanese bondage designs feature, plus the usual collars, cuffs and neck corsets.

Sh!

57 Hoxton Square, N1 6PD (7613 5458, www.sh-womenstore.com). Old Street tube/rail. **Open** noon-8pm daily.

You don't have to be a woman to pass through the hallowed pink portals of London's only female-oriented sex shop, but you'll need to be chaperoned by one. The capital's best sex shop for toys, Sh!'s strongest feature is its friendly staff who give honest advice. Books, gifts and new kinky artworks are displayed alongside strap-on harnesses and a penis-shaped sex toy demo desk that includes own-range clitoral pumps, dildos and vibrators in numerous materials, styles and prices (our fave is the iPod-activated vibrator, £50, that pulsates in time to your tunes). The Sh! Lil' Softee vibrator is a bargain at £7. Even the fetish and lingerie lines downstairs in the basement have the feminine touch: handcuffs are suede-lined, collars are fit for a princess and bondage tape, crops and whips (some vibrating!) are candy-coloured.

Showgirls

64 Holloway Road, N7 8JL (7697 9072, www.showgirls latexboutique.com). Holloway Road tube or Highbury & Islington tube/rail. **Open** 10.30am-7pm Mon-Sat.

Holloway Road is fertile ground for fetish fiends, with Fettered Pleasures and House of Harlot (for both, *see p113*) close by, and this small but stylish boutique is going from strength to strength with a supreme selection of latex fashion from Jane Doe, Inner Sanctum and more. Stock ranges from the briefest of briefs to slinky dresses, in striking colourways (like red and gold or blue and silver) as well as in classic black. The shop's true selling point is as London's only retail outlet for latex couturier, *Vogue* favourite and fetish award-winner Atsuko Kudo, whose glamorous 'Hitchcock heroine' take on latex means a range boasting stylish lace-print jacket-and-pencil skirt ensembles and accessories like her signature veiled pillbox hat, driving gloves and latex blinkers. A new, select menswear line in the basement offers alternatives to staple rubber shorts and kilts, from top hats and ties to braces, and there's an ample sale rail.

Weddings

London has some of the best and most original bridal shops in the UK. These stores tend to operate on an appointment-only basis and booking ahead is essential. Also bear in mind that it can take up to a year to order a dress. Go along with a positive attitude, a strong idea of your budget and what you want, and an honest friend. Ask about fittings, alterations and extras to avoid any nasty financial surprises later on.

Vintage shops are an excellent starting point for brides and grooms; **Annie's Vintage Clothes** (see p98) has some great gowns and accessories for brides-to-be.

One-stop wedding shop **Confetti** (0870 774 7177, www.confetti.co.uk) is good for wedding planning, affordable stationery, table decorations and even details of bridal fashion trends.

Many footwear designers, including **Beatrix Ong**, **Emma Hope**, and **Jimmy Choo**, have bridal collections and/or services; for these and others, see pp119-127.

Dresses

Jenny Packham
75 Elizabeth Street, SW1W 9PJ (7730 2264, www.jennypackham.com). Sloane Square tube or Victoria tube/rail. **Open** *by appointment 10.30am-5.30pm Tue-Sat.*
With a string of design accolades to her name and a devoted celebrity following, Packham's brand of contemporary bridal glamour is in high demand. Appointments start with a lengthy discussion to determine exactly what the bride is looking for, and staff are experts in advising on styles to flatter. The look is glamorous and Packham cites artist Anthony Burrill and musicians Acid Washed as inspirations for her latest collection. Collaboration with footwear designer Emmy (*see Morgan-Davies p116*) produced a range of crystal-adorned 1920s heels. Just along the road (No.34) you'll find the 'Accessories Boudoir with lingerie, handbags, headdresses (including Swarovski tiaras by Polly Edwards) and handbags to complete the look.
Branch 3A Carlos Place, Mount Street, W1K 3AN (7493 6295).

Luella's Boudoir
33 Church Road, SW19 5DQ (8879 7744, www.luellasboudoir.co.uk). Wimbledon tube/rail. **Open** 11am-6pm Tue, Wed; noon-6pm, 6-8pm (by appointment) Thur; 11am-6pm Fri; 10am-6pm, Sat; noon-4pm Sun.

Temperley London Bridal Room. *See p116*.

TEN Shops for wedding planners

For wedding lists
Looking for an alternative to **John Lewis** (see p23)? **Ganesha** (see p133) has an eco-friendly wedding list service that's worth checking out.

For rings
Many jewellers (see pp131-136) take commissions for wedding rings; try **Cox & Power** or **ec one** (for both, see p133).

For floral bouquets
Take a course with **Bloomsbury Flowers**... or leave it to the experts: see p185-186 **Flowers**.

For traditional accessories
How about a summery parasol from **James Smith** (p128) or a top hat from **Bates the Hatter** (p131)?

For vintage
To create an entire retro look, from hair and make-up to gowns and accessories get along to the annual **London Vintage Wedding Fair** (see p103).

For a bespoke suit
Head to **Savile Row** (see p96) for the ultimate tailored wedding suit.

For make-up
Artists at **Becca** (see p141) and **Cosmetics à la Carte** (see p142) offer blushing brides-to-be lessons in make-up application.

For the party
Party Party (see p222) has everything from tableware to books on flower arranging.

For the cake
Fancy a wedding cake made from cheese? If so, then head to **Paxton & Whitfield** (see p246). For classic options, see p243 **Bakeries & pâtisseries**.

For lingerie
Agent Provocateur has a gorgeous bridal range, with lace, tulle and silk much in evidence; for more innocent, but still sexy and luxurious bridal undies, try **Alice & Astrid** (for both, see p107).

A one-stop shop for every bride and bridesmaid (as well as mums, boys and guests), Luella's Boudoir features a handpicked selection of the very best accessories, lingerie, shoe and jewellery designers. Labels are constantly updated and include Yarwood-White, Freya Rose, Magpie Vintage, Emmy, Jane Taylor Millinery and Sophie Benoit. The staff's wedding expertise is second to none and the shop offers a made-to-order bridesmaid collection with a choice of over 200 colours and the option of bespoke. In collaboration with Cosmopolitan Bride, a wedding fair will offer guests the chance to meet a host of exhibitors (planners, make-up artists, stationers and so forth) all under one roof.

Morgan-Davies
62 Cross Street, N1 2BA (7354 3414, www.morgandavieslondon.co.uk). Angel tube or Highbury & Islington tube/rail. **Open** by appointment 9.30am-6pm Mon-Sat.
The boudoir-like interior of this Islington boutique is flanked with stunning gowns, all of them classic with a contemporary twist. British and European designers stocked include Augusta Jones, Jesus Peiro, Lusan Mandongus, Alan Hannah, Stephanie Allin and Beverly Lister. Shop manager Annalize has the remarkable ability to pick the perfect dress for your physique; keep your mind open, it's often not the one you expect. After initial fittings, you're looked after in the atelier over the road on Upper Street where the seamstresses ensure you're fitted to absolute perfection. The shop also holds a range of accessories including hairbands, brooches and earrings to complement your outfit. Custom shoe brand Emmy (65 Cross Street, N1 2BB, 7704 0012, www.emmyshoes.co.uk) is just across the street.

Temperley London Bridal Room
6-10 Colville Mews, Lonsdale Road, W11 2DA (7229 7957, www.temperleylondon.com). Notting Hill Gate tube. **Open** by appointment 10am-6pm Mon-Wed, Fri; 10am-7.30pm Thur; 11am-6pm Sat.
Tucked away in a quiet Notting Hill mews, Alice Temperley's bridal room delivers superb service and an unparalleled attention to detail – offering champagne at appointments and even retailoring the dress to cocktail length after the big day to ensure you get as much wear and value for money as possible. As well as the extensive showroom of ready-to-wear creations in the label's signature romantic and ethereal style (silk georgette, handsewn pearls and sequins, embroidery), Temperley offers a fully bespoke service, giving a lucky few the opportunity to work with Alice herself to design a dream gown (from £10,000). For listings information for the flagship Temperley boutique, *see p92*.

Maternity & Unusual Sizes

Several high street chains offer trend-led maternity lines, including **Topshop** and **H&M**; **American Apparel** is a good choice for the style-conscious, thanks to an abundance of stretchy, high-quality cotton items. Many of the shops listed below also sell baby clothes and gifts.

Maternity

Blossom Mother & Child
164 Walton Street, SW3 2JL (0845 262 7500 www.blossommotherandchild.com). South Kensington tube. **Open** 10am-6pm Mon-Sat; noon-5pm Sun.
This softly scented maternity wear specialist is a calming and reassuring place for hot and bothered mothers-to-be. As well as advice on everything from nursing bra sizes to local maternity wards, you can arrange a private evening appointment. The collection ranges from more affordable own-label day- (denim, workwear), eveningwear and sexy swimwear through to their popular customised jeans, and high end designs by the likes of Sonia Rykiel and Temperley. The lingerie collection is extensive and there are plenty of things for baby too, as well as luxury toiletries, lotions and potions. A concession can also be found in Harrods (*see p22*).
Branch 69 Marylebone High Street, W1U 5JJ (7486 6089).

Elias & Grace
158 Regent's Park Road, NW1 8XN (7449 0574, www.eliasandgrace.com). Chalk Farm tube. **Open** 10am-6pm Mon-Sat; noon-6pm Sun.
The Primrose Hill fashion set needn't compromise on style with this haven of Vivienne Westwood, Stella McCartney and Luella designs at their fingertips. E&G is ideal for special-occasion clothes but not everything is maternity and so may not take the extra weight on breasts, arms, back and thighs into consideration. But with its adorable baby clothes upstairs (Petit Bateau, Quincy, Bonton) and racks of beautiful pregnancy clothes downstairs (Matthew Williamson dresses; James maternity jeans), this is the first stop for the mum-to-be with cash to flash. The shop also stocks a fantastic array of health and beauty products.

JoJo Maman Bébé
68 Northcote Road, SW11 6QL (7228 0322, www.jojomamanbebe.co.uk). Clapham Junction rail. **Open** 9.30am-5.30pm Mon-Sat; 11am-5pm Sun.

JoJo Maman Bébé. *See p118.*

Affordable and practical, with occasional flashes of French chic, JoJo is one of the most user-friendly maternity ranges around. Bestsellers include maternity jeans (possibly the cheapest to be found), easy-to-wear wrap dresses, kaftans and capsule officewear (linen shirts, trousers, dresses et al). There's loads of choice, plenty of style and it's all amazingly inexpensive – important when you're buying clothes that might not get much wear. Even so, only a selection of its huge stock is in-store – visit the website for further lines, including swimwear, nightwear, knitwear and jackets. It's also a good source of clothes for babies and children, gifts and nursery items.
Branches throughout the city.

9 London by Emily Evans
8 Hollywood Road, SW10 9HY (7352 7600, www.emilyevansboutique.com). Earl's Court tube.
Open 10am-6pm Mon-Sat.
This swanky maternity shop has a decidedly starry following – Kate Moss, Gwen Stefani and Laura Bailey are among the names choosing glamorous designs during their nine months – thanks to the names found here: True Religion, Minna, Faire Dodo and Fierce Mamas for Moody Mamas. There are stylish maternity jeans, cute cashmeres and elegant knitwear, and its own-label collection – 9 London – offers amazingly flattering and stylish evening and day dresses. There's also a range of lingerie and nightwear, lotions and potions and an unmissable children's collection – Tiny9 – for newborns through to nine-year-olds. There's also a concession on the 4th floor of Harrods.

Unusual sizes
On the high street, **New Look** has a line called Inspire, which comes in sizes 16-28, while **Topshop**, **Dorothy Perkins**, and **Next** all cater for both small and tall girls; **Principles**, **Austin Reed**, **Debenhams**, **Wallis** and **Miss Selfridge** all have a Petite range for women under 5ft 3in (in sizes 6-16). Stylish Marylebone High Street shop **Shoon** (94 Marylebone High Street, London, W1U 4RG (7487 3001, www.shoon.com) also stocks several brands that will suit larger female figures, including the luxurious label **Wall**.

High & Mighty
145-147 Edgware Road, W2 2HR (7723 8754, www.highandmighty.co.uk). Marble Arch or Edgware Road tube. **Open** 10am-6pm Mon; 9am-6pm Tue, Wed, Fri, Sat; 9am-7pm Thur; 11am-5pm Sun. **Sells** M.
Since High & Mighty opened its first shop over 50 years ago on Edgware Road, trading as Northern Outsize Menswear, its reasonably priced contemporary and classic styles for men who struggle to fit into conventional high street sizes have gone from strength to strength. Catering to men over 6ft 2in, most trousers go up to 38in leg, and waist sizes up to 60in. Alongside its own labels there's a choice of brands such as Polo Ralph Lauren, Ben Sherman and Umbro. Covering most wardrobe necessities, including made-to-measure suits and wedding hire, there are accessories and shoes as well.
Branches The Plaza, 120 Oxford Street, W1N 9DP (7436 4861); 81-83 Knightsbridge, SW1X 7RB (7752 0665).

Long Tall Sally
21-25 Chiltern Street, W1U 7PH (7487 3370, www.longtallsally.com). Baker Street tube.
Open 9.30am-6pm Mon-Wed, Fri; 9.30am-7pm Thur; 9am-6pm Sat; 11am-5pm Sun. **Sells** W.
Providing sartorial solutions for many a long-legged lass for over 30 years, Long Tall Sally's collections focus on comfortable, conventional and well-cut styles rather than high fashion: labels include Birkenstock, Converse and Dr Martens. Prices are mid range, and there are clothes for every occasion. Tailored for ladies over 5ft 8in, trousers stretch from 34in to 38in, sleeves are longer, waists are cut lower and everything is offered in sizes 10-20. The range covers swimwear, maternity, knitwear, nightwear, accessories and shoes (sizes 7-11). LTS Boutique and Lisa's Collection are a little more elegant (think floaty dresses, sequinned tops and chic waistcoats).

Elias & Grace. *See p117*.

Shoes

Many of the shops listed in the **Indie Boutiques** chapter (*see pp56-76*) stock a select range of stylish shoes, and both **b store** (*see p56*) and **Folk** (*see p59*) have their own lines of directional models for men and women. The **Three Threads** (*see p65*) is also excellent for men's shoes, with one of the biggest range of Pointers in town. **Topshop** (*see p81*), **Selfridges** (*see p27*) and **Liberty** (*see p25*) are also good first ports-of-call with huge ranges.

On the high street, the ubiquitous **Office** (www.office.co.uk) is a good bet for a large selection of on-trend styles for men and women.

If you're in need of unusual sizes, *see p118*; for children's shoes, *see pp262-268*.

General

Beatrix Ong
8 Newburgh Street, W1F 7RJ (7287 2724, www.beatrixong.com). **Open** 10am-7pm Mon-Wed, Fri, Sat; 10am-8pm Thur; noon-6pm Sun. **Sells** W.
With the closure of Beatrix Ong's beautiful Burlington Arcade flagship, this new white 'concept store' on more youthful Newburgh Street is now the only Ong standalone shop in London, though her designs can be found in Liberty (*see p25*) and Harvey Nichols (*see p23*), as well as within Beatrix Ong concessions in Jaeger branches (*see p87*) all over London. Known for her timeless styles that can be worn from season to season, here the ex-Jimmy Choo designer sells limited editions of her elegant footwear alongside the main collection and her range of wedding slippers (arrange for an appointment if you're after customised bridal shoes). Wearable high heels in luxurious materials dominate the collection, for a feminine but strong aesthetic, while the men's range is all loafers and brogues, with the odd deck shoe or desert boot making an appearance. Ong has also recently undertaken exclusive collaborations with Dover Street Market and Nike iD, and has also expanded her accessories range, which includes flashy bags and stylish umbrellas, including one wittily covered in illustrations of cats and dogs.

Black Truffle HOT 50
4 Broadway Market, E8 4QJ (7923 9450, www.blacktruffle.com). Cambridge Heath or London Fields rail. **Open** 11am-6pm Tue-Fri; 10am-6pm Sat; noon-6pm Sun. **Sells** W, C.
Time Out has long sung the praises of Black Truffle, and for good reason. Selling some quirky yet wearable footwear for women and kids, the shop – a lovely space over two levels – has notched up a string of awards. The

SUBSCRIPTION OFFER

Life's too short for quiet nights in…

SUBSCRIBE TO *TIME OUT* AND GET 5 FREE ISSUES!

REASONS TO SUBSCRIBE

- Pay just £2.99 for your first 6 issues – saving you 83%
- Then pay just £39.99 every 26 issues – saving you 49%
- Free, fast delivery to your door
- Save on *Time Out* guides

Time Out. Know More. Do More.

SUBSCRIBE TODAY
CALL **0800 068 0050** (Quoting GD Shops)
VISIT **TIMEOUT.COM/GDSHOPS**

range of shoes is impressive, with brands such as Roby & Pier, Chie Mihara, Baltarini, Melissa, b store, Repetto and Timeless represented. The shop also stocks tasteful bags from the likes of Abro, a small range of clothing (that's especially strong on knitwear) and tasteful accessories (such as Falke tights, Dents gloves, Maniyak hats and affordable jewellery). It may be located on painfully trendy Broadway Market, but the stock here is more safely stylish rather than avant garde, meaning that both designs and materials have longevity. There's also a central London store on Warren Street.
Branch 52 Warren Street, W1T 5NJ (7388 4547).

British Boot Company
5 Kentish Town Road, NW1 8NH (7485 8505, www.britboot.co.uk). Camden Town tube. **Open** 10am-7pm daily. **Sells** M, W, C.
The British Boot Company was the first UK retailer for Dr Martens and became a favourite haunt of bands such as the Sex Pistols, the Buzzcocks and Madness in their late 1970s heyday. As well as the aforementioned DMs, the BBC offers all manner of big-soled, mean-looking, hard-wearing boots and shoes from the likes of Solovair, Gladiators, Grinders, NPS and Tredair. This is also one of the few outlets where you can get your hands on George Cox, the British brand famed for its brothel creepers and winklepickers and newer Robot shoes. The shop even sells vintage versions for true Cox aficionados.

Christian Louboutin
23 Motcomb Street, SW1X 8LB (7245 6510, www.christianlouboutin.fr). Knightsbridge tube. **Open** 10am-6pm Mon-Fri; 11am-6.30pm Sat. **Sells** W.
Celebrity favourite Christian Louboutin has been making truly exquisite footwear since 1992, and his shiny red-lacquered soles on his sought-after stilettos (which often have heels of over four inches) have become something of trademark. He's more recently branched out into making equally covetable bags and creates catwalk shoes for everyone from Rodarte to Richard Nicoll. His London boutique brings a little drop of Paris to the big smoke and stocks key looks from his sleek and sexy collections, including sky-high platforms, Ms Turner-inspired ankle boots, stylish wedges and chic pumps. Prices (from £300) aren't for the faint-hearted, but then, perfection doesn't come cheap. There are plans afoot to stock menswear in this store from winter 2010.
Branch 17 Mount Street, W1K 2RJ (7491 0033).

Emma Hope
53 Sloane Square, SW1W 8AX (7259 9566, www.emmahope.co.uk). Sloane Square tube. **Open** 10am-6.30pm Mon, Tue, Thur-Sat; 10am-7pm Wed; noon-5pm Sun. **Sells** M, W.
Having cut her teeth at Laura Ashley, Emma Hope's own-name designs nod to current trends yet remain every inch a reflection of her own dainty tastes; styles are the more sensible side of feminine, tending towards Kensington classics such as court shoes, ballet pumps and riding boots rather than sexy killer heels (although her snakeskin platforms are a little more in your face). Her unisex Joe sneakers are popular thanks to their natty juxtaposition of unusual uppers such as velvet and embroidered silk with stripes and simple rubber soles. Her straw weave and metallic leather ballet pumps are also bestsellers, while for evening there's a wide selection of slender courts and slingbacks. Men's styles centre around loafers and desert boots. Quality materials and craftsmanship mean steep prices, however, starting around £199 for a pair of sneakers.
Branches 207 Westbourne Grove, W11 2SF (7313 7490); Westfield London, Ariel Way, W12 7GFF (3249 1010).

Georgina Goodman
44 Old Bond Street, W1S 4GB (7493 7673, www.georginagoodman.com). Green Park tube. **Open** 10am-6pm Mon-Wed, Fri, Sat; 10am-7pm Thur. **Sells** W, C.
Georgina Goodman's smart flagship store, which opened in 2008, brings new blood to Old Bond Street. The RCA graduate launched her label back in 2001 crafting made-to-measure footwear from a single piece of untreated leather – and a couture service is still available. Since then, she has gone on to design for everyone from Alexander McQueen to Evans, and began ready-to-wear in 2004. Her personal touch remains thanks to the inscription 'Made in Love' on the sole of every mainline shoe. Goodman is known for using a dramatic mix of textures and colours, with snakeskin, patents and satin often making an appearance, and with inspiration coming from some original sources. Show-stopping killer heels share shelf space with rock-tinged boots and her signature colourful slippers. This level of craftsmanship doesn't come cheap, however, with prices starting at £320 for flats.

Jeffery-West
16 Piccadilly Arcade, SW1Y 6NH (7499 3360, www.jeffery-west.co.uk). Green Park or Piccadilly Circus tube. **Open** 10am-6pm Mon-Wed, Fri, Sat; 10am-7pm Thur. **Sells** M.
With its playboy vampire's apartment feel (red walls, velvet curtains, skulls in the window), this gothic Piccadilly store is the perfect showcase for Marc Jeffery and Guy West's rakish shoes. Still made to exacting traditional standards in Northampton – where both designers grew up – each shoe comes with an interesting twist, such as hand-burnished uppers, diamond broguing or a cleft heel, and are much loved by modern-day dandies about town. Classic shoes include the Punched Gibson in polished burgundy (£220) and the Rochester Center Seam Boot in red and black patent

(£295). Shoe prices start from £210 to around £240, while boots range from around £220 up to £295.
Branch 16 Cullum Street, EC3M 7JJ (7626 4699).

Kate Kanzier
67-69 Leather Lane, EC1N 7TJ (7242 7232, www.katekanzier.com). Chancery Lane tube. **Open** 8.30am-6.30pm Mon-Fri; 11am-4pm Sat. **Sells** W.
Adored for great-value directional footwear, Kate Kanzier is the place to come for brogues (£30), ballerinas (£20), and stylish boots in a huge range of colours. Sexy high-heeled pumps also feature strongly, in patent, suede, leather and animal prints, and with vintage designs dominating. The range is attractively arranged alongside a line of straightforward handbags and clutches in the spacious Holborn shop. The initial amazement at such low prices for such stylish designs is levelled when you inspect the quality a little more closely; however, the shoes are still good value for money – you'll be pushed to find knee-high leather boots as stylish as Kate Kanzier's for under £100 elsewhere – and it's a good bet for a splurge even when the bank balance is low.

Kurt Geiger
198 Regent Street, W1B 5TP (3238 0044, www.kurtgeiger.com). Oxford Circus tube. **Open** 10am-8pm Mon-Fri; 10am-7pm Sat; noon-6pm Sun. **Sells** M, W.
Kurt Geiger has become the uncrowned king of the high street shoe chains in London with its swanky products found in all the classiest department stores (Liberty, Selfridges, Harrods). Its mirror-clad Regent Street flagship store and nearby South Molton Street branch remain the best places to see the full collection, however. Women's shoes covers a wide variety of styles, from the brand's signature, statement-making wedges and platforms to 'utility' urban boots, via a huge number of sexy stilettos, kitten heels, sandles and ballerinas. The men's lines are equally appealing, with a nice selection of Desert-style suede boots, and a wide range of loafers, deck shoes and brogues. A good range of budgets are catered for too, with the Kurt Geiger diffusion lines, KG and Miss KG, catering to those with slightly thinner wallets.
Branches throughout the city.

Laura J
114 Islington High Street, N1 8EG (7226 4005, www.laurajlondon.com). Angel tube. **Open** 11am-6pm Mon-Wed; 11am-6.30pm Thur, Fri; 11am-7pm Sat; noon-5pm Sun. **Sells** W.
This petite boutique, previously called Lollipop London, has more girly charm than you can shake a stick at. Owner Laura Allnatt and her ladies have sourced interesting lines from some of the world's best independent designers. Displays see newer labels such

Georgina Goodman. *See p121.*

as Wilomena, Talie and London-based brand Esska sit alongside more established favourites, such as the Jackson Twins, Velvet Bee and Francesco Morichetti, as well as vintage-style cowboy boot brand Lama Peach. And now taking centre stage in the store is own-brand Laura J designed by Laura Allnatt in store, alongside Cordwainers graduate Rachele Davies, and then constructed in Spain before being shipped back to London. Form an orderly queue for the glamorous heels and fashion-forward boots. A sprinkling of vintage accessories are also for sale from French Kiss Vintage.

Manolo Blahnik

49-51 Old Church Street, SW3 5BS (7352 3863, www.manoloblahnik.com). South Kensington tube or Sloane Square tube then 11, 19, 22 bus. **Open** 10am-5.30pm Mon-Fri; 10.30am-5pm Sat. **Sells** W.

Manolo Blahnik CBE has become one of the most prestigious shoe designers in the world. You have to buzz to gain admittance but once inside the service is impeccable as you rub shoulders with women happy to pay a month's rent for a pair of his timeless shoes. Best known for his killer heels, Blahnik's designs run the gamut from flat slip-ons to boots. The black patent high-heeled Campari model (aka the Mary Jane), immortalised by Carrie Bradshaw in *Sex and the City*, and often seen on the hoofs of Kate Moss, has now been brought back to the collection by popular demand. Blahnik launched his first men's collection in 2008, although this wasn't stocked at this shop when this guide went to press.

Old Curiosity Shop

13-14 Portsmouth Street, WC2A 2ES (7405 9891, www.curiosityuk.com). Holborn tube. **Open** 10am-7pm Mon-Sat. **Sells** M, W.

Built around 1567, this building can justifiably lay claim to being the oldest shop premises in central London – though whether it actually inspired the Charles Dickens novel of the same name is anyone's guess (though Dickens lived in nearby Bloomsbury and was known to have visited the shop). It's a joy to visit, anyhow, with small winding staircases and low wooden ceiling beams. These days, Japanese designer Daita Kimura creates unique handmade shoes in the basement workshop – his avant-garde (and sometimes eccentric) styles for men and women start at around £200; the jazz shoe styles, such as the Paris model, are particularly covetable, while the Hog Toe styles are particularly emblematic of his work. Margo Salby designs are also sold here. Duck as you go in to avoid bumping your head.

Oliver Sweeney

5 Conduit Street, W1S 2XD (7491 9126, www.oliversweeney.com). Oxford Circus tube. **Open** 10am-7pm Mon-Wed, Fri, Sat; 10am-8pm Thur; noon-6pm Sun. **Sells** M.

Tracey Neuls. *See p126.*

Oliver Sweeney makes beautiful men's shoes from his gallery-like new store on Conduit Street. In past collections, he's given classic styles such as the brogue, Chelsea boot and loafer fresh twists including metal stud detailing, a toe-shape inspired by the clean lines of a Ford Mustang and new colourways including petrol blue and wine. The brand has recently been on a drive to keep up with contemporary styles, launch the more trend-led London Collection and the Goodyear Welted line; both collections still adhere to Sweeney's high level of craftsmanship, with top-quality materials. Prices typically range from £140 to £285. As well as the City branch, there's also an Oliver Sweeney concession within Harvey Nichols (see p23).
Branches 133 Middlesex Street, E1 7JF (7626 4466).

Poste Mistress
61-63 Monmouth Street, WC2H 9EP (7379 4040, www.office.co.uk/postemistress). Covent Garden tube. **Open** 10am-7pm Mon-Wed, Fri, Sat; 10am-8pm Thur; 11.30am-6pm Sun. **Sells** W.
Started by the Office Shoes chain as the more high-profile sister to its popular high street shops, Poste Mistress offers reasonably priced quality footwear in a decadent, retro boudoir setting. It's a sure bet if you're after a pair of on-trend shoes that will last you more than one season. As well as its own-brand range, the selection here – arranged attractively on shelves – includes designer favourites b store, Dries Van Noten, Chie Mihara, Eley Kishimoto, Stella McCartney, Hudson, Acne, Opening Ceremony, Miu Miu, Jil Sander and Vivienne Westwood, and there's also a good range of more casual footwear from the likes of Converse and Melissa. The latest label to be stocked is Laura J (see p122). The shop also stocks a small range of stylish accessories.

Terra Plana
64 Neal Street, WC2H 9PQ (7379 5959, www.terraplana.com). Covent Garden tube. **Open** 10am-7pm Mon-Sat; noon-6pm Sun. **Sells** M, W.
Winner of a number of ethical footwear awards over the past few years, Terra Plana has set its sights on original, fashionable yet ecologically sound shoes made from unusual materials, and includes several models that are completely free from animal products and materials. The collections are constructed using traditional artisan methods and includes ankle boots, cowboy boots and mid-heeled shoes made from recycled Saami quilts. The comfortable Work Again Escape shoes are made from 99% recycled materials. And trendy bohemians will go especially mad for the Vivo Barefoot range with their ultra-thin, puncture-resistant soles that mimic a barefoot stroll; recent models from this range include the Evo running shoe and Aquas designs.
Branches 124 Bermondsey Street, SE1 3TX (7407 3758); 32 Brushfield Street, E1 6AT (7426 2158); 155 Kensington High Street, W8 6SU (7937 9405).

FIVE
Trainer flagships

Adidas Originals
6 Newburgh Street, W1F 7RQ (7734 9976, www.adidas.com). Oxford Circus tube. **Open** 10.30am-6.30pm Mon-Sat; 1-5pm Sun.
Retro fiends should make a beeline for this gallery-like space, where many of the sneakers are limited-editions of classic models. There's also a branch on Covent Garden's Earlham Street.

Onitsuka Tiger
15 Newburgh Street, W1F 7RX (7734 5157, www.onitsukatiger.co.uk). Oxford Circus tube. **Open** 11am-7pm Mon-Sat; 1-6pm Sun.
The company behind the Asics brand has gone back to its roots at this store, which specialises in the original Tiger designs that the Japanese manufacturer first made its name with in the 1960s.

Puma
51-55 Carnaby Street, W1F 9QE (7439 0221, www.puma.com). Oxford Circus tube. **Open** 10am-7pm Mon-Sat.
The London flagship of the self-named 'sportlifestyle' brand has the full range of the classic German sneakers.

Rbk
51 Neal Street, WC2H 9PQ (7240 8689, www.reebok.com). Covent Garden tube. **Open** 10am-7pm Mon-Sat; noon-6pm Sun.
Another global brand flagship that stocks the broadest range of Reebok trainers available in the capital; if you like garish colours, you'll be in heaven.

Vans
47 Carnaby Street, W1F 9PT (7287 9235, www.vans.eu). Oxford Circus tube. **Open** 10am-7pm Mon-Wed, Fri, Sat; 10am-8pm Thur; noon-6pm Sun.
The original skate trainers are still going strong and there's no better place to get them than the brand's flagship store.

Tracey Neuls HOT 50
29 Marylebone Lane, W1U 2NQ (7935 0039, www.tn29.com). Bond Street tube. **Open** 11am-6.30pm Mon-Fri; noon-5pm Sat, Sun. **Sells** W.
Footwear hangs from the ceiling on chains, nestles on top of wooden stools and sits in fireplaces in Tracey Neuls' intimate and stylish studio shop on Marylebone Lane. The Cordwainers-trained Canadian is known for challenging the footwear norm with her unconventional yet comfortable designs and uses her equally conceptual shop to show off her wares. The eponymous mainline (from £300) concentrates on her timeless yet trendy shapes in gorgeous tones and textiles, with her signature solid leather heels polished, slicked and even burnt. Her TN-29 brand (around £220) combines old and new so that vegetable tanned leathers are paired with perspex, felt and hand-painted details. September 2008 saw Neuls introduce a third label called Homage, which offers her classic shapes with new rubber soles at a more affordable price (from £170). Not one to let the grass grow, Neul's latest collaboration was struck with furniture company Moroso for Clerkenwell Design Week in 2010, with Neul's rendering her designs in fabrics created by Tord Boontje and Patricia Urquiola.

Bespoke

John Lobb
9 St James's Street, SW1A 1EF (7930 3664, www.johnlobbltd.co.uk). Green Park tube. **Open** 9am-5.30pm Mon-Fri; 9am-4.30pm Sat. **Sells** M, W.
In the shadow of the St James's Palace gate tower, this is a fitting site for one of the finest bespoke shoemakers in the world. The original John Lobb made his name as a cobbler during the reign of Queen Victoria, when he shod the feet of the Prince of Wales, later King Edward VII. Today, the company currently holds two royal warrants and has a fabulous range of classic shoes, boots, slippers and wellies. A pair of made-to-measure leather shoes will cost over £2,000, but this might be considered money well spent if you consider the craftsmanship involved and that the product is likely to last a lifetime. What's more, some of the traditional loafer styles commonly asked for here have come around again, and are now positively trendy.

Trainers
Skate shop **Slam City Skates** (*see p238*) is good for limited-edition Nike SB's and Vans.

1948

Arches 477-478 Bateman's Row, EC2A 3HH (7729 7688, www.nike.com). Shoreditch High Street rail. **Open** 11.30am-6pm Thur, Fri; 10.30am-6.30pm Sat; 11.30am-5pm Sun. **Sells** M, W.

With Oxford Circus's Nike Town catering for the masses, it seems Nike's army of more refined sneaker freaks were feeling a little overlooked. The trainer brand's clubhouse for their most loyal (and obsessive) fans, 1948, is hidden under the railway arches on Bateman Row, a sidestreet connecting Great Eastern Street to Curtain Road. Its black-brick interior is complete with squishy sports-ready flooring made from recycled trainers, white neon football-pitch ceiling sculpture and plasma screens (which customers are often glued to when a big match is on). Another sizeable arch acts as a room for parties and Nike events, and a decked garden makes the most of the odd flash of sun. Originally a pop-up shop stocking Nike's NSW collection, 1948 opened its doors in February 2009 and its steady stream of customers has ensured the store stays open indefinitely.

Kazmattazz

39 Hoxton Square, N1 6NN (7739 4133, www.kazmattazz.com). Old Street tube/rail. **Open** 10.30am-6.30pm Mon-Thur; 10.30am-8pm Fri, Sat; 11am-4pm Sun.

An essential stop for both hardened trainer fanatics and anyone looking for rare pumps. Past treats found among the piles of boxes have included pairs of brown-and-white as well as purple-and-grey Adidas Flavours of the World as well as kicks from Greedy Genius, and new stuff comes in every week, sourced from all over the world. It also stocks more standard Nike (Dunks, Blazers, Air Max), Puma, Converse, Adidas (Stan Smith, Superstars) and Vans models, as well as Timberland boots. The shop is open until 8pm on Fridays and Saturdays, making the place a handy stop-off if you happen to be on your way to the bars and restaurants of Hoxton Square and around.

The Other Side of the Pillow

61 Wilton Way, E8 1BG (07988 870508). Hackney Central rail. **Open** 11am-6pm Thur-Sun. **No credit cards**.

At first the name may seem strange, but not if you're into original Vans skate shoes and trainers, vintage sportswear and NOS (new old stock) designer sunglasses. Then you'll know why this shop, situated on whisper-quiet Wilton Way to the north of London Fields in Hackney, is mining a rich seam of cool. The Vans range from £25 to £150 (for rare and one-off needlepoint designs from the late 1960s), with a whole (retro) fridge full of Vans with exclusive Disney motifs and designs at around £70 a pair. Owners Henry Davies and Maurizio Di Nino have a passion for all kinds of collectables from the 1960s to the mid '90s: cameras, line-dancing shoes, tea sets, '70s NOS Italian socks, or even a first-edition copy of Larry Clark's book *Teenage Lust*.

Size?

37A Neal Street, WC2H 9PR (7836 1404, www.size.co.uk). Covent Garden tube. **Open** 10am-7.30pm Mon-Wed, Fri, Sat; 10am-8pm Thur; noon-6pm Sun.

This hot-spot for London trainer fiends is unbeatable simply for its sheer variety of sneaker brands and colour combinations, thus making the too-cool-to-smile staff a necessary evil for punters looking for something a bit different. Old-school styles abound – there's no better place to pick up all-time classics like Puma Clydes, Adidas Gazelles and Nike Super Blazers. There are countless alternatives to the industry giants, like the more subdued Pointer and Tretorn kicks, an array of British New Balance trainers, plus Asics, skate shoes from Vans, Lakai and DVS. The small ground-level space is devoted to the Converse range, as well as new releases; head to the surprisingly expansive basement for the rest.

Branches 33-34 Carnaby Street, W1V 1PA (7287 4016); 200 Portobello Road, W11 1LB (7792 8494).

Jewellery & Accessories

Shops such as **Paul Smith** (*see p89*), **Beyond the Valley** (*see p37*), **Paul & Joe** (*see p92*), **Diverse** (*see p56*), **Sefton** (*see p65*) and **Goodhood** (*see p59*) have glass cabinets displaying some lovely, affordable pieces by an eclectic range of designers.

The shoe boutique **Black Truffle** (*see p119*) also has an excellent selection of bags, purses, tights, jewellery, hats and more. The bag collection at **Kate Kanzier** (*see p122*) is also extensive, stylish and affordable.

Bags & accessories

Ally Capellino   HOT 50
9 Calvert Avenue, E2 7JP (7613 3073, www.allycapellino.co.uk). Liverpool Street tube/rail or Shoreditch High Street rail. **Open** noon-6pm Tue-Fri; 11am-6pm Sat; 11am-5pm Sun.

There's something quietly satisfying and delightfully unshowy about British designer Ally Capellino's bags, belts, wallets and purses. Her signature pieces include understated, unisex satchels made from waxed cotton or canvas, with leather buckles: a classic 'Jeremy' will set you back under £200. Other offerings run from crisp canvas beach bags with rope handles to more structured yet simple handbags, with brass frames and buffalo leather detailing. To celebrate over 30 years of collaboration with Liberty (*see p25*), Capellino has reworked two of its classics: the 'Frank' rucksack (soft blue leather with tan straps) and 'Sadie' soft brown leather shoulder bag, forming part of an installation in Liberty's stairwell.

Comfort Station
22 Cheshire Street, E2 6EH (7033 9099, www.comfortstation.co.uk). Liverpool Street tube/rail or Shoreditch High Street rail. **Open** 11am-6pm Tue-Sun.

Fine art graduate and designer Amy Anderson is the creative talent behind this ladylike Cheshire Street boutique. Offbeat touches, such as birds painted on the door and a piano-turned-display cabinet, provide the ideal environment to showcase her handmade accessories. Alongside the beautiful, ethically made bags and bone-china crockery covered in wonderfully weird collaged prints is her jewellery line. The collection changes each season, with classically elegant but original designs in gold, silver, cord, wood and onyx: a globe pendant made up of concentric rings that rotate to form a sphere, perhaps, or a silver chain from which a tiny, gold-plated, working hourglass is suspended.

James Smith & Sons
53 New Oxford Street, WC1A 1BL (7836 4731, www.james-smith.co.uk). Holborn or Tottenham Court Road tube. **Open** 9.30am-5.15pm Mon-Fri; 10am-5.15pm Sat.

James Smith & Sons is one of the most visually striking of London's traditional shops. In the niche market of superior quality umbrellas, the store is unrivalled thanks to its lovingly crafted products, all built to last. This charming shop opened in 1830 and its original Victorian fittings are still intact. To say that it sticks out like a sore thumb would be an understatement, but it's impossible to imagine New Oxford Street without it. Alongside the expected traditional brollies (such as a classic City umbrella with a hickory crook), there are high-tech folding models and sun parasols – including a dainty beechwood-handled number that's designed for weddings. Walking sticks and canes are the shop's other speciality, each one cut to the correct length for the customer. Furthermore, if you buy an umbrella here and the elements do get the better of it, James Smith has a repairs service to put it right again. The shop's staff are clearly proud to be carrying on a brand with such a long history.

J&M Davidson
97 Golborne Road, W10 5NL (7313 9532, www.jandmdavidson.com). Notting Hill Gate tube. **Open** 10am-6pm Mon-Sat.

Anglo-French couple John and Monique Davidson's bags and leather accessories are made in their own Bolton factory, and the brand's slightly retro aesthetic has stood them in good stead for over 20 years. In the heart of Westbourne Park, the company faces some stiff competition from the neighbouring fashion boutiques, but holds its own thanks to traditional craftsmanship – high-quality leather, hand-stitching – combined with constantly evolving design. The brand steers clear of fly-by-night trends, however, so that the bags won't date – and helping to justify the prices. Small leather goods include belts, purses and wallets as well as a small range of classically stylish knitwear.

Lulu Guinness
3 Ellis Street, SW1X 9AL (7823 4828, www.luluguinness.com). Sloane Square tube. **Open** 10am-6pm Mon-Fri; 11am-6pm Sat.

Lulu Guinness's much-imitated signature style oozes femininity, matched with an irrepressibly playful streak. There's no mistaking her more extravagant handbag designs: bold, lip-shaped perspex or snakeskin clutches, say, or 'rose basket' bags, overflowing with pink satin appliqué blooms. Cheaper pieces are equally distinctive, running from retro-print laminated canvas vanity cases and make-up bags to gorgeously girly umbrellas (especially covetable),

Jewellery & Accessories

Ally Capellino

FASHION

dh
DINNY HALL
AT WESTFIELD

NOTTING HILL | ISLINGTON | SELFRIDGES | LIBERTY | WWW.DINNYHALL.COM

PROMOTING A PRINCIPLED RESPONSE TO TERRORISM PROTECTING THE RIGHTS OF WOMEN DEFENDING THE SCOPE OF HUMAN RIGHTS PROTECTION PROTECTING CIVILIANS IN WARTIME SHAPING FOREIGN POLICY ADVANCING THE INTERNATIONAL JUSTICE SYSTEM BANNING INDISCRIMINATE WEAPONS OF WAR LINKING BUSINESS PRACTICES AND HUMAN RIGHTS RESPONDING FIRST TO HUMAN RIGHTS EMERGENCIES PROMOTING A PRINCIPLED

HUMAN RIGHTS WATCH
AS LONG AS THERE IS OPPRESSION
TYRANNY HAS A WITNESS

RESPONSE TO TERRORISM PROTECTING THE RIGHTS OF WOMEN DEFENDING THE SCOPE OF HUMAN RIGHTS PROTECTION PROTECTING CIVILIANS IN WARTIME SHAPING FOREIGN POLICY ADVANCING THE INTERNATIONAL JUSTICE SYSTEM BANNING INDISCRIMINATE WEAPONS OF WAR LINKING BUSINESS PRACTICES AND HUMAN RIGHTS RESPONDING FIRST TO HUMAN RIGHTS EMERGENCIES REPORTING FROM CLOSED SOCIETIES WWW.HRW.ORG

HUMAN RIGHTS WATCH

covered in her customary shoes, painted lips and flower patterns. The costume jewellery collection's trinkets run from diamanté-encrusted charms and rings to charming bracelets, strung with little enamel roses. Look out too for the vintage-inspired sunglasses.
Branch 23 Royal Exchange, EC3V 3LR (7626 5391).

Mimi
40 Cheshire Street, E2 6EH (7729 6699, www.mimiberry.com). Liverpool Street tube/rail or Shoreditch High Street rail. **Open** 10.30am-6pm Tue-Sat; 11am-6pm Sun.
Central Saint Martins graduate Mimi Berry is a staple on Cheshire Street, having set up shop here back in 2001. She began by making slouchy leather carry-alls in unconventional colours, but these days her collection covers a wider array of understated designs, taking in more structured styles. Waxed oilskin satchels, roomy leather weekend bags, pillar box-red or black patent laptop bags, and beautifully simple shoulder bags, with gorgeous linings, vie for customers' attentions; there are plenty of designs for both sexes, along with purses, pencil cases and card holders. Prices for bags range from about £100 to about £300. Mimi bags are often stocked in independent fashion boutiques.

T Fox & Co
118 London Wall, EC2Y 5JA (7628 1868, www.tfox.co.uk). Moorgate tube/rail. **Open** 9am-6pm Mon, Tue, Thur, Fri; 9am-7pm Wed.
T Fox & Co began as an umbrella makers back in 1868 (protection from the elements was clearly a priority on any traditional gent's agenda), though it has expanded its range since then. Today, with its leaping fox logo a sure-fire stamp of quality, it also provides smart shirts, ties, shoes and leather goods (wallets, briefcases and the like). Located on the edge of the City, the shop caters to power-broking businessmen out to impress with their attire and accessories. A bespoke tailoring service is also available, but the real treat is a trip to the shop itself: the ground-floor's attractive modernist interior is complemented by a Victorian clubroom upstairs.

Hats

Bates the Hatter
73 Jermyn Street, SW1Y 6JD (7734 2722, www.bates-hats.co.uk). Piccadilly Circus tube. **Open** 9.30am-5.30pm Mon-Fri; 10am-6pm Sat.
Once, a man was not considered fully dressed if he went out without his hat. Having kept the tradition of gents' hats alive on Jermyn Street for over a century, Bates the Hatter clearly knows its niche, advising customers: 'Always wear a hat in inclement and sunny weather.' And sure enough, the shop sells headwear that covers all weather conditions: the straw panama is perfect for summer, while the deerstalker is ideal for those winter hunting expeditions. Well-crafted flat caps are a timeless classic, and chaps would do well to keep Bates in mind for formal occasions – Steed from *The Avengers* would be proud to wear the company's bowler hat, and the classy black top hat is a stunner in grey or black. This old-fashioned shop, with its wonderful topper-shaped sign, is one of London's finest surviving gems.

Bernstock Speirs
234 Brick Lane, E2 7EB (7739 7385, www.bernstockspeirs.com). Aldgate East tube or Shoreditch High Street rail. **Open** 11am-6pm Mon-Fri; 11am-5pm Sat, Sun.
Paul Bernstock and Thelma Speirs first met at Middlesex Polytechnic in 1979 and have been attiring east London's best-dressed heads since 1982. Everyone from Julie Christie and Boy George to Cheryl Cole and Victoria Beckham has bought one of their bonnets – creative reworkings of classic styles. Recent collections have featured veiled visors, bobble hats with bows, cotton jersey caps, 'panama trilbys' with a striped jersey brim and beanies in corduroy and tartan. The brand has also collaborated with designers Peter Jensen, Emma Cook, Agnès b, Jean Paul Gaultier and Richard Nicoll, and has a concession in Dover Street Market (*see p39*).

Philip Treacy
69 Elizabeth Street, SW1W 9PJ (7730 3992, www.philiptreacy.co.uk). Sloane Square tube. **Open** 10am-6pm Mon-Fri; 11am-5pm Sat.
Philip Treacy competes only with Stephen Jones for the title of London's most fashionable milliner. Much-loved by the late, great fashion editor Isabella Blow, he established his first studio in the basement of her house on Elizabeth Street in 1991 and his petite shop has since become a Belgravia hotspot a few doors down. Known for his ornate, attention-grabbing creations that often don't resemble a hat at all, designers like Karl Lagerfeld and Alexander McQueen have called on his services. Recent collections have featured leopard-print trilbys, logo-embroidered baseball caps for men, fantastically feathered fascinators and neon berets for women. Treacy also designed and art directed Grace Jones's Hurricane tour in 2009.

Jewellery

Ben Day
18 Hanbury Street, E1 6QR (7247 9977, www.benday.co.uk). Liverpool Street tube/rail. **Open** 11am-6pm Tue-Fri; 11am-5pm Sat, Sun.
Ben Day has built up a loyal following for his exquisite, opulent creations. His workshop and shop are housed in

James Smith & Sons. *See p128.*

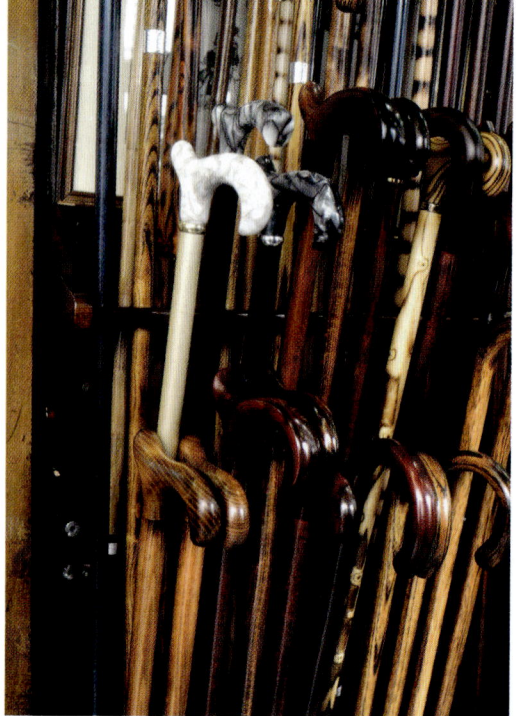

one of Spitalfields' atmospheric Huguenot buildings – the perfect setting for Day's almost medieval designs, which feature flawless South Sea pearls (blue, silver, gold and black), smooth pebbles of amethyst, shimmering pink kunzite or heavy drops of vivid green chysoprase. Each piece is a handmade one-off, adding to the air of exclusivity; for those who want something even more personal, Day will undertake bespoke work. Men are not forgotten, with a range of accessories that includes unusual cufflinks and signet rings.
Branch 3 Lonsdale Road, W11 2BY (3417 3873).

Berganza
88-90 Hatton Garden (entrance in Greville Street), EC1N 8PN (7404 2336, www.berganza.com). Chancery Lane tube or Farringdon tube/rail.
Open 10am-5pm Mon-Sat.
Among the look-at-me sparkle and glitter of Hatton Garden, Berganza has a more subtle appeal, with its array of antique rings, rescued from home and abroad. Rings are displayed in beautifully tattered velvet boxes in the shop window, next to hand-written labels describing their provenance. Georgian, Victorian, Edwardian and art deco treasures are all represented, in addition to a selection of stylish 1940s and '50s one-offs. Other pieces might include dapper sapphire and diamond Edwardian cufflinks or a turn-of-the-century enamelled locket, with a midnight-blue pansy surrounded by pearls. Prices start at just over £200.

Cox & Power
35C Marylebone High Street, W1U 4QA (7935 3530, www.coxandpower.com). Baker Street tube. **Open** 10am-6pm Mon-Sat.
Sleek, beautifully crafted contemporary designs are the stock-in-trade at Cox & Power. Candy-bright gemstones mounted on simple silver and gold bands, strings of glinting sapphire beads and textured, invitingly tactile men's rings and cufflinks are among the goodies, while price tags start in the hundreds but soon run into the thousands. Wedding and commitment rings can be customised according to taste: choose the shape, finish and colour of the gold (from £295) and, if you really want to see how the whole process works, you can spend half a day in the workshop alongside goldsmith Power and even take part in the making of your jewellery (from £1,000, plus the cost of the jewel created).

ec one
41 Exmouth Market, EC1R 4QL (7713 6185, www.econe.co.uk). Farringdon tube/rail.
Open 10am-6pm Mon-Wed, Fri; 11am-7pm Thur; 10.30am-6pm Sat.
Husband-and-wife team Jos and Alison Skeates have a magpie's eye for good design, which makes for delightfully varied browsing. Over 50 designers are showcased: temptingly inexpensive trinkets include

T Fox & Co. *See p131.*

native New Yorker Alex Bittar's colourful lucite bangles, Lindsay Pearson's silver and gold button friendship bracelets and Adore Hawaii's sweet little heart necklaces. Among the slightly pricier standouts are Fiona Paxton's exquisitely beaded collars and cuffs (donned by various fashion-forward starlets) and Swedish designer Celestine Soumah's beguilingly simple silver designs. Wedding and engagement rings are equally varied in price and style, running from simple stacking bands to shimmering, diamond-encrusted extravaganzas.
Branch 56 Ledbury Road, W11 2AJ (7243 8811).

Electrum Gallery
21 South Molton Street, W1K 5QZ (7629 6325, www.electrumgallery.co.uk). Bond Street tube.
Open 10am-6pm Mon-Sat.
Talent-spotting new jewellery design is made easy at Electrum Gallery, where a good deal of stock is conveniently under one roof. Now under new management, Electrum's new sister gallery is the mixed-media (glass, ceramics and textiles) Contemporary Applied Arts (*see p168*). At the South Molton Street shop, around 100 designers are represented at any one time, so the range of styles and budgets is huge. Gerda Flöckinger, CBE, works with fused 18ct yellow gold (from £700), while Jo Hayes-Ward uses computer-aided design to create works in stainless steel and aluminium as well as precious metals. A new star arrival to Electrum's sparkling firmament is Karola Torkos, a young, up-and-coming designer with two collections: one working with colourful plastics, and the other with precious metals (from £100).

French's Dairy
13 Rugby Street, WC1N 3QT (7404 7070, www.frenchsdairy.com). Holborn or Russell Square tube. **Open** 11am-6pm Mon-Fri; 11am-5pm Sat.
Lovers of costume jewellery flock to Maggie Owen's jewel of a shop located off Lamb's Conduit Street. Behind the beautifully tiled frontage of London's first dairy, the shop (designed by architect William Smalley, with parquet flooring lifted from the V&A's jewellery department) showcases a lovely collection of bold, contemporary jewellery by the likes of French designer Philippe Ferrandis (whose distinctive necklaces started the story), along with innovative and talented designers such as Anton Heunis, Extasia, Simon Harrison and Patrice. The collection is enhanced by must-have lifestyle products: silk scarves, luxurious laptop bags and elegant fragrances. A second shop opened in Chancery Lane at the end of 2008.
Branch 3 Chichester Rents, WC2A 1EG (7242 4555).

Kabiri HOT 50
37 Marylebone High Street, W1U 4QE (7224 1808, www.kabiri.co.uk). Baker Street tube.
Open 10am-6.30pm Mon-Sat; noon-5pm Sun.
Kabiri's admirable mission statement is to showcase the best in jewellery, regardless of its price, provenance or how well known the designer is – though many of its unknowns go on to become very successful indeed. Collections change with dizzying speed, but there's always plenty for smaller budgets, like the perspex necklaces and brooches, as well as the mid-range market, including the colourful, disco-inspired beaded bracelets, necklaces and earrings by designer Brokenfab. Prices climb into quadruple figures for investment pieces: Brazilian designer Carla Amorim's rose gold and hefty gemstone rings and Vicente Gracia's gloriously outré pieces, adorned with tiny animal heads with gems for eyes, are among the pricier treasures. Kabiri also has a concession in Selfridges.
Branches 18 The Market, The Piazza, WC2E 8RB (7240 1055).

Kirt Holmes
16 Camden Passage, N1 8ED (7226 1080, www.kirtholmes.com). Angel tube. **Open** 11am-6pm Tue-Thur; 11am-7pm Fri; 10am-6pm Sat; noon-5pm Sun.
Kirt Holmes is an established fixture on Camden Passage (*see p106* **Streetwise**), where Holmes's own vintage-look handiwork is complemented by French designer Corpus Christi and Alex Monroe's feminine fripperies. Inside the smart boutique you'll also find a selection of real vintage jewellery dating from the 1920s, courtesy of Eclectica (once a near-neighbour on Camden Passage, now an online shop). Holmes's trademark chain mail and beading is still in evidence, though it evolves with each collection, and the designs have been more geometric in recent seasons, with precisely cut translucent haematite shards as pendants. Earrings start at around the £120 mark.

Lara Bohinc
149F Sloane Street, SW1X 9BZ (7730 8194, www.larabohinc107.co.uk). Sloane Square tube. **Open** 10am-6pm Mon-Fri; 10am-7pm Wed; noon-5pm Sun.
This Slovenian-born designer's talent for creating distinctive, dramatic pieces has stood her in good stead with the usually fickle fashionistas but her appeal went stellar when it was discovered that Samantha Cameron gave a Laratella bracelet (£249) from Bohinc's Essentials range to Michelle Obama. Elle MacPherson, Madonna and SJP are also fans. Glossy and sleek, with a high-fashion edge, Bohinc's creations make a real statement: think heavy, intricate yellow gold collars, sinuous interwoven bracelets and flowing, looped rose gold or platinum plate necklaces, all much imitated on the high street. Luxurious, supremely stylish bags, belts, shoes and sunglasses complete the look.

Lesley Craze Gallery
33-35A Clerkenwell Green, EC1R 0DU (7608 0393, www.lesleycrazegallery.co.uk). Farringdon tube/rail.
Open 10am-5.30pm Tue-Sat.

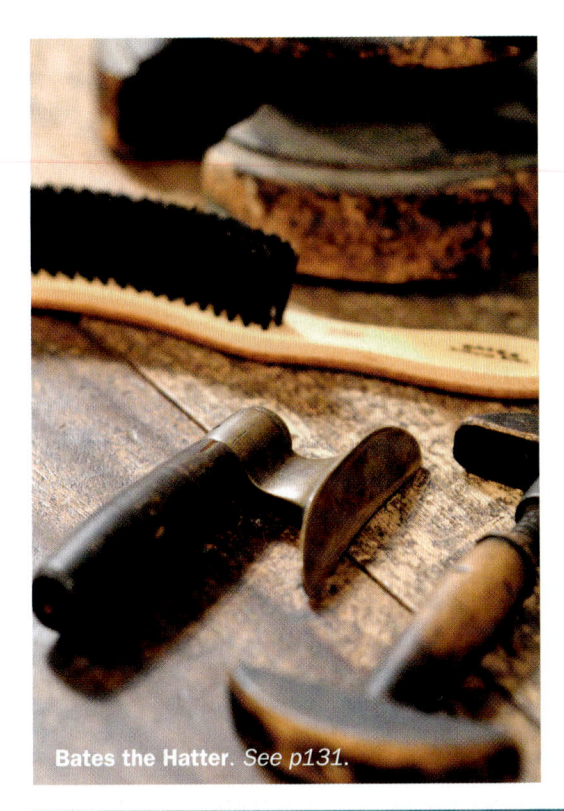

Jewellery & Accessories

Bates the Hatter. See p131.

FASHION

ec one. See p133.

All manner of inventive jewellery is showcased at this well-established Clerkenwell gallery, alongside delicate metalwork, decorative objects and textiles. Yoko Izawa's knitted lycra and nylon yarn rings are among the quirky, highly individual offerings, while Josephine Cullen creates dramatic rings and earrings from Whitby jet – usually associated with ornate Victorian mourning jewellery, but in Cullen's hands transformed into something elemental, especially when combined with gold and glittering crystals. Regular exhibitions highlight the work of selected designers, such as Australian jeweller Felicity Peters, who studied the Etruscan art of granulation to create her works of 18ct gold beads attached to onyx, tanzanite and tourmaline.

Tatty Devine
236 Brick Lane, E2 7EB (7739 9191, www.tattydevine.com). Liverpool Street tube/rail or Shoreditch High Street rail. **Open** 11am-6pm Tue-Sun.
This east London company made its name with plastic fantastic jewellery: guitar plectrum charm bracelets, say, or kitsch anchor necklaces. Despite many imitators, it's still going strong – tribute to the designers' boundless inventiveness, which keeps it one step ahead of the competition. Think pastel-hued ric rac bangles, Dali-esque moustache necklaces, bow tie rings, pressed silk flower hairbands, volume-dial brooches and, for those with more cash to splash, intricately-cut lace-effect collars, which look a treat worn over a plain jumper. There are collaborations with the likes of Rob Ryan of Ryantown (*see p171*) and artists Gilbert & George, and the shop also stocks Smart Women products and Andrea Garland's beauty soaps, lotions and potions (handmade from scratch in Hackney). There's now also a branch in Covent Garden.
Branch 44 Monmouth Street, WC2H 9EP (7836 2685).

Wright & Teague
35 Dover Street, W1S 4NQ (7629 2777, www.wrightandteague.com). Green Park tube.
Open 11am-5pm Tue-Sat.
Despite the boutique's Mayfair setting, much of Gary Wright and Sheila Teague's much-imitated-but-never-matched jewellery is affordable for the average person: silver bangles hung with a single charm, say, or beaten silver studs. Prices rise for yellow and rose gold designs and rings set with gemstones. There's a pleasingly organic feel to many of the designs, which shun fussy detailing in favour of clean, simple lines. Some of the ranges look to other cultures and societies, and the latest – Nuba – features colours, signs and symbols inspired by Africa. The men's collection includes chunky chain bracelets, inscribed rings, pendants and tactile, pebble-like silver cufflinks.

Health & Beauty

Skincare & Cosmetics	**138**
Perfumeries & Herbalists	**146**
Eyewear	**153**

Health & Beauty

London is now home to a selection of top-notch health and beauty boutiques that appeal to Londoners for their straight-talking approaches and high-quality products, and which eschew synthetic ingredients for purer concoctions with divine natural scents. In this field, Australian skincare brand **Aesop** (see below) excels; the 'thinking person's' skincare brand opened shop on Mount Street in 2008, and now has three branches in the capital, with the latest opening on east London's trendy Redchurch Street in spring 2010.

Meanwhile, beauty and cosmetics shops have become more sophisticated, as consumers have become more savvy. Visit Primrose Hill's **Lost in Beauty** (see p142) for cult make-up lines, or **Space NK** (see p144) – now a common feature on London's retail landscape – for brands such as Eve Lom.

London's perfumeries now rival those in Paris for their indulgent atmosphere, and here, as with skincare, things have stepped up a notch, quality-wise, with **Miller Harris** (see p146) and US newcomer **Le Labo** (see p146) pioneering the trend for non-synthetic scents that can be sampled in their stylish boutiques. The city's handful of herbalists, meanwhile, contains some lovely old gems – Green Park's **DR Harris** (see p150) first opened for business in 1790, while **G Baldwin & Co** (see p150) has been a feature of the Walworth Road since 1844.

Aesthetics are now as important a priority as eyecare at London's opticians and eyewear shops; visit **archiv** (see p153) or **Opera Opera** (see p156), and you'll positively want to wear specs.

Skincare & Cosmetics

Skincare specialists

Space NK (see p144), **Cosmetics à la Carte** (see p142), **Lost in Beauty** (see p142) and the **HQ hair & beauty store** (see p142) all have good ranges of skincare products.

Aesop London
91 Mount Street, W1K 2SU (7409 2358, www.aesop.net.au). Bond Street or Green Park tube. **Open** noon-5pm Mon; 10am-6pm Tue-Sat.

Aesop's first stand-alone store in London opened in 2008, in a former jeweller's shop in Mayfair, and is dominated by a huge circular sink (plucked from an old fish-paste factory) over which customers are encouraged to lather up body washes and smear on face creams. Lining the apothecary shelves, amid the mottled mirrors and glass globe lights, is the entire collection of the Australian brand's skin, hair and body products. A brand for the thinking person who wants to avoid heavily packaged and marketed products, the brand eschews the dubious claims made by other skincare ranges, preferring instead to focus on quality and scrupulously researched natural ingredients and gorgeous scents, such as geranium, primrose and mandarin. Highlights of the range include

the Geranium Leaf body cleanser, the zingy Tahitian Lime cleansing slab and the Parsley Seed skincare range – although we defy you to find a scent you don't like here. Animal, a body wash for dogs, is a surprise big seller, but the Moroccan Neroli Shaving Serum might be used more often. Success has seen follow-up branches in east and west London.
Branches Aesop Westbourne, 227A Westbourne Grove, W11 2SE (7221 2008); Aesop Shoreditch, 5A Redchurch Street, E2 7DJ (7613 3793).

Fresh
92 Marylebone High Street, W1U 4RD (7486 4100, www.fresh.com). Baker Street or Regent's Park tube.
Open 10am-7pm Mon-Wed, Fri, Sat; 10am-8pm Thur; 11am-5pm Sun.
Boston-based company Fresh does a very fine line in sophisticated health and beauty products, made with premium ingredients and dressed up in irresistible packaging. Co-founders Lev Glazman and Alina Roytberg are pioneers of sugar as a beauty ingredient, and the sensual Sugar range is among the brands most covetable; the heavenly Brown Sugar Body Polish contains real brown sugar crystals and essential oils, while the SPF15 Sugar lip treatment combines reparative oils and natural waxes with the sweet stuff. Products certainly don't come cheap but the quality is clearly high. The most indulgent purchase has to be a pot of Crème Ancienne (£155/100g); it's made entirely by hand in a monastery in the Czech Republic and is so rich that it banishes any dryness instantaneously. Pretty apothecary-style eaux de parfum are also available, in enticing flavours such as Redcurrant Basil and Citron de Vigne (also available as shower gel and body lotion). The brand also now has a make-up collection inspired by the wanton 'aristocratic indulgence of the 18th century' (Firebird mascara £17; Imperial Bedroom face palette £32) plus a range of anti-ageing skincare products – we loved the rich-but-not-greasy Black Tea Age-delay face cream, with its distinctive scent.

Ortigia. See p141.

The Painted Lady invites you to revive and relax the old fashioned way. Specialising in vintage and contemporary hair cuts, up dos and one-to-one styling sessions, you'll find her enticingly tucked away in the heart of Shoreditch.

65 Redchurch Street, E2 7DJ
E.   www.thepaintedladylondon.com
T.   + 44 (0)207 729 2154

the Painted Lady

xrealhair

6-8 cale street, chelsea green, london, sw33qu
020 7589 0877

realhair best london cut – Timeout 09

realhair has summer covered this year whether it be achieving that sun kissed, holiday hair with their baliage colour specialists or perhaps the 'realhair shine service', an intense glossing service to make the most of your hair in the summer sunshine, or even their celebrity brow specialist from the US to give you that instant non surgical facelift.

realhair are offering 25% off all introductory cut and colour appointments in July / August – 0207 589 0877

andrew jose • london

The Andrew Jose salon has an outstanding reputation for cutting, colouring, men's hair, Afro Caribbean, natural hair extensions and innovations in blow dry's. Named by TimeOut as one of London's best hairdressers.

no.1 Charlotte St. London W1T 1RB   t: 020 7323 4679
www.andrewjose.com

Nova Brazilia
infinite blow dry
exclusively at andrew jose • london

Skincare & Cosmetics

Kiehl's
29 Monmouth Street, WC2H 9DD (7240 2411, www.kiehls.com). Covent Garden or Leicester Square tube. **Open** 10am-7pm Mon-Sat; noon-5pm Sun.
The London flagship of the New York skincare company that started up in 1851 goes from strength to strength, with branches popping up on all the best shopping routes. Using only naturally derived ingredients that are beneficial to the skin and using the minimum amount of preservative, Kiehl's products are suitable for some of the most sensitive skins. As well as products for face, body and hair, there are ranges for men (from pre-shave to lip care), babies and children, and even sun protection. The lip balms and rich Crème de Corps (from £8.50) are cult products, recently joined by the non-oily, vitamin-enriched facial fuel for tired-looking skin.
Branches 20 Northcote Road, SW11 1NX (7350 2997); 186A King's Road, SW3 5XP (7751 5950); Units 14-15 Royal Exchange, EC3V 3LP (7283 6661).

Liz Earle Skincare
38-39 Duke of York Square, King's Road, SW3 4LY (7730 9191, www.lizearle.com). Sloane Square tube. **Open** 10am-7pm Mon, Thur-Sat; 10.30am-7pm Tue; 11am-5pm Sun.
Isle of Wight-based former beauty writer Liz Earle launched her eponymous skincare brand in 1995, but it's only since the opening of her shop on Duke of York Square in 2007 that the brand has become better known to beauty editors and savvy shoppers. Based on botanical ingredients, most grown organically or harvested from sustainable wild sources, the streamlined range of products is, like Korres and Ortigia, pleasingly gimmick-free, as well as being notable for its absence of mineral oils and liquid paraffin waxes. Items are lovingly arranged in the spacious, well-staffed and fresh-feeling shop (think dove-grey tones, slate, greenery and wood), which is full of helpful leaflets and books on skincare and green beauty. The new Superskin Moisturiser for mature skin contains cranberry and borage seed oils and rosehip oil to nourish and restore skin, while the Instant Boost Skin Tonic Spritzer uses the naturally active ingredients of pure aloe vera, camomile, cucumber and essential oils. Cleanse & Polish Hot Cloth Cleanser (a cream used with a muslin cloth; £13 for a starter kit) has an avid following. The selection of 'minis' (from £4.75) in the shop are a great way to introduce yourself to the range, and facials are also available (signature facial, £85/90mins).

Neal's Yard Remedies
15 Neal's Yard, WC2H 9DP (7379 7222, www.nealsyardremedies.com). Covent Garden or Leicester Square tube. **Open** 10am-7pm Mon, Tue, Thur-Sat; 10am-7.30pm Wed; 11am-6pm Sun.
A forerunner of the organic movement in the early 1980s, Neal's Yard has retained a loyal following, despite competition from younger companies with similar ideologies. In recent years, the brand has expanded onto (smart) main shopping streets, such as Upper Street and King's Road, and there are now 20 stores in London alone, most with luxury treatment rooms offering a wide range of therapies. The prettily packaged products, in their distinctive blue-glass bottles to safeguard the ingredients, smell delicious without being overpowering, and prices are fairer than many organic products. Made in an eco-factory in Dorset, they run the gamut from lovely French soaps, hand washes and bath oils to sun creams, deodorants and essential oils, plus a mother-and-baby range. There's also a dispensary for a huge range of dried herbs. Our top picks are the quick-absorbing Orange Flower Facial Oil, the Rehydrating Rose Daily Moisture Cream, the gently foaming Palmarosa Facial Wash and the Melissa Hand Cream. The range of remedies designed to 'feed the skin from within' includes the Mahonia Clear Skin Formula, a tonic to be taken orally, and the Organic Beauty Oil, containing essential fatty acids to improve skin elasticity and hydration. There is also a men's range: NYR Men.
Branches throughout the city.

Ortigia
55 Sloane Square, SW1W 8AX (7730 2826, www.ortigia-srl.com). Sloane Square tube. **Open** 10am-6.30pm Mon-Sat.
Sicilian brand Ortigia made something of a splash in the capital when it opened in 2008, for its exotically presented soaps and skincare, which come in handmade packaging covered in designs inspired by Italian palazzos, mosaics and tiles (making them perfect for gifts). Ortigia uses plants indigenous to Sicily to create its luxurious but well-priced toiletries. There are 13 fragrances incorporating aromatic oils such as lavender, pomegranate, Sicilian lime, orange blossom and bergamot (the essential oil derived from the bitter orange tree), with base materials such as olive oil and almond oil strengthening the natural agenda. Each range includes bath oil, salts, soaps, room sprays and candles. The new Geranium collection is sure to be a bestseller, and the classically packaged Almond Milk body cream is divine. The firm's first stand-alone London boutique opened in spring 2008 in a fittingly elegant building in Sloane Square; a Marylebone shop followed suit shortly after.
Branch 23 Marylebone High Street, W1U 4PF (7487 4684).

Cosmetics & beauty shops

Becca
91A Pelham Street, SW7 2NJ (7225 2501, www.beccacosmetics.com). South Kensington tube. **Open** 10am-6pm Mon-Sat.

With its rich brown colour scheme and seductive lighting, Becca has a luxurious, decadent feel. Australian founder Rebecca Morrice Williams, a former make-up artist, launched the brand when she couldn't find the perfect foundation, and is still very 'hands-on' in her approach; a key aspect of Becca is its inclusive approach – it caters for all skin colours and complexions. The focus is on achieving a radiant complexion, with a three-step system that begins with primer – a key product here, available in Hydrating or Mattifying versions – and a tinted base of Luminous Skin Colour or Shimmering Skin Perfecter. We're big fans of the Beach Tint 'crème stain' for cheeks and lips, which imparts a dewy, natural-looking glow, as well as the mineral powder foundation. The final step is a dusting of very fine finishing powder. The smudge-proof, waterproof Ultimate Mascara can be removed just with warm water. Make-up artists are on hand to give you a revamp (from £45) or lesson (£90; £45 redeemable against products), and there's a bridal service.

Cosmetics à la Carte
19B Motcomb Street, SW1X 8LB (7235 0596, www.cosmeticsalacarte.com). Knightsbridge tube.
Open 10am-6pm Mon, Tue, Fri, Sat; 9.30am-7pm Wed, Thur; 11am-5pm Sun.
Cosmetics à la Carte, in the same hands for 30 years, has enjoyed a steady following from local Sloane families throughout its lifetime; grandmothers bring their teenage granddaughters here for their first make-up lesson, thirtysomethings drop in for a seasonal make-up bag refresher, while brides-to-be visit in preparation for the big day. The small, stylish shop offers 'made-to-measure' make-up (it was the first company to do so) and skincare. Gone are the days of buying an eyeshadow trio because you like two of the shades. The click-in Colourbox system here allows you to fill up a palette with whichever shade you fancy (eye, lip and cheek colours cost between £12 and £25). And the Rose Dew Hydrating Primer does an excellent job at smoothing out fine lines. Having trouble finding your perfect foundation? If one of the ready-made shades doesn't match your complexion perfectly, you can have one specially mixed for £45. Make-up artists are on hand to give advice, even if you don't opt for one of the renowned lessons (£50-£180). Recent additions to the collection include the Skin Veil primer, Cover Tint mineral make-up, 'flush blush' and a new range of colours for the excellent 'outliner' eyeliner pots.

HQ hair & beautystore
2 New Burlington Street, W1S 2JE (0871 220 4141, www.hqhair.com). Oxford Circus tube.
Open 10am-6pm Mon, Sat; 10am-7pm Tue, Fri; 10am-8pm Wed, Thur.
The wealth of products within this store, teamed with knowledgeable advice from in-house experts – not least Dominic Webb the products guru – mean you're sure to find just what you're looking for. It's a store that doubles up as a salon offering hairdressing and beauty services including waxing, spray tanning and even the odd holistic health indulgence, like the Hopi ear candles treatment. Product lines are extensive with the clutch of new arrivals including YonKa, the French skincare range, Frédéric Fekkai hair products, Dermalogica, OPI and Slikit cordless ceramic straightening irons, plus the luxury make-up range Becca (*see p141*). As well as the original website, there's one dedicated to the boys: www.hqman.com.

Lost in Beauty
117 Regent's Park Road, NW1 8UR (7586 4411, www.lostinbeauty.com). Chalk Farm tube.
Open 10am-6.30pm Sat; noon-5pm Sun.
Kitted out with vintage shop fittings, this chic Primrose Hill boutique stocks a well-edited array of beauty brands, including Phyto, Caudalie, Dr Hauschka, Alexandra Soveral, Dr Alkaitis, Environ, REN, Shu Uemura, Art of Hair and Butter London nail polish with supremely covetable colours; other cult brands stocked include Becca make-up (*see p141*), the retro-packaged Rosebud Salve, Chantecaille make-up and skincare, Bumble & Bumble hair products, Jimmyjane candles and Belmacz Oyster Pearl translucent face powder. Make-up artist Georgie Hamed (a regular on glossy fashion shoots) offers private lessons and parties. Prices start from £50 and head upwards. There's also a choice selection of vintage jewellery.

Pak's
25-27 & 31 Stroud Green Road, N4 3ES (7263 2088, www.pakcosmetics.com). Finsbury Park tube/rail. **Open** 9am-8pm Mon-Sat; 10am-6pm Sun.
Established 27 years ago, Pak's is an Aladdin's cave of African and Afro-Caribbean hair and beauty products, with many exclusive and hard-to-find ranges. The flagship is a shop of two halves; the Wig Centre, on the left, offers an extensive array of wigs, weaves and extensions, both synthetic and human, alongside fake ponytails and hair pieces. Colours range from natural blond to black as well as kaleidoscopic blues, reds and pinks. The right-hand side Hair Centre is stocked to the rafters with hair and beauty products. Alongside names like Bedhead and Aveda are excellent moisturising haircare ranges Soft n' Free and Soft & Beautiful and various relaxers. Hair serums, oils, shines and polishers are a particular strength. Men are also catered for with shaving oils, aftershaves and ingrowing hair treatments. The store also has a wide range of combs, brushes, straightening irons and rollers.
Branches throughout the city.

Screenface
48 Monmouth Street, WC2H 9EP (7836 3955, www.screenface.com). Covent Garden, Leicester

Easton Regal.
HAIRDRESSING

bookings@eastonregal.com / www.eastonregal.com / 020 7250 1441
Easton Regal Hairdressing / 84 Clerkenwell Road / London / EC1M 5RF

Situated on the edge of St John's Square, at what is arguably the pulse of Clerkenwell, Easton Regal brings something unique to this vibrant part of East London. The salon itself exudes luxury. This is high end hairdressing with a creative touch. The show-piece buildings architecture reflects the calm and confident ambience inside. The Easton Regal Team never impose a style that's impractical to recreate at home. Using a blend of both classically disciplined and contemporary techniques, we personalise and polish hairstyles to flatter the individual's unique qualities. Precision, trend-aware haircuts are complimented with cosmetic colouring and offered alongside indulgent power treatments.

We also have celebrity session stylists taking up guest residency at Easton Regal. Our most popular treatments include the Permanent Blow dry and revolutionary Micro Mist Machine and not forgetting our incredibly successful in house nail and browbars.

Please feel free to pop in for a complimentary consultation, call us on 0207 250 1441 or check out our website for full details on us and the services we provide, www.eastonregal.com

TEN Green shops

Aravore Babies
Crocheted and knitted organic clothes with skincare products from Erba Viva, and a baby wish-list service. See p265.

Eco
From sustainably sourced designer homewares to ecological paints by earthBorn. The basement design consultancy advises amateur eco warriors. See p163.

Equa
Fairtrade and organic fashion collections; shoes from Veja Volley and Beyond Skin; vegan wallets and beauty products from Ila; and jewellery from Made. See p69.

Family Tree
Carefully chosen designer gifts, homewares and accessories with an eco slant, with plenty of Fairtrade and organic cotton. See p41.

JoJo Maman Bébé
Organic, sustainable or recycled materials and a commitment to sustainably tackling poverty in rural northern Mozambique. See p118.

Square or Tottenham Court Road tube.
Open 10.30am-6pm Mon-Sat; noon-5pm Sun.
Professional make-up artists seek out Screenface for its high-quality, long-lasting make-up and tools of the trade. Fardel face and body paints, Blink mascara, Lord & Berry eye and lip liners and Screenface's own range of make-up. Haircare is of a similarly high standard (Joico, Fudge, Phyto), as are the make-up brushes and other tools. Special effects are big business: fake blood, adhesives and removers, plus all types of facial hair, from handlebar moustaches to mutton chops. The latest products include French skincare range Embyolisse and, for those looking for knockout effects for that forthcoming fancy dress party, torn skin gelatine prosthetic and werewolf double fangs.
Branch 20 Powis Terrace, Westbourne Park Road, W11 1JH (7221 8289).

Space NK
8-10 Broadwick Street, W1F 8HW (7287 2667, www.spacenk.com). Oxford Circus or Piccadilly Circus tube. **Open** 10am-7pm Mon-Fri; 11am-5.30pm Sat.

Skincare & Cosmetics

Space NK

With some 30 stores across London, Space NK could have easily swerved off the rails into soulless super-chain territory. The fact that it hasn't pays testament to founder Nicky Kinnaird's commitment to unearthing the latest cult beauty products from across the world. And not just any old products either – at Space NK, you can count on a meticulously edited range of top-quality items, produced by specialists in their field (Acqua di Parma, Nars, Nia 24, Tocca, Skeen, Michael Van Clarke, Laura Mercier among others). You'll find winners such as the legendary cleanser from celebrated facialist Eve Lom; perfect lipsticks by dedicated lip colour specialist Poppy King (aka Lipstick Queen); skincare by dermatologist Dr Brandt; By Terry make-up and skincare from Terry de Gunzburg, who created YSL's celebrated light-reflective concealer Touche Eclat. And Space NK is showing no signs of resting on its laurels, with new lines of products being added all the time; recent additions include Life NK – Space NK's very own line of everyday essentials, including candles and travel goodies – and organic make-up by Kjaer Weis.
Branches throughout the city.

Lemon Balm
High-quality herbal and organic skincare as well as natural soaps, top-notch eco candles and bath salts. *See p151.*

Natural Mat Company
Renowned for mattresses made of all natural materials, such as organic coir, latex straight from the rubber tree, unbleached cotton, and mohair. *See p264.*

123 Boutique
Recycled clothing like ripped T-shirts painstakingly reworked into leftfield designs, and a self-titled fashion label that's completely sustainable. *See p42.*

Terra Plana
Award-winning, original, fashionable but ecologically sound shoes made from unusual materials (including Saami quilts). *See p125.*

Unpackaged
Buy only what you need, reduce what you use, reuse old containers and recycle all you can… *See p250.*

Perfumeries & Herbalists

Perfumeries

See also p150 **Farmacia Santa Maria Novella**, and the shops in the **Skincare & Cosmetics** section on pages 138-145; **Space NK** (*see p145*) is particularly good for scents.

Angela Flanders
96 Columbia Road, E2 7QB (7739 7555, www.angelaflanders-perfumer.com). Hoxton or Shoreditch High Street rail. **Open** *10am-3pm Sun; by appointment Mon-Thur.*
Perhaps thanks to her former job as a costume designer, entering Angela Flanders' shop is a little like stepping back into Victorian London. The small perfumery is redolent of her own creations, all of which are simply presented in packaging that exudes an air of Victoriana. The 16 signature scents, available in eau de toilette, eau de parfum, perfumed candles, room sprays, fragrant burning oils and perfumed lamp grains, include the woody Coromandel, vanilla-scented Parchment and summery Hesperides. There's also a range of colognes for men and women based on historic scents, scented accessories like linen water and moth bags made of French herbs. In addition to the signature scents, there are six florals, and four new 'dark' fragrances – rich, exotic scents like fig & amber. Fragrances are also available in a more concentrated form, in a handbag-sized 30ml bottle.

L'Artisan Parfumeur
17 Cale Street, SW3 3QR (7352 4196, www.artisanparfumeur.com). South Kensington tube. **Open** *10am-6.30pm Mon-Sat.*
It's no surprise to find that the heritage of L'Artisan Parfumeur is Parisian. The pretty Kensington store is discreet, stylish and unique. Scents – 'based on memories' – are grouped by 'family' ('Fresh' includes Ananas Fizz, a youthful pineapple scent, while 'Precious Wood' features scents like the spicy Timbuktu). Fragrances are arranged in tealight holders filled with scented muslin, which allow the perfume notes to breathe more easily than a tester spray. What's more, all the fragrances are designed to be used by both sexes. New scents are regularly added to the collection: recent additions include Havana Vanille, the heady and tropical Fleur de Liane and Al Oudh, inspired by the Arabian peninsula, while additions to the organic body care Jatamansi range – scented with rose and bergamot – include candles and room sprays. A new London store was about to open as this guide went to press; visit the website for details.

Le Labo [HOT 50]
28A Devonshire Street, W1G 6PS (3441 1535, www.lelabofragrances.com). Baker Street tube. **Open** *10am-6.30pm Mon-Wed, Fri, Sat; 10am-7pm Thur; noon-5pm Sun.*
Joining New York, Tokyo and Los Angeles, London now has its very own Le Labo perfume boutique. You may have seen the austere bottles in Liberty, or spotted the ultra-hip perfume bar in Paris's Colette, but if you've never heard of it, even better – the brand has cultivated a cult following among those who crave designer quality but balk at purchasing anything mass-produced (Le Labo's scents are freshly mixed at point of sale). Handsome co-founder Edouard Roschi cites London's eclectic vibe as to why it was the natural next step, and accordingly he's taken over a 'superbly ugly' former estate agent's in Marylebone and kitted it out with a slick interior and Japanese mixing den. Perfume starts at £38 a bottle, and everything smells amazing, from the delicate Ambrette 9 to the 'power bomb' Ciste 18.

Miller Harris
21 Bruton Street, W1J 6QD (7629 7750, www.millerharris.com). Bond Street or Green Park tube. **Open** *10am-6pm Mon-Sat.*
To celebrate the 10th anniversary of Miller Harris, creator and founder Lyn Harris created four new fragrances in each of the four main fragrance families: citrus, floral, woody and oriental. Her use of only the finest natural materials in her unisex eaux de parfum, eaux de toilette, body oils and body lotions, together with the gorgeous packaging, makes the perfumes some of the best quality and most covetable on the market, and have earned her a slew of discerning fans. Harris, who undertook years of formal training in both Paris and Grasse, sources raw ingredients from all over the world. Her iris comes from Florence, the violet leaf from France, jasmine from Egypt, while the particular orange flower she favours is Tunisian. Harris eschews the idea of a signature scent, instead using the phrase 'wardrobe of scents' to describe her philosophy of choosing scents depending on mood and occasion. Perfumes from the original range of 12, divided up by 'family', are still some of the bestsellers; all are completely individual and evocative – we're big fans of Fleur Oriental, Geranium Bourbon and Figue Amère. Those looking for their own exclusive perfume can, if they can afford it, take advantage of the bespoke service.
Branch 14 Monmouth Street, WC2H 9HB (7836 9378); 14 Needham Road, W11 2RP (7221 1545).

Ormonde Jayne
12 The Royal Arcade, 28 Old Bond Street, W1S 4SL (7499 1100, www.ormondejayne.com). Green Park tube. **Open** *10am-6pm Mon-Sat.*

Perfumeries & Herbalists

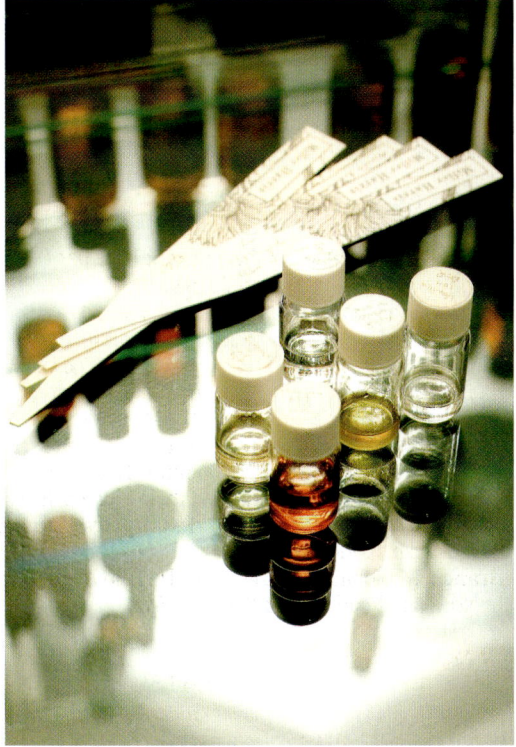

Miller Harris

HEALTH & BEAUTY

Antique gold wallcoverings and black glass chandeliers give the Ormonde Jayne store a sumptuous look that befits the rich scents created by Linda Pilkington. Pilkington is passionate about her trade, sourcing ingredients herself in the Far East and Africa. All components are free from mineral oils, parabens and GM products, and staff are happy to discuss which scents would best suit you. There are just 14 to choose from; our favourites include the elegant Champaca, with pink pepper and bamboo, and Ormande Woman. An extended range of scents is now available in the form of Parfum d'Or Naturel – concentrated, alcohol-free gold perfume purées with a base of natural sugars; smooth it over the décolletage and shoulders for an incandescent effect with a lasting fragrance. There are also body lotions, bathing oils, scented candles and travel sets, consisting of four purse-size 10ml vials of fragrance.

Les Senteurs
71 Elizabeth Street, SW1W 9PJ (7730 2322, www.lessenteurs.com). Sloane Square tube or Victoria tube/rail. **Open** 10am-6pm Mon-Sat.
The shelves of James Craven's pretty Belgravia boutique are laden with wares by prestigious perfumers, including stalwarts like Annick Goutal, Creed, and lesser-known makes from traditional French and Italian perfume houses, such as Frédéric Malle's Editions de Parfums. One of the shop's attractions is the care given to those selecting gifts for others. Craven builds up a profile of the intended recipient by asking questions about looks, personality, favourite colours and even food. This personal approach is what sets the family-run business apart from other perfume shops. Les Senteurs always supplies a sample with each sale so that the perfume can be tested before the bottle is opened.

Herbalists

Chinalife
101-105 Camden High Street, NW1 7JN (7388 5783, www.acumedic.com). Camden Town tube.
Open 9am-8pm Mon-Sat; 9am-6pm Sun.
Created with the aim of bridging the gap between Eastern and Western healthcare, Chinalife is a modern holistic health shop with wooden shelves piled high with a selection of teas, supplements and aromatherapy oils. Stylishly packaged skincare and body ranges feature all-natural active ingredients: some familiar (gingko and ginseng), others, like the anti-ageing reishi or moisture-boosting Chinese angelica, less well known in the West. We particularly like the herbal foot bath, the flower water sprays and the jasmine face mask for dry skin. Tea-lovers are spoilt for choice, with an impressive array of medicinal blends and flower- and berry-filled sachets. A chic tea bar also offers exotic concoctions infused with pomegranate syrup and crushed rosebuds and fragrant,

Ormonde Jayne. *See p146*.

Perfumeries & Herbalists

Les Senteurs

HEALTH & BEAUTY

Lemon Balm

spice-infused lattes. At the shop's rear, canvas panels suspended from the ceiling create an airy room where a therapist can help you feel right as rain with an energising lifestyle package, where acupuncture and Chinese Meridian massage fulfil their promises. Next door at the AcuMedic clinic, a team of experts from China can offer solutions to just about anything, from infertility through to smoking addiction.

DR Harris
29 St James's Street, SW1A 1HB (7930 3915, www.drharris.co.uk). Green Park or Piccadilly Circus tube. **Open** 8.30am-6pm Mon-Fri; 9.30am-5pm Sat.
In a city overtaken by characterless chain pharmacies, DR Harris has remained unfazed – it's hung on tight to its identity since 1790 and even boasts a royal warrant. A visit is much like stepping back through a door into times past. Polished wooden cabinets are filled with bottles and jars with old-fashioned shaving brushes and manicure kits. Its own elegantly packaged products have appealing names; there's Almond Oil Skinfood (£12.95/50ml), Bay Rum Aftershave (£20.95) and Old English Lavender Cologne (£28.50/100ml). Keep your eyes peeled too for Marvis toothpaste and Roger & Gallet soaps. Traditional it may be, but DR Harris appeals to modern sensibilities – none of the products are tested on animals and beauty editors continue to clamour over cult favourites such as the bright blue Crystal Eye Gel.

Farmacia Santa Maria Novella
117 Walton Street, SW3 2HP (7460 6600). South Kensington tube. **Open** 10am-6pm Mon-Sat.
The minuscule London outpost of the famed Florentine pharmacy, founded by Dominican friars, sells beautifully packaged lotions, perfumes, eaux de colognes, exfoliating powders, pot pourri, scented paper and soaps. The shop can't compete with the Italian version, located in a 13th-century frescoed chapel, but the products from one of the world's oldest herbal pharmacies (the company was officially founded in 1612, though its origins date back as far as 1221) are the same; in fact, the lavender smelling salts and 'anti-hysteria' Acqua de Santa Maria Novella are practically unchanged formulas. Other renowned items include orange blossom water and pomegranate perfume. A new branch opened in Piccadilly Arcade at the end of 2009.
Branch 1 Piccadilly Arcade, SW1Y 6NH (7493 1975).

G Baldwin & Co
171-173 Walworth Road, SE17 1RW (7703 5550, www.baldwins.co.uk). Elephant & Castle tube/rail.
Open 9am-6pm Mon-Wed, Fri, Sat; 9am-7pm Thur.
This old-school apothecary, specialising in natural beauty products and health remedies, from oils and balms to herbs, has been open on the Walworth Road

since 1844, making it one of London's oldest herbalists; there were originally 12 branches, but this is the only remaining shop. Swing by for top-notch dispensing advice and you might bump into long-time customers Michael Caine or Terence Stamp. Products include health tinctures, supplements, barks and flower remedies. You can also buy soap-making mould kits (£40.99, makes six bars) and a range of unfragranced Baldwin bases to make your own face creams, shampoos or shower gels. The Synergy Range is based on the finest quality essential oils combined with luxurious carrier oils.

Lemon Balm
76 Parkway, NW1 7AH (7267 3334, www.lemonbalmonline.com). Camden Town tube.
Open 10.30am-7pm Mon; 10am-7pm Tue-Fri; 10am-6pm Sat.
This natural health and beauty shop/complementary therapies clinic opened in spring 2008. The lovingly arranged shop has a fresh and soothing vibe and is stocked with a plethora of high-quality herbal and organic skincare brands – such as Figs & Rouge, Ruby Red, Trilogy and Damask – as well as bath and beauty products, aromatic flower-water sprays from the company's own label, natural soaps, top-notch eco candles, eco salt baths and house-blended herbal teas (try the Skin Tea to clarify skin and hair or Wild Meadow Tea if you have a spot of indigestion). Owner Paula Grainger tries hard to stock brands from small-scale producers based in the UK. Lemon Balm is also a lovely space in which to search for a unique and indulgent present; gift sets come in three sizes, priced from £15 to £48, and you can also create your own personalised gift box, from £10. The clinic offers massage, aromatherapy, acupuncture, reflexology, homeopathy and more from independent therapists, as well as Western herbal medicine from Grainger herself.

Nelsons
73 Duke Street, W1K 5BY (7629 3118, www.nelsonspharmacy.com). Bond Street tube.
Open 9am-6.30pm Mon-Fri; 10am-5.30pm Sat.
There's a cure for every ailment at this homeopathic pharmacy – which was the first of its kind when Ernst Louis Ambrecht opened it in 1860. In the 1930s, Dr Edward Bach began to sell his famous Bach Original Flower Remedies here. On other shelves you'll find pills and potions such as Menopause Care Tincture, Pills for Brain Fatigue and Tennis Elbow Bursitis and the Pure & Clear range for blemished skin. If you don't find what you're after, the friendly pharmacist will talk over symptoms and tailor-make a medicine for you using the vast 'potency bank' of more than 2,000 remedies. There's a peaceful clinic in the basement for massages, food-sensitivity testing, Alexander Technique lessons and homeopathy.

Nelsons

NEW DESIGNER FRAMES
EVERY SEASON

AUERBACH & STEELE

AUERBACH & STEELE OPTICIANS
129 KING'S ROAD, CHELSEA SW3 4PW
020 7349 0001

DESIGNER FRAMES • CONTACT LENSES
SUNGLASSES • OPEN 7 DAYS
WWW.AUERBACH-STEELE.COM

LINDBERG

Eyewear

Chains **Dolland & Aitchison** (which has now merged with Boots Opticians; 223 Regent Street, W1B 2EB, 7495 8209, www.danda.co.uk), **Optical Express** (65-72 The Strand, WC2N 5LR, 7436 5029, www.opticalexpress.com), **Specsavers** (Unit 6, 6-17 Tottenham Court Road, W1T 1BG, 7580 5115, www.specsavers.com) and **Vision Express** (263-265 Oxford Street, W1C 2DF, 7409 7880, www.visionexpress.com) also offer a wide range of frames, including budget-friendly options.

arckiv

Arch 67 Stables Market, NW1 8AH (07790 102204, www.arckiv.net). Camden Town or Chalk Farm tube.
Open 1-6pm Tue-Fri; 11am-6pm Sat, Sun.
Supplying frames and lenses to the theatre, TV and film industries, arckiv specialises in beautiful and unusual designs, antique and modern: find monocles and lorgnettes, flying and biking goggles, glam rock or space-age designs, as well as the usual suspects (Mikli, Ray-Ban, Persol) and a few high-end names associated with fashionable over-sized sunglasses (Pucci, Courrèges, Cardin). They also supply anti-reflection lenses (clean, single vision, bifocal and varifocal) from £15 (with an additional fee if you supply your own frames) and can add metallic and other coatings. So, if you're looking for a pair of frames to make you stand out from the crowd…

Cutler & Gross

16 Knightsbridge Green, SW1X 7QL (7581 2250, www.cutlerandgross.com). Knightsbridge tube.
Open 9.30am-7pm Mon-Sat; noon-5pm Sun.
Cool and quirky is the name of the game at this long-established Knightsbridge outlet, known for its innovative hand-built frames. A new collection is introduced twice a year, perhaps Warhol-inspired or the classic retro styling of the 'Belle du Jour' range. (The glasses supremo has even been handling Victoria Beckham's impressive eyewear collection.) C&G is renowned for its clever use of colour in its optical frames, while sunglasses run the gamut from leather-trimmed aviators to oversized tortoiseshell numbers. What characterises all of the frames is the high quality. The iconic Vintage eyewear range, meanwhile, draws rock and film stars to the fabulous sister shop at no.7, which has period gems dating back to the 1920s. Current bestsellers include 1960s Persols, '70s Porsche and '80s Cazals with prices from £200 to £3,000.
Branch (Cutler & Gross Vintage) 7 Knightsbridge Green, SW1X 7QL (7590 9995).

The Eye Company
Eyewear Specialists

www.eye-company.co.uk

159 Wardour Street,
London,
W1F 8WH

020 7434 0988

Be Amazed!

36 Beauchamp Place
London SW3 1NU
Tel: +44 207 581 6336
Fax: +44 207 584 5836
e-mail: info@36opticians.co.uk

Eye Company

159 Wardour Street, W1F 8WH (7434 0988, www.eye-company.co.uk). Oxford Circus or Tottenham Court Road tube. **Open** *10.30am-6.30pm Mon-Wed, Fri; 10.30am-7.30pm Thur; 11am-6pm Sat.*
Supplying the film and TV industry, Soho's Eye Company is a hip independent intent on challenging the mediocrity of the high-street chains. Its select range of mint-condition vintage frames (some dating back to the 18th century), its stylish own-brand frames and its selection of cherry-picked numbers from the likes of Cutler & Gross, Oliver Peoples and Rayban make you positively want to have to wear glasses – although the sunglasses provide plenty of excitement for those with 20/20 vision. If you have a favourite pair of frames that need a little TLC, Eye Company can also repair or copy your frames, or even design you a pair from scratch. Naturally the full optical treatment is also available, including eye tests, contact lens fitting and after care.

Eye Contacts

10 Chalk Farm Road, NW1 8AG (7482 1701, www.eyecontactscamden.co.uk). Camden Town or Chalk Farm tube. **Open** *10.30am-6pm Mon-Sat; 11am-6pm Sun.*
Tucked away in the lee of the Camden Lock railway bridge, this relaxed optician's has been tending to the optically challenged of NW1 since Camden's 1980s heyday. Spec-themed stained-glass windows provide a nice touch of colour to a stylish, pared-back bare-brick space housing a small but well-chosen frame selection. Orgreen, Alain Mikli and ic! Berlin are displayed alongside less familiar designers such as Belgium's Mix and Etnia from Spain. British designs include Cutler & Gross (*see p153*) and Booth & Bruce. Eye tests are reasonably priced and friendly staff are on hand to help with the difficult frame-choosing process.

Kirk Originals

29 Floral Street, WC2E 9DP (7240 5055, www.kirkoriginals.com). Covent Garden tube. **Open** *11am-7pm Mon-Sat; noon-5pm Sun.*
Set up by Jason Kirk after he found some glasses made by his great uncle over 90 years ago, this shop takes a witty approach to the art of specs (check out the fun website). Kirk's own-brand frames dominate, mixing simple old-school styling with bright colours. Ranges include a Heroes selection named after members of a fictional Kirk family tree, such as Sir Reginald Kirk (sported by David Mcalmont) and the fabulous Sculpture range (acetate and acrylic, six new shapes, nine new colourways). The Victor Eclipse and Sunshine sunglasses collections are equally covetable, and the coffee's not bad either.

Mallon & Taub

35D Marylebone High Street, W1U 4QB (7935 8200, www.mallonandtaub.com). Baker Street or Regent's Park tube. **Open** *10am-6.30pm Mon-Wed, Fri, Sat; 10am-7pm Thur; 11am-5pm Sun.*
The ethos behind Mallon & Taub is to 'dress the eyes and have fun doing so', and Joan Mallon and Shanah Taub have made every effort to deliver. The philosophy seems to be echoed in the boutique's stylish interior: slate floors, weekly fresh flowers, and friendly and knowledgeable staff to talk customers through eye-care issues as well as new developments – new high-tech varifocals, perhaps, or glasses geared for high-energy sport. Specs on offer include all the main brands including Oliver Peoples, Alain Mikli and Cutler & Gross (*see p153*) as well as Booth & Bruce, Maui Jim, Fred and Robert Marc. There's also a nice range of sunglasses.

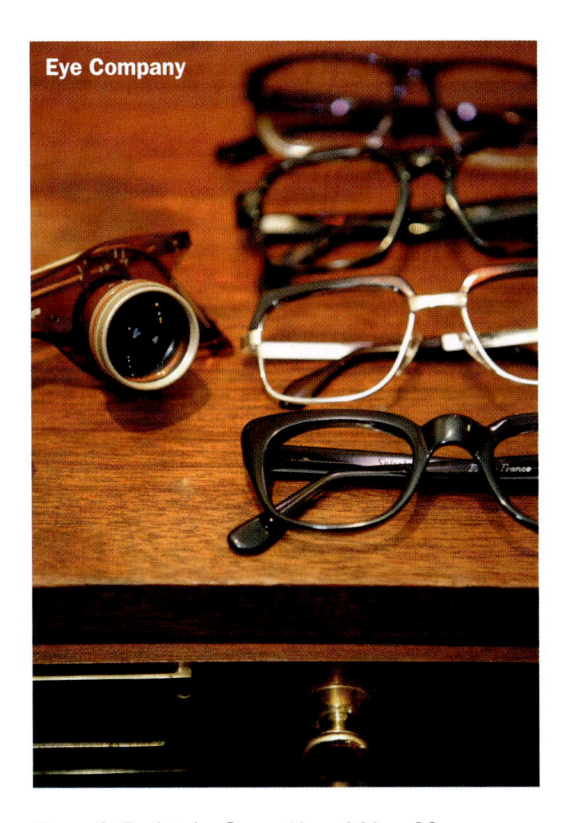

Michel Guillon

35 Duke of York Square, SW3 4LY (7730 2142, www.michelguillon.com). Sloane Square tube. **Open** *10am-7pm Mon-Thur, Sat; 9.30am-7.30pm Fri.*
The USP here is the quality of eye care: Michel Guillon provides a comprehensive service that includes extra eye checks and nutritional advice. Drawing on 25 years of scientific research, Guillon is an expert in contact lens research, providing lenses for people normally unable to wear them. Sporty types too can benefit from the shop's dynamic vision testing, designed to improve visual reactions. The Ab Rogers-designed interior is a hint at the high-tech service available here: striking

blue cabinets house a changing range of designer frames that includes Japanese Yellows Plus and elegant Gold & Wood (spec providers to the stars), as well as Guillon's own brand.

Opera Opera
98 Long Acre, WC2E 9NR (7836 9246, www.operaopera.net). Covent Garden tube. **Open** 10am-6pm Mon-Sat.
Dispensing for three decades from its corner site near the Royal Opera, this family-run business exudes an old-fashioned sense of pride in optical craftsmanship, and even has its own factory turning out the shop's Harpers range. Control of production not only allows touches like old-fashioned hinges, but also means the shop is geared for bespoke frames – whether to replicate some treasured old specs or copy something you've seen perched on a famous nose (John Lennon, Johnny Depp, Buddy Holly). The shops stocks frames based on designs from the '30s through to the '80s; its range of rare vintage and retro sunglasses is unbeatable, if you have the cash to splash.

Spex in the City
1 Shorts Gardens, WC2H 9AT (7240 0243, www.spexinthecity.com). Covent Garden or Leicester Square tube. **Open** 11am-6.30pm Mon-Fri; 11am-6pm Sat; 1-5pm Sun.
This small and friendly Seven Dials outlet, run by Gillian Caplan, offers sight tests, lens fitting, fabulous frames and, perhaps most importantly, really good style advice. Optician Caplan prides herself on taking as much time as necessary to help you into the right frames, taking into account face and eye shape, even hairstyle. A carefully chosen range includes frames by European designers Freudenhaus and Alain Mikli, Australian Roger Henley plus Brits Booth & Bruce, John Richmond and Oliver Goldsmith. Also check out Caplan's expanding line of own-brand frames as well as the ultra cool sunnies by the likes of Black Flys, Versace and Diesel.

36 Opticians
36 Beauchamp Place, SW3 1NU (7581 6336, www.36opticians.co.uk). Knightsbridge or South Kensington tube. **Open** 10am-6pm Mon-Sat.
There's an eclectic range of over 4,000 frames at this appealing Knightsbridge store run by opticians Ragini Patel and Sveta Khambhaita. The enormous range stretches from the simple (with super-low starting prices to match) to the exclusive limited-edition handmade beauties by the likes of US designer Barton Perreira (as seen in one of the coolest ad campaigns featuring Giovanni Ribisi) along with a host of other fabulously famous-name frames for the four-eyed. A growing range of cool accessories includes stylish lorgnettes (the opera-style glasses with a handle on one side) and spectacle loops made of stone.

Best for...

Timeless models
36 Opticians (*see right*);
Cutler & Gross (*see p153*).

Vintage sunglasses
Eye Company (*see p155*);
Opera Opera (*see right*).

Eye care
Eye Contacts (*see p155*);
Mallon & Taub (*see p155*);
Michael Guillon (*see p155*);
Spex in the City (*see right*).

Directional styles
archiv (*see p153*);
Cutler & Gross (*see p153*).

Ecentric frames
Kirk Originals (*see p155*);
Opera Opera (*see right*).

Home

Furniture & Homewares	**159**
Vintage Furniture & Homewares	**175**
Gardens & Flowers	**183**

tribe
CONTEMPORARY RUGS

ISLINGTON
52 CROSS STREET LONDON N1
T : 020 7226 5544

HAMPSTEAD
92 HEATH STREET LONDON NW3
T : 020 7433 3676

www.tribe-london.com

Home

British furniture manufacturing is on the rise, and London now rivals Milan as the centre of cutting-edge design. Rather than seeking to reproduce bland room sets in soulless showrooms and glossy magazines, more people are looking for unique pieces, with the division between design and art becoming increasingly blurred at shops such as **SCP** (*see p164*). Design classics never go out of style, however, and London's stylish furniture shops – many of which are clustered around Islington and Clerkenwell, as well as Brompton Road – excel in this area.

Individually made objects once only found in crafts outlets or bought direct from makers are now sold in the large interiors stores; but if you're still one for browsing the boutique independents, you're in for a treat – London's small home accessories shops are better than ever before. East London's **Cheshire Street**, **Columbia Road** and **Redchurch Street** host a fair number of them – don't miss **Caravan** (*see p167*), **Labour & Wait** (*see p168*), **Shelf** (*see p45*) and **Treacle** (*see p171*).

London is also a fantastic place to hunt for antiques, although the landscape has shifted in recent years. Camden Passage, once lined with creaky dealers, has yielded to new (albeit lovely) independent shops, selling everything from chocolate to jewellery – although some of the old guard remain, especially in idiosyncratic **Pierrepoint Arcade** (*see p100*). Church Street in Marylebone, home of the excellent **Alfie's Antique Market** (*see p100*), has blossomed into antiques row. Meanwhile, shops selling more affordable 20th-century furniture are flourishing, with some excellent neighbourhood shops, such as the **Peanut Vendor** (*see p182*) and **Fandango** (*see p181*).

Note that many of the shops listed in the **Concept Stores & Lifestyle Boutiques** chapter (*see pp35-45*) have a good range of furniture and items for the home, while **Orla Kiely** (*see p92*) and **Paul Smith** (*see p89*) also have increasingly well-established homewares lines.

Furniture & Homewares

Contemporary & design classics

Aram
110 Drury Lane, WC2B 5SG (7557 7557, www.aram.co.uk). Covent Garden or Holborn tube.
Open *10am-6pm Mon-Wed, Fri, Sat; 10am-7pm Thur.*

Back in the 1960s, design champion Zeev Aram introduced the likes of Alvar Aalto, Marcel Breuer, Le Corbusier and Arne Jacobsen to UK homes through his long-gone King's Road store. This impressive five-storey space replaced it, stocking furniture, lighting, textiles and other home accessories. Alongside the classics, Aram also stocks contemporary works by both established designers – Ronan and Erwan Bouroullec, Hella Jongerius and Massimo Morozzi – and emerging ones. Lighting

Aram. See p159.

comes from top manufacturers such as Artemide and Flos, furniture from brands like Herman Miller and Hitch Mylius. Head to the basement for funky accessories and tableware. Aram is the biggest stockist of Interlübke's storage systems, and the only UK stockist of authorised Eileen Grey designs. It also often stocks special editions.

Aria [HOT 50]

Barnsbury Hall, Barnsbury Street, N1 1PN (7704 1999, www.ariashop.co.uk). Angel tube or Highbury & Islington tube/rail. **Open** 10am-6.30pm Mon-Sat; noon-6pm Sun.

Aria is located in an atmospheric space in Islington's Barnsbury Hall. Many of the building's original features have been restored and they now contrast beautifully with the über-modern lines of contemporary furniture and homewares. High-quality designers' pieces are here, as are more unusual pieces like Fornasetti's black and white hand-painted wall plates (£135) and the Bourgie table light by Ferruccio Laviani (£199). This mix, teamed with a very nice in-store café, makes Aria a pleasure to visit. Chairs are a speciality, with Starck and Patrick Jouin well represented. Smaller stand-outs include a Fisheye Kompact camera (£49.95) and pretty Taika bowl (£16.50) that would make a great gift, especially if it had some of Aria's very tempting selection of toiletries (Cowshed, Savon de Marseilles) nestled inside it.

Atelier Abigail Ahern

137 Upper Street, N1 1QP (7354 8181, www.atelierabigailahern.com). Angel tube or Highbury & Islington tube/rail. **Open** 10am-6pm Mon-Sat; noon-5pm Sun.

This tiny interiors shop may not have a huge range, but what it lacks in quantity is more than made up for in quality. The selection is both inventive and original, with much of it from emerging international designers. A beautiful Kathy Dalwood concrete cast, part of a collection that focuses on historical characters, reinterprets 18th-century haute porcelain but retains mould lines from the casting process, indicating contemporary concerns about texture (from £320). British graduate Andrew Oliver is similarly playful, but with very different results; his lighting range (from £700) is a delightful addition to his drunken table range, unique one-off furniture pieces inspired by practical experimentation with salvaged furniture. Textiles are particularly strong; as well as some striking merino wool ottomans (£755), there are Impressionist paintings transposed on to linen by Argentinian-born artist Haby Bonomo (from £65). Colour ranges are muted but striking, summing up a store that's a delightful departure from the sparse lines of many design stores.

Furniture & Homewares

B&B Italia
250 Brompton Road, SW3 2AS (7591 8111, www.bebitalia.com). South Kensington tube.
Open 10am-6pm Mon-Sat; noon-5pm Sun.
Few London interiors stores exhibit the pzazz of B&B Italia; if you've ever fancied yourself as a catwalk model, the long runway that guides you into the cavernous showroom offers plenty of opportunity to try out a few moves. B&B's sleek furniture is displayed in classic room-sets that are bigger than most London flats. Over its 40 years, the Italian brand has maintained a strong interest in working with inventive designers – 2008 saw new versions of Patricia Urquiola's Back and Lazy 100 chairs, and a raft of additions to Antonio Citterio's Maxalto range, including a new thermo-treated ash wood variant to the Apta collection of storage units, tables and bookcases. Alongside these traditionally proportioned pieces are more sculptural forms – Jean-Marie Massaud's Terminal 1 Daybed, for example, is a great example of a contemporary chaise longue.

Conran Shop
Michelin House, 81 Fulham Road, SW3 6RD (7589 7401, www.conran.co.uk). South Kensington tube. **Open** 10am-6pm Mon, Tue, Fri; 10am-7pm Wed, Thur; 10am-6.30pm Sat; noon-6pm Sun.
While Terence Conran pioneered the idea of modernism in Britain back in the 1960s, he's always had an impressively sharp eye for the decorative too, and nowhere is this more evident than at the Fulham Road flagship. The furniture here ranges from design classics, such as the Eames Dar chair, to collaborations with established designers, such as the colourful Oswald sofa with Squint (*see p164*), to more prosaic but well-designed armchairs, tables, storage units and beds. Much stock is exclusive and Conran mixes them in among classics to create inspirational room settings on the ground floor. The basement is home to a vast array of lighting (with some innovative designs), tableware and accessories and a great range of inventive kids' things.
Branch 55 Marylebone High Street, W1U 5HS (7723 2223).

Designers Guild
267-271 (store) & 275-277 (showroom) King's Road, SW3 5EN (7351 5775, www.designersguild.com). Sloane Square tube then 11, 19, 22 bus. **Open** *Store* 10am-6pm Mon-Sat; noon-5pm Sun. *Showroom* 10am-6pm Mon-Sat.
Interior designer Tricia Guild launched this shop in 1970 when it quickly became the best of its type, with colourful fabrics and wallpapers offering modern takes on traditional patterns. The store now also has a great selection of homewares, including a range of 98 paint colours selected to complement the fabrics, wallpapers, home furnishings, tableware, rugs, stationery and all the

Atelier Abigail Ahern. *See p160.*

other design-led accessories. It also stocks a great range of contemporary and vintage furniture, which you can choose to cover with fabrics from the vast Designers Guild range or select from other brands such as Jasper Conran and William Yeoward, even combining different fabrics on the same piece. Cushions go from around £50, while bedlinen starts at £60 for a single duvet set.

Eco
213 Chiswick High Road, W4 2DW (8995 7611, www.eco-age.com). Turnham Green tube.
Open 10am-6pm Tue-Sat; 11am-4pm Sun.
Founded by Nicola Giuggioli, with help from his sister Livia and her actor hubbie Colin Firth, Chiswick's green-minded lifestyle shop was opened to prove that ecologically sound items can also look fantastic. It's a hotspot for all things green; from sustainably sourced designer homewares, ecological paints by earthBorn, wallpaper by the likes of Graham & Brown. There are plenty of surprises here – who'd have thought a blanket or a towel could be made from bamboo? But if you've only a few quid to spare, pencils made from recycled CD cases are just £2 and Maison Belle cleaning fluid starts at £3.95. The basement design consultancy advises amateur eco warriors.

Geoffrey Drayton
85 Hampstead Road, NW1 2PL (7387 5840, www.geoffreydrayton.com). Warren Street tube.
Open 10am-6pm Mon-Sat.
Geoffrey Drayton has been pioneering modern furniture, lighting and homewares in London for almost five decades. The shop's success (it has recently expanded into the shop next door) is partly down to the knowledgeable staff and partly to a terrific range of high-end, made-to-order classic furniture from the world's best brands and designers. B&B Italia, Cassina, Interlübke, Kartell, Knoll, Vitra and Ycami are all stocked, along with smaller makers like E15 and Rexite. Classics stocked include Ludwig Mies van der Rohe's Barcelona chair and Harry Bertoia's Diamond chair (both manufactured by Knoll), and there's a good range of beds and stylish storage furniture. Limited editions crop up regularly.

Green & Fay
137-139 Essex Road, N1 1QP (7704 0455, www.greenandfay.net). Essex Road rail.
Open 10am-6pm Tue-Sat; 11am-4pm Sun.
With over 30 years of experience in the furniture sector, Green & Fay offers design staples, innovation (supporting British design as well as showcasing leading international names) and a gallery-style space within which to be inspired by it all; find carefully selected artworks, luxurious bedlinen, stylish lamps and sofas, tableware and chairs. The capsule collection of original mid 20th-century furniture is particularly covetable. Buyers are constantly looking out for ways of supporting eco-producers using recyclable and sustainable materials as well as promoting creative community-led initiatives from around the world; for instance, with every pair of shoes purchased, Toms will give a new pair of shoes to a child in need. Green & Fay is also about to introduce a range of well-designed kitchen furniture to its Islington store.

Heal's
196 Tottenham Court Road, W1T 7LQ (7636 1666, www.heals.co.uk). Goodge Street tube. **Open** 10am-6pm Mon-Wed; 10am-8pm Thur; 10am-6.30pm Fri; 9.30am-6.30pm Sat; noon-6pm Sun.
Heal's may be the grand old dame of interiors stores, but its happy combination of excellent sourcing, helpful staff and a layout that's constantly being reinvented means it manages to stay relevant. Heal's commitment to sourcing new designers is impressive, while established names such as Orla Kiely, Clarissa Hulse, LSA and the Designers Guild are also well represented among the mirrors, rugs, bedlinen, clocks, cushions, art and photography available. The store's ground floor is the most fun for casual browsers, offering a cornucopia of table- and kitchenware, toiletries and gift items, plus a terrific lighting department boasting such delights as Tom Dixon's Beat pendant shades range. First and second floors house the bulk of the furniture, and for mid-century modernist fans, there's a great selection of vintage Danish furniture.
Branches 234 King's Road, SW3 5UA (7349 8411); 49-51 Eden Street, KT1 1BW (8614 5900).

Lifestyle Bazaar
11a Kingsland Road, E2 8AA (7739 9427, www.lifestylebazaar.com). Old Street or Liverpool Street tube/rail. **Open** 11am-7pm Mon-Sat; noon-5pm Sun.
Lifestyle Bazaar, the creation of London-based design team Laurent Nurisso and Christopher Curtis, was originally based in central London's Newburgh Street, before moving to more design-centred Shoreditch. The shop specialises in a selection of fun and stylish homeware items, such as antler wall hooks and Hamlet skull tea-light holder, which are perched on or around larger pieces such as storage systems, lighting and retro-contemporary chairs. There are lots of bright and original ideas, with products sourced from around the world. There's a nice selection by big-name designers too, including Starck and Marcel Wanders, but this is definitely a place to discover new names and, with any luck, pick up future design classics.

Mint
2 North Terrace, SW3 2BA (7225 2228, www.mintshop.co.uk). South Kensington tube.
Open 10.30am-6.30pm Mon-Wed, Fri, Sat; 10.30am-7.30pm Thur.

Mint feels like a Dalí painting come to life, with its hand-picked and specially commissioned furniture, glassware, textiles and ceramics arranged like an avant-garde curiosity shop. Owner Lina Kanafani fills her two-level space with international designs, and form and colour play a large part in her selections. Much of Mint's stock could be considered as art with a capital 'a', a fact reflected in the prices. Louise Hindsgavl's porcelain stunning one-off piece Everyday Scenario, Surgery Suggestion (£1,400), would be hard to define as anything other than sculpture, and Ezgi Turksoy's limited edition sterling silver spoons (from £550) are hardly everyday items, but the vintage pieces add to the sense of the unique, and there are plenty of smaller, more affordable items too; Katie Lilly's hand-decorated plates are adorable (£60).

SCP

135-139 Curtain Road, EC2A 3BX (7739 1869, www.scp.co.uk). Old Street tube/rail or Shoreditch High Street rail. **Open** 9.30am-6pm Mon-Sat; 11am-5pm Sun.

SCP attempts to showcase the very best of contemporary furniture, lighting and homewares. Overseeing it is Sheridan Coakley, who sources globally and stocks a clutch of respected designers – among them Robin Day, Terence Woodgate, Matthew Hilton, Konstantin Grcic, Donna Wilson and Michael Marriott. Furniture and storage solutions are all bold lines and slick minimalism, exemplified by Kay + Stemmer's Edith and Agnes shelving and Jasper Morrison's global lights. Accessories broaden out to take in everything from the highly decorative to the fun and quirky, such as Reiko Kaneko's Egg soldier cup, which has four sword-wielding soldiers attacking the egg. SCP also retails the George Nelson Bubble lights by Modernica. Produced by Howard Miller until 1979, these shades are part of the permanent collection of the Museum of Modern Art in New York – you can own one for £305.
Branch 87-93 Westbourne Grove, W2 4UL (7229 3612).

Skandium

247 Brompton Road, SW3 2EP (7584 2066, www.skandium.com). South Kensington tube.
Open 10am-6.30pm Mon-Wed, Fri, Sat; 10am-7pm Thur; 11am-5pm Sun.

With two shops in London – a two-storey space in Marylebone and this 700sq m flagship – Skandium fans are spoilt for choice. Most people know the store for its gorgeous ranges of home- and tableware, but there's also classic furniture from manufacturers like Asplund, Artek, Fritz Hansen, Swedese and Knoll and even broader European wares from the likes of German design house Vitra and big names Cappellini and Cassina. Lighting comes courtesy of top names like Louis Poulsen, Secto and Le Klint. What makes Skandium special, however, is its commitment to excellence in contemporary design; Arne Jacobsen's 1969 Vola mixer tap in 18 colours is stocked, as are vacuum cleaners, bird tables, hooks, phones, plus a range of coffee-table books on Scandinavian design, to ensure attention to detail across the home. Skandium has a concession in Selfridges.
Branch 86 Marylebone High Street, W1U 4Q (7935 2077).

Squint

178 Shoreditch High Street, E1 6HU (7739 9275, www.squintlimited.com). Liverpool Street or Old Street tube/rail. **Open** 10am-6pm Mon-Fri; by appointment Sat; 1-5pm Sun. **No credit cards**.

Squint's products – easily recognisable by the colourful and distinctive patchwork designs – are now stocked in Harrods, Liberty, the Conran Shop (*see p161*) and the Designers Guild (*see p161*), but this is its only stand-alone shop and showroom, where you can see a selection of its bespoke and the bestselling 'ready to go' Chesterfield sofas (from £4,500), iconic Egg chairs and other upholstered furniture. The beautiful coverings – made up of both contemporary and vintage textiles – cover the items completely, including chair legs and even entire chests of drawers, and all of the pieces are handmade in England. In addition to furniture, a small range of mirrors and lighting products are sold in the stylish space. The Shoreditch Collection launched in May 2010 features a range of contemporary shapes inspired by designs from the '50s and '60s.

Tobias & the Angel

68 White Hart Lane, SW13 0PZ (8878 8902, www.tobiasandtheangel.com). Hammersmith tube then 209 bus or Barnes Bridge rail. **Open** 10am-6pm Mon-Sat.

This lovely shop has the kind of interior many of us strive to create at home: careful, but unfussy, cosy yet airy. The furniture, a sleeker Scandinavian take on English country, is all handmade to measure in its workshop in Surrey. Constructed in wood (including solid pine and oak), the range includes tables, chairs, drawer units, chicken-wire linen cupboards, desks and benches – painted in a choice of colours and priced per square foot. The freestanding furniture, such as the superb housekeeper's cupboard, provides a flexible alternative to a fitted kitchen. Chairs and sofas are covered in antique and vintage cloth, which is also for sale in lengths, as is a lovely hand-block-printed cloth. The accessories are particularly attractive, from pretty cushions to delightful cat doorstops. The place also has a good selection of lamps, shades, bags, aprons and table linen. Come Christmas, it's the place to head to for unusual decorations for the tree.

Twentytwentyone HOT 50

274 Upper Street, N1 2UA (7288 1996, www.twentytwentyone.com). Angel tube or Highbury & Islington tube/rail. **Open** 10am-6pm Mon-Sat; 11am-5pm Sun.

Furniture & Homewares

Shop talk
Richard Ward, owner of Wawa

Tell us about the shop
'The core of the business is sofas and seating, which I design and we manufacture. This area of east London has historically been full of furniture-makers, and this shop used to be a workshop. As the other workshops have been sold and turned into loft conversions, we turned from a workshop into a shop and showroom. We have been Wawa for ten years now. Everything is made to order and we have a comprehensive range of fabrics that people keep complimenting and coming back for. We have extended our range to lighting, mirrors and bags, which are all made in England.'

Who shops here?
'We get quite a broad range; we just sent one sofa to Copenhagen and another to Belgium! We're very lucky because, more by accident than design, we are adjacent to Columbia Road flower market (see p50 and p173 **Streetwise**), so we get a huge range of diverse shoppers, locals and the more widely scattered.'

What else do you do?
'I am designer, proprietor and tea maker all in one. I used to make the sofas too but now we have a workshop in Upminster where that happens. But this is a full-time job!'

Have you noticed changes in the London shopping scene over the past few years?
'We've stuck around long enough to gather momentum and not be overly affected by the recession. I don't think it's harder to run a small business now than it used to be. People are still keen to support independent shops and are always pleased to know things are made locally, which is very rewarding. What we do is different because it's a bespoke service. It's like having a suit made; we make the sofa to fit their requirements, making it bigger or smaller, fatter or thinner to suit them. And we use the fabrics of their choice, from an economical £40 per metre to silks at £400 per metre.'

What is the most enjoyable aspect of owning a shop?
'It has to be the customers and the fact that they come back or write to us and tell us that they're recommending us to their friends. Knowing that our designs are being used and cherished and that people are delighted with the finished product. We're lucky because our main trading day is Sunday, so people are always ready to chat and relax and come in with their children. We're fortunate to have such lovely customers.'

What are your favourite shops in London?
'I love the Ginger Pig butchers (see p244) in Victoria Park; they're very knowledgeable and helpful and the merchandise is exceptional. I shop for clothes at the independents on Exmouth Market.'

What do you envisage for your business for the future?
'I'd like it to carry on in the same sort of form. The thing I like is being in touch with the public, so it's always going to be important for that to continue. And I love being very much a part of it. We're thinking about a larger premises locally, but there are a lot of things to consider.'

▶ For **Wawa**, see p167.

Twentytwentyone. See p164.

Twentytwentyone furniture and homewares shop has long been held in high esteem by *Time Out* for its mix of vintage originals, reissued classics and contemporary designs. Big-name brands such as Arper, Artek, Cappellini, DePadova, Flos, Swedese and Vitra are stocked, but founders Simon Alderson and Tony Cunningham are also keen to foster new talent; the Ten/twentytwentyone range, for instance, features ten designs created by ten leading British designers. Stock is divided between two locations; the River Street showroom houses most of the larger items, while the Upper Street outpost – brilliant for home accessories and gifts – has been expanded and now includes a basement showroom to display lighting, as well as a few larger items.
Branch 18C River Street, EC1R 1XN (7837 1900).

Unto This Last
230 Brick Lane, E2 7EB (7613 0882, www.unto thislast.co.uk). Shoreditch High Street rail. **Open** 10am-6pm daily.
Nestled snugly in an old East End workshop that exudes Dickensian quaintness, this small furniture maker produces a distinctive range of birch plywood and laminate pieces, transforming raw materials into decidedly modern furniture. Named after the 1862 John Ruskin book advocating the principles of local craftsmanship, Unto This Last does exactly that – combining simple design with sophisticated computer software to produce well-priced cabinets, bookcases, chairs and beds, plus a small range of accessories like tealight holders, fruit bowls and placemats. The finished products have a beautifully fluid, organic appearance, and are bold enough to act as statement pieces. We particularly liked the Square shelves (from £180) that can be free-standing or wall-mounted. Look out too for the undulating Wavy Bench (£280) and the 4ft Standing lamp (£90).
Branch Arch 72, Queens Circus, SW8 4NE (7720 6558).

Wawa
3 Ezra Street, E2 7RH (7729 6768, www.wawa. co.uk). Hoxton or Shoreditch High Street rail.
Open by appointment Mon-Fri; 10am-2.30pm Sun.
Wawa sells bright and bold made-to-order sofas designed and handmade by Richard Ward, whose love of curves, lines and colour is obvious in his work (think contemporary takes on old classics). Each sofa is unique and upholstered with great attention to detail using hand-tied springs. Prices start at around £680 for an armchair, rising to around £2,000 for a chaise longue; choose your fabric from the large collection that takes in ranges by the Designers Guild, Andrew Martin and Lelieve, while Lucy Wassell, who works in the same studio, creates textiles to commission. The shop also stocks a gorgeous selection of plates and trays, as well as mirrors, lamps and lampshades, tableware and clocks. Head to the showroom on a Sunday to have a mooch around the flower market afterwards. *See also p165* **Shop talk**.

Accessories & specialists

Caravan HOT 50
3 Redchurch Street, EC2 7DJ (7033 3532, www.caravanstyle.com). Liverpool Street tube.
Open 11am-6.30pm Tue-Fri; 1-5pm Sat-Sun.
Stylist and author Emily Chalmers's Redchurch Street boutique is a treasure trove of cool interiors ideas, vintage finds and unusual decorative pieces. Think glossy French industrial lamps, battered leather suitcases, stunning vintage teapots, tiny cameo brooches, big black ornamental crows, woollen knitted dog toys, light-reactive singing birds and gold angel wings for decorating candles. From its whitewashed walls to its hotchpotch display cabinets, Caravan showcases its owner's magpie tendencies and eye for detail. A browsing ground for interior designers, gift-hunters, party planners and vintage aficionados, Caravan is bursting with ideas and fantastically offbeat takes on style and design (concrete bulb-shaped pendant lights at £49, for example). Why bother with pricey interior designers and style tomes when all the benefits of a stylist's keen eye are here for the taking?

Casa Mexico
1 Winkley Street, E2 6PY (7739 9349, www.casamexico.co.uk). Bethnal Green tube/rail or Cambridge Heath rail. **Open** 10am-6pm daily.
For all things Mexican, this Bethnal Green store is a must-visit: the product list covers the usual kitchenware – from little *cazuelas* (bowls) to *chimineas* (wood-burning stoves) – lamps, rugs and blankets, and 'ranch-style' furniture (made from seasoned pine) but also features Mexican folk art, reproduction Mayan and Aztec terracotta masks and funerary urns, sisal and straw bags and baskets, ponchos, pots and planters for the garden and a range of handmade tiles. Of course, no Mexican outpost would be complete without a full range of Day of the Dead products, and Casa Mexico doesn't disappoint: skull pennants, skull candle-holders, Loteria de Luna playing cards, and that essential articulated clay skeleton.

Celia Birtwell
71 Westbourne Park Road, W2 5QH (7221 0877, www.celiabirtwell.com). Royal Oak or Westbourne Park tube. **Open** 10am-1pm, 2-5.30pm Mon-Fri; by appointment 10am-1pm, 2-5pm Sat.
The work of this celebrated textile designer has long been in vogue. Her latest foray into bright, breezy colourful interiors, Pop Story, keeps her in the trendy bracket, while the delightful classic lines Beasties, Jacobean and Kew are hardy perennials. This lovely little shop is mainly about the textile collection, launched in partnership with her former husband, fashion designer Ossie Clarke, in the 1960s, and which later became a witty range of furnishing fabrics and wallpapers, but you will also find a lovely range of gifts, watering cans,

gardening tools, notebooks, wrapping paper and cards. Classic collection prints cost from £45/m, and voiles, silk cushions (£75 each) and upholstered chairs are also available, as is a bespoke upholstery service.

Contemporary Applied Arts
2 Percy Street, W1T 1DD (7436 2344, www.caa. org.uk). Goodge Street or Tottenham Court Road tube. **Open** 10am-6pm Mon-Sat.

The CAA is consistently inventive with its exhibitions of its 300-plus makers. The applied arts here embrace the functional in the form of unique pieces of jewellery, textiles and tableware as well as ceramics, glass, metal, paper, silver and wood, but there are also purely decorative pieces such as wall-hangings made of recycled ceramic and mosaic shards. The ground-floor gallery space houses solo or themed exhibitions, while the large basement shop area has pieces for all pockets, from both established members and newcomers. If you can't find exactly what you're looking for, CAA will probably be able to direct you to a maker who undertakes commissions with whom you can discuss your specific requirements.

Divertimenti
227-229 Brompton Road, SW3 2EP (7581 8065, www.divertimenti.co.uk). Knightsbridge or South Kensington tube. **Open** 9.30am-6pm Mon, Tue, Thur, Fri; 9.30am-7pm Wed; 10am-6pm Sat; noon-5.30pm Sun.

Cooks will salivate in this fantastic store. If you need something to blanch, zest, grate, glaze or dust, then you're almost guaranteed to find it here. There's a good range of top-quality kitchen classics like the Waring Juice Extractor and the Kitchen Aid Artisan, and a dazzling array of knives; professional sets in a fabric roll by Wusthof are perfect for any wannabe Gordons. Attractive chunky earthenware is another speciality – the Mediterranean colours of the Poterie Provençal give an instant hit of sunshine. Venture downstairs for staggeringly pricey cookers by La Cornue, plus copper pans, enormous mortar and pestles, super-thick wooden chopping boards and old-fashioned ice-cream scoops. The baking section is exhaustive. If you don't think you merit fancy cooking tools yet, then enlist in its cookery school to hone your skills.

Branch 33-34 Marylebone High Street, W1U 4PT (7935 0689).

Ella Doran Design
46 Cheshire Street, E2 6EH (7613 0782, www.elladoran.co.uk). Shoreditch High Street rail. **Open** by appointment Mon-Wed; 11am-6pm Thur, Fri; noon-6pm Sat, Sun.

Ella Doran's striking placemats, coasters, trays and mugs feature a colourful range of photos – from the iconic Routemaster bus bells and American diner booths to exotic vintage plates and lots of flora and fauna. The prints appear on bigger things too though, among them the covetable duck down cushions, tote bags, wallpaper and even made-to-measure blinds (from £200), so that you can have prints of a brick wall or a forest clearing covering your windows. A collaboration with Fulton has led to a particularly appealing range of umbrellas – the Smartie Love and Sunlight Through Leaves models are sure to brighten up a rainy day – while new ranges Sweetie Love (cake tins, china mugs, aprons and tea towels) and Geo Play (cushions) are also worth checking out.

Labour & Wait
18 Cheshire Street, E2 6EH (7729 6253, www.labourandwait.co.uk). Shoreditch High Street rail. **Open** 11am-5pm Wed, Fri; 1-5pm Sat; 10am-5pm Sun.

This retro-stylish store sells the sort of things everybody would have had in their kitchen or pantry 60 years ago: functional domestic goods that have a timeless style. Spend any time here and you'll be filled with the joys of spring cleaning. Who'd have guessed that a scrubbing brush (made of wood and Tampico fibre) could be so appealing? For the desk proud, there's a pig and goat hair bristle computer brush, while for the kitchen there are some great simple classics like a steel-wall mounted bottle opener, enamel jugs and pans in retro pastels and Sori Yanagi's steel kettle. You can garden beautifully with ash-handled trowels, pale suede gauntlets and a dibber and label set. Our favourite, though, is the chubby flowerpot brush. There is a small range of classic vintage clothing (work jackets, aprons) and some great old-fashioned gifts for children, such as a pinhole camera kit and vintage-style satchels, plus a lovely range of notebooks. Hard to leave empty handed.

Limelight Movie Art
313 King's Road, SW3 5EP (7751 5584, www. limelightmovieart.com). Sloane Square or South Kensington tube. **Open** 11.30am-6pm Mon-Sat; 1-5pm Sun.

Limelight Movie Art sells original movie artwork from all over the world. The clientele includes collectors looking for the work of a particular graphic artist, such as Saul Bass or Ercole Brini, as well as film buffs or fans hunting down images of their favourite star. Buying a piece of movie artwork can prove a wise investment, as it's a product that never seems to go out of fashion. Foreign posters can be less expensive – *Certains l'aiment chaud* (rather than *Some Like It Hot*) can be bought for £950. All the posters, lobby cards and inserts on sale are in excellent condition.

Rug Company
124 Holland Park Avenue, W11 4UE (7229 5148, www.therugcompany.info). Holland Park tube. **Open** 10am-6pm Mon-Sat; 11am-5pm Sun.

The designer collection here reads more like a fantasy wardrobe than a selection of rugs, with collaborations

Furniture & Homewares

Celia Birtwell. *See p167.*

Ella Doran Design. *See p168.*

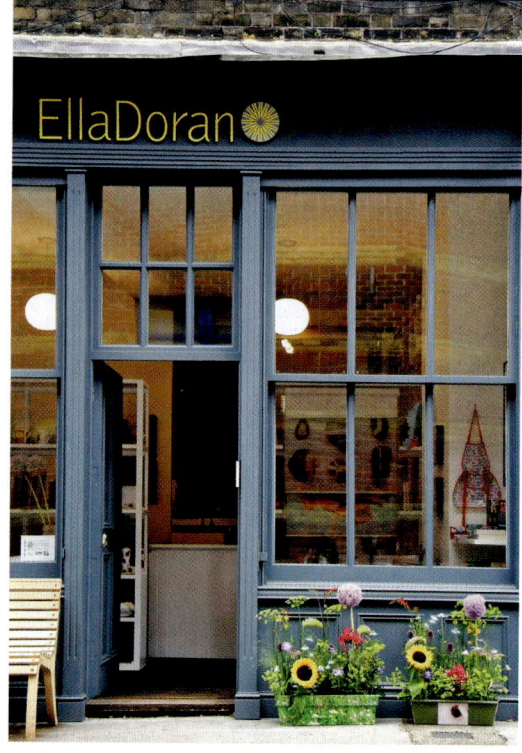

from Vivienne Westwood, Diane von Furstenberg, Paul Smith and Matthew Williamson among others. Founded in 1997 by Christopher and Suzanne Sharp, the Rug Company is dedicated to traditional methods of rug-making; the hand-knotting is done by weavers in Kathmandu, using hand-spun wool from Tibet and northern India. It also sells antique rugs, sourced from around the globe. Bespoke commissions are undertaken.

Ryantown
126 Columbia Road, E2 7RG (7613 1510, www.misterrob.co.uk). Hoxton or Shoreditch High Street rail. **Open** noon-5pm Sat; 9am-4.30pm Sun. Printmaker Rob Ryan opened this lovely gallery/shop in summer 2008. Tiles, printed tissue paper, screen-prints, paper cut-outs, cards, wooden keys, limited-edition prints, vases, Easter egg cups, even skirts and T-shirts, all bear his distinctive, fun graphics and words – with phrases such as 'I thought you didn't like me' or 'The stars shine all day as well' printed on many of the covetable items. Collaborations have seen his work appear on skateboards, necklaces and even Paul Smith pumps. Aside from his shop work, Rob has also recently customised a Lomo 'Diana' camera, relocated his entire workshop to Somerset House for two weeks, and auctioned his work for the Marine Conservation Society; details of his latest exploits can be found on his blog http://rob-ryan.blogspot.com.

Treacle
110-112 Columbia Road, E2 7RG (7729 0538, www.treacleworld.com). Hoxton or Shoreditch High Street rail. **Open** noon-5pm Sat; 9am-3pm Sun. Treacle started off as a cake shop, quickly expanding to cater for those looking to uphold the traditions of the great British teatime by selling a range of retro paraphernalia, such as cake stands, tea pots and baking equipment (including Kitchen Aid mixers and blenders and a stylish selection of tea towels and hand-knitted tea cosies). There's an impressive stock of original china tea sets from the British post-war era (with brands such as Midwinter and Meakin often featuring), mixed alongside some innovative contemporary brands, such as Yoyo Ceramics and Donna Wilson. The cupcakes should help to appease any market crowd-provoked stress.

W Sitch & Co
48 Berwick Street, W1F 8JD (7437 3776, www.wsitch.co.uk). Oxford Circus tube. **Open** 9am-5pm Mon-Fri; 9.30am-1pm Sat. **No credit cards**. This strangely old-fashioned shop has been trading in this Soho townhouse for more than 100 years. Managed by Ronald Sitch and his sons James and Laurence, its business is the reproduction and restoration of antique lights, though there are also fittings for sale. The company's own range of wall lights and lanterns are made using traditional methods. This may be a small-scale operation, but its prestige and skill are far-reaching – W Sitch supplied the light fittings for the film *Titanic* and it also looks after the wall brackets that grace the state dining room at No.10. For the rest of us, W Sitch will repair, rewire and repolish most period lighting or convert a favourite vase into a lamp.

Bathrooms & kitchens

Aston Matthews
141-147A Essex Road, N1 2SN (7226 7220, www.astonmatthews.co.uk). Angel tube or Essex Road rail. **Open** 8.30am-5pm Mon-Fri; 9.30am-5pm Sat. This bathroom emporium has been trading since 1823 and the showroom, stretched over several shopfronts on the Essex Road, is packed floor to ceiling with a huge selection of bathroomware, showerheads, screens, taps and accessories. Every taste is catered for from Empire-style cast-iron baths, such as the Brunel, through to art deco-inspired taps and the latest Philippe Starck-designed bidet. You'll also find cloakroom-sized basins and, for very bijou spaces, corner WCs. The extensive range means anyone with lavatory pretentions will be happy here, yet the store maintains the reassuring, competent feel of an old-fashioned plumber's merchants.

CP Hart

Arch 213, Newnham Terrace, Hercules Road, SE1 7DR (7902 5250, www.cphart.co.uk). Lambeth North tube or Waterloo tube/rail.
Open 9am-5.30pm Mon-Sat.
A visit to CP Hart's flagship showroom underneath the Waterloo arches is rather like going on an exciting outing. Filled with gleaming room-sets, a fountain of shower heads and sanitaryware that is more Salvador Dali than Thomas Crapper – this is a place like no other. Here, bathrooms are courtesy of Starck, Foster, Massaud, Hayón and Citterio. For boutique hotel style decadence, there's the Hayon freestanding bath, which, with its dark tapered legs and integral tray, looks more like a piece of antique furniture. Walk up steps to the Seaside Waterfall bath and you could be in an Indian Ocean spa. Showering has possibilities you never knew existed: FeOnic sound technology turns glass shower screens into speakers, and Power Glass has invisibly wired LED lights that appear to float. If your main bathroom concerns are to wash and go, there are simple classics such as CP Hart's own London range – ideal for period homes. Our only gripe is that nothing is priced, not even on the website, but for products alone, expect to pay from £8,000 for an average bathroom. The design service is £500, redeemable if you spend over £7,000.
Branch 103-105 Regent's Park Road, NW1 8UR (7586 9856).

Czech & Speake

39C Jermyn Street, SW1Y 6DN (7439 0216, www.czechspeake.com). Green Park or Piccadilly Circus tube. **Open** 9.30am-6pm Mon-Fri; 10am-5pm Sat.
Located on the street that's renowned for purveying the finer things in life to gentlemen of means – shirts, cologne, cigars – Czech & Speake is perhaps the poshest bathroom shop in London. Its bathroom furniture is terribly smart and includes a mahogany Edwardian-style range of fittings and bath panels. From its art deco-inspired Cubist range, an octagonal black lacquer-framed mirror costs £1,400 plus VAT, while a set of chrome basin taps will set you back £705 plus VAT (more for the platinum option, obviously). We spotted a chrome toilet brush for £315 plus VAT and a pair of robe hooks for £150 plus VAT – both beautifully designed, but you'd have to spend a lot of time in your smallest room to justify it. If you can't afford the hardware, you can always treat yourself to some of the elegant own-brand lotions and potions, including the No. 88 bath oil in a chic black frosted bottle for £40. Also stocks Edwardian kitchen fittings.

Plain English

41 Hoxton Square, N1 6PB (7613 0022, www.plainenglishdesign.co.uk). Old Street tube/rail.
Open 10am-5pm Tue-Sat.
Plain English's beautiful kitchens are based on 17th- and 18th-century examples and handmade in Suffolk. Designs are beautifully simple; the London-popular Spitalfields is timeless without being olde worlde, and adapted to suit contemporary living. The Shaker kitchen was designed for the Shaker Shop in London while the Longhouse was inspired by a Georgian butler's pantry. The designs differ slightly, but are very much in the same restrained – and yes, plain – mould. Look around and the displays ooze craftmanship and longevity. Drawers are dovetailed and cupboards can have 'Wapping holes' or a 'Spitalfields hole fret' for ventilation. Three coats of Farrow & Ball paint are applied before installation plus a final coat once the kitchen is in place. You'll pay £35,000 for an average kitchen, including appliances and fitting.

Water Monopoly

16-18 Lonsdale Road, NW6 6RD (7624 2636, www.watermonopoly.com). Queens Park tube/rail.
Open 9am-6pm Mon-Thur; 9am-5pm Fri.
The Water Monopoly certainly has the wow factor. The company, based in a converted stables, specialises in restored English and French antique sanitaryware. Choose from over 200 baths and basins, from copper tubs to polished-iron wash stands, all expertly restored to your chosen finish. Our last visit unearthed a French 1930s art deco double basin and an Edwardian canopy shower bath complete with body sprays. There's no need to worry about dodgy old plumbing – each item comes complete with fittings converted for modern pipes, and smart new taps in classic designs, such as its Bistrot range, work perfectly with the antique baths and basins. As well as original pieces, there's a selection of reproductions such as the beautiful freestanding Paris bath based on a French stone tub (from £5,200 plus VAT). Children – or exhibitionists – will appreciate the Porthole bath (£3,250 plus VAT) with its two glazed portholes on the side.

Streetwise Columbia Road, E2

Come on a Sunday for the popular flower market and a winning array of quirky, one-off shops.

If you can drag yourself out of bed on Sunday morning and stagger down to east London's Columbia Road, you'll find London's sweetest-scented and most colourful market, with flower stalls, trendy locals and an excellent range of boutique-style shops. If you want to avoid the crowds and you're not after any blooms, many of the shops also open on Saturday afternoons – though the lively Sunday exchanges are often the best part of the experience.

The market is open from 8am until 2pm. Given the early start needed to bag the choicest bouquets, you might need sustenance first: starting from the Haggerston Park end of the street, turn right when you reach Ezra Street, at the corner of the Royal Oak pub. Here is a lovely little square with a festival vibe. It's a great place to gather, eat delicious treats and listen to the buskers. Grab some breakfast at characterful **Jones Dairy Café**, (www.jonesdairy.co.uk) or wander down to the yard where stalls tout vintage items.

If you're looking for upmarket homewares, **Wawa** (see p167 and p165 **Shop talk**) sells customised handmade sofas, lamps and accessories. On your way back up Ezra Street to Columbia Road, you pass the Courtyard. There you can drool at the retro items in **Ben Southgate** (see p102), which sells restored furniture and ephemera, and check out the art in **Columbia Road Gallery** (no.7, 07812 196257, www.columbiaroadgallery.com).

Back on Columbia Road, you'll be swept along by the market throng. When you've had your fill of flower traders, check out the attractive shops that run either side of the street.

This end of Columbia Road is best for art. **Elphick's** (no.160, 7033 7891, www.elphicksshop.com) deals in mixed media work; Rob Clarke's slightly unsettling bird paintings start at around £180. **Nelly Duff** (no.156, www.nellyduff.com) has an affordable array of more graphic art, and **Start Space** (no.150, 7729 0522, www.startspace.co.uk) showcases large-scale paintings and photography.

L'Orangerie is an accessories shop on the corner of Barnet Grove (no.162, 8983 7873). Gems include chunky bead necklaces, trendy straw sun-visors and fat glass rings, while the staff are very friendly. At no.152 is **Open House** (07979 851593), a pretty shop selling reproduction home- and gardenwares. **Marcos & Trump** (no.146, 7739 9008) has a decadent interior displaying carefully chosen vintage women's clothes and accessories. Retro-inspired beauty boutique the **Powder Room** is at no.136; pop inside for reasonably priced hair dos, manicures and make-up sessions.

Sweet-toothers can indulge at old-fashioned sweetshop **Suck & Chew** (no.130, 8983 3504) and cupcake and retro kitchenware shop **Treacle** (nos.110-112; see p171).

Columbia Road institution **Milagros** (no.61, 7613 0876, www.milagros.co.uk) offers a wonderful selection of Mexican curiosities and trinkets. Particularly covetable are the *retablos* (allegorical folk art) and the Day of the Dead paper banners.

Ryantown (no.126, see p171) is one of the newer – and loveliest – additions to the street. Rob Ryan's crafty motifs cover tiles, perspex keys, giant floor-standing rulers, screenprints and mugs.

Supernice (no.106, 7613 3890, www.supernice.co.uk) has Blik wall art (removable stickers) in a great range from robots to birds on telegraph wires. Thomas Paul melamine plates and trays sell from £6. Opposite Supernice at no.49 is the **Fleapit café**, which proffers delicious veggie food.

You're coming to the end of the main drag, but don't miss **Vintage Heaven** (no.82, 01277 215968, http://vintageheaven.co.uk) just before the junction with Cosset Street. Poke around to find vintage kitchen and garden treasures. Further on, at no.2, past the residential flats, at the junction with Hackney Road, is **Two Columbia Road** (see p106), a stalwart for 20th-century furniture.

The ultimate sourcebook for interior and garden design and decoration

Find it all on...

THE HOUSE DIRECTORY

"Streets ahead of the competition"
The Good Web Guide

www.thehousedirectory.com

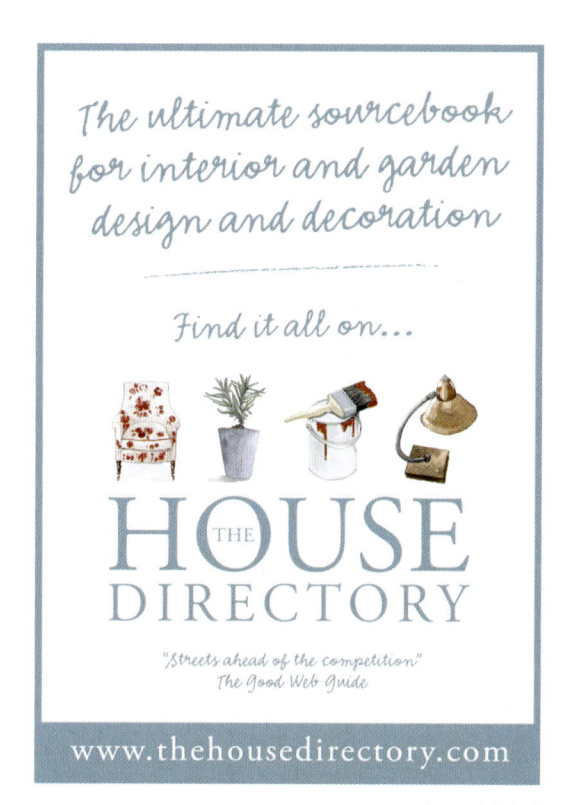

Warren Evans
Handmade quality beds and mattresses

The Sunday bed
~~£890~~ £395

'Best Retailer' **The Observer** Winners 2008, 2009
'Best Green Companies' **THE SUNDAY TIMES** Winners three years running

OPEN 7 DAYS FREE PARKING (Except Bromley)

☎ 020 7693 8987
🖱 warrenevans.com

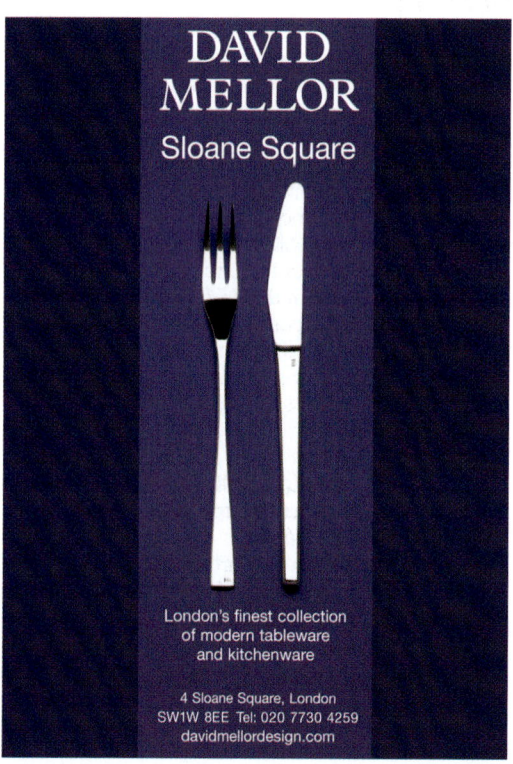

DAVID MELLOR
Sloane Square

London's finest collection of modern tableware and kitchenware

4 Sloane Square, London
SW1W 8EE Tel: 020 7730 4259
davidmellordesign.com

Offset your flight with **Trees for Cities** and make your trip mean something for years to come

www.treesforcities.org/offset

Trees for Cities
Charity registration number 1032154

Vintage Furniture & Homewares

Antiques

Antique Trader at Millinery Works
85-87 Southgate Road, N1 3JS (7359 2019, www.milleryworks.co.uk). Old Street tube/rail then 76, 141 bus. **Open** 11am-6pm Tue-Sat; noon-5pm Sun.
This former Victorian hat factory is packed with Arts and Crafts and Aesthetic Movement furniture and objects from Gothic Reform to the Cotswold School – all of which can be picked up at reasonable prices. Even the most basic dining tables and chairs are sturdy and of good quality. Expect to pay £2,000 for an oak Arts and Crafts table and four chairs by an unknown maker. Specialised pieces that you wouldn't be surprised to see in the V&A are a real draw – and some are strictly POA. Top-drawer makers include Godwin, Dresser, Rennie Mackintosh and 'Mouseman' Thompson. Heal's bedroom furniture is often in stock and look out too for smaller items such as Liberty & Co dressing-table sets and Glasgow Style ceramics. There are regular exhibitions as well as excellent Arts and Crafts shows twice a year.

Bloch & Angell Antiques
22 Church Street, NW8 8EP (7723 6575, www.angellantiques.com). Edgware Road tube or Marylebone tube/rail. **Open** 10am-5.30pm Tue-Sat.
'Decorative without being fussy' is how Tony Bloch describes his stock. He also 'doesn't do small', so it's just as well he has a large, attractive space to house his expansive collection of furniture and objects. He specialises in Scandinavian, French and English pieces from the Georgian era to the 1950s. Typical items include 18th-century rustic farmhouse tables alongside bold pieces of sculpture and early industrial furniture, lockers and cupboards. You'll also find pairs of 1930s leather armchairs for around £2,200 and good-quality chaises longues. Bloch shares the space with Andrew Angell, who specialises in old shop fittings, vintage advertising signs and tins.

Chesney's
194-202 Battersea Park Road, SW11 4ND (7627 1410, www.chesneys.co.uk). Bus 344. **Open** 9am-5.30pm Mon-Fri; 10am-5pm Sat.
An international fireplace empire that began when Paul Chesney and his brother Nick realised the value of discarded antique fireplaces 25 years ago. Chesney's Battersea showroom stretches over four shopfronts, providing ample space to display an impressive variety of antique and reproduction chimneypieces. Made in China from limestone and marble, there are over 50 period-inspired styles (£500-£25,000) to choose from. Modern designs come courtesy of partnerships with designers such as Jasper Conran and Jane Churchill. Chesney's also has a licence to recreate a collection of chimneypiece replicas from the archives of Sir John Soane's Museum. A bespoke service is also available; call for details.
Branch 734-736 Hollway Road, N19 3JF (7561 8280).

Core One
The Gas Works, 2 Michael Road, SW6 2AD (7371 5700, www.coreoneantiques.com). Fulham Broadway tube. **Open** 10am-6pm Mon-Fri; 11am-4pm Sat.
This large industrial building is an unlikely setting for a group of antique and 20th-century furniture dealers. Head through the gates, keep going past the rusting gasometer, and you're there. Dean Gipson, whose Dean Antiques (7610 6697, www.deanantiques.co.uk) covers 2,000sq ft of Core One, has a great eye. Everything has a solid feel and a wow factor, from a 19th-century French oak workshop table to a pair of stone obelisks. Mirrors are another strength, from Regency convex to French brasserie-style. DNA Design has a mixture of antique and later furniture. Elegant pieces include dining tables, marble-topped consoles and Venetian mirrors. Other dealers here include Roderic Haugh Antiques Ltd (English and French furniture and objects, 7371 5700) and De Parma, the 20th-century furniture dealer (*see p178*).

Floral Hall
Corner of Crouch Hill & Haringey Park, N8 9DX (8348 7309, www.floralhallantiques.co.uk). Finsbury Park tube/rail then W7 bus or 91 bus. **Open** 10am-5pm Tue-Sat; also by appointment. **No credit cards**.
With its old-fashioned window, Floral Hall is a constant in Crouch End, its shop floor creaking with faded French grandeur. Gilt overmantel mirrors may not be in top-notch nick but, with prices starting from around £300, they are ideal for those in search of the battered look – and a bargain. Early 20th-century chandeliers range from £250 to £2,000 and there's normally some nice furniture pieces too – an art deco bedside table, say, or a pair of French café chairs, as well as a good range of original lamps. Call before visiting in August as, in true French style, the shop usually closes.

French House
41-43 Parsons Green Lane, SW6 4HH (7371 7573, www.thefrenchhouse.co.uk). Parsons Green tube. **Open** 10am-6pm Mon-Sat.
The French House has the sort of stock you'd like to discover in France yourself. Most of the furniture is displayed in its original state with two prices: restored and as seen. The on-site workshop has been integrated into the showroom so you can watch the experienced upholsterer at work; for your own piece, you can choose from a selection of lovely French fabrics, exclusive to the shop. A restored 1860s chaise longue will cost around

£1,800. Large gilt mirrors are good enough to hang as they are. Thanks to monthly buying trips, there's always something new and unusual to check out. Pretty 19th-century single bed prices start at £600, more masculine *lits bateaux* from around £950.

La Maison
107-108 Shoreditch High Street, E1 6JN (7729 9646, www.lamaisonlondon.com). Shoreditch High Street rail. **Open** 10am-6pm Mon-Sat.
This classy shop makes you want to get under the sheets – and stay there. The beds here are the stuff of French costume dramas and perfect for *liaisons dangereuses*. If you don't know your Louis XVI from your Louis Philippe, the charming staff will guide you through some bedroom history. Don't be put off by the rather cramped dimensions of the antique doubles; La Maison provides a seamless extension service. Single Louis XVI beds go for £500 and doubles from £700. Armoires start at £900 and bedside tables at £350. The shop also sells its own reproduction beds – expect to pay around £2,000 for a simple Louis XV-style double.

Lacquer Chest & Lacquer Chest Too
71 & 75 Kensington Church Street, W8 4BG (7937 1306, www.lacquerchest.com). Notting Hill Gate or Kensington High Street tube. **Open** 9.30am-5.30pm Mon-Fri; 10.30am-4.30pm Sat.
Gretchen Anderson and her husband Vivian have been in the business for well over 40 years and the ordered clutter of their 18th- and early 19th-century household antiques creates a more intimate atmosphere than that found in the shop's smarter neighbours. Think William Morris rush chairs, Welsh milking stools and early 19th-century, three-legged cricket tables (£500-£2,500). Gretchen is passionate about her stock – she loves pieces with an intriguing tale, such as her collection of 19th-century Scottish metal piggy banks, engraved with messages such as 'Dinna spare the cream mither'. Most of the business is carried out behind the scenes, however; five floors hold an extraordinary library of antiques, with pieces hired out to film makers and stylists.

LASSCo
Brunswick House, 30 Wandsworth Road, SW8 2LG (7394 2100, www.lassco.co.uk). Vauxhall tube/rail. **Open** 10am-5pm Mon-Sat; 11am-5pm Sun.
This 18th-century Vauxhall mansion and its vast warehouse are packed with architectural relics from the capital and beyond, such as Victorian stained-glass windows, a cell door from the Clerkenwell House of Detention (£975 plus VAT), and mahogany museum cupboards from the British Museum by way of Chiddingstone Castle (£1,600). The stunning first-floor 'saloon' of the house is the flooring department. Baltic pine floorboards from an ex-Salvation Army building were £38/sq m. The Parlour houses baths and basins of the sort Hercule Poirot might have used and there are also ornate art nouveau radiators. Head downstairs for butlers' sinks and 1930s free-standing larders.

20th-century design

Ben Southgate
4 The Courtyard, Ezra Street, E2 7RH (07905 960792, www.bsouthgate.co.uk). Hoxton or Shoreditch High Street rail. **Open** 9am-3pm Sun.
Ben Southgate spent over a decade as a furniture restorer before opening this stylish grown-up boys' paradise among the blooms of Columbia Road. Stock includes vintage board games from around £30, the kind of 1950s football tables you see in French bars and cafés, clubby 1930s and '40s leather armchairs, enamel lampshades and polished medical cabinets (around £1,250). Prices are reasonable; huge 1940s eight-drawer plan chests sell for around £600. As well as restoring the items he sells, Southgate will take on a range of private restoration commissions, including French polishing, upholstery, cane repairs and desk leathering. *See also p173* **Streetwise**.

Birgit Israel
301 Fulham Road, SW10 9QH (7376 7255, www.birgitisrael.com). South Kensington tube. **Open** 10am-6pm Mon-Sat.
Birgit Israel's smart, timeless 20th-century furniture store attracts collectors, interior designers and stylists looking for period pieces in mint condition. Lights are a particular passion, with the likes of Murano glass-tiered chandelier and Venini glass disk wall lights often gracing the shop with their presence. Furniture is understated – what Israel calls 'casual luxury' – encompassing, for example, a set of four 'Eden Roc hotel' chairs (£1,750), say, or a pair of acrylic cube tables, fresh from the 1960s (£645). The store also makes cushions and furniture to order. An interior design consultancy is available and you can arrange a wedding list here. Israel's clothing boutique is just along the road.

D&A Binder
34 Church Street, NW8 8EP (7723 0542, www.dandabinder.co.uk). Edgware Road tube or Marylebone tube/rail. **Open** 10am-6pm Tue-Sat.
D&A Binder looks rather like the ghost of Grace Brothers past. It's where old shop fittings come to rest, no longer needed for perfumery, haberdashery and wigs. David Binder sells to the likes of Hackett and Agent Provocateur but private individuals shop here too – the huge 1920s mahogany shirt cabinets are perfect for the shirted man about town. Chrome and glass display cabinets from the 1940s work well in modern bathrooms. Museum cabinets are often in stock too. Look out for 1920s hat moulds and corsetry advertising figures for manufacturers like Regent Corsetry or a 1950s Sunflex

Vintage Furniture & Homewares

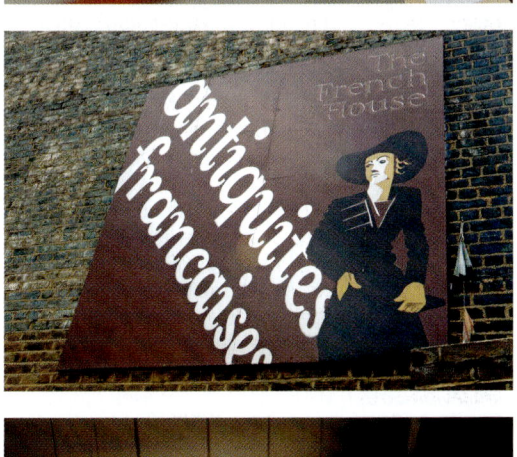

French House. *See p175.*

display for stockings. And, of course, chrome shoe stands will do a fine job displaying your treasured Manolos.
Branch 101 Holloway Road, N7 8LT (7609 6306).

De Parma
The Gas Works, 2 Michael Road, SW6 2AN (7736 3384, www.deparma.com). Fulham Broadway tube. **Open** 10am-6pm Mon-Fri; 11am-4pm Sat.
Gary de Sparham concentrates on mid 20th-century design in this hip white space in south-west London. Almost everything is Italian and, in the main, by well-known designers such as Ico Parisi, Gio Ponti, Adnet, Fortana Arte and Fornasetti. Special pieces have been spotted here in the past, such as a 1969 Maurice Calka fibreglass 'Boomerang' desk, one of only 35 (£34,000), and a 1940s Osvaldo Borsani commode in black lacquer and sycamore (£5,200). But there are also more affordable items available, such as a chic 1940s black lacquered armchair (£1,450). De Parma also has a small selection of artworks and photography for sale.
Branch 247 Fulham Road, SW3 6HY (7352 2414).

Dog & Wardrobe
Unit 3B Regent Studios, 8 Andrew's Road, E8 4QN (07855 958741, www.thedogandwardrobe.com). London Fields rail or 55 bus. **Open** 10am-5pm Sat; by appointment Mon-Fri.
Jane Money and Vishal Gohel's tiny retro furniture and design emporium is hidden just past Broadway Market and beside the canal, in a ground-floor unit of artists hub Regent Studios. Crammed with artfully presented vintage furniture (with lots of 1960s-style chairs and tables) and curios such as retro alarm clocks, desk lamps, stylish coat stands, framed insects, animal skulls, shopkeepers' display cabinets, classic tins and bottles, old typewriters, as well as a selection of framed contemporary art. Get

Furniture arcades & covered markets

Alfie's Antique Market
13-25 Church Street, NW8 8DT (7723 6066, www.alfiesantiques.com). Edgware Road tube or Marylebone tube/rail. **Open** 10am-6pm Tue-Sat.
Alfie's occupies a building that started life as the Edwardian department store, Jordan's. After falling into disrepair, it reopened as an antique market in 1976 and is now home to around 60 dealers, including vintage clothes store the **Girl Can't Help It**. For 20th-century furniture, venture into the area known as the Quad, as well as **Decoratum's** (7724 6969, www.decoratum.com) vast space in the basement. On the first floor, don't miss **Dodo** for '20s and '30s advertising posters and signs, and Louise Verbier, which has mirrors, lighting and mercury glass. **Vincenzo Caffarella**'s (7724 3701, www.vinca.co.uk) impressive showroom of 20th-century Italian lighting takes up the second floor mezzanine. Finally, rest up at the pleasant rooftop café, before one last rummage through the vintage trimmings at the charming **Persiflage**.

Bermondsey Square Antiques Market
Corner of Bermondsey Street & Long Lane, SE1 (7525 6000). Borough tube or London Bridge tube/rail. **Open** 6am-1pm Fri. **No credit cards**.
Following the redevelopment of Bermondsey Square the ancient antiques market – traditionally good for china and silver as well as furniture and glassware – continues in an expanded space that now accommodates 200 stalls that now include food, fashion and craft stalls. Arrive early.

Camden Passage/Pierrepont Arcade
Camden Passage, off Upper Street, N1 5ED (www.camdenpassageislington.co.uk). Angel tube. **Open** *General market* 7am-6pm Wed, Sat.
Boutiques and estate agents have now encroached on this once-thriving antiques enclave, with the Mall being the latest casualty to developers, its future uncertain. But some antiques dealers remain: for a good old rummage, turn off the Passage and explore the antique and vintage clothes shops in the still bustling Pierrepont Arcade. **Aquamarine Antiques** (www.aquamarineantiques.co.uk) has military costumes and taxidermy. **Key Leyshon** (7226 8955, www.kays-canteen.com), at no.15, has well-priced silver-plated flatware. For antique maps and prints, check out **Finbar Macdonell** (www.finbarmacdonnell.co.uk) at no.10.

Grays Antique Market & Grays in the Mews
58 Davies Street, W1K 5LP & 1-7 Davies Mews, W1K 5AB (7629 7034, www.graysantiques.com). Bond Street tube. **Open** 10am-6pm Mon-Sat.
Stalls in this smart covered market – housed in a terracotta building that was once a 19th-century lavatory showroom – sell everything from antiques, art and rare books to jewellery and vintage fashion. The place was set up in 1977 and is now home to around 200 dealers – making it one of the world's largest and most diverse markets of its kind. There's a good café on site. *See also p196* **Bernard J Shapero** – one of the antiquarian booksellers here.

Vintage Furniture & Homewares

LASSCo. *See p176.*

HOME

Planet Bazaar. *See p182.*

Vintage Furniture & Homewares

Sales & events

The cream of London's auction houses and antiques fairs.

Bonhams
101 New Bond Street, W1S 1SR (7447 7447, www.bonhams.com). Bond Street or Oxford Circus tube. **Open** *9am-5.30pm Mon-Fri.*
Auction house set up in 1793 with regular antiques sales throughout the year.

Christie's
85 Old Brompton Road, SW7 3LD (7930 6074, www.christies.com). South Kensington tube. **Open** *9am-7.30pm Mon; 9am-5pm Tue-Fri; viewing only 10am-4pm Sat, Sun.*
The world's first fine art auctioneers, with sales and auctions that total an average of £2.8 billion a year.

Criterion Auctions
Wandsworth; *41-47 Chatfield Road, SW11 3SE (7228 5563, www.criterionauctions.co.uk). Clapham Junction rail.* **Open** *2-7pm Fri; 10am-6pm Sat, Sun; viewing 10am-5pm Mon; auction 5pm Mon.*
Islington; *53 Essex Road, N1 2SF (7359 5707). Angel tube.* **Open** *2-7pm Fri; 10am-6pm Sat, Sun; viewing 10am-5pm Mon; auction 5pm Mon.*
Criterion has 100 antique sales a year, and weekly specialised sales.

Decorative Antiques & Textiles Fair
Battersea Park, SW11 4NJ (7616 9327, www.decorativefair.com). Sloane Square tube then Renault courtesy car. **Open** *28 Sept-3 Oct.*
Thrice-yearly specialist event for the discerning decorator. Antique textiles and interior design.

Lots Road Auctions
71 Lots Road, SW10 0RN (7376 6800, www.lotsroad.com) Fulham Broadway tube. **Open** *6-8pm Wed; 10am-6pm Thur; 9am-4pm Fri; viewing 10am-4pm Sat; auctions 1pm Sun (contemporary furniture, lighting and mirrors), 4pm Sun (antiques).*
A full catalogue is available online.

Midcentury Modern
Dulwich College, SE21 7LD, (www.modernshows.com). West Dulwich rail. **Open** *March, Nov.*
The only design show that made it into *Time Out*'s top 10 London attractions in 2009. Specialising in Scandinavian, European and American mid-century furniture and decorative arts. Twice yearly.

Olympia Fine Art & Antiques Fairs
Olympia Exhibition Halls, Hammersmith Road, W14 8UX (7370 8211, www.olympia-antiques.com). Kensington Olympia tube. **Open** *11am-7pm daily 3-13 June.*
A vast array of items from many periods; the summer fair is the largest, with around 260 dealers from all over the world.

Sotheby's
34-35 New Bond Street, W1A 2AA (7293 5000, www.sothebys.com). Bond Street or Oxford Circus tube. **Open** *9am-5pm Mon-Fri.*
Masters at auction since 1744, with lots ranging from contemporary Turkish art to A Celebration of the English Country House.

here early on a Saturday for rich pickings before E8's fashionistas wake up, and then head to the market for brunch. Money and Gohel also provide a design service.

The Facade
99 Lisson Grove, NW1 6UP (7258 2017, www.thefacade.co.uk). Edgware Road tube or Marylebone tube/rail. **Open** *10.30am-5pm Wed-Sat.*
Walking into the Facade feels like entering a sort of a crystal hanging garden. Specialising in decorative antiques from 1890 to 1950, there is a definite emphasis on lighting. Its ceilings drip with chandeliers of all sizes – some supremely elegant, some coloured, tasselled and bordering on the kitsch. There are stacks of gilded and painted mirrors and the odd piece of furniture, including over-gilded chairs and a range of coffee tables. At the back of the shop there are weird and wonderful standard lamps – churchy plaster angels holding lights, bronze rose bushes with light bulbs in their blooms and mad pineapple wall sconces.

Fandango
2 Cross Street, N1 2BL (7226 1777, www.fandangointeriors.co.uk). Angel tube or Highbury & Islington tube/rail. **Open** *noon-6pm Wed-Sat; by appointment Mon, Sun.*
The selection of 20th-century furniture and objects is very thoughtful. The shop specialises in post-war design from the 1950s and '60s, such as an orange Theo Ruth sofa or a Neil Morris cloud table, and you'll usually find pieces by well-known designers such as Arne Jacobsen. But it's not all about names here. Stock is interesting even if it is anonymous. There are attractive 1940s Murano glass chandeliers that have been resin-coated to bring them up

to date and give them more masculine appeal (£1,400) and neon works of art by Chish and Fips. Fandango has a restoration workshop, and will email images of pre-madeover pieces before they arrive in the shop.

Gallery 1930
18 Church Street, NW8 8EP (7723 1555, www.susiecooperceramics.com). Edgware Road tube or Marylebone tube/rail. **Open** 10am-5pm Tue-Sat.
The shop is a must for deco enthusiasts and a particularly good hunting ground for those furnishing small flats, with dinky occasional tables and silver or chrome deco photograph frames, nostalgically filled with pictures of silver screen stars like Grant and Garbo (from £65). The drinks trays from the 1920s and '30s – mirrored or in black Vitriolite – make classy wedding gifts. For more movie glamour, there's 1930s polished steel film-set lighting on wheels – some lights are huge (prices range from £700 to £1,500) and all are reconditioned and rewired. Susie Cooper ceramics are always in stock, as are other big names such as Clarice Cliff and Lalique.

Origin Modernism
25 Camden Passage, N1 8EA (7704 1326, www.originmodernism.co.uk). Angel tube.
Open 10am-6pm Wed, Sat; noon-6pm Thur, Fri; also by appointment. **No credit cards**.
People always have room for a chair, Chris Reen believes, which is why you'll always find a good selection of seating in his Camden Passage shop. Reen will happily talk you through the interesting modernist stock here and explain why, for instance, a deliberate mistake might be visible in a design. Furniture and lights dating from 1930 to 1950 are usually Scandinavian, American or British and well-preserved examples of the period. Expect to find names such as Eames and Breuer, Alvar Aalto, Cees Braakman and George Nelson. Previous visits have revealed an Alvar Aalto Type 69 chair, a Marcel Breuer B56 stool and Willy van der Meeren F1 chairs for sale.

Peanut Vendor
133 Newington Green Road, N1 4RA (7226 5727, www.thepeanutvendor.co.uk). Canonbury rail or 73 bus. **Open** 10am-7pm Tue-Thur; 10am-6pm Fri, Sat; noon-6pm Sun. **No credit cards**.
This local fave sells a well-edited range of charming yet affordable early to mid 20th-century furniture. The affable owners Barny and Becky have a passion for good design and recognised a gap in the London market for aesthetically pleasing furniture that doesn't cost the earth. The eclectic selection normally includes classic designs, such as Ercol pieces; enamel hanging light shades, 1960s coffee tables and folding stools, original wall hooks, art deco mirrors, G-Plan sideboards, old telephones, enamel bread bins and school-style chairs

also crop up regularly. All items are originals, sourced and hand-selected from the country's auction houses and antiques warehouses. Note that the place is sometimes closed on Tuesday mornings.

Planet Bazaar
Arch 86, The Stables Market, Chalk Farm Road, NW1 8AH (7485 6000, www.planetbazaar.co.uk). Chalk Farm tube. **Open** noon-6pm Mon-Fri; 10am-6pm Sat, Sun; also by appointment.
Proprietor Maureen Silverman remarks that Planet Bazaar's atmospheric digs beneath Victorian railway arches are the sort of place that people pop into to cheer themselves up as much as to do any shopping. You can see why. The place is crammed with everything from 1950s to '70s telephones (from £65) to funky '60s Danish wooden lamps (from £95). Downstairs you'll find rosewood coffee tables and the sort of sideboards that would have been laden with platters of cheese and pineapple in *Abigail's Party*. There's a variety of lighting priced from £65. Pop art is usually in stock, with prints by Jamie Reid, who did iconic artwork for the Sex Pistols.

Themes & Variations
231 Westbourne Grove, W11 2SE (7727 5531, www.themesandvariations.com). Notting Hill Gate tube.
Open 10am-1pm, 2-6pm Mon-Fri; 10am-6pm Sat.
Liliane Fawcett's enduringly chic gallery has a strong focus on French and Italian decorative arts and furniture, especially from the 1970s. It takes its name from Italian designer Piero Fornasetti's series and is the exclusive UK agent for the Fornasetti studio. Plates from the series, featuring a woman's head in one of 365 positions, are £95. Stylish post-war and contemporary furniture is a speciality. On a recent visit the arrival of a Mark Brazier-Jones 'Carter' chandelier (£4,625 plus VAT) was causing much excitement. The gallery has an annual themed exhibition, bringing together 20th-century pieces with furniture and objects from contemporary designers.

Two Columbia Road
2 Columbia Road, E2 7NN (7729 9933, www.twocolumbiaroad.com). Hoxton or Shoreditch High Street rail. **Open** noon-7pm Tue-Fri; noon-6pm Sat; 10am-3pm Sun.
Well-selected pieces are the order of the day here, whether it's 1970s chrome pendant lights or collectable Charles Eames wooden chairs. Some 20th-century shops can feel like a bit of a mixed bag, but there's a definite style here. The appealing corner site is owned by Tommy Roberts (who made his name with the cult Carnaby Street interiors shop Kleptomania in the 1960s) and is run by his son Keith. Expect to find well-known names such as Arne Jacobsen and Willy Rizzo among the stock as well as more affordable pieces (Danish 1960s leather sofas in slender, elegant shapes for around £850, and rosewood desks of the same period for £1,500).

Gardens & Flowers

Columbia Road Market (*see p50* and *p173* **Streetwise**) is London's dedicated plant market, and the best bet for a combination of variety and keen prices, although your local street market is likely to sell you workaday bedding plants and blooms for even less. **New Covent Garden Flower Market** (Covent Garden Market Authority, Covent House, SW8 5NX, 7720 2211, www.cgma.gov.uk) covers three-and-a-half acres and sells blooms from all over the world; there's a £4 entrance fee if you bring your car, but it's free for pedestrians. Turn up before 7am for the best choice.

Garden centres & nurseries

Clifton Nurseries
5A Clifton Villas, W9 2PH (7289 6851, www.clifton.co.uk). Warwick Avenue tube. **Open** *Apr-June* 8.30am-7pm Mon-Sat; 10.30am-4.30pm Sun. *June-Sept* 8.30am-6pm Mon-Sat; 10.30am-4.30pm Sun. *Oct-Mar* 8.30am-5.30pm Mon-Sat; 10.30am-4.30pm Sun.
Visiting London's stateliest centre, established in 1851, fills the amateur gardener with longing and enthusiasm. From the gorgeous stucco mansions of Little Venice you enter a horticulturalist's paradise, via a shady drive lined with topiarised box trees in lavish pots. Fortunately, good looks aren't Clifton's only selling point. Helpful and knowledgeable staff are able to steer you toward sensible purchases for your patch. There's also a huge flowering shrub and perennial section. Take some time to sit on the bench in the fragrant rose garden collection and breathe deeply. The centre's impressive exotics are pampered in a large hothouse – head inside for carnivorous plants, fragrant gardenias, cacti and succulents, and fleshy tender tropicals. Non-gardeners might like to enquire about the legendary Clifton design and landscaping service. Cut flowers, as well as tools and accessories, are sold and Clifton also runs a plantfinder service. What's more, there's a Daylesford organic café on site.

Ginkgo Garden Centre
Railway arches, Ravenscourt Avenue, off King Street, W6 0SL (8563 7112, www.ginkgogardens.co.uk). Ravenscourt Park tube. **Open** *Mar-Dec* 9am-6pm Mon-Sat; 10am-5pm Sun. *Jan, Feb* 9am-5pm Mon-Sat; 10am-5pm Sun.
Glamorous Ginkgo – well set out and beautifully tended – sits beside Ravenscourt Park, so pulls in fair-weather gardeners with its grandiloquent clipped box and bay trees and gorgeous climber and burgeoning cottage-garden perennials. It's also strong on Mediterranean splendour for the sunny terrace; olives that would do well in big planters, little citrus trees and architectural spiky agaves give instant impact. The range of containers is impressive, as are the terrace and conservatory furniture and ornaments. Staff dispense advice and will also pot out containers to order; the Ginkgo design, landscape and maintenance business provides for larger projects, and even the café gets a mention for its excellent coffee.

Petersham Nurseries
Church Lane, off Petersham Road, Petersham, Richmond, Surrey TW10 7AG (8940 5230, www.petershamnurseries.com). Richmond tube/rail. **Open** *Summer* 9am-5pm Mon-Sat; 11am-5pm Sun. *Winter* 9am-5pm Tue-Sat; 11am-5pm Sun.
There isn't a corner of this celebrated nursery that isn't ravishing, especially in its flowery summer garb. Idyllically set amid Petersham's pastures, the nurseries are a series of antique timber frame greenhouses around which pots and raised beds, old-fashioned hand carts and timber boxes filled with annuals, hardy perennials, shrubs, climbers and herbs put up a stunning cottage garden display. There are big blowsy dahlias and

Clifton Nurseries

planters full of sweet peas and nasturtiums in high season, fruit trees and bushes for autumn planting and bulbs, conifers and evergreens for winter interest. It really is a feast for the eyes – and the stomach too, as Petersham Nurseries is home to Skye Gyngell's fantastic café. It's best to walk from the bus stop or the Twickenham ferry to get here, as Richmond Council will only give permanent consent for this treasure to remain if fewer people arrive by car. Be as green as your fingers and leave the motor behind.

Garden shops

Daylesford Organic (30 Pimlico Road, SW1W 8LJ, 7730 2943, www.daylesfordorganic.com) has an achingly cool garden shop for timber furniture, vintage garden tools, aged pots, organic seeds and cut flowers.

Hortus
26 Blackheath Village, SE3 9SY (8297 9439, www.hortus-london.com). Blackheath rail. **Open** *Summer* 9.30am-6pm Mon-Sat; 10am-5pm Sun. *Winter* 9.30am-6pm Mon-Sat; 10am-4pm Sun.
A garden design and maintenance business is run from this rather lovely village store. Hortus aims to sell unique designs from small producers that are not available on the high street. The stock changes seasonally and includes the shop's own range of tools and accessories. Everything is functional first and beautiful second, and the owners personally test the tools before they're put on sale. Trowels and secateurs from Burgon & Ball and Duchy, swings and containers made from recycled tyres, trug baskets, lamps, ceramics and glassware, picnicware and quality outdoor furniture, including hand-printed deckchairs, are stocked inside. In the fragrant garden at the rear you can buy a selection of roses, herbs, perennials and city-suitable shrubs, all well tended and healthy looking. Modern stone water features and bird-baths complete the look.

Judy Green's Garden Store
11 Flask Walk, NW3 1HJ (7435 3832). Hampstead tube. **Open** 10am-6pm Mon-Sat; noon-6pm Sun.
This 'garden boutique' located down a small cobbled street is Hampstead right down to its delicate roots. The tumble of seasonal blooms spilling out of their pots outside (perhaps pelargoniums, lavender, nemesias or angelonias) would all look artful in the designer vases and pots that you'll find indoors. As well as these cottage-garden favourites, the shop sells a range of orchids and an ever-changing selection of accessories, ranging from the functional (watering cans, handmade garden tools, outdoor furniture) to the absolutely essential (bags and aprons from Cath Kidston). The wellington boots from Le Chameau and Hunter make excellent gifts for gardeners struggling with London's clay-heavy soil.

Petersham Nurseries. *See p183.*

Flowers

Absolute Flowers
12-14 Clifton Road, W9 1SS (7286 1155, www.absoluteflowersandhome.com). Warwick Avenue tube. **Open** 8am-7pm Mon-Sat; 10am-6pm Sun.
Absolutely sumptuous arrangements are created by the artists bustling about the art deco tiled interior of this chic, black shop, which acts as a perfect backdrop to the richly coloured glass vases and containers stacked to the ceiling. The shop specialises in English blooms, and bouquets are kept simple with minimal foliage. Homewares and accessories are also sold. Expect to pay premium prices for the bouquets – a fact that won't come as too much of a surprise, given the genteel neighbourhood the shop is located in. Staff are helpful but the place gets very busy, so you may have to wait before being attended to.

Angel Flowers
60 Upper Street, N1 0NY (7704 6312, www.angel-flowers.co.uk). Angel tube. **Open** 9am-7pm Mon-Sat; 11am-5pm Sun.
Belgian Marco Wouters founded this bright and breezy shop in 1995, having previously travelled and worked in Spain and the Far East, observing the exotic plants he now uses in their natural environments. His blooms are imported from Dutch and Belgian flower markets four times per week and there's always a massive variety available with which to make a dramatic bunch. There are hot tropicals and orchids, and buckets full of cottage-garden lovelies in season. The shop is very handsome, with its vintage lights and containers filled with colour, so it's difficult to leave without at least a pretty posy.

Bloomsbury Flowers
29 Great Queen Street, WC2B 5BB (7242 2840, www.bloomsburyflowers.co.uk). Covent Garden tube. **Open** 9.30am-5pm Mon; 9.30am-5.30pm Tue-Fri.
A classy shop opposite the Freemasons Hall, where seasonal flowers are carefully chosen to appeal to all the senses. Stephen Wicks and Mark Welford, who call themselves the Bloomsbury Boys, create dramatic and unusual arrangements that are made up while you wait. A long way from your standard bouquet, the designs may involve scented herbs and shiny evergreens. Good-quality standards like orchids, lilies, roses, peonies and summer sweet peas stand alongside more unusual choices such as bergamot and rosemary, part of an imaginative range that changes throughout the year. Day and evening flower design courses are on offer – see the website for details.

Jane Packer Flowers
32-34 New Cavendish Street, W1G 8UE (7935 2673, www.jane-packer.co.uk). Bond Street tube. **Open** 9am-6pm Mon-Sat.

La Maison des Roses. *See p186.*

Jane Packer – the florist of choice for many stars – has now become something of a household name. This sleek Marylebone store fronts her equally successful school of floristry, for evening and one-day courses, where students sit with their clippers and wire learning the tricks of the trade. There's a range of own-brand candles and toiletries, unusual plants in modern containers and vases, ready-assembled arrangements in boxes and a selection of Packer's books. What's more, bouquets of flowers – or the bestselling rose hatboxes – can be ordered for same- or next-day delivery, along with top-quality chocolates and champagne, if you want to push the boat out. A classic and dependable choice.

La Maison des Roses

48 Webbs Road, SW11 6SF (7228 5700, www.maison-des-roses.com). Clapham South tube or Clapham Junction rail. **Open** 10am-6pm Tue-Sat.
A beautiful and soothing shop, which seems a world away from the metal vases and stuffed-full displays of ordinary florists, where our national flower scents the rarefied air. The rose wallpaper and soft furnishings, and the bouquets, nosegays and bushes of blooms wherever you look, add to the charm. Given the flower's short season in this country, imported flowers make up most of the stock – all of it in the winter – but there's always a heady variety of species, and a lovely range of bouquets, including stunning rose hearts. Scented candles, soaps, bath oils and room sprays add to the all-pervading aroma. Dried and preserved roses are also for sale.

McQueens

70-72 Old Street, EC1V 9AN (7251 5505, www.mcqueens.co.uk). Old Street tube/rail.
Open 8.30am-6pm Mon-Fri; 9am-noon Sat.
Graydon Carter might have forgotten to invite you to the *Vanity Fair* post-Oscars party this year, but pop along to McQueens and you can at least see the sort of designs that Hollywood's power elite had as their backdrop. Drop-dead gorgeous arrangements are prepared on site by impossibly glamorous students studying at this floristry school. The shop and school is very Old Street industrial chic, softened with exquisite window displays. There's usually an enormous range of stems that can be hand tied into a bunch, with the glamourpusses – strelitzia, protea et al – alongside the more stolid natives, such as moluccella (bells of Ireland) and hydrangea.

Scarlet & Violet

76 Chamberlayne Road, NW10 3JJ (8969 9446, www.scarletandviolet.com). Kensal Green tube.
Open 9.30am-6pm Mon-Sat.
This exquisite flower shop takes your breath away the moment you walk in the door. An abundance of flowers are displayed casually in old jugs, buckets, glass jars and even milk bottles. The artless containers serve in fact to draw the eye to the extraordinary artistry displayed in the bunches made up in the very personal style of the owner, Victoria Brotherson. Old-fashioned and traditional country garden flowers are plentiful, including nodding peonies, and tall sticks of hollyhocks and delphiniums. Highly recommended, Vic opened her shop in 2006 and is at her happiest when arranging for parties in people's houses.

Wild at Heart

Turquoise Island, 222 Westbourne Grove, W11 2RH (7727 3095, www.wildatheart.com). Notting Hill Gate tube. **Open** 8am-6pm Mon-Sat.
The Ledbury Road Wild shop sells homewares, clothing and gifts with a floral theme. Pop around the corner to Westbourne Grove for the florist: in the middle of the street stands Turquoise Island, with a designer public loo on one side and Wild at Heart on the other. It's vibrant with peonies, delphiniums, hydrangeas and sweet peas in summer, daffs, tulips and anemones in spring. Traditional English blooms are close to the Wild heart, so it's a seasonal look you'll find in its fragrant tied bunches. Head office is the WaH flowers and interiors shop in Pimlico, and there are also concessions in Liberty and Harrods.
Branch 54 Pimlico Road, SW1W 8LP (3145 0441).

Leisure

Books	**189**
CDs & Records	**201**
Electronics & Photography	**208**
Crafts, Hobbies & Parties	**214**
Musical Instruments	**225**
Sport & Fitness	**232**
Pets	**240**

French's Theatre Bookshop

Playscripts • Libretti • Audition Material • Accent CDs •
Free Theatre Books Lists • Speech Training Resources

52 Fitzroy Street London W1T 5JR
Tel: 0207 255 4300
Fax: 0207 387 2161
9.30 - 5.30 Mon - Fri, 11 - 5 Sat
email:
theatre@samuelfrench-london.co.uk

www.samuelfrench-london.co.uk

THE BOLINGBROKE BOOKSHOP
147 Northcote Road
London SW11 6QB
020 7223 9344

bolingbroke_bookshop@hotmail.com
Opening hours:
9.30 a.m. - 6.00 p.m. Mon to Sat & 11.00 a.m. - 5.00 p.m Sunday

---

Take Time Out to broaden your horizons at...

www.oxfam.org.uk

Oxfam

CHARLOTTE KNEE PHOTOGRAPHY

Professional photographer offering a bespoke and affordable service, specialising in portraits and headshots.
www.charlotteknee.com / info@charlotteknee.com / 07726 543 901

Leisure

Despite reports of the decline of the independent music and book trade, things aren't necessarily as bleak as the gloom merchants make out. Yes, there have been some sad closures over recent years, but there have also been notable openings – in particular the massive East End outpost of **Rough Trade** (*see p201*) and a new, larger branch of art bookshop **Artwords** (*see p192*). Music stores and bookshops have been at the forefront of the trend for more experience-led shopping, having traditionally been places where customer-staff interaction is particularly valued; now, enjoying a free in-store gig at Rough Trade or **Pure Groove** (*see p206*) is a regular experience for many a music buff, while London's bookshops have frequent in-house talks and events, and continue to excite those who enjoy the quality browsing experience that can never be replicated by online shops.

Photography and electronics buffs keen to get their hands on the latest gadgetry will also have a field day in the capital, while second-hand camera shops proferring vintage models cater to those who feel that modern equipment lacks the romance of yesteryear.

Londoners have become a crafty lot. Knitting and other traditional handicrafts have fitted in nicely with the eco-conscious move towards cottage industries. Modern haberdasheries can now be found in various spots around London, and Islington's popular knit shop, **Loop** (*see p220*), moved into its spacious new home on Camden Passage in 2010.

We've also become bike-crazy, with fixed-gear and single-speed bikes now a common sight on the city's roads; Soho's **Tokyo Fixed** store (*see p234*) is the latest trendy emporium for 'fixie' obsessives, while **Bobbin Bicycles** (*see p232*) has led the way in the revival of classic 'sit-up-and-beg' models.

Books

General & local

Central branches of the big chains include the massive **Waterstone's** flagship (203-206 Piccadilly, SW1Y 6WW, 7851 2400, www.waterstones.co.uk), which has a bar/restaurant, and the academic bookseller **Blackwell's** (100 Charing Cross Road, WC2H 0JG, 7292 5100, www.blackwell.co.uk).

The **British Library Bookshop** (British Library, 96 Euston Road, NW1 2DB, 7412 7735, www.bl.uk/bookshop) stocks some good literature and history titles based on the collections.

Broadway Bookshop

6 Broadway Market, E8 4QJ (7241 1626, www.broadwaybookshophackney.com). London Fields rail or 26, 55 bus. **Open** 10am-6pm Tue-Sat; 11am-5pm Sun. This Hackney independent benefits from its position on the canal end of popular Broadway Market. A smart layout and intelligently weighed stock boost its appeal further. The shop is a thoughtful enterprise, promoting small publishers like Eland and stocking lots of *New York Review* titles, plus interesting reprints of forgotten gems. There's plenty of top-drawer literary fiction and a large travel section that's strong on London and local history. The second-hand collectibles have become more popular since last year, with punters keen to get their hands on old Penguins and 1930s and '40s hardbacks. The shop is also a permanent exhibition space, promoting local artists.

Daunt Books HOT 50
83-84 Marylebone High Street, W1U 4QW (7224 2295, www.dauntbooks.co.uk). Baker Street tube.
Open 9am-7.30pm Mon-Sat; 11am-6pm Sun.
Though not strictly a travel bookshop, this beautiful Edwardian shop will always be seen first and foremost as a travel specialist thanks to its elegant three-level back room complete with oak balconies, viridian-green walls, conservatory ceiling and stained-glass window – home to row upon row of guide books, maps, language reference, history, politics, travelogue and related fiction organised by country. France, Britain, Italy and the United States are particularly well represented; go downstairs to find more far-flung destinations. Travel aside, Daunt is also a first-rate stop for literary fiction, biography, gardening and much more. James Daunt's commitment to providing proper careers for his workers ensures an informed and keen team of staff.
Branches 51 South End Road, NW3 2QB (7794 8206); 193 Haverstock Hill, NW3 4QL (7794 4006); 112-114 Holland Park Avenue, W11 4UA; 158-164 Fulham Road, SW10 9PR (7373 4997).

Foyles HOT 50
113-119 Charing Cross Road, WC2H 0EB (7437 5660, www.foyles.co.uk). Tottenham Court Road tube.
Open 9.30am-9pm Mon-Sat; 11.30am-6pm Sun.
Probably the single most impressive independent bookshop in London, Foyles built its reputation on the sheer volume and breadth of its stock (with 56 specialist subjects in the flagship store) and, going against the tide of bookshop closures, now boasts four stores in central London. Its five hugely comprehensive storeys accommodate other shops too: there's Ray's Jazz and café and a fine concession of Unsworth's antiquarian booksellers. Fiction at Foyles should be lauded along with an impressive range of teaching materials, computing software and the comprehensive basement medical department. Elsewhere, there's an extensive music department, a large gay-interest section, an impressive range of foreign fiction, law and business, philosophy and sport. The shop hosts regular events featuring well-known faces like Billy Bragg, Sophie Dahl and John Gray (visit the website for more details).
Branches Southbank Centre, Riverside, SE1 8XX (7440 3212); St Pancras International, Euston Road, N1C 4QL (3206 2650); Westfield, W12 7GE (3206 2656).

Hatchards

187 Piccadilly, W1J 9LE (7439 9921, www.hatchards.co.uk). Piccadilly Circus tube. **Open** 9.30am-7pm Mon-Sat; noon-6pm Sun.

Holding court with Fortnum & Mason and other Piccadilly royalty is London's oldest surviving bookshop, dating back to 1797. Its old-school charm and refined aura have helped it maintain an ambience all its own (even though it's now owned by HMV). The grand shop is extensive in its stock, but particularly good for travel and biography, new hardback fiction and signed editions. Benjamin Disraeli, Lord Byron and Oscar Wilde are former fans. These days, celebrated authors come to sign the books – recent visitors include Antonia Fraser, Ian McEwan and Philip Pullman. Mowbray's religious booksellers is located on the third floor. Hatchards prides itself on its knowledgeable staff and professional service.

John Sandoe HOT 50

10 Blacklands Terrace, SW3 2SR (7589 9473, www.johnsandoe.com). Sloane Square tube. **Open** 9.30am-5.30pm Mon, Tue, Thur-Sat; 9.30am-7.30pm Wed; noon-6pm Sun.

John Sandoe founded the shop in 1957 and, though he has passed away, his legacy is one of the best local independents in London with a loyal and ever-growing clientele, professional staff and enviably broad stock.

New and classic releases rub spines with more unusual items – books with no ISBN or that have been privately printed, for example. These are bought safe in the knowledge that certain customers will be interested – a testament to the personal relationship here between staff and visitors. There's a high proportion of quality hardbacks, a very full travel section upstairs and a fun children's section in the basement. Half the ground floor is devoted to art, photography and architecture.

London Review Bookshop

14 Bury Place, WC1A 2JL (7269 9030, www.lrbshop.co.uk). Holborn or Tottenham Court Road tube. **Open** 10am-6.30pm Mon-Sat; noon-6pm Sun.

If you're looking for a place to inspire you to get reading then this is it, from the inviting and stimulating presentation to the clear quality of the books chosen. Politics, current affairs and history are well represented on the ground floor, while downstairs, books on CD lead on to thorough and exciting poetry and philosophy sections – everything you'd expect from a shop owned by the *London Review of Books*. The LRB's events programme has seen authors such as Martin Amis, Christopher Hitchens and Anne Enright visit, while all sorts of writers and journalists stop by at the adjoining London Review Cake Shop, a breezy coffeeshop that displays original art. The shop also sells second-hand books, mainly modern first editions, and co-publishes signed limited editions by writers such as Julian Barnes and Ian McEwan.

Owl Bookshop

209 Kentish Town Road, NW5 2JU (7485 7793). Kentish Town tube/rail. **Open** 9am-6pm Mon-Sat; noon-5pm Sun.

A clever rearrange has made Kentish Town's Owl Bookshop easier to negotiate: classic fiction has been given room to expand and there are now some armchairs to help you relax while you mull over your choices. Trading for a good three decades, the shop covers food and drink, gardening, sport and fiction, with all stock judiciously laid out. There's a strong children's section to the right as you come in and a smart selection of stationery and magazines for sale. Owl also stocks some DVDs (mainly cult and classic films) and CDs (particularly classical, world music and jazz). You can combine fiction and non-fiction in the popular four-for-three promotions. All in all, a valuable local resource in this part of north London.

Special interest

London's main art galleries, such as **Tate Britain**, **Tate Modern**, the **Design Museum**, as well as the **National Gallery** should also be first ports-of-call for books on art.

Foyles

Artwords Bookshop HOT 50

65A Rivington Street, EC2A 3QQ (7729 2000, www.artwords.co.uk). Old Street tube/rail. **Open** 10.30am-7pm Mon-Sat.

Partly thanks to its location in artist-dense Hoxton but also due to its knowledgeable staff, Artwords has its finger firmly on the pulse when it comes to contemporary visual arts publications. As well as offering a vast collection of up-to-date books from the UK, the shop regularly imports new works from Europe, North America and Australia. Stock relating to contemporary fine art dominates, but there are also plenty of architecture, photography, graphic design, fashion, advertising and film titles, plus a range of DVDs and industry and creative magazines – including the Eastern European import Piktogram, the painting-specialist TurpsBanana and the interdisciplinary Cabinet. *See also right* **Shop talk**.
Branch 20-22 Broadway Market, E8 4QJ (7923 7507).

Atlantis Bookshop

49A Museum Street, WC1A 1LY (7405 2120, www.theatlantisbookshop.com). Holborn or Tottenham Court Road tube. **Open** 10.30am-6pm Mon-Sat.

London's oldest independent bookshop on the occult (it opened back in 1922) sells new and secondhand titles on everything from angels and fairies, vampires, werewolves, earth mysteries and magic, to yoga, meditation, feng shui, healing, green issues, spiritualism and psychology. The shop also hosts regular events such as 'Discovering the Runes (for beginners)' and the popular 'Psychic Café' series. The physical shop is petite in size, but a much larger range of stock is available from the company's e-shop (see the website listed above). The shop's in-store noticeboard is a useful resource for finding out about practitioners of alternative therapies, as well as external events.

Bookmarks

1 Bloomsbury Street, WC1B 3QE (7637 1848, www.bookmarks.uk.com). Tottenham Court Road tube. **Open** noon-7pm Mon; 10am-7pm Tue-Fri; 10am-6pm Sat.

From each according to his ability, to each according to his reads: Bookmarks is London's premier socialist bookshop, going strong for more than three decades, despite constant threats from, well, global capitalism (Amazon is 'the Starbuck's of the booktrade', say staff). Bookmarks (almost a pun) sees itself as a home for ideas and an enabler of those ideas in a practical manner, regularly 'taking ideas to the movement' by setting up stalls at rallies, providing information about activism and hosting author events; Patrick Cockburn, Sara Paretsky and Melissa Benn (Tony's wife) have all been guests. The shop's spacious, airy interior (replete with replica Soviet sculpture) holds a fabulous collection of left-wing writing – lots of history and politics of course, but also a small but well-chosen fiction section, left-wing second-handers and a great, thought-provoking children's section. As official bookshop for near-neighbour the TUC, there are also many trade union publications.

Books for Cooks

4 Blenheim Crescent, W11 1NN (7221 1992, www.booksforcooks.com). Ladbroke Grove/Notting Hill Gate tube. **Open** 10am-6pm Tue-Sat.

The astute book shopper will have noticed the number of London bookshops opening coffeeshops to attract customers. Books for Cooks puts them all to shame – it has its own kitchen in the back, where recipes from a massive stock of cookery books are put to the test and sold from midday (no reservations). The most successful of them are compiled into the shop's own publications (£5.99 each). The front room is stacked high with books covering hundreds of cuisines, chefs and cookery techniques, as well as food-related fiction, culinary history, foodie biographies and nutrition. The Authors' Lunch and Dinner series is going strong – the likes of Tessa Kiros, Jay Rayner and Mark Hix demonstrate how to make a three-course meal from one of their books; workshops and evening classes are another way to get stuck in (see website for details).

Forbidden Planet

179 Shaftesbury Avenue, WC2H 8JR (7420 3666, www.forbiddenplanet.com). Covent Garden or Tottenham Court Road tube. **Open** 10am-7pm Mon-Wed, Fri; 10am-8pm Thur; noon-6pm Sun.

Self-confessed geeks (and otherwise) get together at London's mega-store for sci-fi, fantasy and comic-related books and memorabilia. Forbidden Planet stocks thousands of books – covering science fiction, animation, graphic arts, computer games, film, horror, sport, superheroes, and more – as well as a huge range of graphic novels, from classic Marvel comics, to obscure small publishers from around the world, to Viz manuals. The store also stocks a good number of signed books, as well as a huge range of DVDs, action figures, posters, clothing, games, and other genre-related merchandise. What's more, author events take place here regularly. A first port-of-call for *Star Wars*, *Buffy the Vampire Slayer* and *Doctor Who* obsessives.

Gay's the Word

66 Marchmont Street, WC1N 1AB (7278 7654, www.gaystheword.co.uk). Russell Square tube.
Open 10am-6.30pm Mon-Sat; 2-6pm Sun.

In 2010, as Camden council threatened a rent hike of 25%, the future looked uncertain for Britain's only dedicated gay and lesbian bookshop (established in 1979). Its last financial crisis was back in 2007 when the shop launched a shelf-sponsorship programme called Cash for Honours, which drew support from loyal

Books

Shop talk
Ben Hillwood-Harris, owner of Artwords

Tell us about the shop
'We sell books, magazines and DVDs on the contemporary visual arts – everything from architecture, fashion and graphic design to the theory and history of art. We specialise in newly published books and stock a wide variety from overseas. We also publish a small number of books, and we host events in-store.

'The Rivington Street branch was our first shop, which we set up in 2001. I had been employed by another business as shop buyer and manager. Over time I became frustrated by the limitations on what I could and couldn't stock. So I developed a plan to open my own shop. I identified Shoreditch as the ideal location and started looking for a shop for rent – basically there was nothing there, or they were too big and expensive, but mainly very little retail shops in the Shoreditch Triangle at the time; but I managed to find a small space that had retail usage. I'm still here now!

'We opened another branch on Broadway Market [see p137 **Streetwise**] last summer.'

What are your most popular publications?
'Not surprisingly, books that are predominantly visual are the most popular, so monographs make up some of our biggest sellers. The most anticipated magazine is *Apartamento*, but we also have high demand for *Lula* and *Acne Paper*.

'There is an official statistic that a certain percentage of books sold (60%, I think) are bought as gifts for others. This is probably true.'

Have you noticed changes in the London shopping scene over the past few years?
'Yes, in a way there is a growing market for the independent shop owner. I think there's an increasing number of people who are interested in books and in the more exclusive, unique side of things. These are people who look for limited editions and signed copies. We're finding more and more people who are interested in quality rather than availability, in spite of the recession.'

What is the nicest aspect of owning a shop?
'Finding the right book for the right customer is always an enjoyable experience – tracking down an obscure or one-off title, and sourcing amazing new books and magazines that I know will appeal to our customers. And I love where I work… I think [Rivington Street] is the most walked down road in Shoreditch! The sun rises at one end and sets at the other.'

What are your favourite shops in London?
'I go to Sister Ray (*see p201*) on Berwick Street for music, and I love the sailing shop Arthur Beale (*see p237*) on Shaftesbury Avenue. The shop General Woodwork Supplies (76-80 Stoke Newington High Street, N16 7PA, 7254 6052) caters to all DIY needs. For amazing world and independent cinema rentals there's the Film Shop on Broadway Market (no.33, E8 4PH, 7923 1230, www.thefilmshop.co.uk). Obviously Rough Trade East (*see p201*) for music; and near us is a great little designer shop for men's and women's clothes called Start (*see p65*).'

Any plans for the future?
'A new, larger shop on Rivington Street and then an additional shop in west London.'

▶ For **Artwords**, *see left*.

customers including Sarah Waters, Ali Smith and Simon Callow. Stock covers fiction, history and biography, as well as more specialist holdings in queer studies, sex and relationships, children, and parenting. In addition to regular author readings and book-signings (think Adam Mars-Jones, Armistead Maupin, Neil Bartlett, Clare Summerskill), there are weekly lesbian and monthly trans discussion groups.

Gosh!
39 Great Russell Street, WC1B 3NZ (7636 1011, www.goshlondon.com). Tottenham Court Road tube.
Open 10am-6pm Mon-Wed, Sat, Sun; 10am-7pm Thur, Fri.
There's never been a better time to take up reading comics – and there's nowhere better to bolster your collection than at this Bloomsbury specialist. Half of the basement room is given over to comics while the other holds a fine stash of Manga. It's graphic novels that take centre stage, though, from early classics like *Krazy Kat* and *Little Nemo* to Alan Moore's Peter Pan adaptation *Lost Girls*. The legendary Moore is one of many high-profile authors to have signed here. Bryan Talbot (*Alice in Sunderland*) is another. Gosh! has begun to sell exclusive bookplated editions of some works – authors sign tip-in sheets that collectors can then add to their copies; plates upcoming when we visited included Mike Mignola and Duncan Fregredo's *Hellboy: Darkness Calls*, Nick Abadzis's *Laika* and Gilbert Shelton's *Complete Fabulous Furry Freak Brothers Omnibus*. Classic children's books, of the *This is London* vein, are also a plus point here.

Grant & Cutler
55-57 Great Marlborough Street, W1F 7AY (7734 2012, www.grantandcutler.com). Oxford Circus tube.
Open 10am-6.30pm Mon-Wed, Fri; 10am-7pm Thur; 10.30am-6.30pm Sat; noon-6pm Sun.
Offering an exhaustive collection (some 55,000 items) of foreign-language books, reference works and teaching aids in more than 150 languages, Grant & Cutler is an essential resource for language students and their profs. Much of the material is for hardcore study, but there are interesting translations too. French is still the biggest section, with Spanish snapping at its toes; the Eastern European languages section is also strong (and includes items like the UK driving theory test in Polish). Elsewhere there's Scrabble in several languages and international films on DVD. G&C was set up in 1936 as a lending library, which may explain its dull decor. Amuse yourself by working out how many languages your shop assistant speaks.

Koenig Books
80 Charing Cross Road, WC2H 0BF (7240 8190, www.koenigbooks.co.uk). Leicester Square tube.
Open 10am-8pm Mon-Wed, Fri, Sat; 10am-9pm Thur; noon-6pm Sun.
An inspiring, German-owned independent bookshop specialising in art, architecture and photography tomes. Koenig's first London branch is based in the Serpentine Gallery, and the other is the newest addition to the capital's traditional literary artery – Charing Cross Road. The latter shop is done out stylishly in black and every book is given respectful prominence – products are displayed with their covers rather than spines facing customers to ensure their full effect. Both branches of Koenig have full access to the stock of mammoth arts bookshop Buchhandlung Walther Koenig in Cologne, so can order you just about anything you can think of.
Branches Serpentine Gallery, Kensington Gardens, W2 3XA (7706 4907); Whitechapel Gallery Bookshop (managed by Koenig Books), 77-82 Whitechapel High Street, E1 7QX (7522 7897).

Magma
117-119 Clerkenwell Road, EC1R 5BY (7242 9503, www.magmabooks.com). Chancery Lane tube or Farringdon tube/rail. **Open** 10am-7pm Mon-Sat.
There's all the design, architecture, graphics and creative magazines you could want here, but the main stock is large-format art and design books. Its objective is to blur the boundary between bookshop and exhibition space, making visits interactive and educational experiences. As well as the usual look-at-me coffee-table books, there are lots of in-depth essay collections, plus obscure and fun tomes. If you can visualise it, there's probably a book on it here, with stock covering everything from Banksy to less predictable items like Custom Kicks (about customised trainers). There are also numerous unbookish design-related items, such as the blank toys that you can make your own and a popular T-shirt range. Try the nearby arty products sister store for trendy bicycle clips, Moomin-print kitchenware or tiny Ikimono cameras designed to fit to your keychain.
Branches 8 Earlham Street, WC2H 9RY (7240 8498).

John Sandoe. *See p191.*

Persephone Books

59 Lamb's Conduit Street, WC1N 3NB (7242 9292, www.persephonebooks.co.uk). Holborn or Russell Square tube. **Open** 10am-6pm Mon-Fri; noon-5pm Sat.

The main office of this publisher and bookseller is piled high with lovingly restored reprints of unfairly neglected women writers, mainly from the interwar period. These beautiful objects are covered in identical plain eggshell blue, but each book's endpapers comprise wonderful re-creations of patterns – wallpapers, fabrics, clothing or suchlike – contemporary with the book; but, more importantly, they make for fascinating reading. Some are by well-known names – Penelope Mortimer, Katherine Mansfield, Virginia Woolf – while others offer the chance to get to know quick-witted women who, by virtue of the time in which they lived, were not given the respect they might otherwise have gained in their own lifetimes. There's *William – an Englishman*, Cicely Hamilton's 1919 exploration of war; or *Someone at a Distance* (1953), in which Dorothy Whipple traces the effects of a man's infidelity on his family. Persephone's bestseller is *Miss Pettigrew Lives for a Day* (1938) by Winifred Watson.

Stanfords

12-14 Long Acre, WC2E 9LP (7836 1321, www.stanfords.co.uk). Covent Garden or Leicester Square tube. **Open** 9am-7.30pm Mon-Wed, Fri; 9am-8pm Thur; 10am-8pm Sat; noon-6pm Sun.

Escape the throngs of tourists on Long Acre by ducking for a breather into this inspirational travel shop. Stanfords is almost as essential to your trip as suntan lotion. In addition to every kind of travel guide, you'll find background literature on every conceivable destination, a specially selected fiction range, world music and cinema, a children's section and navigation software in the basement. The selection of equipment like medical kits, binoculars and torches (all upstairs) has also grown in recent years. Check out the giant maps on each shop floor, then go to the basement and have your very own customised map or aerial photograph printed out in poster form. Adding even more character, Stanfords stocks atlases and antique maps and guides. A café is now open at the back of the ground floor.

Travel Bookshop

13-15 Blenheim Crescent, W11 2EE (7229 5260, www.thetravelbookshop.com). Ladbroke Grove or Notting Hill Gate tube. **Open** 10am-6pm Mon-Sat; noon-5pm Sun.

Success hasn't gone to the head of this Blenheim Crescent establishment. Since finding fame as the inspiration for Hugh Grant's store in Richard Curtis's *Notting Hill*, it's continued to open up the world to residents of its chi-chi neighbourhood. At the front is the Europe room; turn right for the excellent UK and London room or go straight ahead for well-lit Africa, Asia, Australasia and Americas sections. All are filled with travel guides and background reading. There's a small but pretty children's section, a range of colourful cards, a decent selection of road maps and, as you would expect, a fab choice of coffee-table travel books. Knowledgeable staff display clippings of recent reviews to help with your choices. Collectors may wish to peruse the cabinets of first- and early-edition travel books.

Secondhand & antiquarian

The book stalls underneath Waterloo Bridge, near BFI Southbank, are a hotspot for browsers.

Any Amount of Books

56 Charing Cross Road, WC2H 0QA (7836 3697, www.anyamountofbooks.com). Leicester Square tube. **Open** 10.30am-9.30pm Mon-Sat; 11.30am-8.30pm Sun.

This Charing Cross stalwart seems to have smartened up a little over the last year; fear not, the bare floorboards

Magma. See p194.

and wooden shelving remain, but the stock seems easier to negotiate than in times past. Specialising principally in arts and literature, Any Amount is jam-packed with decent quality books on all subjects. Prices range from £1 to £2,000 (including, amusingly, a 'medium-rare' section). The shop had a scoop in 2007 by acquiring the library of Angela Carter; more recently, the books of noted *bon viveur* Norman Douglas made their way here. Diversifying a little never hurts business either, and the shop has developed a sideline selling collections of leather bindings to interior decorators, set designers and posh drinking establishments.

Bernard J Shapero
32 St George Street, W1S 2EA (7493 0876, www.shapero.com). Bond Street or Oxford Circus tube. **Open** 9.30am-6.30pm Mon-Fri; 11am-5pm Sat.
Bernard J Shapero's interesting collection of antiquarian and out-of-print texts is enticingly displayed over four floors in these smart Mayfair premises. Specialisms here include travel (with a comprehensive collection of Baedeker guides), natural history, literature and colour-plate books. The shop's newest department deals with books from and about Russia and there are also rare maps and atlases and monographs of early photography. The shop began in Grays Antiques Market in 1979 and moved to Notting Hill before settling here over a decade ago; the range, presentation and, above all, quality of its beautiful volumes are second to none. One for the serious collector – though by no means unapproachable to the rest of us.

Goldsboro
7 Cecil Court, WC2N 4EZ (7497 9230, www.goldsborobooks.com). Leicester Square tube. **Open** 10am-6pm Mon-Sat.
Goldsboro stands out from the crowd along this street of antiquarian booksellers. As the largest signed first-edition specialist in the UK, its premises may not bulge with the weight of stock as at most Cecil Court repositories, but everything here has been autographed by its author. Writers regularly sign consignments of first editions (mostly from the 1960s onwards), which often sell for the same price as unsigned editions elsewhere: there were around 200 such copies of Salman Rushdie's brand-new *The Enchantress of Florence* on our visit; other big names include Ian Rankin and Wilbur Smith. Goldsboro is also responsible for one of the

world's largest first-edition book clubs; there's a new title each month and many are exclusive to the store and bound in limited-edition slipcases.

Henry Sotheran
2-5 Sackville Street, W1S 3DP (7439 6151, www.sotherans.co.uk). Green Park or Piccadilly Circus tube. **Open** 9.30am-6pm Mon-Fri; 10am-4pm Sat.

A fine old-fashioned antiquarian bookshop, Henry Sotheran combines its well-founded association with quality, class and tradition – established in York back in 1761, the business moved to London nearly 200 years ago, in 1815 – with a surprisingly relaxed ambience. The extraordinary range of stock covers English literature (specialising in first and important editions of works from the 17th to the 20th centuries), children's and illustrated titles, travel and exploration, art and architecture, science and natural history. Departments are run by specialists, so novices can be assured of being guided by informed hands, while opportunities for collectors are abundant (past acquisitions have included the libraries of Laurence Sterne and Charles Dickens). Prices fittingly often run into the thousands here – a first edition of *The Origin of Species* sold for £82,000 recently – though they start at around £20. In recent years, greater emphasis has been placed on the shop's fine collection of prints and posters downstairs, where two or three exhibitions are put on per year – prints by William Blake were a recent attraction.

Jarndyce
46 Great Russell Street, WC1B 3PA (7631 4220, www.jarndyce.co.uk). Tottenham Court Road or Holborn tube. **Open** 10.30am-5.30pm Mon-Fri.

In Dickens's *Bleak House* Jarndyce and Jarndyce was the law case that consumed all the money the litigants were fighting over. In contrast, the stock in this charming bookshop, which is housed in a building dating back to the 1730s and located opposite the British Museum, is most reasonably priced, with exciting finds from £10. The shop does maintain its links to the great man himself, though, with a suitably large collection of Dickens that had been freshly catalogued on our last visit. The owners believe strongly in the durability and good value of an 18th- or 19th-century hardback – the focus of this fine institution. Other specialisms here include pamphlets, street literature, women writers and chapbooks from the period. Proprietor Brian Lake is known for his publication *Fish Who Answer the Telephone* (co-edited with Russell Ash) and other amusingly titled publications.

Marchpane
16 Cecil Court, WC2N 4HE (7836 8661, www.marchpane.com). Leicester Square tube. **Open** 11am-6pm Mon-Sat.

Opened in 1989, London's longest-serving specialist for children's books, Marchpane, is the only bookshop we know with its own BBC Dalek. Other features are signed photos of Russian cosmonauts, punk fanzines and circuit board fixtures. Since 2008, the shop has also housed a fully functional Scalextric track downstairs (the owner is making up for not having had one as a child). Stock includes classics such as *Winnie-the-Pooh* and *The Wind in the Willows*, and the shop specialises in Lewis Carroll, with a collection of illustrated editions of *Alice's Adventures in Wonderland*, but you don't need to be a serious collector to appreciate the stock, which starts at around £5 and includes some real gems. Downstairs, near the gramophone and chaise-longue, are drawers housing periodicals from the 1930s to '60s.

Nigel Williams
25 Cecil Court, WC2N 4EZ (7836 7757, www.nigelwilliams.com). Leicester Square tube. **Open** 10am-6pm Mon-Sat.

Nigel Williams stocks mainly 20th-century first editions costing between £15 and £15,000. On the ground floor is a wonderful collection of rare children's books, including what staff call 'the three Bs' – Biggles, Bunter and Blyton – and a host of popular 20th-century authors and illustrators such as AA Milne, Arthur Rackham and Heath Robinson. There's also the 'Wodehouse Wall' – which staff conjecture is the largest collection of PG

Persephone Books. See p195.

Wodehouse in the country – and a growing poetry section. Approximately 10% of the stock is signed. The owners believe that collecting first editions needn't be expensive and advise potential purchasers to collect the kind of thing they take pleasure in: a good place to start is the shop's pleasingly unpretentious basement collection, which places strong emphasis on popular genres like crime and detective fiction. Whether it's John Fowles or Dick Francis you're after, books here are all less than £250, sometimes as low as £10.

Quinto/Francis Edwards
72 Charing Cross Road, WC2H 0BE (7379 7669). Leicester Square tube. **Open** 9am-9pm Mon-Sat; noon-8pm Sun.
A stalwart of Charing Cross Road, in 2010 Quinto and Francis Edwards moved from their premises at 48A just up the road to 72, but their remit remains the same: to sell antiquarian, rare, second-hand and collectible books and to continue their deservedly famous monthly wholesale change of stock, with new books brought regularly from Hay-on-Wye; lines of customers still extend down the street at 2pm on the chosen Sunday. There's a rolling stock of around 50,000 titles, so you'll feel like you've earned your find, especially if you're rooting around the assortment of titles in the basement. Francis Edwards concentrates more on military history.

Simon Finch Rare Books
26 Brook Street, W1K 5DQ (7499 0974, www.simonfinch.com). Bond Street tube. **Open** 10am-6pm Mon-Fri.
Simon Finch's four floors of printed material contain non-stop surprises in the fields of English and European literature, science, early printing, art, photography and architecture. Simon Finch certainly has an eye for intriguing items, from HG Wells's *The First Men in the Moon* signed by the second man on the moon, Buzz Aldrin, to Twiggy's modelling card from 1968. The ground floor houses mainly 20th-century works, while older books are held on the first. Finch produces several catalogues a year; prices start at around £20 or £30, so it's worth popping in even if you're not a serious collector. Once you've got past the door buzzer, staff are welcoming.

Skoob
Unit 66, The Brunswick, WC1N 1AE (7278 8760, www.skoob.com). Russell Square tube. **Open** 10.30am-8pm Mon-Sat; 10.30am-6pm Sun.
In 2008, Skoob returned to business in the Brunswick Centre and we're delighted to say it's still going strong. The 2,500sq ft of floor space may be in a basement with concrete walls and exposed piping, but the operation is light and airy, and recent reshuffles have made it more logical to navigate the 60,000 titles on display, which cover almost every subject imaginable – from philosophy, biography, maths and science to languages, literature and criticism, art, history, economics and politics. Holdings are regularly refreshed with stock from the 750,000-strong shop in Oxford that's also run by personable owner Chris Edwards, and as other bookshops round the country collapse, Skoob buys their stock. Unlike its name, Skoob is not backward in coming forwards, and long may it continue. There's a discount for students, Wedge card holders and cinema-goers.

Travis & Emery
17 Cecil Court, WC2N 4EZ (7240 2129, www.travis-and-emery.com). Leicester Square tube. **Open** 10.15am-6.45pm Mon-Sat; 11.30am-5pm Sun.
Specialist second-hand music shops are thin on the ground in London; it's no surprise that the best one should be in Cecil Court, home of antiquarian publications and convenient for customers popping in for a browse before going to the nearby Coliseum Opera House. It stocks mostly collectors' music: libretti for operas, music history and theory books and collectable programmes and play-bills. Travis & Emery is strong on piano, violin, flute and organ music, but all music is catered for. Staff are musicians and very knowledgeable – ask them if you can't find something as they may have it in the basement storeroom. Upstairs is mainly sheet music, with reference works behind the counter. It's good for out-of-print music, and is popular with students; much of the second-hand stock is as good as new.

Simon Finch Rare Books

Streetwise Cecil Court, WC2

The central London passageway that's fervent browsing territory for bibliophiles and history buffs.

Bookended by rumbling Charing Cross Road and St Martin's Lane, this picturesque pedestrian cut-through is known for its line-up of antiquarian book, map and print dealers. But Cecil Court was once a leader in a brasher form of entertainment. The nascent film industry set up shop here in the late 19th century, when it became known as Flicker Alley – some of the earliest moving pictures shown in this country would have been projected on to the walls of its quaint townhouses. Until fairly recently, there was a steel door within **Greening Burland** (no.27, 7836 0999), a specialist in mystery, crime and science fiction – a reminder that cinematic film was flammable and needed to be kept in isolation. specialises. Today the only movie connections are in the form of inspiration as a period location: the passage is reputed to have been the model for Diagon Alley in the *Harry Potter* franchise, and Renée Zellweger's Beatrix Potter sees her first edition of *Peter Rabbit* in a Cecil Court shopfront in the film *Miss Potter*.

Antique map and book specialist **Tim Bryars** (no.8; 7836 1901), who is also secretary of the Cecil Court Association, has researched the alley's history, and the antique maps he sells emphasise the lack of development in the area at the time the alley was laid out in the 1670s.

The street deserves a mention in the annals of British crime history. The 18th-century residents were regularly engaged in highway robbery, forgery and arson, and in 1735 Elizabeth Calloway set fire to her brandy shop for insurance. The fire destroyed 15 houses in neighbouring St Martin's Court and caused the death of William Hogarth's mother. In more recent times, the street was the site of the 1961 murder of antiques shop assistant Elsie May Batten – the first crime to be solved with the use of Identikit, then a novel import from America.

Although there were booksellers here by the early 20th century – the Foyles brothers opened at no.14 in 1904, before relocating to their current flagship premises (*see p190*) – it wasn't until the 1920s that they moved in en masse. Mystical and spiritual specialist **Watkins** (no.19 & 21; 7836 2182) is the oldest store, on site since 1904. But the longest-serving individual resident is **David Drummond at Pleasures of Past Times** at no.11 (7836 1142), who set up shop here more than 40 years ago. Drummond was dubbed 'the last of the eccentric booksellers' by Simon Callow, and calls himself 'the doyen of the Court'. President of the Cecil Court Association, he caters to a thespian crowd, selling tatty but valuable playbills, magic books and assorted theatrical ephemera. Past customers have included Sir John Gielgud and Alec Guinness. Sword swallowers and 'Punch & Judy men' have also passed through the shop over the years.

Because each Cecil Court shop is unique, they don't seem to tread on one another's toes. For example, at no.16, **Marchpane**'s (*see p197*) collection of children's literature, with its emphasis on Lewis Carroll, is quite different to **Nigel Williams**'s stock, at no.25 (for both, *see p197*), where you'll find lots of annuals. Besides, the latter has a huge collection of Wodehouse, as well as modern firsts in the basement, while the former boasts its own Dalek. Similarly, **Tindley & Chapman** at no.4 (7240 2161) and **Goldsboro** at no.7 (*see p196*) both specialise in first editions, but the former concentrates on second-hand items, while the latter operates an impressive signed-copy book club. A stone's throw away, **Travis & Emery** (no.17; *see p198*) stocks new and old books on music, opera programmes, photographs and playbills.

▶ www.cecilcourt.co.uk

INTOXICA!

231 Portobello Road London W11 1LT
www.intoxica.co.uk intoxica@intoxica.co.uk
T: 0207 229 8010 F: 0207 792 9778

SECOND-HAND & NEW VINYL
originals - reissues - 45s - LPs
60s soul - beat - psych - jazz
70s funk - blues - beats & breaks
soundtracks - punk - weird stuff

nearest tube Ladbroke Grove
open 7 days a week

flashback

Buy Online Direct At
WWW.FLASHBACK.CO.UK
Experts In All Genres Of Rare & Collectable Vinyl, From Jungle to Prog, Rock to Jazz
50 Essex Rd, Islington, London, N1 8LR
(+44)(0)20 7354 9356
144 Crouch Hill, Crouch End, London, N8 9DX
(+44)(0)20 8342 9633

"After the glass-and-chrome titans of Oxford Street, frenetic with escalators and decibels and security guards, Harold Moores is a Dickensian haven ..."
- *An Equal Music*, Vikram Seth

SERVICE WITH A SMILE

HAROLD MOORES RECORDS

SHOP OPENING HOURS:
Monday to Saturday 10am to 6:30pm

Mail orders by phone, fax or via our website.
Worldwide post-free delivery for all CD orders

T 020 7437 1576   F 020 7287 0377
E sales@hmrecords.demon.co.uk   W www.hmrecords.co.uk

Harold Moores Records Limited
2 Great Marlborough Street, London W1F 7HQ

Revival Records

What? A New Record Store??

Now Open at:
30 Berwick St,
Soho W1

BUY SELL TRADE

"We **REALLY DO** pay the highest prices for your unwanted Vinyl and CDs"

020 7437 4271
revival.records@gmail.com

CDs & Records

General

Brill
27 Exmouth Market, EC1R 4QL (7833 9757, www.clerkenwellmusic.co.uk). Angel tube or Farringdon tube/rail. **Open** *7.30am-6pm Mon-Fri; 9am-6pm Sat.*
It's no misnomer: this small CD store/café has a strong local following and is a great place to add to your collection without being patronised by record fascists. Stock is CD-only; not all back-catalogue records make the cut and new releases only do if they're suitably interesting. You'll find a rock section that mixes classic albums by Pavement with newer releases from Fleet Foxes, a soul rack where the Marvin Gayes and Al Greens of this world snuggle up to the Corinne Bailey Raes and Marie Knights, and eclectic jazz, reggae, pop, country and world sections. Overseeing the operation is Jeremy Brill himself, as affable as he is informed, cheerfully dispensing fresh (Fairtrade) coffee, Brick Lane bagels and Flower Power bakery cakes for consumption at a smattering of outdoor and window seats.

HMV Megastore
150 Oxford Street, W1D 1DJ (7631 3423, www.hmv.com). Oxford Circus or Tottenham Court Road tube. **Open** *9am-8.30pm Mon-Wed, Fri, Sat; 9am-9pm Thur; 11.30am-6pm Sun.*
Oxford Street's only remaining megastore – now that Virgin/Zavvi and Borders have bitten the dust – the HMV flagship is a first and last stop for CDs, records and DVDs covering all genres. The sensory overload may be too much for those who prefer the more relaxing and personalised atmosphere of some of the small independents, but there's no denying the width and breadth of the stock available here. And with competitive seasonal sales, cut-price box sets and hundreds of rarities and imports, there's little chance you'll leave this world-beating behemoth of a store empty-handed. The vast basement houses broad classical, world music and jazz sections, and staff are always on hand to locate discs for you.

Rough Trade East `HOT 50`
Dray Walk, Old Truman Brewery, 91 Brick Lane, E1 6QL (7392 7788, www.roughtrade.com). Shoreditch High Street rail. **Open** *8am-9pm Mon-Thur; 8am-8pm Fri, Sat; 11am-7pm Sun.*
Celebrating its 35th birthday in 2011, this infamous temple to indie music has never looked more upbeat, its new-found impetus provided by its venture east in August 2007. Rough Trade East's truly inspiring 5,000sq ft loft-style store, café and gig space offers aural beats and treats for Shoreditch's scenesters. The café sells smoothies, sarnies and beer, and rock portraits are hung around the seating area, while nu-psychedelic pop often floats out of the speakers. Both the vinyl and CD collections are dizzying in their range, spanning punk, hardcore, American and British indie, reggae, dub, funk, soul, post punk and new wave, with a large row of dance 12-inches, the highlight of which is the 'bastard pop' mash-up section. With 16 listening posts and a stage for live sets you cannot get much closer to music nirvana.
Branch (Rough Trade West) 130 Talbot Road, W11 1JA (7229 8541).

Sister Ray
34-35 Berwick Street, W1F 8RP (7734 3297, www.sisterray.co.uk). Oxford Circus or Piccadilly Circus tube. **Open** *10am-8pm Mon-Sat; noon-6pm Sun.*
Previously Selectadisc, Sister Ray remains a mecca for Berwick Street's beat obsessives on their lunchbreaks, with its flatscreen TV, customer turntables and turquoise walls – not to mention a hugely broad stock. Much of the music is on vinyl (over 20,000 plates and counting) and the shop's dedication to back-cataloguing genres like drum'n'bass, gothic and industrial, hip hop (with UK talent well represented) and rock albums puts most megastores to shame. Staff are well informed and there are plenty of new release CDs, DVDs, T-shirts and books should the vinyl not appeal, as well as regular instores from hipster bands. If in doubt, check the tacky (and cheap!) Sleeve of the Week outside for inspiration.

Second-hand

Flashback
50 Essex Road, N1 8LR (7354 9356, www.flashback.co.uk). Angel tube then 38, 56, 73, 341 bus. **Open** *10am-7pm Mon-Sat; noon-6pm Sun.*
Just a stone's throw from the cavernous Haggle Vinyl (No.114-116), but a million miles away aesthetically, Flashback's mostly second-hand stock is treated with utmost respect. There are usually a few boxes of bargain basement 12-inches going for pennies outside the front door, but inside stock is scrupulously organised. The ground floor is dedicated to CDs, with rock and pop alongside dance, soundtracks, soul, jazz and metal, while the new stock of urban and dance records, especially 1960s psych, garage and hip hop, is a well-kept secret among DJs. The basement, though, is vinyl only: an ever-expanding jazz collection jostles for space alongside soul, hip hop and an astonishing selection of library sounds (regularly plundered by producers looking for samples). Those not inclined to rummage can search out long lost gems on its website. For a more ramshackle experience, head along to Haggle.
Branch 144 Crouch Hill, N8 9DX (8342 9633).

Harold Moores Records.
See p205.

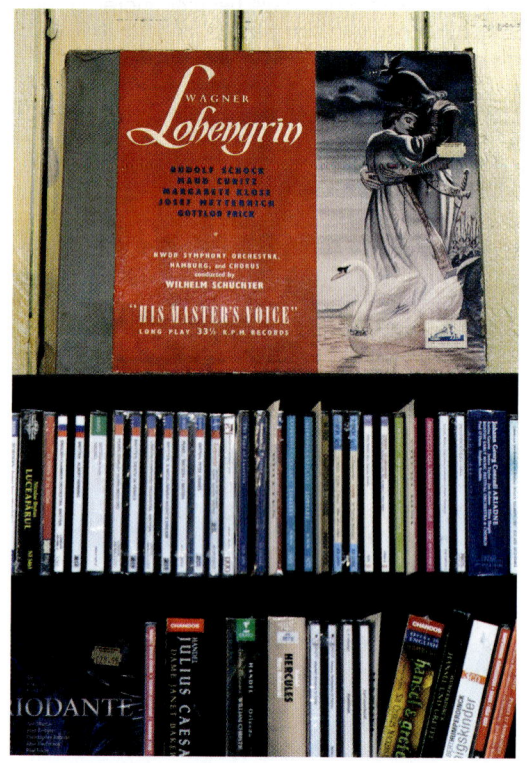

Intoxica!
231 Portobello Road, W11 1LT (7229 8010, www.intoxica.co.uk). Ladbroke Grove tube.
Open 10.30am-6.30pm Mon-Sat; noon-5pm Sun.
One of London's most idiosyncratically decorated shops, Intoxica! – a vinyl-only store – is kitted out with bamboo wall coverings and glowering tribal masks. You wouldn't want to be the last person locking up here, but it makes for a browsing experience that's as big on character as it is on classic records. The ground-floor shelves are stacked with everything from reggae, funk and '60s beat to exotica and easy listening; there's also a good range of alternative and new wave from the 1970s to today and a great soundtrack selection. The basement is packed with soul and blues, and its jazz section is especially big on British artists.

On the Beat
22 Hanway Street, W1T 1UQ (7637 8934). Tottenham Court Road tube. **Open** 11am-7pm Mon-Sat.
Put thoughts of Norman Wisdom's 1967 police comedy to one side: On the Beat is for record collectors of all stripes. Spend 15 minutes thumbing here and you'll definitely come out with something you'd forgotten you always wanted. The well-priced, mostly vinyl collection is crammed into a small room, walls lined with posters and dog-eared music mags that date back decades. In manager Tim Derbyshire's words, the large collection covers 'everything but classical' – you'll find a wealth of old funk and soul albums, a huge number of library sound compilations and a good range of jazz, country, folk and 'girl singers' records; the rock section covers everything from 1960s psychedelia to '90s pop.

Out on the Floor
10 Inverness Street, NW1 7HJ (7485 9958). Camden Town tube. **Open** 11am-6pm daily.
This three-level, three shop operation is a sanctuary for serious record collectors in an area short on decent options. Out on the Floor itself is in the basement and stocks guitar music – there's a particularly interesting selection of heavy metal seven-inches and plenty of punk, prog and 1960s and '70s rock. The ground floor hosts Up at Out on the Floor, home to a well-chosen collection of 12-inch reggae and 1960s soul and a limited array of CDs. Despite the unwieldy name, hand-drawn psychedelic signs for the 12-inches give the place a particular charm. In between the two floors is Backroom Records, catering to the upper end of the collectors' market with a greater emphasis on poster art and silkscreen prints.

Revival Records
30 Berwick Street, W1F 8RH (7437 4271, www.revivalrecords.uk.com) Oxford Circus tube.
Open 10am-7pm Mon-Sat.

Shop talk
Simon Singleton, Manager of Pure Groove

Tell us about the shop
'It's been open for about 20 years, but we've been here [at Smithfields, Farringdon] for just two.
'It's a record shop that's evolved to also be a music hub: we have live performances; we release our own records; and we hold film and comedy nights. We try to make everything we do music-led – it's still at our core.'

Who shops here?
'It's a complete mix. Because of where we are located we get a lot of office workers; young hipsters are attracted to us because of the music we sell, and an older group come because they like the relaxed atmosphere. It's the atmosphere that attracts such a mixed demographic – people like the homeliness of it. Someone once said to me that it feels like a house party here and I really like that idea.'

Have you noticed any changes in the London shopping scene over the past few years?
'Yes, definitely. People are a lot more open to independent stores and far less willing to be spoon-fed the same old brands. For a long time, streets were dominated by the same shops but in recent years the city seems to have grown out and up. There are great shops in further flung places now, like Brick Lane and Bethnal Green; lots have sprung up as people have moved there.
'People have become more open-minded and want shops to reflect them a little more. It's been a renaissance of independence! It's still tough of course; it's very difficult to compete with the internet on prices, which is why shops have become more atmospheric and why people are trying to return a sense of community to shopping, a sense which supermarkets have done their best to stamp out!'

What's the most enjoyable aspect of working in the shop?
'The results – when you see it all come together. There are obviously easier ways to make a living than running a record store, but the feedback we get is great, and doing something that people really respond to is amazing. We come from a leftist musical background and attract open-minded people.'

What are your favourite shops in London?
'One of the problems about working in a shop is that shopping does become a bit of a busman's holiday – I don't do that much of it! I do really like Unpackaged [see p251 and p250 **Shop talk**] for food; I think what they are doing there is similar to what we are aiming to do and the things we are trying to change about shopping.'

▶ For **Pure Groove Records**, see p206.

Pure Groove Records. *See p206.*

Duncan Kerr, general manager of Revival Records, was involved with Reckless Records for 23 years until all four of its sites closed in 2009. When the company went bust, Revival bought up some of Reckless's old stock and opened on the location of the mini-chain's former dance music branch in Soho's Berwick Street selling everything from rare rock vinyl to classic drum 'n' bass, as well as punk, reggae, jazz and a good range of original Mo' Wax and Blue Note vinyl. Revival will buy most kinds of music and will make house calls for large buys. They also buy CD box sets, limited editions and DVDs.

Classical

Gramex
25 Lower Marsh, SE1 7RJ (7401 3830). Waterloo tube/rail. **Open** *11am-7pm Mon-Sat.*
Browsing here is as comfy and laid-back as flicking through a friend's collection; battered sofas and cuppas abound. The vast selection of quality used LPs and CDs is so constantly in flux that hundreds of records are cluttered on the central table at any given time while they await sorting. This is done by affable owner Roger Hewland, whose alleged photographic memory is probably the only thing stopping the store sliding into chaos. The majority of the ground-floor CD stock is taken up with an alphabetised catalogue of composers past and present, with opera also well represented (both on CD and DVD) and an assortment of mainstream and modern jazz, comprising almost half the stock. Venture down to the shoebox basement and you'll find the home of the store's vinyl collection. There's a 10% discount on purchases over £100 too.

Harold Moores Records
2 Great Marlborough Street, W1F 7HQ (7437 1576, www.hmrecords.co.uk). Oxford Circus tube. **Open** *10am-6.30pm Mon-Sat.*
Harold Moores is not your stereotypical classical music store: young, open-minded staff (including Tim Winter of Resonance FM) and an expansive stock of new and second-hand music bolster its credentials. This collection sees some great old masters complemented by a range of eclectic contemporary music, including plenty of avant-garde and electronic work from independent labels like Touch. Soft lighting, carpets and wood panelling create a cosy atmosphere, and there's plenty to appeal to amateur enthusiasts as well as aficionados. There's a suitably studious basement dedicated to second-hand classical vinyl, including an excellent selection of jazz music.

MDC Music & Movies
Unit 3, Level 1, Festival Riverside, Royal Festival Hall, South Bank, SE1 8XX (7620 0198, www.mdcmusicandmovies.co.uk). Waterloo tube/rail. **Open** *10am-10pm daily.*

Best for...

Listening posts
Rough Trade East (*see p201*);
Sister Ray (*see p201*).

In-store events
Pure Groove (*see p206*);
Rough Trade East (*see p201*).

A relaxing vibe
Brill (*see p201*); **Harold Moores** (*see left*); **Pure Groove** (*see p206*).

Obscure vinyl
Flashback (*see p201*); **Harold Moores** (*see left*); **Intoxica!** (*see p202*); **Sister Ray** (*see p201*); **Vinyl Junkies** (*see p207*).

Bargains and special offers
HMV Megastore (*see p201*).

MDC enjoys one of the most privileged shopping locations in London, a riverside installation on the South Bank. The white walls, reverent atmosphere and abundance of light lend the store a slightly sterile air, but it remains a top place to browse CDs. These include classical music in all its forms, with entire shelves dedicated to the likes of Wagner and Vaughan Williams, not to mention a huge range of albums from modern composers like Karl Jenkins, John Tavener and Hans Zender. There are improved jazz and world sections, plus a recently extended selection of foreign and arthouse DVDs, which have taken over half the store. Opera buffs, however, may be better off making a beeline for the branch by the English National Opera's Coliseum.

Jazz, soul & dance

BM Soho
25 D'Arblay Street, W1F 8EJ (7437 0478, www. bm-soho.com). Oxford Circus tube. **Open** 11am-7pm Mon-Wed, Sat; 11am-8pm Thur, Fri; noon-6pm Sun.
Junglist Nicky Blackmarket's BM Soho has kids queuing up to snag his latest promos. Don't come expecting anything other than upfront club music: the ground floor stocks house, minimal and techno, while the basement remains London's most reliable dispenser of new and pre-release drum'n'bass, with dubstep, bassline and UK garage represented too. Both are kitted out in futuristic black metallic that only amplifies the apocalyptic bass sounds emanating from the sound system. Come on a Friday afternoon when turntablists nod into their headphones trying out white labels for the weekend's sets and it can feel like you're already clubbing. DJs also head here for last-minute equipment – slip mats, needles, mixers and speakers reside at the back.

Honest Jon's [HOT 50]
278 Portobello Road, W10 5TE (8969 9822, www.honestjons.com). Ladbroke Grove tube.
Open 10am-6pm Mon-Sat; 11am-5pm Sun.
This legendary record shop's owner had the good foresight to lend former hired hand James Lavelle £1,000 to set up Mo' Wax records in the early 1990s. Prints of old blaxploitation posters crowd the technicolour walls, a sign that jazz, soul, revival reggae and global sounds remain the house specialities. Honest Jon's has also branched out into many of the genres that for years relied on this very store for their samples: hip hop is especially well represented and even more peripheral dance genres like dubstep get a look in. The majority of the store's CD and vinyl collection is reserved for luminaries such as Parliament, Prince and Burning Spear.

Phonica
51 Poland Street, W1F 7LZ (7025 6070, www.phonicarecords.co.uk). Oxford Circus or
Tottenham Court Road tube. **Open** 11.30am-7.30pm Mon-Wed, Sat; 11.30am-8pm Thur, Fri; noon-6pm Sun.
The doors are always flung open at this lively dance vinyl hubbub. Recline on the battered leather sofas and egg-shaped chairs that give the chic space a 1970s gangster feel, or finger through rack upon rack of pristinely selected records favouring the deeper and edgier side of club music. The balanced selection journeys around the world taking in nu jazz, krautrock, minimal techno, exotica, dubstep and nu disco flavours, but fluorescent-clad kids best head for the front rack of French electro labels. CDs are displayed on antique wooden tables, boasting the latest alt-indie and electronic releases. Box sets take pride of place in a glass cabinet, while tees suspend above the vinyl racks. The staff – DJs-about-town – are happy to help you dig out a hard-to-find disc.

Pure Groove Records [HOT 50]
6-7 West Smithfield, EC1A 9JX (7778 9278, www.puregroove.co.uk). Farringdon tube/rail.
Open 9am-11pm Mon-Fri.
Once Archway's tiny testament to all things indie, alternative and cutting edge in guitar and electronic music, Pure Groove upped sticks to a minimalist space next to Smithfield Market a couple of years back. Describing itself as a 'record shop/music bar/gallery space', its stylish, multimedia treasure trove of vinyl, poster art and CD gems will strike fire in the loins of London's chic elite. A visually stimulating jigsaw of record and CD cases connected with metal pincers suspends from one wall, displaying the shop's top 100 leftfield singles, 12-inches

Sounds of the Universe

and CDs. Garish graphics hang over the till while black-and-white photographs are exhibited in the centre of the shop, hanging over magazines stacked neatly on black cubes. The rear, housing T-shirts, cotton bags and posters, doubles as a stage for the regular live-band sets and film screenings. Simply stunning. *See also p202* **Shop talk**.

Sounds of the Universe
7 Broadwick Street, W1F 0DA (7734 3430, www.soundsoftheuniverse.com). Tottenham Court Road tube. **Open** *11am-7.30pm Mon-Sat.*
Bright and breezy, this stylish sound store in the heart of Soho has universal appeal. Its affiliation with reissue kings Soul Jazz records means its remit is broad. This is especially true on the ground floor (new vinyl and CDs), where grime and dubstep 12-inches jostle for space alongside new wave cosmic disco, electro-indie re-rubs, Nigerian compilations and some electronic madness. A good number of listening posts offer insights into a diverse mix of new releases from Venetian Snares to Soul II Soul legend Jazzie B, while the second-hand vinyl basement is big on soul, jazz, Brazilian and alt-rock.

Vinyl Junkies
94 Berwick Street, W1F 0QF (7439 2923, www.vinyl-junkies.com). Piccadilly Circus tube. **Open** *11am-7.30pm Mon-Sat; noon-5pm Sun.*
Vinyl Junkies takes the business of record buying very seriously indeed. The stock is on black plastic only – as the name suggests – and the extensive selections of battle records, breaks samples and a capella compilations is a sure sign of the place's affection for its male-heavy, DJ clientele. Eyes are initially drawn to the numerous reggae and dancehall seven-inches tacked to the walls, but there's also a comprehensive collection of house music in all its geographical subdivisions (New York, Chicago, Detroit, West Coast). And there's also a smattering of hip hop, disco, eclectic electronica and second-hand thrown in for good measure. Turntables are available for sampling potential purchases through headphones – which you'll definitely need, what with staff spinning deafening floor fillers that shake the walls all day.

Soundtracks, shows & nostalgia

Dress Circle
57-59 Monmouth Street, WC2H 9DG (7240 2227, www.dresscircle.co.uk). Leicester Square tube. **Open** *10am-6.30pm Mon-Sat; noon-5pm Sun.*
This OTT luvvy-magnet and temple to show tunes is still a West End hit after more than 30 years. It continues to wow professional thesps and drama queens alike with its staggering collection of show tunes on CD and DVD (featuring popular classics like *The Sound of Music* and plenty of more obscure gems). A range of posters celebrates productions past and present; Stephen Sondheim, Barry Manilow and Barbara Cook are regulars here. The downstairs boasts a range of scores as comprehensive as you'll find anywhere in the capital, alongside a book range from reference to autobiographies.

Electronics & Photography

The early stretch of Tottenham Court Road is electronics heaven, and includes the **Sony Centre Galleria** (no.22-24), Toshiba-supplier **Gultronics** (no.52) and the four-storey palace that is **Ask** (*see below*).

General

Ask
248 Tottenham Court Road, W1T 7QZ (7637 0353, www.askdirect.co.uk). Tottenham Court Road tube.
Open 10am-7pm Mon-Wed, Fri, Sat; 10am-8pm Thur; noon-6pm Sun.
Ask is a virtual palace in comparison with the other shops along this stretch of Tottenham Court Road, providing four floors of stock, more staff than you can shake a stick at and a lofty feel. Boasting a clean online service, which allows you either delivery or a pick-up service, the company supplies some 10,000 different lines, with the emphasis on popular items like home-cinema packages, hi-fi equipment, laptops (no Macs though), digital cameras, sat navs, MP3 players and DAB radios from big-name brands. Staff are helpful but not overly pushy – and they're trained by the manufacturers themselves so they're kept up to date with new technology and are always willing to impart their knowledge. Competitive prices, frequent special offers and a 'try before you buy' policy are further pluses.

Maplin
166-168 Queensway, W2 6LY (7229 9301, www.maplin.co.uk). Bayswater or Queensway tube. **Open** 9am-8pm Mon-Fri; 9am-6pm Sat; 10am-5pm Sun.
The size of the shop often dictates the size of gear on offer, so expect plasma screens, speakers, satellite kits and hard drives aplenty at the 31 spacious Maplin stores located in the London area. Yet this only scratches the surface – the real beauty of the nationwide chain is the sheer scale of random kit available, from motherboards to computer cables, wireless phone line extenders to USB turntables and roll-up pianos. Turntables, mixers, amps and disco lighting do a roaring trade with the capital's DJs while gadget fiends are well catered for with metal detectors, a variety of flying toys, underwater CCTV surveillance systems (honestly) and solar-powered battery chargers. All in all, there's a mind-boggling choice, so use the power of the internet to narrow your preferences before setting off (the more central shops tend to be smaller).
Branches throughout the city.

Computers

Apple Store HOT 50
235 Regent Street, W1B 2EL (7153 9000, www.apple.com). Oxford Circus tube.
Open 9am-9pm Mon-Sat; noon-6pm Sun.
Apple's grandiose London flagship is as hip and beautiful as one might expect. All the latest Apple products can be found here – compact MacBook and MacBook Pro laptops, iMac desktops, the full range of iPods, Apple TV systems and covetable Apple Cinema HD display units. The iPhone was joined in the 'must-own' category by the iPod touch, the breathtaking MacBook Air and now the supercool iPad. Head up the imposing glass staircase to the 'Genius Bar', where you can get free one-to-one technical support. A new three-storey Apple store is due to open on the site of Covent Garden's Rock Garden in late summer 2010.
Branches Westfield London, W12 7GF (8433 4600); Brent Cross, Upper West Mall, NW4 3FP (8359 1050).

Apple Centre
78 New Oxford Street, WC1A 1HB (7692 6810, www.squaregroup.co.uk). Tottenham Court Road tube. **Open** 10am-5.30pm Mon, Fri; 10am-7pm Tue-Thur; 10am-5pm Sat.
Just around the corner from the electronics main drag on Tottenham Court Road, the Apple Centre is an authorised reseller of Apple products, hard, soft and in between. iMacs start from £969, MacBooks from £816 and MacPro from £1,940. The centre also sells all the iPods and iPhones you could want, as well as a tempting selection of accessories. To get the full effect, high quality Bose and B&W speakers are on offer, as well as headphones from manufacturers such as Sennheiser, JVC and Bose again. There are extended warranties available on most products. The store provides training courses in using Apple products, and Quark Xpress and Adobe software.

Micro Anvika
6-17 Tottenham Court Road, W1T 6BH (7467 6090, www.microanvika.com). Tottenham Court Road tube. **Open** 9.30am-8pm Mon-Fri; 9.30am-6pm Sat; noon-6pm Sun.
There are three Micro Anvika stores on Tottenham Court Road and all are excellent computer retailers; this one stocks a broad range of makes from major manufacturers (Sony, Hewlett Packard, Samsung) and Macolytes are well served, but the Chenies Street branch specialises in Apple products and sells many Mac-compatible accessories. Apart from computers, the stores offer digital cameras and camcorders, iPods, MP3 players and iPhones, sat navs and TVs, DVDs and home-cinema systems. The staff are trained by the manufacturers, so know the products well.
Branches 53-54 Tottenham Court Road, W1T 2EJ (7467 2030); 245 Tottenham Court Road, W1T 7QT (7467 6080); 13 Chenies Street, WC1E 7EY (7467 7085).

Electronics & Photography

Audio Gold. *See p210.*

Hi-fi

Audio Gold
308-310 Park Road, N8 8LA (8341 9007, www.audiogold.co.uk). Finsbury Park tube/rail then W7 bus. **Open** 10.30am-6.30pm Mon-Sat.
A mix of new, second-hand and hireable audio products, Audio Gold is one of the best places in London to track down old-school equipment – from ghetto blasters to gramophones, this store has it covered. The extensive 'prop hire' section celebrates all the 'strange and beautiful' machines the owners have picked up over the years, which is ideal for the media industry (film shoots or magazine articles especially) looking to set the scene with an original Walkman or a 1980s clock-radio. The list of manufacturers covered includes typical brands (Sony, Toshiba, Denon, Tivoli) but by and large they are names from a realm that's beyond the high street's vocabulary: turntables by Linn, speakers by Quad, amps by Sugden and so on. Audio Gold also buys your second-hand equipment – as long as it works, of course.

Grahams
Unit 1, Canonbury Yard, 190A New North Road, N1 7BS (7226 5500, www.grahams.co.uk). Essex Road rail or 271 bus. **Open** 10am-6pm Tue, Wed; 10am-8pm Thur; 9am-6pm Fri, Sat.
Secreted away in the backstreets of De Beauvoir Town, Grahams certainly won't be doing any casual business with passing pedestrians. Those who come here make the pilgrimage because they are ready to compile a hi-fi/home-cinema system with much care and deliberation and are willing to spend a large sum of money in the process. Probably the longest-established of all competitors in town (its predecessor, Grahams Electrical, opened in Clerkenwell in 1929), the shop is guided by a policy of uncompromising quality, whatever the cost; consequently, the large majority of its components (amps, speakers, HD TV equipment, wireless streaming audio and so on) demand four-figure sums. The carefully crafted list of manufacturers includes B&W, Linn, Loewe, Miller & Kreisel, Spendor, Classe and many others of the same lofty and rarefied standard. The staff and owners are so proud of the company that their profiles can be found online so you can put names to faces before walking through the front door.

Oranges & Lemons
61-63 Webb's Road, SW11 6RX (7924 2040, www.oandlhifi.co.uk). Clapham Junction rail.
Open 11am-7pm Mon, Tue, Fri; 11am-9pm Thur (7-9pm by appointment only); 10am-6pm Sat.
Laid-back and friendly, Oranges & Lemons is one of the best places in which to buy separates or home-cinema equipment in south London. It's keen to insist that hi-fi and home cinema are, fundamentally, about fun, and this is reflected in the store and its website. As with many of

Aperture Photographic. *See p212.*

Electronics & Photography

Classic Camera. *See p212.*

the other stores listed here, HD systems are available but, unlike some of the others, the new visual technology has not overtaken the audio side of things. The test rooms are cosy, serving as both a pleasant environment for your shopping experience and a guide to how the audio set-up will work in an average living room. Systems of any size and complexity can be compiled – right up to a full, wireless multi-room AV solution – but you could also come here to upgrade just one component of an existing system. Bear in mind that the shop can often reach 'chaotic' proportions so you may not get a test room immediately – you can, however, book a demonstration in advance online, by phone or in-store.

Photography

Aperture Photographic
44 Museum Street, WC1A 1LY (7242 8681, www.apertureuk.com). Holborn or Tottenham Court Road tube. **Open** 11am-7pm Mon-Fri; noon-7pm Sat
Frequented by camera enthusiasts and paparazzi downloading their latest scoops, this camera shop-cum-café has a great atmosphere. The photographic side centres on an excellent selection of vintage and new, manual and autofocus Nikons, Leicas, Canon autofocus and Hasselblads, along with a sprinkling of other makes. Prices are reasonable too, while offers for unwanted gear are among the more generous in town. The café serves coffees, teas and juices, as well as sandwiches and cookies, giving you something to chew on while jawing over the relative merits of Leica lenses and Canon zooms. Staff are enthusiasts, and happy to answer questions.

Camera City
16 Little Russell Street, WC1A 2HL (7813 2100, www.cameracity.co.uk). Tottenham Court Road tube.
Open 10am-5.30pm Mon-Fri; 10am-2pm Sat.
One of a cluster of second-hand photography outlets to be found within a stone's throw of each other, this tiny shop is a good place to look for hard-to-find vintage accessories ranging from flash adaptors to small-but-important things like a replacement tripod bush. It also stocks old Nikon, Canon, Olympus and Pentax cameras, and has a postal service if you can't come personally. Apart from retail sales, the store provides a fast developing service for tourists who have to catch the evening plane, and a well-regarded and generally speedy repair service to digital and film cameras.

Classic Camera
2 Pied Bull Yard, off Bury Place, WC1A 2JR (7831 0777, www.theclassiccamera.com). Holborn tube.
Open 9.30am-5pm Mon-Fri; 10am-4.30pm Sat.
This isn't the place for anyone on a tight budget, since 90% of the stock is Leica, and they don't come cheap – we're talking £3,000 plus for a camera. The rest of the

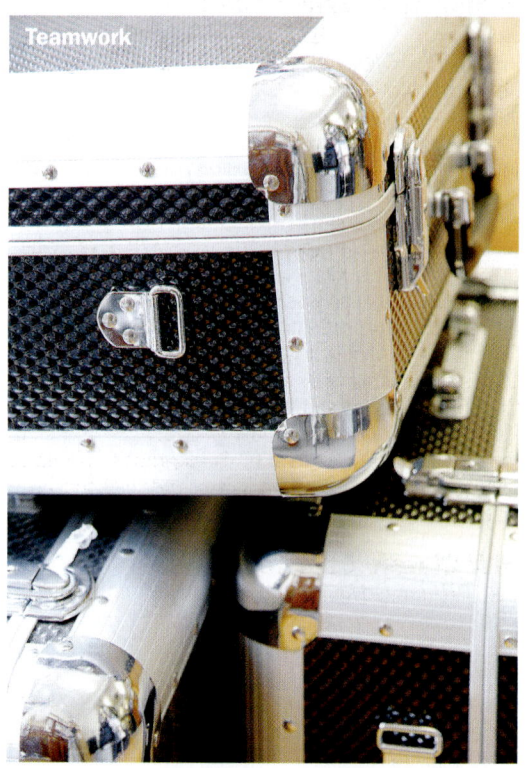

Teamwork

stock isn't exactly light on the wallet either, mixing up Voigtlander, Nikon and top-of-the-range Panasonic cameras with Zeiss lenses. Apart from cameras and lenses, there are binoculars by Leika, Zeiss, Nikon and Minox, and accessories including Billingham bags and Gitzo tripods, as well as a nice selection of photographic books by famed Leica users such as Korda and Brassai. They service and repair Leica cameras too, promising to try and fix anything made by the German company.

Kingsley Photographic
93 Tottenham Court Road, W1T 4HL (7436 8700, www.kingsleyphoto.co.uk). Goodge Street or Warren Street tube. **Open** 9am-5.30pm Mon-Fri; 10am-5.30pm Sat.

This tiny shop squeezes in a surprisingly extensive range. Nikons are to the fore, though there's also a selection of Leicas and a diverse mix of second-hand gear. But it's the staff that make this such a highly-regarded place. They are all keen, knowledgeable photographers who discuss products with genuine enthusiasm for the art and craft rather than as a means towards upping their sales bonus. There's a large selection of photographic accessories, including bags, tripods and albums, plus binoculars and telescopes. Catering to film loyalists, it still stocks photographic paper as well as digital accessories and printers.

Lomography Gallery Store   HOT 50
3 Newburgh Street, W1F 7RE (7434 1466, www.lomography.com). Oxford Circus tube. **Open** 10am-7pm Mon-Wed, Fri, Sat; 10am-9pm Thur; 11am-5pm Sun.

Parallel to the rise of the digital revolution, the Lomography movement was a phenomenon that began in the 1990s when a group of art students from Austria rediscovered the Lomo LC-A 35mm Soviet-era compact; and so began a nostalgia for the 'good old days', when Polaroid cameras were considered cutting-edge and no holiday pic collection was complete without the odd cut-off head or unfocused shot. Opened in 2009, with its logo 'The Future is Analogue', Lomography stocks a collection of reissued 'toy' cameras such as the Diana (Hong Kong), the Chinese Holga and the Russian Lomo, as well as fisheyes, pinholes and some lovely accessories. Check out the Lomowall with over 14,000 'Lomographs'. Would-be Lomographers can attend workshops and neighbourhood walkabouts when they test-drive the cameras.

MW Classic Cameras
Unit 3K, Leroy House, 436 Essex Road, N1 3QP (7354 3767, www.mwclassic.com). Angel tube then 38, 73, 341, 476 bus. **Open** 11am-6pm Mon-Fri; 11am-4pm Sat.

The owners of MW Classic Cameras, Mahendra Modi and David Woodford (hence the company name), are enthusiastic and knowledgeable. They sell rare and collectable cameras and photographic equipment, with a wide range of brands stocked, including Hasselblad, Pentax, Rollei and Voigtlander, as well as an interesting selection of old Soviet-era cameras. Of course, pride of place goes to Leica, and there are many collectable examples for sale. MW also sells some fascinating examples of old plate and box cameras. There's a mail-order service available if you can't make it to the shop.

Nicholas Camera Company
15 Camden High Street, NW1 7JE (7916 7251, www.nicholascamera.com). Mornington Crescent tube. **Open** 10am-6pm Mon-Sat.

An interestingly shambolic shop with mountains of stock, the Nicholas Camera Company sells all sorts of old and modern cameras dating from as far back as the 1800s. It's best to have a clear idea before you go in of what you want – rather than browsing you have tell the shopkeeper what you want and he goes and looks. In addition to the more familiar SLR names, you'll find large-format cameras by the likes of Linhof, Sinar, Horseman and medium-format giants such as Hasselblad and Mamiya. There are also accessories, darkroom kits and a growing array of used digital equipment.

Teamwork
41-42 Foley Street, W1W 7JN (7323 6455, www.teamworkphoto.com). Goodge Street tube. **Open** 9am-5.30pm Mon-Fri.

Teamwork specialises in high-end digital camera backs and medium- to large-format models, as well as meters, lighting and lots more accessories and equipment (panoramic cameras, tripods and monopods, camera and computer bags, backgrounds and props). There is a large amount of Hasselblad equipment. Although the shop caters mainly to a professional market, the knowledgeable and helpful vendors are more than happy to advise and help amateurs too – just not where compact cameras are concerned. A selection of quality used equipment is for sale, and the company has a rental equipment service for cameras, lighting equipment and computers.

York Cameras
18 Bury Place, WC1A 2JL (7242 7182, www.yorkcameras.co.uk). Holborn tube. **Open** 9am-5pm Mon-Fri; 10am-3pm Sat.

Staffed by a team of seasoned experts, each of whom is a dedicated photographer too, York Cameras is a Canon Pro Centre, and stocks an impressive selection of both new and used cameras as well as lots of accessories. The shop was first established in 1971 (on York Road at the time, which explains the name), and moved to its current address in 2000. A smaller selection of used Nikon gear is also for sale, including some interesting rarities, as well as Sigma lenses, Hoya filters, and Lowepro and Tamrac gadget bags. Factor in the attentive service, and it's little wonder the shop attracts a loyal, discerning clientele.

Crafts, Hobbies & Parties

Art & craft supplies

Atlantis European
Britannia House, 68-80 Hanbury Street, E1 5JL (7377 8855, www.atlantisart.co.uk). Aldgate East or Whitechapel tube or Shoreditch High Street rail. **Open** 9am-6pm Mon-Sat; 10am-5pm Sun.

Creatives will be find themselves in heaven at this vast emporium just off Brick Lane, which is filled to the brim with thousands of tubes of paint covering a wide variety of quality and prices, as well as paper of every texture and hue, tools, brushes, pens, pencils, crayons, solvents, spray paints, glues, canvases, stretchers, easels, frames and portfolios – in other words, pretty much everything and anything that arty folk might ever need, and at competitive prices too. What's more, staff are helpful and friendly and there's a 10% discount for students, making it a first port-of-call for young artists in the making. There's also a framing shop downstairs, for when you've finished that masterpiece.

Cass Art
66-67 Colebrooke Row, N1 8AB (7354 2999, www.cassart.co.uk). Angel tube. **Open** 10am-7pm Mon-Sat; 11am-5.30pm Sun.

Known for its low prices and much loved by impecunious artists and designers (there's a discount for those with student cards), Cass Art has a stellar array of artistic materials in its outlets across the capital. Its flagship store in Islington, located just behind the Islington Green end of Essex Road, spans three large floors, selling everything from sketchbooks, Moleskin notebooks, sheet paper and brushes to easels, wooden mannequins, canvases and portfolios, in a pleasant, airy and browser-friendly setting. There are inks, markers, oils, acrylics, watercolours and pastels in a rainbow of colours and a good crafts section downstairs.
Branches 13 Charing Cross Road, WC2H 0EP (7930 9940); 24 Berwick Street, W1F 8RD (7287 8504); 220 Kensington High Street, W8 7RG (7937 6506).

Green & Stone
259 King's Road, SW3 5EL (7352 0837, www.greenandstone.com). Sloane Square tube, then 11, 19, 22 bus. **Open** 9am-6pm Mon-Fri; 9.30am-6pm Sat; noon-5pm Sun.

Browsing the paints and palettes at this old-fashioned establishment is like stepping back in time. Founded in 1927, it is one of Chelsea's longest-standing retailers,

Cass Art

Crafts, Hobbies & Parties

and the emphasis is on quality: you'll find only the finest art supplies here. Expect a comprehensive selection of calligraphy tools and paper, along with print-making paraphernalia, graphic design gear and brushes of every size and specification. A picture-framing and mounting service is also available. Downstairs in the basement is a huge array of easels, as well as rolls of canvases and unprimed linens, a craft and modelling section and assorted portfolios.

L Cornelissen & Son HOT 50
105 Great Russell Street, WC1B 3RY (7636 1045, www.cornelissen.com). Tottenham Court Road tube. **Open** 9.30am-5.30pm Mon-Sat.
For those who like their umber raw, burnt or somewhere in between, legendary artists' supply shop L Cornelissen & Son, specialising in gilding, printmaking and restoration, has offered up hundreds of pigments since 1855. With its original antique shop fittings and stoppered glass jars, the quaint shop resembles an old apothecary, and is one of a dying breed. Its illustrious customers have included Ford Madox Brown, Dante Gabriel Rossetti and, more recently, Damien Hirst. As well as top-quality printing and painting materials, the shop also sells calligraphy equipment, paper, painting sets and feather quills. It also offers a worldwide mail order service.

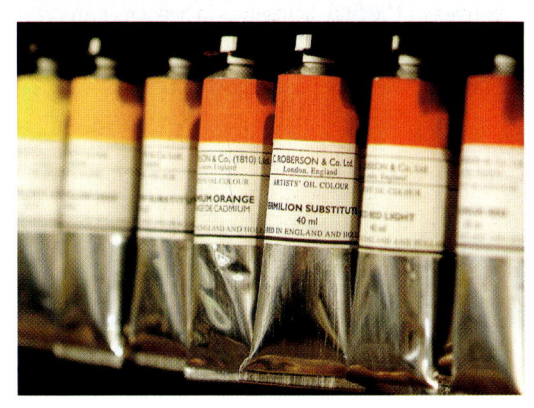

London Graphic Centre
16-18 Shelton Street, WC2H 9JL (7759 4500, www.londongraphics.co.uk). Covent Garden or Leicester Square tube. **Open** 10am-6.30pm Mon-Fri; 10.30am-6pm Sat; noon-5pm Sun.
One of the capital's major suppliers of art and graphics materials, this large corner building in Covent Garden is LGC's flagship, offering a huge array. Whether you're a keen novice or an established professional, you'll find all you need in the way of fine art supplies, graphics materials, lightboxes, papers, portfolios and bags (including Freitag and Manhattan Portage bags), books and magazines, Pantone colour guides, modelling clays and tools, spray paint – the list goes on. The shop also houses sporadic exhibitions, and is good for gift items for arty types – think Lomography cameras, old-fashioned wind-up tin toys, Eames mugs and Moleskin notebooks. **Branches** 13 Tottenham Street, W1T 2AH (7637 2199); 86 Goswell Road, EC1V 7DB (7253 1000).

Shepherds Bookbinders
76 Southampton Row, WC1B 4AR (7831 1151, www.bookbinding.co.uk). Holborn or Russell Square tube. **Open** 10am-6pm Mon-Fri; 10.30am-5pm Sat; 11.30am-4.30pm Sun.
Previously Falkiner Fine Papers, this old-fashioned shop, lined with wooden shelves, is a romantic's haven. The

range of decorative paper for craft projects, bookbinding and present-wrapping is superb: Bengali Fairtrade papers in sari-like colours, intricate, Japanese silk-screened designs and some truly glorious 1930s prints, with designs from the likes of Eric Ravilious. If you want actual bookbinding services, head to the bindery in Victoria; here you can get a photograph album bound in one of 150 choices of book cloth. If you want to do the binding yourself, however, you can find the sewing thread, glue, paper-making equipment and tools you'll need here and at the new Soho branch (which also undertakes restorations and framing).
Branches 76 Rochester Row (The Bindery), SW1P 1JU (7233 6766); 46 Curzon Street, W1J 7UH (7495 8580).

Beading & jewellery-making

Bead Shop
21A Tower Street, WC2H 9NS (7240 0931, www.beadworks.co.uk). Covent Garden or Leicester Square tube. **Open** *10.30am-7pm Mon-Sat; 11am-5pm Sun.*
This long-established shop attracts professional designers and bead enthusiasts from around the globe. A dazzling variety of beads is stocked, from humble resin stalwarts to ostentatious Swarovski crystal pearls; other beads are made from precious metals, glass (a huge selection), pearl, silver, porcelain, plastic, wood, bone or carved lacquer, and pendant beads on wire loops are also stocked. So whether you're after Indian glass beads, Chinese enamelled, African turquoise beads or the vintage-style carved-rose plastic variety, this is the place to visit. Threads, wires and tools for putting it all together are also available, along with bargain packs of mixed beads. Jewellery-making classes are also offered.

Buffy's Beads
Unit 2.3, Kingly Court, W1B 5PW (7494 2323, www.buffysbeads.com). Oxford Circus tube.
Open *11am-7pm Mon-Sat; noon-6pm Sun.*
This minimalist, airy shop is tucked away on the top floor of the sadly underused Kingly Court shopping centre, and seems only to attract those in the know. Polished gemstone beads, Czech and Swarovski crystals, freshwater mother of pearls, sterling silver findings, and other superior types of beads and pendants are housed in antique drawers; husband and wife team Rosie and Andrew Pollard, who started the business after being frustrated by the shortage of reasonably priced gemstones and freshwater pearl beads available, also sell a hand-picked selection of tiaras, rings, chains and ribbons, as well as jewellery-making tools. Staff are all jewellery-makers themselves, and are on hand to offer friendly, informative service.

Fabrics

Soho's Berwick Street has been home to some of the best textile shops in town for decades.

Berwick Street Cloth Shop

14 Berwick Street, W1F 0PP (7287 2881, www.theberwickstreetclothshop.com). Oxford Circus or Piccadilly Circus tube. **Open** 9am-6pm Mon-Fri; 9am-5pm Sat.

This Soho store – a leading supplier of fabrics to the film, theatre, interior design, fashion and bridal industries – carries a prime selection of fabrics, running from delicate beaded tulle and gossamer-thin, intricate lace to strokably soft velvets and fake furs, and is run by a team of knowledge and helpful staff. Taffettas, wool blends, silk jacquards, denim, rubber and latex round off the varied stock. BSCS's sister companies, Broadwick Silks (9-11 Broadwick Street, 7734 3320, www.broadwicksilks.com) and the Silk Society (44 Berwick Street, 7287 1881, www.thesilksociety.com), are both a stone's throw away, and carry some show-stopping brocades, feather fabrics and specialist sequins.

Borovick Fabrics

16 Berwick Street, W1F 0HP (7437 2180, www.borovickfabricsltd.co.uk). Oxford Circus tube. **Open** 8.30am-6pm Mon-Fri; 8.15am-5pm Sat.

This family-run business, located behind the flower stalls of Berwick Street market, was established in the 1930s, and is today a central stomping ground for stylists, fashion students from Central Saint Martins, and general crafty types, who flock here for the wide selection of glitzy and more sensible fabrics, zips, sequins, buttons and thread. Materials range from corduroys and cottons to frou-frou netting, metallic lycras, furs and look-at-me leatherettes – as well as feather boas. The bridal fabrics (Borovick is a leading supplier for the industry) feature smarter offerings, including crushed velvets and silks, laces, taffetas, satins, brocades, embroidered tulles and beaded fabrics.

Cloth House

47 Berwick Street, W1F 8SJ (7437 5155, www.clothhouse.com). Oxford Circus or Tottenham Court Road tube. **Open** 9.30am-6pm Mon-Fri; 10.30am-6pm Sat.

This charming little store – one of the more tasteful of Berwick Street's fabric shops – lures customers in with artful window displays. Inside, the premises are neat as a pin, with wooden floors, bolts of fabric, spools of coloured thread and enticing trays of buttons. Downstairs, more rolls of gingham, cotton poplin, wools and hand-loomed silk await, and there's a great selection of patterned fabrics, with everything from pretty Laura Ashley styles to Liberty-esque lines. It's not cheap, but, with fabrics

Button Queen. See p218.

sourced from all over the world, it is deeply tempting. There's another branch at no.98, which is strong on silks.
Branch 98 Berwick Street, W1F 0QJ (7287 1555).

Joel & Son Fabrics
75-83 Church Street, NW8 8EU (7724 6895, www.joelandsonfabrics.com). Edgware Road tube.
Open 9am-5pm Mon-Sat.
Describing itself as 'the biggest couture fabric store in England', Joel & Son is an Aladdin's Cave of treasures. Its stock includes high-end fabrics from the likes of Loro Piana, Ermenegildo Zegna and Valentino, but that's just the tip of the iceberg: well-priced printed cottons, silks, satins, embroidered chiffons, lace, taffettas, voiles and velvets are all to be found amid the glorious profusion of goods, as are men's suit materials, African dresswear fabrics, beaded fabrics, denims and jerseys. A team of knowledgeable and polite staff will help you find what you're after from the thousands of rolls on offer.

Haberdashery & buttons

John Lewis (*see p23*) has a strong haberdashery department, while **Cloth House** (*see p217*) and **Persiflage**, at Alfie's Antiques Market (*see p178*), have great selections of vintage buttons.

Button Lady
12 Heath Street, NW3 6TE (7435 5412, www.buttonladyhampstead.co.uk). Hampstead tube.
Open 10.30am-5pm Tue-Fri, Sun; 10.30am-6pm Sat.

VV Rouleaux. See p220.

The window at this minuscule boutique is crammed with buttons of every description, overflowing from little tins, stands and cardboard boxes. The affable owners know all the prices (there are no tags), and are happy to advise according to your budget, and describe the buttons' histories. Exquisite antique finds glint amid the piles of stock: tiny enamelled designs, hand-painted with roses, say, or Bohemian pressed glass buttons. The art deco button collection has some particularly stylish options to revitalise your garments. As well as buttons, velvet and silk scarves, shawls and pashminas are also stocked, along with smart bags, hats and jewellery.

Button Queen
76 Marylebone Lane, W1U 2PR (7935 1505, www.thebuttonqueen.co.uk). Bond Street tube.
Open 10am-5pm Mon-Fri; 10am-2pm Sat.
A long-established retailer with a great reputation for knowledge and expertise, Button Queen is an emporium of antique and modern buttons of all shapes and sizes, from 19th-century picture buttons, 1920s antique art nouveau designs and art deco plastics to Bimini glass buttons, enamels and oversized contemporary styles. Shelves are filled with boxes of different buttons, made from horn, silver, glass, jet and plastic. If you've lost an unusual or antique button, staff will try to source a replacement; a button-covering service is also offered, and the company can even arrange to have buttons dyed to match the colour of a fabric. For men, there are blazer buttons, dinner jacket buttons and plastic tailors' buttons.

Kleins
5 Noel Street, W1F 8GD (7437 6162, www.kleins.co.uk). Oxford Circus tube.
Open 10am-5pm Mon-Fri.
Tucked away behind a black, unassuming-looking Soho shopfront, Kleins offers a glorious welter of trimmings: lace trim, ribbons, shoulder pads, military-styling frogging and iron-on badges and motifs of every description. Purse and bag frames, buckles, buttons, dyes (including shoe dyes), zips and metal corset stays, bra fittings and wires are among the other useful bits and bobs, and there's a good array of haberdashery tools for sale too, such as tape measures, sewing machine oil and bulbs, tracing wheels, pliers, scissors and pin cushions. The craft sets (for making purses, hats, et al) are good gifts options.

MacCulloch & Wallis
25-26 Dering Street, W1S 1AT (7629 0311, www.macculloch-wallis.co.uk). Bond Street or Oxford Circus tube. **Open** 10am-6pm Mon-Wed, Fri; 10am-7pm Thur; 10.30am-5pm Sat.
Frequented by designers and tailors, this long-established Mayfair shop, which first opened its doors in 1902, offers a huge selection of fabrics, zips, thread and buttons, as well as dressmaker's dummies and corsetry, bra and

Crafts, Hobbies & Parties

Loop. *See p220.*

millinery supplies – such as corset lace, bra cups and hat blocks. Trimmings run from ostrich feather fringes to handmade velvet roses and rainbow-bright acrylic pom-poms; upstairs, there's a good array of sewing machines (mainly Bernina). There's also a nice range of 'Stitch-It' kits, so you can make your own elephant and owl soft toys. Note that VAT is added to prices at the till.

VV Rouleaux

102 Marylebone Lane, W1U 2QD (7224 5179, www.vvrouleaux.com). Bond Street tube. **Open** 9.30am-6pm Mon, Tue, Fri, Sat; 10.30am-6pm Wed; 9.30am-6.30pm Thur.
A superb place to visit when you're in need of visual inspiration, VV Rouleaux, opened by florist Annabel Lewis some two decades ago, is an enduring favourite with interior designers, fashion stylists and wedding planners. It's best known for its huge variety of vibrantly coloured ribbons (now also sold in John Lewis), braids, trimmings, feathers, butterflies and colourful corsages. Downstairs you'll find furnishing trimmings, including ties, tassels and fringing, as well as jewellery, vintage bridal headdresses, veils and flowers. The shop is a good bet for stylish Christmas fabrics, ribbons and wreaths, and staff are happy to offer decorating tips and ideas.
Branch 54 Sloane Square, WS1W 8AX (7730 3125).

Knitting & needlecraft

For boutique **House of Weardowney** – purveyor of stylish hand-knitted garments – *see p69*.

Fabrications

7 Broadway Market, E8 4PH (7275 8043, www.fabrications1.co.uk). London Fields rail or 26, 55, 106, 277 bus. Open noon-5pm Tue-Fri; 10am-5.30pm Sat.
Barley Massey's studio/shop/gallery is an outlet for her distinctive textile designs. Among the regularly changing offerings, you might find Massey's cushions made from vintage fabrics, and knitted lambswool creatures or items of food (the latter recently made for an entertaining window display). There's a quirky haberdashery section, with a small but unusual selection of wool, needles and patterns, and the shop also does a good line in seasonal items, cards and gifts, as well as Hackney mementoes, such as 'I love Hackney' badges. Regular classes are held for those keen to learn the crafts of knitting and needlework.

I Knit London

106 Lower Marsh, SE1 7AB (7261 1338, www.iknit.org.uk). Waterloo tube/rail. **Open** 11am-9pm Tue-Thur; 11am-7pm Mon, Fri; 11am-6pm Sat; noon-5pm Sun.
Gerard Allt and Craig Carruthers' cool, convivial knitting shop goes from strength to strength. A laid-back atmosphere (think squishy sofas and a drinks fridge), coupled with an amazing selection of wools and yarns, makes this salon-style shop a one-off in the knitting world. There's a special emphasis on British independent yarn producers, while more unusual offerings include glossy vinyl 'jelly yarn'. Knitting patterns from the 1950s and '60s are stocked, along with a decent range of how-to books. With regular film screenings, knitting get-togethers (including a sociable Sunday 'Knit Roast' in a pub) and beginners' classes, there's no excuse not to get crafty.

Loop HOT 50

15 Camden Passage, N1 8EA (7288 1160, www.loopknitting.com). Angel tube. **Open** 11am-6pm Mon-Sat; noon-5pm Sun.
Far less hidden away since its move from Cross Street to Camden Passage in June 2010, Loop is a joy to browse. Assorted yarns in a kaleidoscope of colours awaits, with textures ranging from the softest kid mohair to chunky alpaca wool. You'll also find eco-friendly, hand-dyed yarns by brands such as Be Sweet, as well as Mango Moon's colourful recycled sari yarn. Other products include rosewood knitting needles, crochet, knitting and pom-pom kits, and gorgeous velvet ribbons. A cherry-picked selection of colourful tea-cosies and knitted accessories by young designers is also on sale. If you feel inspired, there are classes for beginners and improvers.

Playlounge

Crafts, Hobbies & Parties

Prick Your Finger
260 Globe Road, E2 0JD (8981 2560, www.prickyourfinger.com). Bethnal Green tube/rail. **Open** *noon-7pm Tue-Fri; 11am-6pm Sat.*
This stylish little 'modern haberdashery' was set up by two Central Saint Martin graduates, Rachael Matthews and Louise Harries, to promote all things knitted. The pair have a dislike for synthetic materials and disposable clothes, and you can rest assured that all the yarns sold here are from small British producers. Recycled cotton and silk blends, knitting kits, needles and patterns are among the other goodies, and there are regular classes and events to initiate beginners in the art of knitting and crocheting, and to assist intermediates with their own projects. Check out the blog for some off-the-wall knits – a double-neck guitar, perhaps, or a woolly cauliflower.

Models & games

See also p192 **Forbidden Planet**.

Comet Miniatures
44-48 Lavender Hill, SW11 5RH (7228 3702, www.comet-miniatures.com). Clapham Common tube or Clapham Junction rail. **Open** *9am-5.15pm Mon-Sat.*
A first port-of-call for all sci-fi, film, TV, military and weaponry-related paraphernalia, and for model-making kits. There's an extensive selection of figures and toys for people who now regret throwing out their childhood collections of *Star Wars* figures, Transformers, plastic Godzillas and Knight Rider cars. Collectables range from replica C-3PO and RD-D2s to a 14in-high figure of the T-600 cyborg from *Terminator* to a metal model of the Starbug from *Red Dwarf*. There's also a good range of books and magazines for sci-fi gee… er, fans, and a range of kits for those who want to try their hand at building their figures, robots and vehicles.

Compendia
10 Greenwich Market, SE10 9HZ (8293 6616, www.compendia.co.uk). Cutty Sark DLR. **Open** *noon-5.30pm Mon-Fri; 10am-5.30pm Sat, Sun.*
A specialist in traditional games, such as board games, dominoes, playing cards and jigsaw puzzles, Compendia. As well as the usual suspects, like backgammon and chess, there are a range of more obscure games, such as mancala (an African game often compared to chess), the Japanese board game Go and Mexican train dominoes (a Latin American variant on the classic game). On other shelves, there are traditional British pub games like skittles and shove ha'penny, and poker and casino games. Board games include Pass the Bomb, Treasure Island and Settlers of Catan. What you won't find here are computer games or games that require plugs or batteries.

Playin' Games
33 Museum Street, WC1A 1JR (7323 3080). Holborn or Tottenham Court Road tube. **Open** *11am-7pm Mon-Sat; noon-6pm Sun.*
A handsome independent boutique located near the British Museum, in which traditional board games, war and fantasy role-playing games, jigsaw puzzles, card games, travel games and books sit side-by-side. Names like Twister, Monopoly and Cluedo will spark nostalgia; others – like the War on Terror and the Hungry Caterpillar game – are new offerings for the enthusiastic game-player. If you're inspired to start playing again, try the Champagne Murder dinner party set at £18.99. Head to the basement for a good selection of out-of-print board games, as well as Dungeons & Dragons sets. The shop also stocks limited-editions, such as a *Lord of the Rings* themed chess set.

Playlounge
19 Beak Street, W1F 9RP (7287 7073, www.playlounge.co.uk). Oxford Circus or Piccadilly Circus tube. **Open** *10.30am-7pm Mon-Sat; noon-5pm Sun.*
Compact but fun filled, this groovy little shop has action figures, gadgets, books and comics, e-boy posters, T-shirts and clothing that appeal to children and adults alike. Pick from a full set of Gorillaz statuettes (£63) or a box of Tragic Toys for Girls & Boys figurines (£14.95), the product of Tim Burton's twisted imagination. For soft toys, how about a huge Plush Moomin (£24.95) or a character from the Uglydoll range (including a good selection of Little Uglies for £9.95). Those nostalgic for illustrated children's literature shouldn't miss out on the selection of *Dr Seuss* PopUps and *Where the Wild Things Are* books. The website – designed like a game of snap – is a hit too.

Parties & magic

Angels
119 Shaftesbury Avenue, WC2H 8AE (7836 5678, www.fancydress.com). Leicester Square or Tottenham Court Road tube. **Open** *9.30am-5.30pm Mon, Tue, Thur, Fri; 10.30am-7pm Wed.*
Angels is the undisputed doyenne of fancy dress hire for adults and children in the capital. The range – spanning everything from splendid Tudor robes to a sequinned showgirl outfit from *Octopussy* – and quality are unparalleled. Some of the costumes have even found their way to the six-floor hire shop from the massive collection of handmade costumes Angels has created for films over the years. The expanding range of packet costumes, sold via the website, are also very good, with Playboy bunnies, sumo wrestlers and Marie Antoinette lookalikes new for 2008. There's also a selection of cheap superhero costumes for sale (Superman, Spider-Man), starting at £30.99. Outfits for

hire from the shop start at £80 plus VAT and include matching accessories, plus £100 deposit.

Davenports Magic Shop
7 Charing Cross Underground Shopping Arcade, WC2N 4HZ (7836 0408, www.davenports magic.co.uk). Charing Cross tube/rail. **Open** 9.30am-5.30pm Mon-Fri; 10.15am-4pm Sat.
Davenports was established back in 1898, and today is staffed by professional magicians who are able to demonstrate the most suitable magic for your level of experience and budget. The equipment for beginners, such as trick card decks, starts from £6; for more advanced magicians, there's everything from trick Top Hats to craftytables. Posters and collectibles (such as a hand-painted representation of Tommy Cooper mounted on a wooden backplate) are also for sale, and there's a wide range of how-to instruction DVDs and books (including an interesting secondhand section). If you really want to learn the tricks of the trade though, then enrol in one of Davenports magic courses (see the website for details).

International Magic
89 Clerkenwell Road, EC1R 5BX (7405 7324, www.internationalmagic.com). Chancery Lane tube. **Open** 11.30am-6pm Mon-Fri; 11.30am-4pm Sat.
This delightful family-run shop, in operation for over 45 years, is an Alladin's Cave for wannabe and professional magicians and those who just want to learn a few party tricks to impress and baffle their friends. Impromptu tricks and gimmicks include a huge range of playing cards and coin tricks, while the large selection of stage tricks range from floating lightbulbs to vanishing cabinets. Arcane books and tutorial DVDs will show you the ropes, and, for those who want to go one step further, there's the opportunity to undertake courses, catered for a range of different levels, plus hear lectures by professional magicians, such as Dave Buck and Kostya Kimlat.

Party Party
9-13 Ridley Road, E8 2NP (7254 5168). Dalston Kingsland or Dalston Junction rail or 67, 76, 149 bus. **Open** 9am-5.30pm Mon-Thur; 9am-6.30pm Fri, Sat.
This cheap and cheerful three-floored party shop – the area's best – is packed to the brim with dressing-up outfits and props (wigs, beards, gorilla outfits, hats, masks, professional outfits, Halloween costumes, fat suits) and party supplies. There's a large area dedicated to equipment for cake-making and decorating – everything from icing and candles to cake stands and pillars – and a massive range of balloons, glitter, banners, confetti, flags of the world, bunting and decorations. A must-visit if you're planning a hen party, wedding or birthday celebration, and for colourful tableware and instruction books on flower arranging and cake decorating.
Branch 206 Kilburn High Road, NW6 4JH (7624 4295).

Preposterous Presents
262 Upper Street, N1 2UQ (7226 4166, www.preposterouspresents.co.uk). Highbury & Islington tube/rail. **Open** 10am-6pm Mon-Sat; 12.30-4.30pm Sun.
This old-school jape player's paradise has been an Upper Street stalwart for over 30 years. It started as a business proffering alternative postcards, expanding to stock humorous gifts and then fancy-dress garb. Today, it's a den of fripperies and fancy-dress that supplies whoopee cushions, water bombs, itching powder and a whole load of fake blood. The staff know their stuff, and can help you find the wig or mask of your wildest dreams. The place is unsurprisingly packed out around Halloween, with skeleton outfits, witches paraphernalia and axe in the head-type special effects a speciality, but it's also excellent for fancy-dress garb of all kinds, with a whole host of moustaches, eye-patches, wigs, 'Thatcher years' masks and more. The place to visit any time you're feeling in the need of a lift. Or a flower that squirts.

Stationery

Blade Rubber Stamps
12 Bury Place, WC1A 2JL (7831 4123, www.bladerubber.co.uk). Holborn tube. **Open** 10.30am-6pm Mon-Sat; 11.30am-4.30pm Sun.

Angels. *See p221.*

Crafts, Hobbies & Parties

A stone's throw from the British Museum, this shrine to wooden-handled rubber stamps has something for every eventuality and taste, from arty stamps depicting chandeliers and cityscapes to images of Henry VIII, London buses, Alice in Wonderland characters, cutesy puppies and telephone boxes. Handy potential purchases include homework stamps ('Check spelling', 'Keep trying') and adorable love-letter writing kits. Unmounted sheets of rubber stamps, ink pads in every imaginable shade, glitters, glues, stencils, stickers, sticks of sealing wax, and a range of magazines and books complete the stock. Blade also has a made-to-order service for personalised stamps.

Mount Street Printers & Stationers
4 Mount Street, W1K 3LW (7409 0303, www.mountstreetprinters.com). Bond Street or Green Park tube. **Open** 9am-6pm Mon-Fri.
With a telltale whiff of glue and ink permeating up from the printworks downstairs, this shop means business – and claims to offer the fastest stationery turnaround in town. You'll find everything from crisp white invitation cards to thank-you notes with matching tissue paper-lined envelopes. Even the most imaginative commissions are affordable, and the company takes particular pride in its special design techniques, which include ornate die-stamping and engraving. A small selection of ready-made stationery runs from invitation and correspondence cards to visitors' books. Mount Street is now home to a host of stylish designer shops; *see also p94* **Streetwise**.

Paperchase
213-215 Tottenham Court Road, W1T 7PS (7467 6200, www.paperchase.co.uk). Goodge Street tube.
Open 8.30am-7.30pm Mon-Wed, Fri; 8.30am-8pm Thur; 9am-7pm Sat; 11.30am-6pm Sun.
The ground floor at Paperchase's three-floor flagship store sells greetings cards of every description, along with all manner of present-wrapping paraphernalia (tissue paper, gift wrap, bows, tags and lengths of velvety ribbon). Photograph albums and frames, notebooks (including Moleskins), pencil cases, diaries and gift items are artfully arrayed towards the front of the store, while the little shelves at the back are filled with writing paper and envelopes in a multitude of colours and sizes. Upstairs, prices climb, with luxury Filofaxes, pens, leather bags and passport wallets (including Mimi; *see p131*) and a select homewares range. The top floor stocks top-notch art materials.
Branches throughout the city.

Tobacconists

G Smith & Sons
74 Charing Cross Road, WC2H 0BG (7836 7422, www.smithsandshervs.com). Leicester Square tube.
Open 9am-6pm Mon-Fri; 9.30am-5.30pm Sat.
The smoking ban hasn't stopped business from booming at G Smith & Sons, a traditional-looking stalwart of Charing Cross Road. Established in 1869, it was the first licensed tobacconist on this strip and its site can legally only house a tobacconist. The walk-in humidor will take your breath away, holding a plethora of cigars, including the Carlos Torano, Café Royale, George IV and La Invicta brands plus Puros Indios and Te-Amo lines and the more familiar Montecristos. Pipe and roll-your-own smokers can choose from 50 blends of loose tobacco; beautifully packaged tins of snuff are also sold.

JJ Fox
19 St James's Street, SW1A 1ES (7930 3787, www.jjfox.co.uk). Green Park tube. **Open** 9am-5.30pm Mon-Fri; 9.30am-5pm Sat.
A prestigious, family-owned tobacconist with expert and enthusiastic staff, who hold great pride in the brand's heritage – the business was started as far back as 1881, and is reportedly the oldest cigar merchants in the world. JJ Fox only stocks cigars with an unquestioned provenance and that meet the highest standards. Among the 20 Cuban brands are the popular Montecristo No.4s and Bolivar Belicosos, while Dominican Republic tobacco brands include Ashton. The great pipe selection features Dunhill and Meerschaum models. There's also a good range of vintage cigars, gift items – such as limited-edition humidors, pipe-shaped cufflinks, and pewter flasks – and the shop has an excellent website. One for the seriously discerning and enthusiastic smoker.

Streetwise **Broadway Market, E8**

Come to see and be seen on east London's most style-conscious street.

One of London's oldest chartered street markets, running between Regent's Canal and London Fields, Broadway Market got a new lease of life a few years back, and is now the centre of the universe for London's skinny-jean wearing, fixed-wheel bike riding young creatives and style-obsessives. Now, every Saturday, Hackney locals gather to chill out with a decent coffee from **Climpson & Sons** (no.67; 7812 9829; http://webcoffeeshop.co.uk), and then stock up on organic fruit and veg, breads, cheeses, meats and pastries, as well as to browse the stalls selling vintage clothes, new threads from up-and-coming designers, fresh-cut flowers and much more. The market is also pleasingly eco-edged, with a ban on plastic bags and a stall selling souvenir cotton totes.

Alongside the stalls are a number of traditional shops – a hardware store, a butcher's, an old-style barber shop, and even a pie and mash shop, **F Cooke** (no.9, 7254 6458) – where you'll pay less than a quid for a cup of rosie lee – as well as some fabulous boutiquey shops and galleries, many of which are also open during the week.

Starting from the top (London Fields end), on the right-hand side, you can browse the well-edited collection of contemporary art and photography books at **Donlon Books** (no.77, 8980 4859, www.donlonbooks.co.uk), peruse gorgeous vintage homewares at **Stella Blunt** (no.75) or pick up some spanking fresh fish and seafood at the **Fin & Flounder** (no.71; www.finandflounder.com).

A little further down, at no.49, is new haberdashery shop **Our Patterned Hand** (www.patternedhand.co.uk), while next door, **MacBlack & Vine** (no.47, 7254 0219, www.macblackandvine.co.uk) displays a regularly changing stock of classic and retro furniture, as well as fine wine. Superb deli **L'Eau à la Bouche** (nos.35-37; 7923 0600, www.labouche.co.uk) – known simply as La Bouche – is now in a larger space, and stocks an unexpectedly wide range of British, French and Spanish (among others) meats, sausages, cheeses and dried goods, as well as tasty filled ciabattas to eat at tables out front (although good luck in nabbing one). **Buggies & Bikes** (see p262) sells funky kids' clothes, organic baby lotions and even paddling pools. Further down, at **Fabrications** (no.7; see p220), you'll find contemporary 'eco-friendly' textiles and designs by new and established designers/makers, as well as regular exhibitions and events. Next door **Rebel Rebel** (no.5; 7254 4487, www.rebelrebel.co.uk) sells inspirational, hand-tied bouquets.

Vintage fans will want to check out **La Vie Boutique**, on the opposite side, at no.18 (7254 5864) – home to a vast range of fashion, from floaty dresses to bags, jewellery, sunglasses and shoes. The former Art Vinyl shop is now a branch of contemporary art bookshop **Artwords** (no.13; see p192 and p193 **Shop talk**); stocking books on fine art, architecture, photography, graphic design and fashion, and with an extensive range of magazines, the place is normally swarming with creatives.

Further along the strip, independent bookseller the **Broadway Bookshop** (no.6; see p189) specialises in literary fiction and hosts regular readings, while next door is one of Broadway Market's best shops, **Black Truffle** (no.4; see p119), where handmade designer shoes sit amid unusual handbags, gloves and other accessories in a deceptively large space.

Head left around the corner of French café La Vie en Rose to seek out retro furniture and design emporium the **Dog & Wardrobe** (see p178), hidden away at the bottom of Regent Studios.

After all the excitement, treat yourself to a bottle of one of over 100 Belgian beers at the **Dove** pub (nos.24-28, 7275 7617, www.dovepubs.com).

Musical Instruments

Most shops listed in this section deal in second-hand as well as new equipment. There are many music shops clustered around Denmark Street (see p231 **Streetwise**) and Charing Cross Road.

All-rounders

Barbican Chimes Music Shop
Silk Street, EC2Y 8DD (7588 9242, www.chimesmusic.com). Barbican tube or Moorgate tube/rail.
Open 9am-5.30pm Mon-Fri; 9am-4pm Sat (9am-5pm during term time).
An invaluable resource for Guildhall students and soloists performing at the Barbican, Chimes – at the base of Cromwell Tower, right next to the main entrance of the Barbican – has a large stock of sheet music, manuscript paper, reeds, strings, bows, mouthpieces, classical CDs, books and more. There's also a limited selection of guitars (classical, acoustic, electro-acoustic) and ukes, plus rhythm instruments and novelty children's items. The South Ken branch has more for-hire instruments, while the Academy Chimes, located at the Royal College of Music, stocks printed and examination music, but is a bit more of a tourist museum shop.
Branches Academy Chimes Music Shop, Royal Academy of Music, York Gate Building, Marylebone Road, NW1 5HT (7873 7400); Kensington Chimes Music, 9 Harrington Road, SW7 3ES (7589 9054).

Chappell of Bond Street
152-160 Wardour Street, W1F 8YA (7432 4400, www.chappellofbondstreet.co.uk). Oxford Circus or Tottenham Court Road tube. **Open** 9.30am-6pm Mon-Fri; 10am-5.30pm Sat.
It's retained its old name, but in 2006 Chappell moved from Bond Street (its home for nearly 200 years) to this amazing three-storey temple (four, if you include the Lost Loft and its guitar fashion range of pick pockets, straps and tees) in Soho. The shop is the leading Yamaha stockist in the UK, with a great range of digital, acoustic and hybrid pianos, electric and acoustic guitars, brass, woodwind and electronic equipment. Prices start at around £20 for a recorder and head into the stratosphere (around £19,000) for a double bass. The basement houses the store's collection of sheet music is reputedly the largest in Europe, and the shop also supplies music books and backing tracks.

Umbrella Music
Unit 6, Eastgate Business Park, 10 Argall Way, E10 7PG (0845 500 2323, www.umbrellamusic.co.uk). Leyton tube then 58 or 158 bus, or Stratford tube/rail/DLR then 158 bus. **Open** 10am-6pm Mon-Sat.
The long-established Umbrella Music school has now relocated to the Eastgate Business Park just off Leyton's Lea Bridge Road. It still stocks a very reasonable collection of new electronic keyboards, acoustic and digital pianos, guitars (classical, bass, electric and electro-acoustic), plus plenty of beginners-level brass, woodwind, strings, drums (including the SpongeBob three-piece junior set) and percussion, amplifiers, recorders, ukes and banjos. It also holds studio equipment (mics, stands, PAs and mixing desks, computer soft- and hardware), plenty of sheet music, runs a 'hire and try' scheme, hosts education courses and has an on-site workshop for basic repairs.

Guitars, banjos & ukuleles

See also above **Barbican Chimes Music Shop** and **Chappell of Bond Street**, and p230 **Hobgoblin**. Denmark Street is a first port-of-call for guitar shops – see p231 **Streetwise**.

Bass Gallery
142 Royal College Street, NW1 0TA (7267 5458, www.thebassgallery.com). Camden Town tube or Camden Road rail. **Open** 10.30am-6pm Mon-Sat.
An alternative to the Denmark Street gang (see p231 **Streetwise**) – and with an ever-growing reputation with the bass space – is north London's Bass Gallery. Opened in 1992, Camden's Bass offers a wide range of new, used and vintage instruments as well as amps and accessories. Staff here pride themselves on their friendly service and expertise and make a point of trying to keep ahead of the curve by road-testing new products before deciding what to stock. There's an in-house workshop where guitars are built that also offers set-ups, repairs and maintenance. The store will also sell your old gear for you.

Chandler Guitars
300-302 Sandycombe Road, Kew, Surrey TW9 3NG (8940 5874, www.chandlerguitars.co.uk). Kew Gardens tube/rail. **Open** 9.30am-6pm Mon-Sat.
The fact that Chandler Guitars has survived for so long in its remote, sleepy Kew Gardens locale is a testament to the quality of the service and instruments here. The catalogue covers new electric guitars from Paul Reed Smith and Fender, high end acoustics models by Atkin Dreadnought and Breedlove, as well as a superb range of vintage models (acoustic, classical, left-handed). There are plenty of pedals, amps and accessories too and the workshop will sort out any setting up modifications or repairs. Chandler is the servicing workshop of choice when the Red Hot Chili Peppers or Dave Gilmour are in town.

LEISURE

Duke of Uke

Musical Instruments

Duke of Uke HOT 50
22 Hanbury Street, E1 6QR (7247 7924, www.dukeofuke.co.uk). Aldgate East tube or Liverpool Street tube/rail or Shoreditch High Street rail.
Open noon-7pm Tue-Fri; 11am-6pm Sat, Sun.
When eccentric musician Matthew Reynolds decided that London needed a specialist ukulele shop he ploughed his life savings into Duke of Uke. The shop stocks a fair few banjos, guitars, mandolins and harmonicas, but its USP is its baffling range of ukuleles. Artists such as Arcade Fire, Conor Oberst, Patrick Wolf, Beirut, Jeremy Warmsley and Stephin Merritt have all brandished ukes on stage, and the shop has become popular for its jam sessions, with recent visitors including Kitty Daisy & Lewis, Le Volume Courbe, Vincent Vincent and the Villains, the Duke Spirit and, of course, the Ukulele Orchestra of Great Britain. The website is a useful starting point with details of Duke of Uke workshops, forthcoming events and miscellanea such as a bit of banjo history and the odd photograph and YouTube clip of banjo performances.

London Guitar Studio/ El Mundo Flamenco
62 Duke Street, W1K 6JT (7493 0033, www.londonguitarstudio.com, www.elmundoflamenco.co.uk). Bond Street tube. **Open** 9.30am-6pm Mon-Sat; 10am-5pm Sun.
If you're looking for an acoustic guitar, whether classical or flamenco, the London Guitar Studio is the place to come. A wide range of traditionally made instruments by manufacturers such as Alhambra, Goya, Vicente Sanchis and Granados can be found here, along with cases, strings, music, stands and tuners. There's also a decent selection of recordings, books and DVDs to provide inspiration and, perhaps not surprisingly, El Mundo Flamenco can supply the rest of the essential extras – from the shoes (150 nails are tapped into the sole one by one) all the way up to the fans, flowers, castanets and hats.

Wild Guitars
393 Archway Road, N6 4ER (8340 7766, www.wildguitars.com). Highgate tube. **Open** 10am-7pm Mon-Sat.
Opened in 1996, Wild Guitars specialises in rare, vintage and often bizarre second-hand guitars, amps, effects and echo machines. Dave Wild – owner, ex-guitar- and guitar repair-man – opened his shop with the intention of providing a service for professional musicians, and WG remains a firm favourite with north London's rock aristos (including members of Coldplay, Babyshambles and Pink Floyd). Expect HiWatt, old Vox, Selmer, Gibson, Fender and Epiphones, and but stock moves quickly and new pieces are coming in all the time, so for a full list of what's in stock, take a look at the regularly updated website.

Pianos & organs

J Reid & Sons
184 St Ann's Road, N15 5RP (8800 6907, www.jreidpianos.co.uk). Seven Sisters tube or South Tottenham rail. **Open** 8am-5.30pm Mon-Fri; 10am-5pm Sat. **No credit cards**.
Britain's largest piano store has been selling pianos since the 1920s and here you'll find brand new Bluthners, Bösendorfers, Kawais and Yamahas; reconditioned Steinways and Bechsteins; shiny new Czech uprights (Petrof, Weinbach, Zeidel, Riga Kloss); and scores of restored second-hand models. Reid also makes its own brand grands and uprights – Reid-Sohn – which are built in Korea. The company runs a busy workshop repairing and restringing pianos, but if you decide your current piano is no longer suitable, Reid will also value, sell or part-exchange your model or another. The shop also offers rentals and hire-to-buy schemes, deducting any hire charges from a subsequent purchase.

Markson Pianos
8 Chester Court, Albany Street, NW1 4BU (7935 8682, www.marksonpianos.com). Great Portland Street or Regent's Park tube or C2 bus. **Open** 9.30am-5.30pm Mon-Sat; 10am-4pm Sun.
As well as selling pianos, this family-run business has been providing restoration, polishing and tuning services for over 100 years. Pianos from the British manufacturer Kemble are sold alongside Bechstein's high-end professional uprights and grands. Other brands include Yamaha, Waldstein, Steingraeber, Petrof and Bösendorfer. Designer pieces from makers like Sauter and Pleyel cost well into the thousands, although there are plenty from around £500. The store sells a number of pre-owned models that have been fully examined and set-up, with necessary parts being replaced and any repairs, such as casework damage, being dealt with by their own repairers and polishers.

Pro audio/electronics

Westend DJ
10-12 Hanway Street, W1T 1UB (7637 3293, www.westenddj.com). Tottenham Court Road tube. **Open** 9.30am-6.30pm Mon-Sat; noon-6pm Sun.
An exhaustive range of cutting-edge DJ and audio-visual equipment and accessories is stocked at Westend DJ. The complete hardware catalogues for all of the leading brands, including Technics and Pioneer, are all available, plus industry names like Stanton, Numark and Denon. As well as the latest turntables, mixers, CD decks, video decks, effects units, amplifiers and speakers, you can pick up headphones, slipmats, styli, microphones, stands, record boxes and a whole lot more. Service is informative and not pushy; and it may well

Bridgewood & Neitzert

be possible to barter for a deal if you're buying a package of several items. It's worth browsing the comprehensive website before you visit.
Branches Microworld, 256 Tottenham Court Road, W1T 7RD (7631 1935); Atlantic Electronics Ltd, 970 North Circular Road, NW2 7JR (8208 6988).

Stringed instruments

Bridgewood & Neitzert
146 Stoke Newington Church Street, N16 0JU (7249 9398, www.londonviolins.com). Stoke Newington rail or 73 bus. **Open** 10am-6pm Mon-Fri; 10am-4pm Sat.
Having started out as makers of lutes, viols and baroque violins, this respected duo has an impeccable knowledge of the stringed instrument. Bridgewood & Neizert sells violins, violas, cellos and double basses in both modern and classical styles with prices for a modern violin starting at around £200, and rising to the thousands for high-end models. They also stock a wide variety of specialist strings. There are five full-time members of staff to deal with guaranteed repairs and restorations of modern as well as period instruments (including lutes and viola d'amores) and B&N also offers valuations, commission-based sales and part exchange services.

John & Arthur Beare
30 Queen Anne Street, W1G 8HX (7307 9666, www.beares.com). Bond Street tube. **Open** (preferably by appointment) 10am-5pm Mon-Fri.
With over 140 years' experience in selling Stradivaris, Guarneris and other Italian masters, J & A Beare's collection of instruments is of the highest calibre. Many of the world's top musicians (Yo-Yo Ma and Isaac Stern included) frequent the place. In 1998, Beare's joined forces with Morris & Smith, London dealers, and together the firm offers expertise and advice in the buying and selling of stringed instruments and bows as well as valuations for insurance purposes. The majority of the violins, violas and cellos are antiques, but there are a few new items. There are experts on hand to appraise and advise on restoration and repair.

Woodwind, brass & percussion
See also p230 **Hobgoblin**.

Foote's
10 Golden Square, W1F 9JA (7734 1822, ww.footesmusic.com). Piccadilly Circus tube. **Open** 9am-6pm Mon-Fri; 10am-6pm Sat.
Founded in 1920 by Charles Ernest Foote, this central London store houses a great selection of instruments: maple ply snare drums, Schlagwerk cajons handmade in Germany, a host of World and Latin percussive instruments (ganzas, tambourines, berimbaus, pandeiros,

Hobgoblin. *See p230.*

bells, whistles and more), as well as woodwind brass and string instruments. Staff are knowledgeable and passionate about the instruments they play and sell. A decent stock of books, DVDs and CDs covers a wide range of instruments; the online site is useful but a store visit is recommended. There's a rent-to-buy scheme as well as hands-on tuition offered (on request) in an in-store demo room.

TW Howarth
31-35 Chiltern Street, W1U 7PN (7935 2407, www.howarth.uk.com). Baker Street tube or Marylebone tube/rail. **Open** 10am-5.30pm Mon-Fri; 10am-4.30pm Sat.
Britain's leading outlet for woodwind instruments and accessories operates across three separate storefronts selling in clarinets, saxophones, bassoons and oboes. It stocks specialist CDs, accessories and sheet music, and has four full-time staff who look after repairs. Yamaha remains the market leader, but the best saxes and clarinets are French (Selmer, Buffet, LeBlanc), while the best bassoons tend to be German (Gebrüder Mönnig, Oscar Adler and the like). The shop also sells second-hand instruments and runs a rental scheme. Over the road (No.34) the Early Music Shop specialises in musical instruments and sheet music from the 18th century, and stocks harps, viols, flutes, baroque cellos, zithers, crumhorns, folk and world instruments.

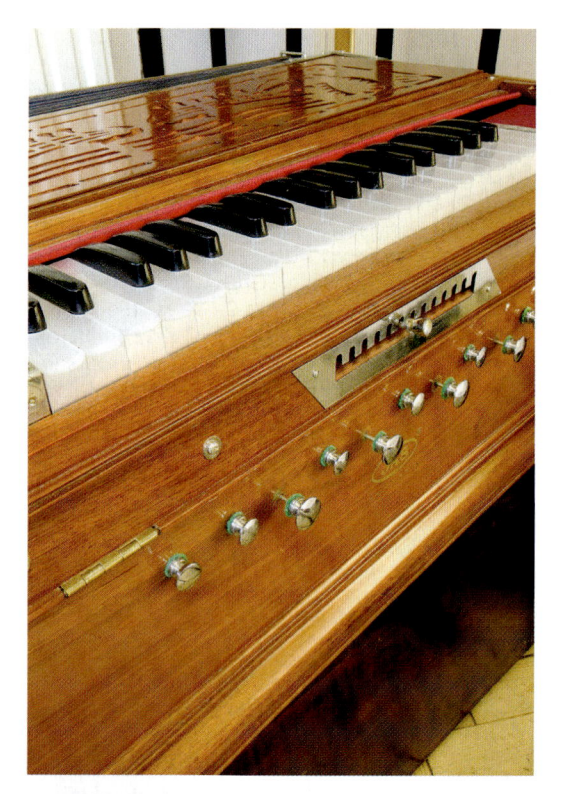

World, early music & folk

See also p229 **TW Howarth** and p231 **Streetwise** for the **Early Music Shop**.

Hobgoblin
24 Rathbone Place, W1T 1JA (7323 9040, www.hobgoblin.com). Tottenham Court Road tube. **Open** 10am-6pm Mon-Sat.
The diverse stock at this remarkable folk shop covers a mix of traditional, world and folk instruments covering woodwind (bagpipes, flutes), stringed instruments (fiddles, harps, zithers) and fretted instruments (banjos, mandolins, ukuleles) as well as free reed (melodeons, harmonicas), percussion and guitars. More unusual finds like the Irish bodhrán drum, a double-reed Chinese flute or the Spanish cajon make this shop unique. Vintage and second-hand items are for sale, as are a host of books, CDs and accessories (amps, cases, tuners), and a luthier makes lutes, ouds and guitars and does repairs. The website lists a host of items that have been reduced to clear.

Jas Musicals
14 Chiltern Street, W1U 7PY (7935 0793, www.jas-musicals.com). Baker Street tube.
Open 11am-7pm daily.
Marylebone's Chiltern Street is the central London outpost of the original Southall shop that was opened over 25 years ago by Harjit Singh Shah. His original intention was to apply high-class Western technology to Indian instruments while maintaining traditional standards, and those impressed with the success of this enterprise have included Jimmy Page, Talvin Singh, John McLaughlin, Zakir Hussain and David Gray. As well as stocking tablas, dhols, harmoniums, tanpuris and sitars, the shop offers a repair service and a host of accessories, instrument bags, music and books. Prices are surprisingly inexpensive compared to most Western musician instruments.
Branch 124 The Broadway, Southall, Middx, UB1 1QF (8574 2686).

Ray Man
54 Chalk Farm Road, NW1 8AN (7692 6261, www.raymaneasternmusic.co.uk). Camden Town or Chalk Farm tube. **Open** 1-5pm Mon; 10.30am-6pm Tue-Sat; 11am-5pm Sun.
A family-run business for over 30 years, Ray Man sells a unique variety of traditional instruments from all over Asia, Africa, the Middle East and South America. More recognisable items like sitars and darbuka drums share the space with Chinese zithers and Indian fiddles. There are also several smaller and more affordable objects such as the Vietnamese frog box and Indian monkey drums, tam tam and nipple gongs, singing bowls, bells, cymbals and shakers. The Vietnamese jaw harps (as heard on Morricone spaghetti western soundtracks) fit nicely into your pocket. Ray Man also runs a service that tracks down specialist overseas instruments.

Jas Musicals

Musical Instruments

Streetwise **Denmark Street, WC2**

Central London's Tin Pan Alley has been a magnet for musicians and rock stars for decades.

Located between Charing Cross Road and St Giles High Street, virtually every door on Denmark Street leads to a room packed with new or vintage guitars, pedals, amps and accessories. Whether you're seeking a 1930s Gibson acoustic, a £20 ukulele or a neon-green lightning bolt DIME-series Dean electric, no other street offers such variety.

From a 17th-century estate turned 18th-century slum, Denmark Street grew into a row of theatres, instrument shops, music printers and cheap domiciles for musicians, earning it the nickname 'Tin Pan Alley'. During the 1960s, it became a launching pad for the UK rock scene: the Beatles and Jimi Hendrix recorded their first tracks in makeshift basement studios here, the Rolling Stones recorded their debut album at Regent Sound Studio, and David Bowie – who couldn't afford a flat at the time – lived out of a van here. The late Malcolm McLaren had one of the divier basements.

Today, most of the recording studios have gone, but the remaining guitar shops are still a magnet for rock stars and music fans. Redevelopment of the surrounding area (the nearby cross rail project is underway, while the new St Giles High Street development was nearly finished as this guide went to press) is also likely to increase passing trade, preserving the street's musical heritage.

Starting at the St Giles High Street end, at no.4, is **Regent Sound Studio** (no.4, 7379 6111), Europe's largest Fender dealer, which also stocks Gretsch, Music Man, Squier, Vox, Tokai, Hofner and Danelectro guitars, basses, amps and accessories.

Next door, **Rockers** (no.5, 7240 2610) offers everything from beginner-level to professional thrash-ready new guitars by Fender, Gibson, ESP, Ibanez and Dean. Staff will let you demo your chosen axe with a HIWATT amp and you'll be melting faces in no time. Plug in, and rock out!

Moving on, **Vintage & Rare Guitars** (no.6, 7240 7500, www.vintageandrareguitars.com) is a treasure trove of 1950s and '60s pre-CBS Fender and Gibson electrics, vintage Martin and Guild acoustics and collectable instruments. Also for sale are rare handmade 'boutique' fuzz and effect pedals from LovePedal and Death by Audio. The Sex Pistols lived in the building behind the shop.

A new arrival, at the Charing Cross Road end, is the **Early Music Shop** (no.11, 7632 3960), where you can pay a tenner for a plastic Yamaha soprano recorder and up to £3,500 for a Paetzold sub bass model, moving through handmade wooden recorders by the likes of Blezinger and Mollenhauer. It also stocks harps, baroque cellos, zithers and more.

On the other side of the street, at no.20, **Wunjo** (7379 0737, www.wunjoguitars.com) houses three rooms of wall-to-wall new and used guitars, ranging from £150 acoustic starter packs and mid-priced Danelectro models to vintage Fender, Gibson, Gretsch, VOX, custom-built electrics, a wide selection of acoustics and a fair range of basses.

Heading back towards St Giles High Street, you'll come to **Bass Cellar** (no.22, 7240 3483), selling standard, fretless, five-, six-, seven-string and lefty models by Fender, Rickenbacker, Warwick and others, as well as a host of bass rigs. Acoustic and classical guitarists, meanwhile, shouldn't miss London's largest Martin dealer, **Hank's**, at no.24 (7379 1139, www.hanksguitarshop.com).

After establishing its original Tin Pan Alley shop in 1958, family-owned and -operated **Macari's** (no.25, 3301 5481, www.macaris.co.uk) moved to Charing Cross Road, but reopened a Denmark Street branch in 2009. The shop is the UK's official Gibson and Marshall dealer with guitars and amps starting at £69. The owner's father co-founded Colorsound effects pedals, producing the first English-made 'fuzzbox', used by Jimmy Page on *Led Zeppelin I*.

Finally, **Music Ground Inc** (no.27, 7836 5354, www.musicground.com) is packed to the gills with vintage electric guitars from Gibson, Fender, VOX and National, to 'odd-ball' European brands.

Time Out London's Best Shops **231**

Sport & Fitness

Of all the major department stores, **Harrods** (see p22) has the biggest selection of sports and fitness equipment, with much of the store's fifth floor given over to golf simulators, ski, riding and biking equipment and plenty of designer sportswear to complete the look. **John Lewis** (see p23) stocks table tennis, snooker and pool tables, as well as exercise machines and accessories for other sports. **Selfridges** (see p27) has a range of GoCycle electric bikes and a concession for Cycle Surgery.

The **howies** (see p60) range of T-shirts, jackets, thermal underwear and cycling gear is sought after as much for the stylish designs as the practical innovations; the brand is a favourite among surfers, bikers and other outdoor enthusiasts.

See also the trainer shops listed in the **Shoes** chapter (pp119-127).

Cycling

London's bike shops are getting better and better, with more and more small business (as well as branches of the big chains, such as Cycle Surgery), opening all the time; below is a selection of the best.

Bikefix
48 Lamb's Conduit Street, WC1N 3LJ (7405 1218, www.bikefix.co.uk). Holborn tube. **Open** 8.30am-7pm Mon-Fri; 10am-5pm Sat.
If you're looking for a machine that'll make fellow cyclists stop and stare, or need a three-wheeler to take your ice-cream business into the parks, head for Bikefix. The fantastically quirky and original selection of bikes includes utility models, recumbents and folding bikes – the recumbent style is significantly more aerodynamic as well as being eye catching. But if you're not keen on eccentric bike models, there's also an excellent choice of more familiar-looking rides, from less well-known manufacturers such as Fahrrad Manufaktur. Bike Fix first started as a repair and maintenance workshop, and it continues to fix bikes, on a first come, first served basis.

Bobbin Bicycles `HOT 50`
397 St John Street, EC1V 4LD (7837 3370, www.bobbinbicycles.co.uk). Angel tube. **Open** 11am-7pm Tue-Fri; 11am-6pm Sat.
If your preference is for the more elegant days of cycle touring, rather than the modern penchant for squeezing into lycra, then Bobbin is the shop for you. Husband-and-wife team Tom Morris and Sian Emmison sell traditional city cycles, many of them vintage, from premises that steer a different route to the traditional bike shop, with accessories to match the striking colour range of their machines. Models for sale include the Pashley Roadster, Gazelle Gent's Tour Populair and Electra Unisex Amsterdam. Test rides are encouraged – there's a traffic-free square nearby – but call ahead to book as the shop gets very busy.

Brick Lane Bikes
118 Bethnal Green Road, E2 6DG (7033 9053, www.bricklanebikes.co.uk). Bethnal Green tube/rail or Shoreditch High Street rail. **Open** 9am-7pm Mon-Fri; 11am-7pm Sat; 11am-6pm Sun.
Fixed-wheel and single-speed bikes have become essential urban-hipster accessories in recent years, and you'll find a wide selection at Brick Lane Bikes. The stock includes Charge Plugs and Surly Steamrollers, but the kit that gets die-hards drooling will be hanging above your head: new frames from esteemed Leeds firm Bob Jackson, plus a variety of vintage track and road frames in most shapes and sizes, all of which can be built to order. Prices for custom-builds are highish and customer service can range from fairly helpful to crushingly indifferent; it helps to have some idea what you're after before going in.

Brixton Cycles
145 Stockwell Road, SW9 9TN (7733 6055, www.brixtoncycles.co.uk). Brixton tube/rail. **Open** 9am-6pm Mon-Wed, Fri, Sat; 10am-7pm Thur.
A Brixton fixture since the 1980s, this co-operative offers a fine range of bicycles and a well-regarded workshop. Bikes from Trek and Specialized keep commuters happy, as do the Bromptons. The workshop can also undertake custom-builds, including fixed-wheel and single-speed machines. It provides a daily on-the-spot repair service in the first hour of opening, otherwise you'll need to book, up to a month in advance. The service options range from a £35 (plus parts) checkover to a £120 service (plus parts) that sees the bike taken apart, cleaned, lubricated and put back together again. Brixton Cycles also stocks a range of skateboards.

Condor Cycles
49-53 Gray's Inn Road, WC1X 8PP (7269 6820, www.condorcycles.com). Chancery Lane tube. **Open** 9am-6pm Mon, Tue, Thur, Fri; 9am-7.30pm Wed; 10am-5pm Sat.
The USP of this family-run London legend, in business since 1948 and still in excellent health, is its own range of road bikes, built to order on a bespoke basis. Having chosen a model, prospective purchasers are propped on a fitting jig and measured for the correct frame and components, with clued-up staff adding appropriate parts according to the buyer's budget. But while Condor

Sport & Fitness

Bikefix

is heaven for the serious road cyclist, there's plenty for casual riders too. The basement showroom also has some off-the-peg bikes from other manufacturers, and the range of accessories on the main floor is perhaps the best in town.

Mosquito Bikes
123 Essex Road, N1 2SN (7226 8765, www. mosquito-bikes.co.uk). Angel tube or Essex Road rail. **Open** 8.30am-7pm Mon-Fri; 10am-6pm Sat.
Stockist of high-end road and mountain bikes from manufacturers such as Surly, Kinesis and Litespeed, Mosquito Bikes is a dream shop for the serious cyclist. It's not cheap however, with frame-building masters like Pegoretti, Milani and Merlin generally charging well into four figures for their products. Since you're spending a lot on the bike, it should fit your body, and as part of its service Mosquito will professionally fit your custom-built bike to your frame, having determined your cycling history and aspirations, measured you from top to toe, and checked your flexibility and feet. The workshop operates a booking system and provides a standard service for £75.

Sargent & Co
74 Mountgrove Road, N5 2LT (7359 7642, www.sargentandco.com). Finsbury Park tube/ rail. **Open** 10.30am-6.30pm Wed-Sat.
Owner Rob Sargent has an off-kilter sense of humour – 'No mountain bikes, high breads (sic), or modern carp (sic)' – but his message is clear: to promote, revive and facilitate the pastime of cycling. Sargent's love of all things cyclical means that his lovely Finsbury Park shop, guarded by Cassius the cat, is bedecked with frames (photo- as well as bike-) and accessories from the glory days of cycling. Services include a puncture repair or a wash-and-brush-up to a full customisation or restoration. 'All carried out at very competitive prices, usually with a smile, and occasionally a cup of tea.' *See also right* **Shop talk**.

Tokyo Fixed `HOT 50`
4 Peter Street, W1F 0AD (7734 1885, www.tokyofixedgear.com). Piccadilly Circus tube. **Open** 11am-8pm daily.
The fixed-wheel cycling scene – or cycling on a bike that has no freewheel so cannot coast – has seen an explosion in popularity and, in response, bike nuts Tokyo Fixed have moved from exporting keirin frames from Tokyo (back in 2007), to opening their two-storey Soho store in 2009. The shop stocks all things fixed-wheel, including frames, wheels, high-end brands such as Nari Furi and CCP, books, jewellery, mags and bags. Fixed-wheel bikes first became popular with cycle couriers due to their simplicity and ease of maintenance, but have more recently become something of a craze, and one that Tokyo Fixed intends to foster in the city.

Sport & Fitness

Shop talk
Rob Sargent, owner of Sargent & Co

Tell us about the shop
'We've been open for two years; we specialise in classic and vintage cycles – basically restoring, rebuilding, repairing and selling. We can build a bike up from a frame in about two days and all our bikes are steel bikes.

'We exist to promote the pastime of cycling; there is a quote on our website from 1917 that puts it very nicely: "Most of our workaday jobs and cares do not tire the muscles but clog them with poisons. Cycling in the pure air gets the blood moving, cleansing and tingling. Cycling is rhythmic, and it is a truism that all 'patterned' exercise is pleasant, efficient and beneficial."

'Before I worked here I was a bit of an aspiring artist, and I had my own workshop, but it was really just for me. I painted the commuter ferries on the river to bring money in, so the shop makes a nice change from standing in the shipyard, painting!'

Why do you only make/repair steel bicycles?
'Well, I want to make bikes that last. It seems that other materials are used purely because the manufacturers realise [that they don't last], and actually want them to break down after a couple of years so that people are forced to buy new bikes.

'From the beginning of the trend for using aluminium, it seems that bikes haven't been made to be lasting machines anymore. I don't tend to work with any bikes made after 1990.'

What's a typical day in the shop?
'It's got to start with a cup of fresh coffee in the morning, otherwise I'm disorientated and rude to customers… I warm up by the afternoon and then open a can of beer at about 6pm!

'We do repair work for people in the area but the best work is with our bespoke bikes, built up and made to order. We are not an ordinary bike shop – more of a bike workshop.'

Have you noticed changes in the London shopping scene over the past few years?
'There's been a huge resurgence in cycling and interest in vintage bikes. It's as though people have had their eyes opened to the fact that they don't have to go around on a grey machine that's been poorly designed and will break down in a small amount of time. Cycling is going through a boom time at the moment, which we are very pleased to be part of.'

What is the most enjoyable aspect of owning a shop?
'Seeing the people who come into the shop with an old bike that they used to ride, or that used to be their father's, and being able to restore or rebuild it to a state that is probably better than it was originally; knowing that they will use and enjoy it is really great.'

What are your favourite shops in London?
'The furniture and repair shop Bennet & Brown (84 Mountgrove Road, N5 2LT, 7704 9200, www.bennetandbrown.co.uk) in Stoke Newington is very good. And the Peanut Vendor (*see p182*) in Newington Green is great for bric-a-brac.'

What do you envisage for your business for the future?
'Apart from winning the Tour de France…? I'd like a bigger shop!'

▶ For **Sargent & Co**, *see p234*.

Outdoor pursuits & multi-sport shops

Covent Garden is the spot for hikers, climbers, campers and snowsports enthusiasts.

Ace Sports & Leisure
341 Kentish Town Road, NW5 2TJ (7485 5367, www.acesportsdirect.com). Kentish Town tube/rail. **Open** 9.30am-6pm Mon-Sat.
Established in 1949, Ace Sports is a proper old-school sports shop that covers all sports but has a particular emphasis on football gear – this is the place to buy your England World Cup shirt (or Brazil or Nigeria); the store stocks plenty of official home and away premiership strips, as well as international shirts, football boots, balls and souvenirs. As well as a rugby section, the store has a small rack of boxing gloves and accessories, a few snooker cues and cricket whites, gloves and pads, as well as tennis and badminton equipment. Most of the products are available online and products can also be sent overseas.
Branch 594 Hertford Road, Enfield EN3 5SX (8804 4500).

Decathlon
Canada Water Retail Park, Surrey Quays Road, SE16 2XU (7394 2000, www.decathlon.co.uk). Canada Water rail. **Open** 9am-9pm Mon-Fri; 9am-7pm Sat; 11am-5pm Sun.
The warehouse-sized London branch of this French chain offers London's biggest single collection of sports equipment. You'll find a vast array of reasonably priced equipment and clothing for all mainstream racket and ball sports as well as for swimming, running, surfing, fishing, horse riding, mountaineering, ice-skating, skiing, even archery and petanque. The company boasts a 'try before you buy' testing service on its golfing woods and irons. Separate premises host bicycle sales and repairs along with all sorts of cycling paraphernalia. There's an extensive range of hiking and camping equipment (tents, clothing and accessories). Deliveries can be made all over the country.

Ellis Brigham
Tower House, 3-11 Southampton Street, WC2E 7HA (7395 1010, www.ellis-brigham.com). Covent Garden tube. **Open** 10am-7pm Mon-Wed, Fri; 10am-8pm Thur; 9.30am-6.30pm Sat; 11.30am-5.30pm Sun.
With countless racks of outdoor clothing upstairs and climbing, hiking, skiing and snowboarding equipment downstairs in the basement, this is the largest of the mountain sports shops on Southampton Street. It also houses London's only ice-climbing wall, 8m (26ft) high. The wall is in a refrigerator, starting in the basement and rising through the ground floor, where

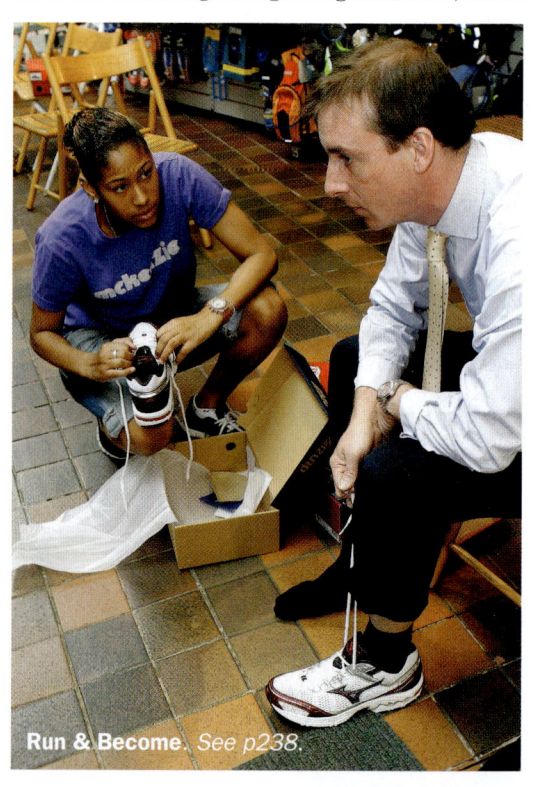

Run & Become. See p238.

there are viewing windows. Two people can climb at any one time (£50 per person per hour, £25-£35 if you have your own kit and don't need instruction). Book at least a day ahead for weekdays, and around six weeks in advance for weekends.
Branches Unit 2003, Westfield Shopping Centre, W12 7GF (8222 6300); 178 Kensington High Street, W8 7RG (7937 6889).

Nike Town
236 Oxford Street, W1W 8LG (7612 0800, www.nike.com). Oxford Circus tube. **Open** 10am-8pm Mon-Sat; 11.30am-6pm Sun.
Four-floor Niketown is big on clothing (and little on clothing too – with tops and shoes for babies as young as three months). It may be low on equipment but it stocks an excellent selection of football boots and has a well-stocked running department as well as a customisation lab on the second floor where, with many of the designs, you can choose your material (cracked leather, metallic) and colour (even colour of 'swoosh') and then personalise it with an embroidered ID. There are also plenty of shirts (baseball, cycling, rugby, football) and accessories (bags, gloves, socks). Nike's 1948 (*see p127*) opened early in 2010 and hosts a raft of events that you'll probably want to show your new togs off at.

Wigmore Sports
39 Wigmore Street, W1U 1QQ (7486 7761, www.wigmoresports.com). Bond Street tube. **Open** 10am-6pm Mon-Wed, Fri, Sat; 10am-7pm Thur; 11am-5pm Sun.
If it's got strings and it swings, you can buy it here. The most impressive racket sports specialist in London, Wigmore Sports has a whole room stacked full of tennis, squash and badminton rackets. This is high-end gear so don't expect to find more than a dozen tennis rackets among the hundreds on display for much under £50; most are over £100. All the extras are here, plus specialist clobber like tennis-specific sunglasses with teal tinted lenses that mute all light except optic yellow. The footwear choice is also extensive, with something for every surface. There's a 24-hour stringing service and an in-store practice wall so you can try before you buy. There's also a concession in Harrods (*see pxxx*).

Specialists

Arthur Beale
194 Shaftesbury Avenue, WC2H 8JP (7836 9034). Tottenham Court Road tube. **Open** 9am-6pm Mon-Fri; 9.30am-1pm Sat.
There are some odd shops in London, but few beat the surprise factor of finding a yacht chandler in Shaftesbury Avenue. Arthur Beale is a retail survivor, hanging on long after many of the other chandlers went bust. It may look old-fashioned – and it stubbornly holds out against this new-fangled internet thing – but the stock is as useful now as it ever was for sailors. On the ground floor you'll find everything from reels of rope, ship's bells, barometers and brass navigation lights to basic boating hardware such as cleats, fairleads and lacing hooks. On the first floor you'll find books, boots and lifejackets.

Bloch
35 Drury Lane, WC2B 5RH (7836 4777, www.bloch world.com). Covent Garden tube. **Open** 10am-6pm Mon-Sat; noon-5pm Sun.
Feet are important for everyone, but vital for a dancer. Bloch, a renowned dance footwear and apparel manufacturer that was founded in 1932, continues to sell shoes for ballet, tap, hip hop, jazz, latin and ballroom, but it has recently gone into partnership with Australian designer Jozette Hazzouri, producing a range of high-fashion shoes and sandals. Its own brand of day shoes features a striking range of colours and funky, dance-inspired designs, and Baby Bloch will ensure your child has shoes to die for before he or she can even crawl – thus ensuring the shoes stay clean as well.

Freed of London
94 St Martin's Lane, WC2N 4AT (7240 0432, www.freedoflondon.com). Leicester Square tube. **Open** 9.30am-5.30pm Mon-Fri; 9.30am-3.30pm Sat.
If you've ever seen a ballet, you'll have seen a Freed pointe shoe. The company was founded in 1929 by Frederick Freed and today supplies shoes to prominent dance companies and schools, including the Royal Ballet, New York City Ballet and the Royal Ballet School. Darcey Bussell and Margot Fonteyn wore Freed shoes. The shoes are mostly still made by hand in the traditional turn shoe method, where most of the stitching is done with the shoe turned inside out. If you can't stand en pointe, the company also produces ballroom, jazz and Latin shoes plus a range of clothing. All products are Freed branded.

LCB Surf Store
121 Bethnal Green Road, E2 7DG (7739 3839, www.lcbsurfstore.com). Shoreditch High Street rail. **Open** 8am-7pm Mon-Fri; 10am-7pm Sat, Sun.
LCB's laid-back vibe and colourful, light interior hit just the right note for a surf shop. The store's owners, Pete and Mark Lindsell, design and manufacture their own distinctive surfboards, the LCB E-series, from glass, Kevlar and carbon fibre, balsa and epoxy resin. The company also produces its own range of LCB clothing for older teens and adults up to 35. Rip Curl wetsuits, Burton snowboards and a range of skateboards round out the stock. There is also an in-store café that serves organic and free trade coffee and juices, with internet access and occasional board-related screenings/events. A new branch is set to open at Mile End Skatepark in 2010.
Branch 23 Chalk Farm Road, NW1 8AG (7482 6089).

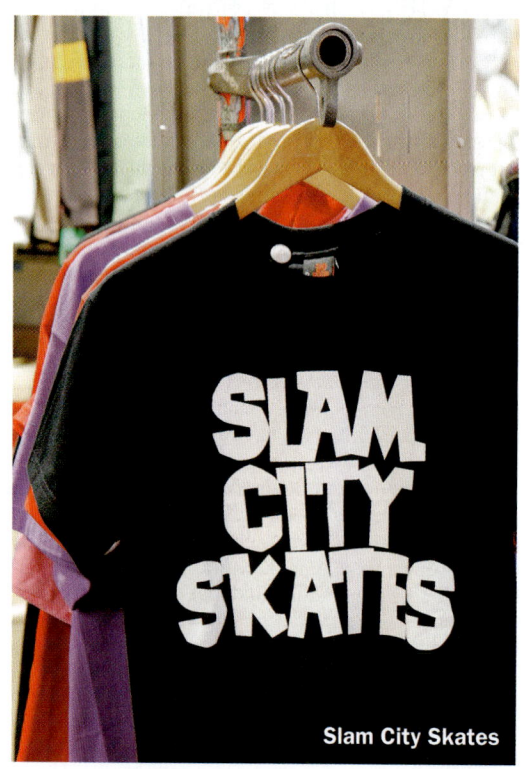

Run & Become

42 Palmer Street, SW1H 0PH (7222 1314, www.runandbecome.com). St James's Park tube.
Open 9am-6pm Mon-Wed, Fri, Sat; 9am-8pm Thur.
Tony Smith opened Run & Become in 1982 on its present site, and improving sales allowed him to buy the next door shop a few years later. Although Tony himself died in 2006, his daughters had already joined him in running the business and it remains family run. The experienced staff, most of them enthusiastic runners, are determined to find the right pair of shoes for your particular physique and running style, with wide selections of road, off-road, fell and spiked shoes for sale, including Saucony, Brooks, ASICS, Puma and Adidas. Apart from shoes, the full gamut of running kit, from clothing to energy snacks to speed monitors, is also available.

Slam City Skates

16 Neal's Yard, WC2H 9DP (7240 0928, www.slamcity.com). Covent Garden tube.
Open 11am-7pm Mon-Sat; noon-5pm Sun.
Slam City Skates is a legendary name on the British skate scene, as much a part of the London skateboarding identity as doing kickflips and railstands on the walkways beneath the South Bank Centre. It's also the best-stocked shop for decks, trucks, wheels and almost any skateboard accessory – with makers such as Death Wish, Alien Workshop and Familia well represented – as well as footwear and clothing, including the shop's own unique T-shirt and hoodie range. All the staff are skaters and you can see some of them doing their stuff on the company website under the 'team' link.
Branch 43 Carnaby Street, W1F 7EA (7287 9548).

Soccer Scene

56-57 Carnaby Street, W1F 9QF (7439 0778, www.soccerscene.co.uk). Oxford Circus tube.
Open 10am-7pm Mon-Wed, Fri, Sat; 10am-8pm Thur; noon-6pm Sun.
Soccer fans are nothing if not tribal, and you can get most of the requisite club and country replica kits here. Arsenal, Chelsea and Spurs team kits are available (from £42.99 to £49.99 for the shirts, £19.99 for the shorts) but West Ham fans will have to make do with the 1958 or '64 kit. Aston Villa, Birmingham City, Bolton Wanderers, Everton, Liverpool, Manchester (United and City), Portsmouth and Wigan strips are also available, plus Newcastle, Norwich and QPR from the lower divisions, and a wide range of national team outfits. There are children's sizes for not much less (£32.99 to £39.99). Apart from shirts, football accessories and training DVDs are for sale and, naturally, football boots – and not just the mainstream brands: come here for Lotto, Uhlsport and Joma.
Branch 156 Oxford Street, W1D 1ND (7436 6499).

Slam City Skates

Streetwise **Lamb's Conduit Street, WC1**

One of central London's most independents-heavy shopping streets.

Partially pedestrianised, with a slew of good pubs and cafés, Lamb's Conduit Street has a gentle pace that seems far from the bustle of the West End. There's a nice mix of traditional and hip retailers, and residents and shopkeepers stick together – there are organised street festivals, and one hell of a fuss was kicked up when Starbucks moved in. Chains remain a rarity, however, and the street's many independents are happily thriving.

Close to Virginia Woolf's old stomping grounds, **Persephone Books** (no.59; see p195) is a treasure. Both a small press and retail shop, it specialises in rescuing and elegantly reprinting neglected women's fiction of the early 20th century.

At no.57 **Kennards** (7404 4030, www.kennards goodfoods.com) displays fruit and veg outside while inside tempting breads and pastries jostle for your attention alongside cheeses and antipasti. The own-made takeaway lunches are top notch.

Just a bit further along, the **Lamb Bookshop** (no.40, 7405 6536, www.thelambbookshop.co.uk) stocks a good range of fiction and an even better selection of children's books – less literary-minded offspring are catered for with Miffy aprons.

In keeping with the old-fashioned feel of the strip, there are a couple of gentlemen's outfitters that seem to belong to a bygone era, selling suits, waistcoats, tweeds and ties. **Sims & Macdonald** (no.46, 7430 1909, www.simsandmacdonald.com) has been on the street for seven decades, while **Connock & Lockie** (no.33, 7831 2479) offers a tailoring service for women as well as men.

A few doors down at no.49 is **Folk** (see p59), which is largely given over to menswear but has a decent selection of women's clothes at the back. The look is casual with a twist and stock is dominated by the in-house label, plus a smattering of other brands such as Humanoid and Sessùn. Footwear by sister label Shofolk includes moccasin-style boots in soft suede and leather.

Just around the corner on Rugby Street is the lovely protected 1920s shopfront of **French's Dairy** (no.13; see p134). The charming jewellery and accessories shop housed within showcases new European designers. Also on offer is a small selection of contemporary women's fashion and an imaginative selection of bags and belts. For more accessories, carry on to 7 Rugby Street where **Susannah Hunter**'s (7692 3798, www.susannahhunter.com) handmade leather bags and furniture are decorated with her signature appliquéd flowers.

Back on Lamb's Conduit Street, Toni Horton's **Something...** (no.58; see p45) is favoured by all those looking for a memorable gift or a treat for themselves: elegant purses and wallets, deliciously scented candles and Provençal soaps, Cath Kidston-esque mugs and cake stands and heart-shaped mirrors, and a selection of girly jewellery and accessories. The garden is opened up in clement weather, with a selection of birdcages and garden lanterns on display in the blue-painted shed. Those who are kitting out a bijou balcony or patio should nip over to fragrant **Dawson Flowers** at no.43 (7404 6893, www.dawsonflowers.net).

One of newest and most exciting shops is concept store **Darkroom** (no.52; see p39); inside the stylish black-walled space you'll find an intriguing selection of covetable items, with unisex fashion, jewellery by Florian and Scott Wilson, Borba Margo bags, designer ceramics and artwork for sale.

Reliable repairs outfit **Bikefix** (no.48; see p232) stocks a good range of accessories, plus unusual urban bikes and fold-ups if you're in the market for a new ride. And to add to the wholesome vibe, as this guide went to press, the **People's Supermarket** (www.peoples supermarket.org) was about to open selling ethically sourced food; an innovative staffing scheme will see those customers working in the shop for four hours a month gain a 20 per cent discount, and a say in how the shop is run.

Pets

Holly & Lil
103 Bermondsey Street, SE1 3XB (3287 3024, www.hollyandlil.co.uk). London Bridge tube/rail.
Open 11.30am-6.15pm Tue, Wed; 11.30am-7pm Thur; 10.30am-6.15pm Fri; 10.30am-5pm Sat.
Holly & Lil's dog collars and leads are all handmade, luxurious and on-trend; there are limited-edition collections – the winning Toto in the BBC's *Over the Rainbow* wore the Rainbow collar, while the calf leather Cross of St George was a must-wear for the 2010 World Cup) – in all materials (leather, tartan, Harris tweed) and all styles ('charm collars' are adorned with beads, tiny multicoloured dice, or semi-precious stones). Prices start at around £40, rising to £120 for the heavily adorned Boho models. The shop also sells a range of harnesses and charity collars (for a cause), and cats get a look in too with their own line of collars. If nothing seems quite fancy enough, owners can commission something ultra-outrageous themselves.

Kings Aquatic & Reptile World
26 Camden High Street, NW1 0JH (7387 5553, www.kingsreptileworld.co.uk). Mornington Crescent tube. **Open** 10am-6pm Mon-Sat; 10am-2pm Sun.
Reptile expert Simon King set up this exotic pet shop, supplying arachnids, snakes, amphibians, invertebrates and reptiles, in 1997. Any squeamish readers out there can relax, though – all the creatures are safely ensconced in their cages. Prices vary widely depending on the rarity of the specimen; a tarantula will set you back between £10 and £200, lizards go for £8 to £800 and baby corn snakes are £45. Kings also breeds rare monitor lizards and runs a pet-sitting service. Crickets, locusts and frozen mice are for sale for pets' snacks, and there are all sorts of cages. A modest selection of cold-water and tropical fish is available downstairs.

Mungo & Maud
79 Elizabeth Street, SW1W 9PJ (7467 0820, www.mungoandmaud.com). Sloane Square tube or Victoria tube/rail or 11 bus. **Open** 10am-6pm Mon-Sat.
A boutique with a touch of French sophistication, this is the ultimate 'dog and cat outfitters'. Fed up with her dog's outmoded accessories clashing with her modern home, dog-lover Nicola Sacher decided to design her own to fill the niche. Stylish and minimalist, pooch products include washable dog beds, collars and leads, and the 'petite amande dog fragrance'; for kitty, there's catnip and embroidered wool cat blankets. Humans won't feel left out and can browse over book titles like *Pug Therapy* and *Is Your Dog Gay?* There are also concessions at Selfridges (*see p27*), Fortnum & Mason (*see p21*) and within Harrods' Pet Kingdom (*see p22*).

Mutz Nutz
221 Westbourne Park Road, W11 1EA (7243 3333, www.themutznutz.com). Ladbroke Grove or Westbourne Park tube. **Open** 10am-6pm Mon, Fri, Sat; 10am-7pm Tue-Thur; noon-5pm Sun.
As the name suggests, the treats from this attractive boutique will drive cats and dogs (or their owners) crazy. On the shelves you'll find toys, leads, handmade jewel-encrusted collars (£50-£200), organic nibbles, toothbrushes – even dog nappies. There are also special dog car seats and, bizarrely, wedding dresses with veils. Cats are equally well catered for, with catnip spray and a three-sided 'scratch lounge'. The nearby same-owned Dog Spa (22 Powis Terrace, W11 1JH, 7243 3399) offers Italian baths: pets are tended to by personal groomers and leave fully coiffed, perfumed and ribbon clad. At the pet supermarket, goodies and titbits can be taken away.

Primrose Hill Pets
132 Regent's Park Road, NW1 8XL (7483 2023, www.primrosehillpets.co.uk). Chalk Farm tube.
Open 9am-6pm Mon-Sat; 11am-5pm Sun.
The UK's finest quality leads and collars are available here (Hunter, Fox & Hounds, Up Country), as well as some very swish numbers from Germany and the US (Timberwolf): they come in all sizes, in leather, fabric or nylon, plain or diamanté. There is also a range of coats (all sizes, some exclusive), beds (faux suede, vet bed), airline-approved pet carriers (Vari-Kennel and Sherpa) and a range of grooming products (including ones for sensitive skins and allergies), plus there's a treatment service for cats and dogs (by appointment). Informed staff give advice on diets, food, supplements and treats and they'll readily point you in the direction of local breeders and shelters.

Holly & Lil

Food & Drink

Food	243
Drink	256

TRAY GOURMET
caterer-traiteur français
SW10

A French Caterer & Delicatessen which is a corner of France on your doorstep. Offering a bespoke catering service to suit your tastes.

Tray Gourmet -
Traiteur Français

240 Fulham Rd
www.traygourmet.com
020 7352 7676

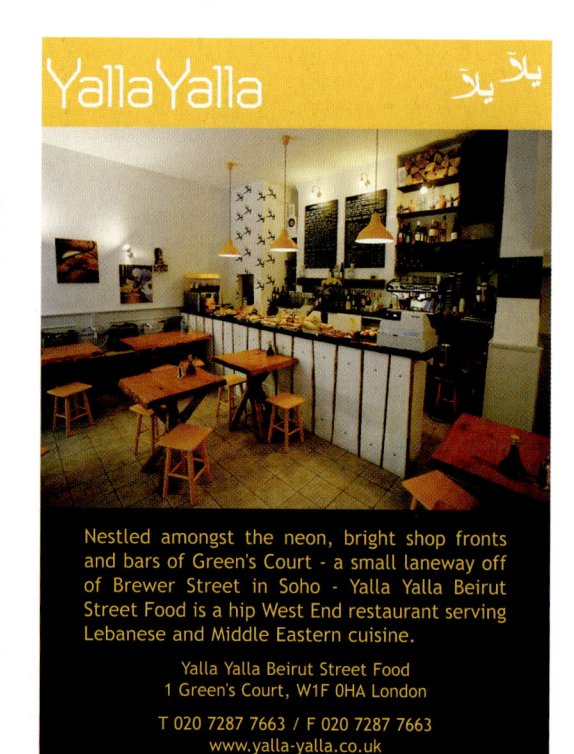

Yalla Yalla
يلاّ يلاّ

Nestled amongst the neon, bright shop fronts and bars of Green's Court - a small laneway off of Brewer Street in Soho - Yalla Yalla Beirut Street Food is a hip West End restaurant serving Lebanese and Middle Eastern cuisine.

Yalla Yalla Beirut Street Food
1 Green's Court, W1F 0HA London

T 020 7287 7663 / F 020 7287 7663
www.yalla-yalla.co.uk

PROMOTING A PRINCIPLED RESPONSE TO TERRORISM PROTECTING THE RIGHTS OF WOMEN DEFENDING THE SCOPE OF HUMAN RIGHTS PROTECTION PROTECTING CIVILIANS IN WARTIME SHAPING FOREIGN POLICY ADVANCING THE INTERNATIONAL JUSTICE SYSTEM BANNING INDISCRIMINATE WEAPONS OF WAR LINKING BUSINESS PRACTICES AND HUMAN RIGHTS RESPONDING FIRST TO HUMAN RIGHTS EMERGENCIES PROMOTING A PRINCIPLED

HUMAN RIGHTS WATCH
AS LONG AS THERE IS OPPRESSION
TYRANNY HAS A WITNESS

RESPONSE TO TERRORISM PROTECTING THE RIGHTS OF WOMEN DEFENDING THE SCOPE OF HUMAN RIGHTS PROTECTION PROTECTING CIVILIANS IN WARTIME SHAPING FOREIGN POLICY ADVANCING THE INTERNATIONAL JUSTICE SYSTEM BANNING INDISCRIMINATE WEAPONS OF WAR LINKING BUSINESS PRACTICES AND HUMAN RIGHTS RESPONDING FIRST TO HUMAN RIGHTS EMERGENCIES REPORTING FROM CLOSED SOCIETIES WWW.HRW.ORG

HUMAN RIGHTS WATCH

Food & Drink

As one of the world's most cosmopolitan cities, London has an unparalleled range of international food shops offering every conceivable type of produce, and with specific neighbourhoods to visit for each; so, for instance, Shepherds Bush is the place to head to for Middle Eastern foodstuffs, Hackney has a host of places selling Turkish and Vietnamese produce, while Soho is home to two much-loved old-school Italian delis (**Lina Stores** and **I Camisa**). London's many food markets are also definite highlights of its culinary landscape; London chefs are often found trawling the famous **Borough Market** (see p46), while **Broadway Market** (see p49) is now *the* Saturday hangout for locals.

Traditional institutions are another highlight: **Allens of Mayfair** (see p244) has been in business since the 1720s, while Jermyn Street's **Paxton & Whitfield** (see p246) has been selling fine cheeses for over 200 years. The newer wave of upscale outfits has solidified the city's enthusiasm for high-quality organic food, with **Daylesford Organic** (see p248), **La Fromagerie** (see p245) and the **Ginger Pig** (see p244) three popular don't-misses. For a more radical approach on how to shop in the 21st century, head to **Unpackaged** (see p251). Meanwhile, treats for the soul come in the form of posh chocolate shops such as **Prestat**, and retro sweet haven **Hope & Greenwood** (for both, see p247).

Food

Bakeries & pâtisseries

De Gustibus
53 Blandford Street, W1U 7HL (7486 6608, www.degustibus.co.uk). Baker Street tube.
Open 7am-4pm Mon-Fri. **No credit cards**.
Dan and Annette Schickentanz started the highly esteemed De Gustibus bakery business in the kitchen of their Oxfordshire home. While the shops tend to look like sandwich joints (and the sandwiches are indeed terrific), it's the modest displays of expertly made breads that really shine. The huge rounds of Six Day Sour are worth a trip across town as this deliciously tangy, even-textured white bread keeps well and upgrades your daily toast and sarnies to gourmet status. A choice of rye loaves and others in the American and Italian traditions mean everyone will be able to find something to satisfy.
Branches 53-55 Carter Lane, EC4V 5AE (7236 0056); 4 Southwark Street, SE1 1TQ (7407 3625).

Konditor & Cook
22 Cornwall Road, SE1 8TW (7261 0456, www.konditorandcook.com). Waterloo tube/rail.
Open 7.30am-6.30pm Mon-Fri; 8.30am-3pm Sat.
Gerhard Jenne caused a stir when he opened this bakery on a South Bank side street in 1993, selling rudie gingerbread people for grown-ups and lavender-flavoured cakes. It's now a mini chain with a few branches (including a swanky café in the Gherkin). The distinctive folds of the whisky and orange bombe make it one of the best-known cakes in the range. Look out especially for seasonal treats such as pumpkin pie in October and mince pies in December, and don't miss the terrific hot chocolate, made with double cream and

Konditor & Cook. See p243.

Valrhona couverture. Quality prepacked lunchtime salads, sandwiches and sausage rolls are also available. **Branches** throughout the city.

Poilâne
46 Elizabeth Street, SW1W 9PA (7808 4910, www.poilane.fr). Sloane Square tube or Victoria tube/rail. **Open** 7.30am-7pm Mon-Fri; 7.30am-6pm Sat.
Founded in Paris in 1932 by Pierre Poilâne, this company achieved international repute under his son Lionel and is now run by granddaughter Appollonia. The London branch produces bread satisfyingly similar to that made in Paris and distributes to many other shops in the capital, including Selfridges and Waitrose. Although prices are premium, the chewy, dense and remarkably sour loaves have long keeping qualities, so score on value.

Butchers

Allens of Mayfair
117 Mount Street, W1K 3LA (7499 5831, www.allensofmayfair.co.uk). Bond Street or Green Park tube. **Open** 6am-5.30pm Mon-Fri; 6am-2pm Sat.
Michael Winner (gourmand) is among the loyal customers of this Mayfair institution operating for nearly 180 years from the same site, though not with the same owners – Justin Preston and David House (both butchers by trade) saved the business from imminent closure when they bought it in spring 2006. Beef and game remain the fortes; in season you'll find snipe, teal and widgeon as well as more common species such as pheasant and grouse, and for a small charge Allens will process birds you have acquired. Meat boxes are also available, including a gourmet weekend selection and a weekly meat box (available online) for two or four people.

C Lidgate
110 Holland Park Avenue, W11 4UA (7727 8243, www.lidgates.com). Holland Park tube. **Open** 7am-7pm Mon-Fri; 7am-6.30pm Sat.
The butchers at C Lidgate have run this store for over 150 years – and have kept the cleavers in the same family's hands for four generations. That's right: the Lidgates truly have butchery in their blood. The meat here is organic and free range, and a great deal of it is sourced from prestige estates, including Prince Charles's Highgrove. But the family have also kept with the times; the window is crammed with tempting dishes like saddle of lamb with pesto, and the scotch eggs (made with quail eggs and wrapped in Lidgate's own cumberland sausage mince) go down a treat.

Ginger Pig
99 Lauriston Road, E9 7HJ (8986 6911, www.thegingerpig.co.uk). Mile End tube then 277, 425 bus or London Fields rail. **Open** 9am-5.30pm Tue; 9am-6.30pm Wed-Fri; 9am-6pm Sat; 9am-3pm Sun.
The east London outlet for the celebrated farm-based butcher of rare breed meats that came to national attention via Borough Market in the late 1990s. You'll find cuts from longhorn cattle, Swaledale and Black Face sheep, Gloucester Old Spot and Tamworth pigs, plus own-made bacon, sausages, pork pies and terrines. All the meat comes from animals that have been raised to a high standard of welfare. There's also an excellent deli downstairs, with sausage rolls, handmade pies and cooked meats, as well as non-meat fodder such as Neal's Yard cheeses, fresh veg, olives, fish, bread, quiches, chutneys and decent wine and beer.
Branches Borough Market, SE1 1TL (7403 4721); 8-10 Moxon Street, W1U 4EW (7935 7788); 27 Lower Marsh, SE1 7RG (7921 2975).

Food

Fishmongers

Sandys
56 King Street, Twickenham, Middx TW1 3SH (8892 5788, www.sandysfish.net). Twickenham rail. **Open** 7.30am-6pm Mon-Wed, Sat; 7.30am-8pm Thur; 7.30am-7pm Fri; 9am-noon Sun.

Easily one of London's best fishmongers, this large, and popular store is an established family-run business, and offers a wide range of species, from Cornish sardines and lemon sole to wild sea trout and Sri Lankan red snapper. The selection of shellfish is also exemplary, with New Zealand mussels, English cockles, live and cooked lobsters and crabs, king scallops and North Atlantic prawns. Smoked produce comes from prestigious Scottish company Inverawe. You'll also find own-made sausages and game in season. As well as the normal services (skinning, boning, filleting et al), the fishmongers will also vacuum pack your fish for you on request.

Steve Hatt
88-90 Essex Road, N1 8LU (7226 3963). Angel tube. **Open** 8am-5pm Tue-Thur; 7am-5pm Fri, Sat. **No credit cards**.

There's nothing new to report about Steve Hatt: just expect first class fresh fish from this long-established fishmonger and you won't be disappointed. A wet fish display stretching along the wide front window affords queuing customers plenty of opportunity to check out what's available and, once you've made your selection, you can have your fish skinned, boned and filleted on request. Labels highlight deals, such as sea trout 'lowest price of the season'. Expect prime examples of wild Scottish halibut, bluefin tuna, gilt head bream, prawns, scallops and fresh samphire. Frozen fish is available, but extras are kept to a minimum.

Cheese shops

La Fromagerie
2-6 Moxon Street, W1U 4EW (7935 0341, www.lafromagerie.co.uk). Baker Street or Bond Street tube. **Open** 8am-7.30pm Mon-Fri; 9am-7pm Sat; 10am-6pm Sun.

A large window piled with regal wheels of comté, gouda, emmental, unpasteurised cheddar and more offers a taster of the delicious delights to be found beyond the black wooden door of this chic deli-café with refrigerated cheese room. Patricia Michelson and team hand-select cheeses from small artisan makers for sale alongside speciality seasonal produce (Brogdale heritage apples, Roscoff onions, San Marzano

C Lidgate

tomatoes), sweet things (orange and almond cake, brownies with Piedmontese hazelnuts), freshly baked breads, quality olive oils and traiteur dishes made on the premises to take away or enjoy in the café. Tasting events are sometimes held; see the website for details.
Branch 30 Highbury Park, N5 2AA (7359 7440).

Neal's Yard Dairy
17 Shorts Gardens, WC2H 9UP (7240 5700, www.nealsyarddairy.co.uk). Covent Garden tube.
Open 11am-7pm Mon-Sat.
A thoroughly British shop with a traditional French attitude to cheese retailing in that, like an *affineur*, Neal's Yard buys from small farms and creameries in Britain and Ireland, and matures the cheeses in its own cellars until ready to sell in peak condition. It's best to walk in and ask what's good today – you'll be given various tasters by the well-trained staff. Also on sale are oat cakes, English apples (in season) and top-drawer books on cheese and other food. Around Christmastime, the queue for stilton and Montgomery's cheddar often runs down the street. The company also has a sizeable shop just off Borough Market.
Branch 6 Park Street, SE1 9AB (7367 0799).

Paxton & Whitfield
93 Jermyn Street, SW1Y 6JE (7930 0259, www.paxtonandwhitfield.co.uk). Green Park or Piccadilly Circus tube. **Open** 9.30am-6pm Mon-Sat.
In business for over 200 years, the last 100 of those on this site, Paxton & Whitfield sells a wide range of British and continental European cheeses, plus excellent hams, biscuits and real ale. Service is exemplary and delightfully unstuffy – a rare pleasure on Jermyn Street. Among the unusual English varieties to look out for are Oxford isis (washed in mead), caradon blue from Cornwall and naturally smoked 'ceodre' cheddar, and the shop now has an extended range of French cheeses, courtesy of Androuet, a traditional Parisian cheese shop. P&W is also known for its celebration 'cheese cakes' – contrasting tiers of artisan cheese rounds made to look like traditional wedding cakes. They also now serve sandwiches at lunchtime.

Confectioners

L'Artisan du Chocolat
89 Lower Sloane Street, SW1W 8DA (7824 8365, www.artisanduchocolat.com). Sloane Square tube.
Open 10am-7pm Mon-Sat.
L'Artisan du Chocolat's Gerard Coleman and Anne Weyns launch a new collection each season as well as special designs for festive occasions such as Valentine's Day, Christmas, Easter and Halloween, making this an ideal destination for those times when you want to give something original and tasteful but lack inspiration. Best known for liquid salted caramels and chocolate 'pearls', they also offer a range of bars made from scratch in Kent using ground cocoa beans, cane sugar and cocoa butter; the green tea bar is particularly innovative, while the ginger and lemongrass bar is designed as a harmonious experience. There are also sugar-free bars available.

La Fromagerie. See p245.

The company also has a concession in Selfridges in London and a stall at Borough Market (*see p246*).
Branch 81 Westbourne Grove, W2 4UL (0845 270 6996)

Hope & Greenwood
20 North Cross Road, SE22 9EU (8613 1777, www.hopeandgreenwood.co.uk). East Dulwich rail.
Open 10am-6pm Mon-Sat; 11am-5pm Sun.
Saturday queues are almost inevitable at this small vacuum for pocket money. Everything from chocolate gooseberries to sweetheart candies is prettily displayed in plastic beakers, cellophane bags, glass jars, illustrated boxes, porcelain bowls and cake tins. Relive sweet childhood memories by indulging in a bag of sherbert Flying Saucers, gobstoppers or rhubarb and custard 'rations', as well as Double Dips, sugar mice, Curly Wurlys, Love Hearts and lots more. Posher chocolates are also available, including the delicious-sounding lavender and geranium truffles. Gift possibilities include retro gumball machines, and the refills for them. Ice-cream is available in the warmer months. There is a second branch in Covent Garden.
Branch 1 Russell Street, WC2B 5JD, 7240 3314.

Paul A Young Fine Chocolates
33 Camden Passage, N1 8EA (7424 5750, www.payoung.net). Angel tube. **Open** 11am-6pm Wed, Thur, Sat; 11am-7pm Fri; noon-5pm Sun.
A gorgeous boutique on Islington's Camden Passage, with almost everything – chocolates, brownies, cakes, ice-cream – made in the downstairs kitchen and finished in front of customers. Young is a respected pâtissier as well as chocolatier and has an astute chef's palate for flavour-combining. Valrhona and Amedei are his favoured couvertures, which he combines in different blends and origins to match his other ingredients. Even in summer there are plenty of temptations, such as Pimm's cocktail truffles featuring cucumber, strawberry and mint flavours, and white chocolate blondies made with raspberries and blueberries. The shop is a first port-of-call for Valentines Day and Mothers Day gifts.
Branch 20 Royal Exchange, EC3V 3LP (7929 7007).

Prestat
14 Princes Arcade, SW1Y 6DS (7629 4838, www.prestat.co.uk). Green Park tube. **Open** 9.30am-6pm Mon-Fri; 10am-5pm Sat.
England's oldest chocolatier – the brand has been around for more than a century – is up-to-the-minute when it comes to promoting the health advantages of chocolate. Prestat's Choxi+ bars (dark, milk, ginger, orange, mint) are processed gently to maximise antioxidant content – the claim is that they contain two to three times more of these nutrients than standard milk or dark chocolate. This bijou boutique, appropriately located in the genteel Princes Arcade, also offers unusual and traditional chocolates in

TEN Shops with cafés

Aperture Photographic
Aperture's (*see p212*) Camera Café is an original spot; offering ciabattas and a full range of beverages, it's popular with London's paps.

Books for Cooks
There are always plenty of keen guinea pigs ready to sample the latest offerings at this bookshop's (*see p192*) 'kitchen laboratory'.

Brill
The café is an integral aspect of this friendly music shop on Exmouth Market. *See p201*.

Daylesford Organic
Breakfast and lunch options are unsurprisingly top-notch at Daylesford's (*see p248*) cafés.

Dover Street Market
The concept store's (*see p39*) Rose Bakery does a heavenly carrot cake.

Fortnum & Mason
Afternoon tea is the order of the day in F&M's (*see p21*) St James's Restaurant – one of the department store's five eateries.

Foyles
The café on the first floor of Foyles' flagship (*see p190*) is full of laptop-using table hoggers, so move quickly if you spot a free space.

London Review Bookshop
The LRB's (*see p191*) Cake Shop isn't just about sweet things – quality lunchtime sandwiches, salads and soups are also on offer.

Rough Trade East
Pull up a stool in the window of RTE's (*see p201*) entrance café, and watch the hipsters pass by on Dray Walk.

Hope & Greenwood.
See p247.

elegant, brightly coloured packaging, making them lovely gift options. Aside from the straight-up options, there are boxes of dark chocolate-covered apricots, indulgent champagne truffles, hot chocolate flakes and a range of chocolate wafers (try the Earl Grey ones). All Prestat's chocolates are manufactured in the UK from top-quality ingredients. There is a Prestat concession within Harrods.

Rococo
5 Motcomb Street, SW1X 8JU (7245 0993, www.rococochocolates.com). Knightsbridge tube.
Open noon-5pm Mon; 10am-6.30pm Tue-Sat.
Don't be fooled by the novelty bags of chocolate maize and mushrooms, Rococo is a serious chocolatier, pioneering artisan manufacture, unusual flavour combinations and ethical practices in the UK. Don't miss the Grenada 71% bar, which betters other 'fairly traded' products both in terms of quality, and the fact that the factory is attached to the estate, ensuring that the growers benefit from adding value to their beans themselves. Beautiful hand-painted eggs made of high-quality couverture are sold at Easter. This branch, the flagship store, is also home to the MaRococo garden café space, a Moorish-style courtyard where you can sip an indulgent hot chocolate. The Chocolate School is also on-site; see the website for details of classes.
Branch 321 King's Road, SW3 5EP (7352 5857); 45 Marylebone High Street, W1U 5HG (7935 7780).

Grocers, delis & health food

Chegworth Farm Shop
221 Kensington Church Street, W8 7LX (7229 3016, www.chegworthvalley.com). Notting Hill Gate tube.
Open 8.30am-8.30pm Mon-Wed; 8.30am-9pm Thur, Fri; 8am-8pm Sat; 9am-6pm Sun.
Stalwarts of many a farmers' market, the producers from this Kent-based organic fruit farm opened their first stand-alone store in 2008. Known especially for the tangy and pure apple and pear juices as well as special blends using rhubarb, raspberries, strawberries, blackcurrants and blackberries, the shop also stocks organic fruit and veg – including their full range of apple and pear varieties (28 types of apple; four types of pear) – and other essentials such as Hurdlebrook Farm yoghurts, daily bread from Flourish, Conscious Food products, Holy Food ready-made dishes, and local farm produce (meat, poultry, eggs) from farms in Kent and East Sussex. Best of all, there's a free (if you spend £15, which isn't hard) same-day delivery service (within a five-mile radius).

Daylesford Organic
44B Pimlico Road, SW1W 8LP (7881 8060, www.daylesfordorganic.com). Sloane Square tube.
Open 8am-8pm Mon-Sat; 10am-4pm Sun.
Everyone shopping at this pristine white marble food hall is likely to be thinner, blonder and richer than you, but pootle about the shelves long enough and you too could

take on that serene glow. Daylesford confidently sets its own rules regarding healthfulness, so while you'll find macca powder on the shelves, there are also fat sausages and salamis, cakes and rustic breads. A typical summer veg display includes white and green asparagus, knobbly green tomatoes and bunches of beetroot. Much is from Daylesford's own organic estates (cheddar, soups, meat, quail eggs) but then, a lot is not, like the unusual varieties of rice, posh French and Italian cheeses and pasta and matching sauces. There are also concessions in Harvey Nichols and Selfridges.
Branches 208-212 Westbourne Grove, W11 2RH (7313 8050); 30 Pimlico Road, SW1W 8LJ (7730 2943).

Earth Natural Foods
200 Kentish Town Road, NW5 2AE (7482 2211, www.earthnaturalfoods.co.uk). Kentish Town tube/rail. **Open** *8.30am-7pm Mon-Sat.*
Not just organic but vegetarian too, this ordered mini-supermarket nevertheless offers plenty of mouthwatering foods, from early morning croissants and seeded loaves, to lunchtime takeaway dishes, pasta for supper, gluten- and wheat-free products, loose teas, coffee, local honey, organic wines, artisan cheeses, and tubs of Booja Booja's excellent vegan ice-creams to scoff in front of the telly. The range of quality oils, vinegars and condiments is impressive, and there's also a good range of herbal remedies and organic skincare products (with brands including Dr Hauschka). It even sells teff flour. What's more, the staff are helpful and courteous.

Leila's
15-17 Calvert Avenue, E2 7JP (7729 9789). Old Street tube/rail or Shoreditch High Street rail. **Open** *Shop* 10am-7pm Wed-Fri; 10am-6pm Sat; 10am-5pm Sun. *Café* 10am-6pm Wed-Sat; 10am-5pm Sun.
Leila McAlister's eclectic store has the nous to distinguish between crusty and gooey brownies and offer customers the choice. There are fresh, seasonal fruit and veg, breads and cheeses, French sunflower oil (sold from large plastic bottles), and bags of marcona almonds. Among the packaged groceries are Chegworth Farm juices, chutneys, jams and the like from Tracklements in Wiltshire. After you've stocked up, head to the café next door for simple but utterly delicious brunch and lunch fodder.

Melrose & Morgan
42 Gloucester Avenue, NW1 8JD (7722 0011, www.melroseandmorgan.com). Chalk Farm tube. **Open** 8am-7pm Mon-Fri; 8am-6pm Sat; 9am-5pm Sun.

Paul A Young. *See p247.*

Sophisticated suppers become dreamily low-effort when you shop at this ultra-foodie set-up. Made-on-the-premises dishes made from organic and free-range products; dishes range from roast aubergine dip to fish cakes, chicken escalope, lamb and fennel meatballs, and superior sandwiches. The array of cakes, pastries, brownies, pasties, tarts and sausage rolls that covers the large table running down the centre of the store is simply spectacular and, frankly, almost impossible to resist. While there, pick up some Newby teas, Regent's Park honey (in season), artisan cheeses, and M&M's wonderful own-made blueberry and thyme jam. Oh, and Flour Station bread to go with it.

Unpackaged HOT 50

42 Amwell Street, EC1R 1XT (7713 8368, www.beunpackaged.com). Angel tube. **Open** 10am-7pm Mon-Fri; 10am-6pm Sat; 10am-3pm Sun.

Buy only what you need, reduce what you use, reuse old containers and recycle all you can – that seems to be the mission statement behind Catherine Conway's impressive enterprise. Locals, as well as others from beyond the borough, bring in their own jars, pots, Tupperware and bags and fill them with fruit, veg and store cupboard ingredients – all organic, Fairtrade or locally sourced – from the beautifully arranged corner shop; alternatively, buy a reusable container from the store. Vats of olive oil are on tap for refills, and you can take your fill of the pulses, nuts, pasta, rice, loose teas, superfoods, such as goji berries, Neal's Yard cheeses, herbs and spices, and much more, all arranged in stylish square containers. Barrels of environmentally friendly cleaning liquids by Ecover can be poured straight into containers brought from home. There are also toiletries by Faith in Nature, loose loo roll made from recycled paper and water filters by Charcoal People. Consumable liquids like juice, cordials, wine and cider are also available. And there's even an in-house nutritionist. *See also right* **Shop talk**.

International

Al-Abbas

258-262 Uxbridge Road, W12 7JA (8740 1932). Shepherd's Bush tube/rail. **Open** 7am-midnight daily.

A short walk from Shepherd's Bush tube, Al-Abbas is one of our favourite Middle Eastern stores in west London, and in fact stocks groceries from all corners of the globe, with Polish, African and Indian essentials, as well as rice, oils, breads and meat. The range of grains and pulses is astonishing and includes the hard-to-find *freekeh* and moth beans. Spice up your cooking with the jalapeños and other fresh chillies or speciality herbs such as *methi*. Teetotallers will appreciate exotic cordials of tamarind and mint and the crates of fresh falafel sitting by the till are hard to resist too.

Rococo. See p248.

Shop talk
Catherine Conway, owner of Unpackaged

Tell us about your shop
'We started here two and a half years ago. Before that we had stalls at Exmouth and Broadway markets, where we tested out the refill idea. It was really popular and people kept coming back and asking for more and more products without packaging. Lots of these products would have been impossible to bring to a market. I had the idea for the shop because as a consumer I wanted to buy goods without packaging and I couldn't find anywhere that let me.

'We want to affect change up and down the supply chain; we use small suppliers and try to be as considerate as we can when we choose who we work with.'

Who shops here?
'Locals and people who are environmentally aware. It's a great shop for people who live alone because they can buy the exact quantities they need. Apparently we throw away a third of what we buy; shopping here means your portion sizes aren't dictated by anyone but you. People who live locally can shop from day to day, and it won't affect the price of the product if they only buy a small amount.'

What are your most popular items?
'Our staples like eggs, bread and milk; also our refillable wine.'

Have you noticed changes in the London shopping scene over the past few years?
'I'm quite new to it as a retailer but as a consumer I can see that there are certainly a lot more options for people food-wise. People have a lot more choice than they used to. There are some really excellent projects out there; we're part of a food-buying group with local businesses to try to help smaller producers get to market. Other schemes include one which aims to grow herbs to order on an Old Street estate. There are lots of ingenious ideas out there.'

Is it more difficult to run a small business now than it used to be?
'It's as difficult as it's ever been. It's hard fighting the might of the high street but that's our job, to show people the value of a really great shopping experience. It's the most enjoyable part too, knowing the people who come in, being part of this community and introducing that community to refillable, handcrafted and beautiful products.'

What are your favourite shops in London?
'I love Darkroom (*see p39*) on Lamb's Conduit Street; that's where my handbag is from. They sell unusual and beautiful products. I also like Brill (*see p201*) on Exmouth Market, Brindisa at Borough Market (*see p46*) and Neal's Yard Dairy (*see p246*). I love Casa Mexico (*see p167*) at the back of Bethnal Green Road.'

Any plans for the future?
'We'd like to move into deliveries and wholesale and to have more shops in London and further afield. Being unpackaged is easy when you live close by, so we need to make it easy for more people.'

▶ For **Unpackaged**, *see left*.

Melrose & Morgan. *See p249.*

Giacobazzi's
150 Fleet Road, NW3 2QX (7267 7222, www.giacobazzis.co.uk). Belsize Park tube or Hampstead Heath rail. **Open** *9.30am-7pm Mon-Fri; 9am-6pm Sat.*

Customers queue patiently at this beloved Hampstead Heath deli to get their hands on Giacobazzi's selection of own-made dishes. Products, from all over Italy, have helpful labels to explain the difference between, say, the various types of pecorino, or Sicilian and Puglian quince pastes. The antipasti counter has more than the usual suspects with options like grilled radicchio and marinated carrot. Filled pastas are made on site, as is truffle butter and desserts. Giacobazzi's can deliver everything you'll need for your meal, from the breadsticks and olives to the seasonal cakes, but for those who can't be bothered to put it together themselves, Giacobazzi's has a restaurant over the road (No.85, 7433 3317).

Green Valley
36-37 Upper Berkeley Street, W1H 5QF (7402 7385). Marble Arch tube. **Open** *8am-midnight daily.*

One of London's best Middle Eastern food halls, Green Valley has a comprehensive meze counter offering myriad possibilities for quick, after-work suppers. The fresh produce area includes squat, round Lebanese pears, dainty aubergines, stumpy cucumbers, plus the likes of dragon fruit, guava and young coconuts, as well as freshly prepared juices. In the freezer you'll find *molokhia* (a high-nutrient green vegetable used especially in soups and stews) and ready-made kibbeh in chicken, lamb and almond varieties. In addition to the eye-catching display of baklava, the sizeable pâtisserie section includes thickly layered gateaux and tubs of rice pudding.

I Camisa & Son
61 Old Compton Street, W1D 6HS (7437 7610). Leicester Square tube. **Open** *8.30am-6pm Mon-Sat.*

This long-established rustic Italian deli was opened by the Fratelli Camisi back in 1929, and this old Soho stalwart is well worth a visit if only for its fresh pasta and accompanying sauces – their pesto is particularly good – but that would be to miss out on the fabulous range of cheeses (pecorino, gorgonzola – both sweet and piccante – parmesan, mozzarella, ricotta), charcuterie (salamis, mortadella, parma ham), freshly marinated olives, vegetables (artichokes, peppers, aubergines, sun-dried tomatoes, mushrooms) under oil, risotto rices, balsamic vinegars, cakes and biscuits, as well as a range of their own-label products. A real taste of Italy indeed.

Japan Centre
14-16 Regent Street, SW1Y 4PH (7255 8255, www.japancentre.com). Piccadilly Circus tube. **Open** *10am-9pm Mon-Sat; 11am-7pm Sun.*

Japan Centre's basement grocery has taken over next door's premises, allowing for the expansion of the

Food

Unpackaged. *See p250.*

FOOD & DRINK

grocery and fresh meat, fish and vegetable ranges, plus the addition of a new trend-setting bakery. Sweet, creamy edamame gateau? It hardly sounds possible but you'll find it here, along with cakes flavoured with red beans and sesame, organic herbs, meats cut specially for *shabu-shabu*, takeaway sushi, myriad types of tofu, rice, snack foods and Fuji apples, as well as a mind-blowing (and occasionally roof-of-mouth-blowing) range of pastes, sauces, seasonings and pickles. The rest of the store is taken up with teas and cookware, as well as books, gifts and accessories.

Lina Stores
18 Brewer Street, W1R 3FS (7437 6482). Piccadilly Circus tube. **Open** 8am-6.30pm Mon-Fri; 8am-5.30pm Sat.

Behind the 1950s green ceramic Soho frontage is Lina Stores, an iconic family-run Italian deli that's been in business for over half a century. Indeed, Jane Grigson used to buy spaghetti in blue wax paper here years before celebrity chefs coasted the streets on scooters. Besides dried pastas (stored in beautiful wooden crates), there's a deli counter chock-full of cured meats, hams, salamis, olives, cheeses, marinated artichokes and fresh pastas. Imported items run from breads to chestnut honey, and Lina is one of the best places to buy truffles in season. Recommended is the fresh pesto and fresh filled pasta, such as artichoke and truffle.

Lisboa
54 Golborne Road, W10 5NR (8969 1586). Ladbroke Grove tube. **Open** 9.30am-7pm Mon-Sat; 10am-5pm Sun.

Among the packaged groceries at this friendly Portuguese deli are tins of sweet potato and guava paste, beans, pastas and the essential strong coffee. You'll also find white anchovies in vinegar, Iberian oils, *pasteis de bacalhau* (salt cod fritters) and *pasteis de nata* (custard tarts). There's a great range of Portuguese and Spanish sausages and cured meats (merguez, chorizo, morcilla) as well as a large variety of Portuguese cheeses, pickles, herbs and oils. Extend the experience by nipping over the road to the popular, ever busy, Lisboa Pâtisserie for coffee and a cake; there's usually a queue, but it's worth the wait.

Olga Stores
30 Penton Street, N1 9PS (7837 5467). Angel tube. **Open** 8am-8pm Mon-Sat; 10am-4pm Sun.

This unpretentious shop may look like many other Italian delis in London, but venture in and you'll find everything from canned tomatoes to whole fresh foie gras, as well as the customary salamis, Italian pasta, olive oils and a good range of Italian wines. It's also a welcome source of creamy burrata cheese. Check the pristine veg and herb section for wonderfully buttery fuerte avocados (when in season); and Olga sells Italian plant seeds too.

Persepolis

28-30 Peckham High Street, SE15 5DT (7639 8007). Peckham Rye rail or 36 bus. **Open** *10.35am-9pm daily.*

Music, handicrafts, tagines, rugs and shisha pipes are stocked alongside edibles at Sally Butcher's colourful Iranian store, an inspiration for food-lovers from the local area and beyond. The Western perspective she brings to proceedings – such as recommending rose petals not just for Persian ice-cream but for pretty party ice cubes – is undoubtedly part of the appeal. And it's a great place to stock up on the likes of fresh Persian dates, *sumak*, dried limes and *verjus*. There's an enormous range of Persian herbs and spices, books and handicrafts, and you'll also find details of a host of Persian literary events.

R García & Sons

248-250 Portobello Road, W11 1LL (7221 6119). Ladbroke Grove or Westbourne Park tube. **Open** *10am-6pm daily.*

In business for over 60 years, R Garcia was established back in 1958 and is one of London's largest Spanish grocer-delis. The meat counter is a joy to peruse, with a mouthwatering array of cured hams and sausages, and the store also stocks an excellent range of sherries, along with cava, sangria, red, white and sweet wines. There are tins of smoked paprika, marcona almonds, olive oils, rices and pastas, sherry vinegar and slabs of turron line the shelves, while the cheese selection includes manchego, *mahon*, *cabralles* and *tetilla*. You'll also fine steel paella pans and terracotta dishes. There is also a café on the premises.

Turkish Food Centre

89 Ridley Road, E8 2NH (7254 6754, www.tfcsupermarkets.com). Dalston Kingsland rail or 30, 56, 236 bus. **Open** *8am-9pm daily.*

Now with ten branches stretching from Catford to Tottenham, this popular supermarket has an excellent range of fresh fruit and veg flown in weekly from Greece, Cyprus and Turkey. Depending on the season, you'll find okra, prickly pears, swiss chard, herbs and *kolngasi* (similar to yam or sweet potato), plus olives in huge vats. An in-house bakery churns out baklava, delicious fresh breads and moreish pastries. There are fresh meats and poultry, savouries and sweets and an enormous range of spices, pulses, nuts, along with apple tea, Turkish delight, and a host of other traditional products, including a selection of rosewater and colognes.

Branches throughout the city.

Turkish Food Centre

Drink

Wine

Bedales
5 Bedale Street, SE1 9AL (7403 8853, www.bedalestreet.com). London Bridge tube/rail. **Open** noon-8.45pm Tue; noon-10.15pm Wed-Fri; 8.30am-5.30pm Sat.

Wine retailing runs in the bloodstreams of the two families that own Bedales. Their shops offer a globetrotting list of uniformly high quality, and they sell it with pride and enthusiasm. The attraction both at the original shop in Borough and the newer one in Spitalfields is the opportunity to try the wines in combination with simple and immaculately sourced food, from cheese plates to charcuterie. The mark-up on every bottle is fixed at £8: the higher you go the better the bargain. While Bedales will admit to favouring Italian and French wines, it stocks and has tastings of wines from around the world, including those harder-to-find wines that you might not be able to source yourself.
Branches 55 Leadenhall Market, EC3V 1LT (7929 3536); 12 Market Street, E1 6DT (7375 1926).

Berry Bros & Rudd
3 St James's Street, SW1A 1EG (7396 9600, www.bbr.com). Green Park tube. **Open** 10am-6pm Mon-Fri; 10am-5pm Sat.

Visit Berry at least once, just to sniff the history. The company has been selling wine here since William III was king (that's late 17th century, for anyone not up on their history), and the cellars are ancient. Berry's impressive list of discerning patrons includes Lord Bryon, William Pitt and Queen Elizabeth II (though probably not personally), all drawn by the heady atmosphere, highly knowledgeable staff and consistently high-quality wines – the shop excels at the traditional favourites of the well heeled, although with prices to match. There's ample choice under £10, however, and its own-label wines (clarets especially) are superb. And despite the shop's heritage (and appealingly creaky floorboards), the brand makes an effort to stay completely up-to-date with innovations in the wine trade.

Lea & Sandeman
170 Fulham Road, SW10 9PR (7244 0522, www.londonfinewine.co.uk). Gloucester Road tube. **Open** 10am-8pm Mon-Sat.

Lea & Sandeman – declared 'best wine merchant in the capital' in 2009 by wine magazine *Decanter* – is so good, you may not know where to start. Charles Lea and Patrick Sandeman only buy wines they are really excited about, whether it's a Vin de Pays d'Oc or a £60 red Burgundy, and their emphasis on drinkability, as opposed to prestige, is very refreshing. Here, Europe is king, but the coverage is global, and there's always the same attention paid to good buying. What's more, the prices here are far lower than you would expect for this part of town, and the modern, airy shop is a highly pleasant space in which to browse. It's no wonder that so many critics regard L&S as the finest wine shop in London.
Branches 167 Chiswick High Road, W4 2DR (8995 7355); 211 Kensington Church Street, W8 7LX (7221 1982); 51 High Street, SW13 9LN (8878 8643).

Roberson
348 Kensington High Street, W14 8NS (7371 2121, www.robersonwinemerchant.co.uk). High Street Kensington tube/Kensington (Olympia) tube/rail. **Open** 10am-8pm Mon-Sat; noon-6pm Sun.

Roberson is a Kensington institution, providing an affluent clientele with a gobsmacking selection, heavily dominated by France, but stretching across the world. Bordeaux and Burgundy account for well over a third of the still wines, with Champagne in abundance and smaller offerings from the Loire and the Rhône at similarly exalted levels. The shop prides itself on its friendly, clued-up and passionate staff and its eclectic decor, making it the perfect antidote to the frequently bland experience of buying wine on the high street. If you love France, and you want something special, Roberson is a top choice in west London.

The Sampler
266 Upper Street, N1 2UQ (7226 9500, www.thesampler.co.uk). Angel tube or Highbury & Islington rail/tube. **Open** 11.30am-9pm Mon-Sat; 11.30am-7pm Sun.

The Sampler is unique in London: a shop where you can taste 80 wines out of the 1,500 on offer. You buy a card (minimum £10), then use it to buy 25ml tastes. Samples cost from 30p to £10-plus for the costliest bottles. The wines are terrific at every level and are sourced from around the globe (Argentina to the USA) including offerings from Greece and India. The wine machines are arranged by grape and the 80 wines are on rotation every two weeks so that, eventually, you'll get to try them all. There are around 100 under £10 and the upper reaches include mature classics. *See also p259* **Shop talk**.

Beer & spirits

Gerry's
74 Old Compton Street, W1D 4UW (7734 4215, www.gerrys.uk.com). Leicester Square or Piccadilly Circus tube. **Open** 9am-6.30pm Mon-Thur; 9am-7.30pm Fri; 9am-6.30pm Sat; noon-5pm Sun.

A London institution with a warehouse-worth of spirits packed into its tiny Soho quarters. It has all the names

Drink

Algerian Coffee Stores. *See p258.*

FOOD & DRINK

you know, and dozens that you don't, including 150 vodkas, 100 rums, plus 120 tequilas. And its selection of oddities is unrivalled. English elderflower vodka? Bulgarian rakia? The fun is in the browsing. Gerry's prides itself on spotting the trends, being the first to bring you absinthe from the Czech Republic, cachaça from Brazil and Pisco from Peru. So the new taste? Fairtrade vodka. There's also a host of liqueurs, vermouths, bitters and sirops to help you create a new trend of your own.

Milroy's of Soho
3 Greek Street, W1D 4NX (7437 9311, www.milroys.co.uk). Tottenham Court Road tube. **Open** 10am-7pm Mon-Sat.
Founded in the 1960s, Milroy's is a whisky-lover's heaven. The range is enormous, with around 400 from Scotland alone. There's a large selection from £14.95, but fine and rare whiskies can cost up to £2,500, including some of Milroy's own bottlings. Other spirits are covered too, with carefully selected Cognac, Armagnac and rums – the brand launched its first own-brand single cask rum (from the Four Square distillery in Barbados) in spring 2010. What's more, staff are knowledgeable and enthusiastic, and the shop runs regular tasting events for those looking to improve their knowledge and appreciation of whisky. Milroy's started life as a wine merchant and wine remains an important part of the operation; the brand is now part of the Jeroboams group of wine merchants.

Real Ale Shop
371 Richmond Road, Twickenham, Middx TW1 2EF (8892 3710, www.realale.com). Richmond tube or Twickenham rail. **Open** 2-8pm Tue-Thur; 1-9pm Fri; 10am-9pm Sat; noon-5pm Sun.
This shop sells a compact but outstanding sampling – around 100 beers, ales, ciders and perries – that takes in not just Europe but the USA as well. The shop is particularly strong on beers from British microbreweries, with many little-known brands on offer, including beers from Ascot Ales, Hepworth, St Mungo and Cotswold Brewery. US lagers include Sierra Nevada, Flying Dog, Dogfish Head and Victory, and the place also now stocks a good range of Italian beers, such as Birra del Borgo and Baladin. The full list of available beers is listed on the website; and if you'd prefer the company to make your choices for you, then join the Ale Club to have 12 bottles of ale delivered to your door each month.

Tea & coffee

Algerian Coffee Stores
52 Old Compton Street, W1V 6PB (7437 2480, www.algcoffee.co.uk). Leicester Square or Piccadilly Circus tube. **Open** 9am-7pm Mon-Wed; 9am-9pm Thur, Fri; 9am-8pm Sat.

Unassumingly nestled in the heart of Soho, Algerian Coffee Stores has traded from its Old Compton Street site for over 120 years and, remarkably, is still using the original wooden counter, shelving and display case. The range of coffees here is improbably large, with a high number of house blends alongside single-origin beans, flavoured beans, rarities and Fairtrade coffees. It also sells some serious teas and brewing hardware. If you're just passing by, the take-away option is the best coffee deal in London: less than a £1 for an espresso, and not much more for a cappuccino or latte; both delicious, and both available with an extra shot for no extra charge.

Camden Coffee Shop
11 Delancey Street, NW1 7NL (7387 4080). Camden Town tube. **Open** 9.30am-5.30pm Mon-Wed, Fri, Sat; 9.30am-2.30pm Thur. **No credit cards**.
The Camden Coffee Shop, established in 1978, has been serving the good customers of Camden and around for more than 30 years and stepping through the door is like stepping back in time. The roasting and grinding of the beans are done on the premises by owner George Constantinou. Using his original machines, George sticks to a small range of six or seven coffees at a time. Prices are low, and the atmosphere is low-key. The Camden Coffee Shop is a treasure; a lovely little bit of old London and, happily, there are no plans for that to change any time soon.

Camden Coffee Shop

Shop talk
Jamie Hutchinson, owner of the Sampler

Tell us about your shop
'We're a wine merchants selling about 15,000 different wines. Our prices range from £6 to more than you'd ever want to spend on a bottle of wine. What makes us unusual is that we offer in-store tasting machines, with up to 80 of our wines on offer to try; it works with a smart card system, like an oyster card, so you can try as you go. We want people to buy wines they actually like, rather than just ones they've had before, or based on a friend's recommendation or (worst of all) just from the label.

'We try to stock as many different styles as we can so that the choice doesn't just reflect our palettes. We have a vast range of speciality champagne (which isn't yet available to try in store) and we spend a lot of time in Champagne meeting tiny growers. We have over 100 Champagnes with everything from organic to bio-dynamic; sweet, dry, bone-dry, old and young.'

Who shops here?
'We are popular with the new "foodie" influence in shopping. People seem to care more and more about what they put into themselves, whether it's an environmental choice or just a case of flavour mixing.'

What are your most popular products?
'One of our most popular bottles all year round is the Clos de la Chapelle Champagne (£23.50).'

Have you noticed changes in the London shopping scene over the past few years?
'Well the top end of the market was quite absent last Christmas, during the peak of the economic crisis, but we've recently seen a return to how it used to be.'

What is the most enjoyable aspect of owning a shop?
'I love it. I was going to say my colleagues but really it's the buying. It's fabulous, going to Spain, France and Italy and meeting the guys who grow these wines. It's a very sociable job, even being in the shop is sociable – it doesn't work if you're not here, it's not like buying online. I love meeting the customers. And we offer them a really good time while they're here.'

What are your favourite shops in London?
'I love Moen's the butchers in Clapham; they're expensive but great. I buy my cheese from Paxton & Whitfield (*see p246*) on Jermyn Street, and I love Neal's Yard Dairy (*see p246*).'

What do you envisage for your business for the future?
'We will be opening a second branch in the summer [2010] in South Kensington and hope to open a third at some point in the not too distant future.'

▶ For the **Sampler**, *see p256*.

HR Higgins

79 Duke Street, W1K 5AS (7629 3913, www.hrhiggins.co.uk). Bond Street tube.
Open 9.30am-6pm Mon-Fri; 10am-6pm Sat.
Established in 1942, HR Higgins is a family-run firm that has a deep commitment to quality in both fine teas and coffee. Teas include some Chinese rarities alongside a full range of both loose tea and teabags. Prices are on the steep side, as you would expect from a holder of a royal warrant (for coffee) operating in Mayfair. A list of the coffees available, from an after-dinner blend to *yirga chefe* produced by the Oromia cooperative in Ethiopia, are listed on the website and can be ordered online. A range of accessories is also available. Enjoy a cup of fne tea or coffee in the café downstairs (which shuts one hour before the shop closes).

Monmouth Coffee House

27 Monmouth Street, WC2H 9EU (7379 3516, www.monmouthcoffee.co.uk). Covent Garden tube.
Open 8am-6.30pm Mon-Sat.
Founded 30 years ago, Monmouth sets itself daunting standards for quality and ethical trading, and meets them consistently. This is pre-eminently a place for single-estate and co-operative coffees. You'll always be able to find a good Kenyan coffee here, and Central and South America are represented by excellent ranges. Founder Anita Le Roy is an industry leader in the campaign to help growers improve quality and earn higher prices. The original shop-café in Covent Garden is tiny and cosy; the Borough space is larger and serves fabulously moreish cakes and savouries to enjoy with your fine brew.
Branch 2 Park Street, SE1 9AB (7940 9960).

Postcard Teas

9 Dering Street, W1S 1AG (7629 3654, www.postcardteas.com). Bond Street or Oxford Circus tube. **Open** 10.30am-6.30pm Mon-Sat.
Whether you're looking for black, white or green tea, you'll find intriguingly unusual examples here. A friendly, classic-looking shop located in an 18th-century Mayfair building, Postcard takes pride in its support for high-quality estates in Sri Lanka, India, China, Japan and elsewhere. You can sit and have a pot at the tasting table to help you choose and, for those who'd like to learn to be more discerning when it comes to the nation's favourite pick-me-up, there are tea tastings at 10am on Saturday mornings. Tea pots are also for sale, tending towards Asian aesthetics rather than traditional English styles.

Babies & Children

| Babies & Children | 262 |

Babies & Children

It pays to stray from central London for the best children's shops. While the department stores and the chains are certainly worth a gander, the most exciting shops for babies and children are neighbourhood independent ones. Their welcoming community feel, with pinboards and play areas, and a certain sense of 'we're in this childrearing lark together' make them more sympathetic to the tentative parent.

The most family-friendly neighbourhood high street is Northcote Road, between Wandsworth and Clapham Commons. These days, however, its independence is increasingly compromised by chains, such as Fat Face and Jigsaw Junior, and the little locals are being squeezed out.

Stoke Newington would appear to be the new Nappy Valley with, it is averred, more buggies per square mile than anywhere else in London, and home to the excellent **Born** (see p263), as well as **Olive Loves Alfie** (see p266).

Closer to the centre, Notting Hill also puts on a good spread. Tucked away in the Portobello Green shopping arcade, a little independent boutique, **Sasti** (see p267) has been keeping west London tots looking adorable on a budget since 1995. Don't miss it. Another sweet thing at the business end of Notting Hill is **Honeyjam** (see p268), a toyshop run by a pair of women well known in the fashion world and having a lot of fun in the toy one. More expensive, but undoubtedly cool and distinctive, the clothes at **Caramel** (see p265) are a big draw.

Finally, for nursery equipment that's all pure and natural, the allergy-free **Natural Mat Company** (see p264) ensures quiet nights all round.

All-rounders & gifts

Concept store **Couverture** (see p39) is also a good bet for stylish clothes, accessories and toys.

Bob & Blossom
140 Columbia Road, E2 7RG (7739 4737, www.bobandblossom.com). Shoreditch High Street rail. **Open** *9am-3pm Sun.*
Dear little knitted and crocheted animals, smart toy cars, spinning tops and bike horns, romper suits and sweetly logoed T-shirts – the selection at Bob & Blossom is nothing if not eclectic. The baby clothing – T-shirts, sleepsuits, hats, trousers and socks – is colourful, often stripy and the legends manage to steer the right side of enchanting; who could fail to say, 'Ahh,' at the sight of a moppet with 'Poppet' written on her tummy? The toddler tees feature some fine skull-and-crossbones designs to counteract the cuteness. B&B does a roaring trade despite only being open to coincide with the Sunday market.

Buggies & Bikes
23 Broadway Market, E8 4PH (7241 5382, www.buggiesandbikes.net). London Fields rail. **Open** *10am-6.30pm Mon-Sat; 11am-5pm Sun.*

Hackney's bohemian Broadway Market (*see p49*) attracts young families in their droves (particularly when the market's in full swing), so this pleasant little shop makes the most of passing trade. As well as innovative double buggies and wooden, pedal-free starter bikes, the stock is made up of unusual pieces of nursery equipment, clothes for babies to 12-year-olds and a range of covetable toys. The proprietor is keen to display the knitwear and needlework of local designers; there are some delightful little cardigans for babies, fine print dresses for toddlers and adorable booties. The basement is given over to baby and toddler activities (drama, yoga, baby massage) and can be hired out for parties, along with the little garden.

Igloo

300 Upper Street, N1 2TU (7354 7300, www.igloo kids.co.uk). Angel tube or Highbury & Islington tube/rail. **Open** 10am-6.30pm Mon-Wed; 10am-7pm Thur; 9.30am-6.30pm Fri, Sat; 11am-5.30pm Sun.

Igloo's highly original range of toys, clothes and accessories is sourced by two mothers with limitless savoir faire. Shelves of toys reach to the ceiling. Favourites include inventive educational ideas for bright sparks, such as ant and worm farms, and telescopes. Passing bundles of lovely wearable clothes for babies and children up to eight, you'll find a spacious Start-rite shoe corner with plenty of seating and another area with more clothes from the likes of Catimini, no added sugar and kidscase, plus fancy-dress outfits. There's a mirrored area for children's haircuts, a table for reading and drawing, party essentials and a gift-wrapping service too.

Branches 80 St John's Wood High Street, NW8 7SH (7483 2332); 227 Kings Road, SW3 5EJ (7352 4572).

Soup Dragon

27 Topsfield Parade, Tottenham Lane, N8 8PT (8348 0224, www.soup-dragon.co.uk). Finsbury Park tube/rail, then 41, W7 bus. **Open** 9.30am-6pm Mon-Sat; 11am-5pm Sun.

This splendidly tot-friendly all-rounder consists of a long, antique space with a stained-glass skylight and wonky wooden floors. The Dragon continues to draw in the majority of Crouch End's young families, and its frequent warehouse sales (see website for details) are not to be missed. There's a lovely little play area and toy kitchen, a wide range of toys and dressing-up kit, and attractive and affordable stripy knits for both babies and toddlers. To add to the Soup Dragon label there are rompers and play clothes from Katvig and Idat. Classic toys from Dejeco and Tomy, plus covetable one-offs such as rocking horses and dolls' houses.

Branch: 106 Lordship Lane, SE22 8HF (8693 5575).

Trotters

34 King's Road, SW3 4UD (7259 9620, www.trotters.co.uk). Sloane Square tube. **Open** 9am-7pm Mon-Sat; 10am-6pm Sun.

Always a pleasure to trot round, this children's shop of many parts has clothes, toys, accessories, toiletries, shoes, books and a hairdressing station (from £13.50). The clothes are adorable, with print dresses from Chelsea Clothing Company and Confiture, stripy tops and cotton shorts from Petit Breton and college-style jumpers, trousers and shirts by Thomas Brown. There are insulated lunch packs and wheelie suitcases, Nitty Gritty headcare treatments and organic suncreams; the shoes at the back are Start-rite and the hairdressing station has a large tank of fish to distract the small clients – first-time customers receive a certificate of bravery.

Branches 127 Kensington High Street, W8 5SF (7937 9373); 86 Northcote Road, SW11 6QN (7585 0572); 84 Turnham Green Terrace, W4 1QN (8742 1195).

Equipment & accessories

Born

168 Stoke Newington Church Street, N16 0JL (7249 5069, www.borndirect.com). Finsbury Park tube/rail, then 106 bus or 73, 393, 476 bus. **Open** 9.30am-5.30pm Tue-Sat; noon-5pm Sun.

A calm, nurturing space with kind staff, specialising in pregnancy products, plus baby equipment, toys and clothes, Born has an organic and fair trade ethos, right down to cotton nappies. Attractions include organic baby clothes (Star range by Kate Goldsmith); toiletries

Bob & Blossom

and massage oils by Weleda, Green People and Born Naked (Born's own brand). Toys are made from renewable materials, products include the attractive Keptin-Jr Organic Comforter, and trendy baby transport systems include the Stokke Xplory buggy, Phil & Ted's Explorer, Bugaboo and Bee, plus Cameleon and Gecko. There's plenty of play space for lively tots, and a comfy sofa for breastfeeding. Born's network of support extends to a weekly mother's meeting on Mondays, plus parenting and breastfeeding groups.

Blue Daisy
13 South End Road, NW3 2PT (7681 4144, www.blue-daisy.com). Hampstead Heath tube/rail. **Open** *9.30am-6pm Mon-Fri; 10am-6pm Sat.*
A typically stylish Hampstead baby boutique, Blue Daisy has the sort of clothes that will up the adorability quotient of even the cutest toddler, from manufacturers such as Mokopuna, Organics for kids and Togz, as well as toys and accessories suitable for babies and toddlers. The stock – organic and Fairtrade where applicable – is loaded with style and ingenuity. It's also well presented; children make straight for the toys alcove to play with the traditional wooden cookers by Tiny Love. Innovative home accessories include the new Kaboost chair booster, the bestselling Cuddledry towels, the Mini-Micro Scooters and Bambino Merino sleeping bags.
Branch 190 West End Lane, NW6 1SG (7435 3100).

Dragons of Walton Street
23 Walton Street, SW3 2HX (7589 3795, www.dragonsofwaltonstreet.com). Knightsbridge or South Kensington tube. **Open** *9.30am-5.30pm Mon-Fri; 10am-5pm Sat.*
Rosie Fisher's hand-painted furniture for the nursery comes with all sorts of child favourites: bunnies, boats, soldiers, fairies, pirate mice and vintage roses. Customers are also encouraged to come up with their own ideas for designs. Dragons, on gentele Walton Street, among a host of other posh children's shops, is a pleasant place to visit; staff are friendly, the mood relaxed and personal service is guaranteed. Curtains, cots, sofas, chaises longues and tiny chairs are made to order, as are the special artwork beds, for which you can expect to pay around £2,000. Personalised chairs and pretty quilts are more affordable. Handsome, traditional toys are also sold.

Natural Mat Company
99 Talbot Road, W11 2AP (7985 0474, www.naturalmat.co.uk). Ladbroke Grove or Notting Hill Gate tube. **Open** *10am-6pm Mon-Fri; 10am-4pm Sat.*
Renowned for mattresses made of all natural materials, such as organic coir, latex straight from the rubber tree, unbleached cotton, and mohair, Natural Mat makes for a toxin-free nursery environment. Infants may safely snooze under quilts, sheets and pillows in duck down and lambs' wool (bathed in essential oils to repel dust

mites) and unbleached cotton, while babies – who spend much of their daily lives asleep – can forget about kicked-off sheet misery in sleeping bags that come in pink, blue, white and natural in lightweight organic cotton or cotton fleece for winter. There are also lambskin fleeces, Welsh wool blankets and West Country willow cribs.

Rub a Dub Dub
15 Park Road, N8 8TE (8342 9898). Finsbury Park tube/rail then 41, W7 bus. **Open** 10am-5.30pm Mon-Fri; 10am-5.30pm Sat; 11.30am-4pm Sun.
Nature's Nest, the dangling travelcot loved by celebrity parents, is a bestseller at Rub a Dub Dub, a store that is always up to the minute with its stock. The knowledgeable owner dispenses advice about the latest fashions in baby transport and nursery equipment with alacrity; apparently Ergobaby backpacks are the newly fashionable way of transporting your child. Top pram systems are still the ever-popular Mountain Buggy and the Phil & Ted double decker. The last word in weather protection is Outlook's Shade-a-babe, a pushchair cover providing UV protection. For indoors there's fun things like wheely bugs in ladybird and bumblebee shapes. Every conceivable brand of eco-friendly nappy and bottom cream is stocked. Look out for the always reliable Kooshies, Bambo nappies and training pants.

Fashion

Many shops listed in the **Maternity** chapter also sell baby togs; **Blossom Mother & Child** is a good bet for baby clothes. *See pp117-118.*

Aravore Babies
31 Park Road, N8 8TE (8347 5752, www.aravore-babies.com). Highgate tube or Crouch Hill rail or 41, 91, W5, W7 bus. **Open** 10am-5.30pm Mon-Sat; noon-4.30pm Sun.
Distinctive, delectable fashions for babies from Aravore aren't cheap, but they'll be much appreciated as gifts for new parents. The crocheted and knitted organic clothes go up to age five. A visit to the shop reveals much to coo over: beautiful handcrafted cream knits in merino wool include gorgeous tops, dresses, mittens and booties, nestling alongside soft shawls and blankets. The spring/summer range is all organic cotton and now includes Green Eyed Monster's fun and functional designs. Aravore also stocks other organic ranges like Green Baby and Bamboo Baby. There are skincare products from Erba Viva, and a baby wish-list service too.

Caramel Baby & Child
77 Ledbury Road, W11 2AG (7727 0906, www.caramel-shop.co.uk). Notting Hill Gate or Westbourne Park tube. **Open** 10am-6pm Mon-Sat; noon-5pm Sun.

FIVE Traditional toy shops

Benjamin Pollock's Toy Shop
London's first port-of-call for classic toys. *See p267.*

Never Never Land
3 Midhurst Parade, Fortis Green, N10 3EJ (8883 3997, www.never-never-land.co.uk). East Finchley tube. **Open** 10am-5pm Tue, Wed, Fri, Sat.
This splendid little toy shop has dolls' houses and their accessories, as well as soft-bodied dolls, Heimess pram toys, tea sets, and wooden firemen.

Petit Chou
15 St Christopher's Place, W1U 1NJ (7486 3637, www.petitchou.co.uk). Bond Street tube. **Open** 10.30am-6.30pm Mon-Sat; noon-5pm Sun.
A wooden toy enclave, selling blocks, pull-alongs, skittles, soldiers and animals in painted wood.

Puppet Planet
Traditional puppets, as well as stuffed toy animals and Crafty Kids craft kits. *See p268.*

Traditional Toys
53 Godfrey Street, SW3 3SX (7352 1718, www.traditionaltoy.com). Sloane Square tube, then 11, 19, 22 bus/49 bus. **Open** 10am-5.30pm Mon-Sat.
The beautiful wooden toys really grab you here, like the tell-the-time clock face and wooden Noah's Arks.

One Small Step One Giant Leap

The bewitching Caramel brand was started by Eva Karayiannis, a trained lawyer whose distaste for 'mass-produced clothing covered in logos' led her to open her own shop in 1999. Her foray into designing togs for children aged 0-12 has certainly paid dividends. The look is relaxed, not aggressively trendy but obviously well finished and fun to wear. All the clothes on sale are Caramel, but accessories such as shoes, hats, hair ties and toys are sourced from carefully chosen smaller brands that are constantly changing. Children's haircuts are done at the Pavilion Road branch, and there are Caramel concessions in Harrods (*see p22*) and Selfridges (*see p27*).
Branches 259 Pavilion Road, SW1X 0BP (7730 2564); 291 Brompton Road, SW3 2DY (7589 7001).

Oh Baby London
162 Brick Lane, E1 6RU (7247 4949, www.oh babylondon.com). Shoreditch High Street rail.
Open 11am-6pm Mon-Fri; 10am-6pm Sat, Sun.
'Been inside for 9 months' reads the logo on Oh Baby's bestselling black-and-white striped babygros for newborns. The witty brand was started as 'an allergic reaction to pastels', on a mission to introduce more jaunty kit for babies and children aged from zero to about six. That said, the new baby gift sets (bib, towel, toy, £22) come in conventional pastel pink and blue – but they're very sweet all the same. We love the striped leggings and pack of toddler pants in bright cotton, and 'The Future is Mine' is making a serious play to become our favourite baby slogan.

Olive Loves Alfie
84 Stoke Newington Church Street, N16 0AP (7241 4212, www.olivelovesalfie.co.uk). Finsbury Park tube/rail then 106 bus or 73, 393, 476 bus. **Open** 9am-5.30pm Mon-Fri; 10am-6pm Sat; 10am-5pm Sun.
A boutique with a strong aesthetic, Olive Loves Alfie houses design-led clothing for newborns, children and teens. There's no clichéd kids stuff in here and the gorgeous stock is wonderfully decorative – the walls are adorned with bestselling babygros from Scandinavian designers Katvig in stylish prints evoking Orla Kiely, which fly out of the shop. The cool educational toy range includes lots of puzzles, jigsaws and games by Djeco. Olive Loves Alfie now also stocks a selection of homewares from Rice and Tokyo Milk, womenswear by Marimekko and Caro kimonos. And if you're wondering about the name, it's what it said on a T-shirt the owner's three-year-old daughter gave to her best friend.

One Small Step One Giant Leap
3 Blenheim Crescent, W11 2EE (7243 0535, www.onesmallsteponegiantleap.com). Ladbroke Grove or Notting Hill Gate tube. **Open** 10am-6pm Mon-Fri; 9am-6pm Sat; 11am-5pm Sun.

You should count your blessings if there is a branch of this specialist children's shoe chain – and consistent winner of the Shoe Retailer of the Year gong – in your neighbourhood. It is a blissful place to take your children for all their footwear needs, from Crocs and sandals to more sensible pairs for school. The best thing is that there's space to spread out, the shoes are displayed with care and the highly regarded Bannock Device is used for fitting. Expect to pay about £12 for a jolly pair of One Small Step canvas sandals and about £36 for Start-rite school shoes.
Branches throughout the city.

Sasti HOT 50
8 Portobello Green Arcade, 281 Portobello Road, W10 5TZ (8960 1125, www.sasti.co.uk). Ladbroke Grove tube. **Open** 10am-6pm Mon-Sat; noon-5pm Sun. Named after the Hindu goddess who looks after all children and small creatures, Sasti is our favourite affordable children's boutique. This season we've been going a bundle on the cherry-print skirts and polka-dot cut-offs and the printed shirts for boys – festooned with grazing Friesian cows and fringed red cowboy trousers. Perennial bestsellers include the little bunny dresses, tutus, bus pyjamas, owl and monster toys, and knitted T-rex. Small girls look very fetching in the sticky-out net skirts. Apart from its own-label clothes, Sasti stocks brands such as Ubang and, from Denmark, Ej sikke lej.

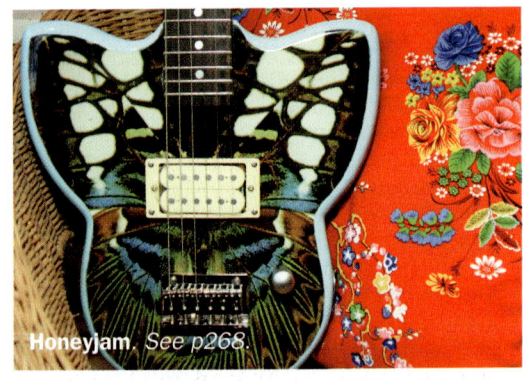

Their Nibs
214 Kensington Park Road, W11 1NR (7221 4263, www.theirnibs.com). Ladbroke Grove or Notting Hill Gate tube. **Open** 10am-6pm Mon-Sat; noon-5pm Sun. With an impressively spacious play area with blackboard, wooden toys, books and pre-school play/learn equipment, a small hairdressing salon (ring for details of shearing sessions) and racks of original clothes, Their Nibs is a top shop for tots. There's a tree of fairies on the front desk and central tables filled with sweet accessories, toys and clothes; fashions are pretty reasonably priced and ballet clothes are now stocked as well. You can pick up a distinctive cream crocheted party dress for a five-year-old for £39, and lovely velour collared T-shirts for boys in chocolate and turquoise cost £20.
Branch 79 Chamberlayne Road, NW10 3ND (8964 8444).

Toys, games & books

Toys and trinkets can often be found in gift shops and concept stores; *see p35*. *See also p221* **Models & games** and **Books** *p189*.

Benjamin Pollock's Toy Shop
44 The Market, Covent Garden, WC2E 8RF (7379 7866, www.pollocks-coventgarden.co.uk). Covent Garden tube. **Open** 10.30am-6pm Mon-Sat; 11am-4pm Sun.

Honeyjam. See p268.

Climb the creaky stairs past Hobbs and into this shrine to playthings from the past. There are music boxes, traditional puppets, hoopla and spinning tops – in fact, many toys so obscure you'll likely never have heard of them before, let alone played with them. Toy theatres make up a good part of the stock, and cost from a couple of quid for one in a matchbox to much more for the really complicated set-ups. If miniature stages aren't your thing, there are more nostalgic toys, such as china and tin tea sets, paper planes and dolls, vintage-style board games, Steiff teddy bears and music boxes. As this guide went to press, plans were in the pipeline for another branch; see the website for details.

Hamleys
188-196 Regent Street, W1B 5BT (0871 704 1977, www.hamleys.com). Oxford Circus tube. **Open** 10am-8pm Mon-Fri; 9am-8pm Sat; noon-6pm Sun.
Both a tourist attraction, with regular school-holiday events for children (check the website), and a ginormous toy shop, Hamleys has all the must-have toys, attractively displayed to boot. Arranged on five noisy floors, with perky demonstrators showing off certain wares on every one, you'll be lucky if you can spend less than an hour in here if you're accompanied by children. There's much to see: the basement has interactive toys, the ground floor is soft toys, floor one is all games, two is for pre-schoolers, three is girls' stuff, four hobbies and five is boys' toys with a café attached.

Honeyjam
267 Portobello Road, W11 1LR (7243 0449, www.honeyjam.co.uk). Ladbroke Grove tube.
Open 9.30am-5.30pm Mon-Sat; 11am-4pm Sun.
Honeyjam is oneΔ of those fashionable toy shops – Claudia Schiffer and Sophie Dahl are fans – that's nevertheless still full of fun, and has a strong line in vintage playthings. There are classic toys that parents will remember from their own childhood, as well as some seriously aspirational role-playing toys, the apotheosis of which has to be the famous toy Aga (made to order). It's all beautifully laid out, with glories to catch the eye at every turn: tea sets, tiddlywinks, anatomically correct dolls, forts and dragon castles, and traditional wooden toys from companies like Bigjigs and Le Toy Van.

Puppet Planet
787 Wandsworth Road (corner of the Chase), SW8 3JQ (7627 0111, mobile 07900 975276, www.puppetplanet.co.uk). Clapham Common tube.
Open 9am-7pm daily; also by appointment.
A specialist marionette shop that's run by Lesley Butler, whose passion for stringed characters is all too evident in the range of stock hanging about here. There are classic Pelham characters, traditional Indian and African marionettes, Balinese shadow puppets and vintage figures. Apart from puppets, the shop also sells Melissa & Doug's wonderful stuffed toy animals and Crafty Kids craft kits, many of which allow you to make your own puppet. There are occasional storytelling events and Punch and Judy parties in store. Best to call in advance if you're making a special trip to the shop as Butler occasionally closes it to put on puppet shows for children's parties.

Victoria Park Books
174 Victoria Park Road, E9 7HD (8986 1124, www.victoriaparkbooks.co.uk). Cambridge Heath or London Fields rail or bus 277. **Open** 10am-5.30pm Tue-Sun.
This amiable bookshop has a true community feel, with one wall featuring book reviews from the school children in the neighbourhood. Owners Jo and Cris De Guia have set out to make the store reflect local tastes and interests, with particular strength in catering to the curriculum requirements of nearby schools. Books are categorised by look and feel as well as content – there's a section for interactive titles, and children can get their hands on cloth, bath and buggy books. Teenagers and adults are also catered for – there's a strong range of parenting books, for example. Everybody's welcome to take a turn in the outside patio, and there are reading events for pre-schoolers on Tuesdays and Fridays.

Indexes & Maps

A-Z Index	**270**
London Underground Map	**287**
Central London Overview Map	**288**

A-Z Index

A

Abercrombie & Fitch p76
7 Burlington Gardens, W1S 3ES (0844 412 5750, www.uk.abercrombie.com).
High Street

Absolute Flowers p185
12-14 Clifton Road, W9 1SS (7286 1155, www.absoluteflowers andhome.com).
Gardens & Flowers

Absolute Vintage p98
15 Hanbury Street, E1 6QR (7247 3883, www.absolute vintage.co.uk).
Vintage & Second-hand

Academy Chimes Music Shop (branch of Barbican Chimes Music Shop)
Royal Academy of Music, York Gate Building, Marylebone Road, NW1 5HT (7873 7400).
Branch

Ace Sports & Leisure p236
341 Kentish Town Road, NW5 3TJ (7485 5367, www.acesportsdirect.com).
Sport & Fitness

Aesop London p138
91 Mount Street, W1K 2SU (7409 2358, www.aesop.net.au).
Health & Beauty

Aesop Shoreditch (branch of Aesop London)
Aesop Shoreditch, 5A Redchurch Street, E2 7DJ (7613 3793).
Branch

Aesop Westbourne (branch of Aesop London)
227 A Westbourne Grove, W11 2SE (7221 2008).
Branch

African Waistcoat Company p97
33 Islington Green, N1 8DU (7704 9698, www.africanwaistcoat company.com).
Tailoring & Bespoke

Agent Provocateur p107
6 Broadwick Street, W1F 8HL (7439 0229, www.agentprovocateur.com).
Lingerie, Swimwear & Erotica

Aimé p66
32 Ledbuy Road, W11 2AB (7221 7070, www.aimelondon.com).
Indie Boutiques

Al-Abbas p250
258-262 Uxbridge Road, W12 7JA (8740 1932).
Food

Albam p66
Old Spitalfields Market, 111A Commercial Street, E1 6BG (7247 6254, www.albamclothing.com).
Indie Boutiques

Albam
23 Beak Street, W1F 9RS (3157 7000).
Branch

Albam
286 Upper Street, N1 2TZ (7288 0835).
Branch

Alexander Boyd p97
54 Artillery Lane, E1 7LS (7377 8755, www.alexanderboyd.co.uk).
Tailoring & Bespoke

Alexander McQueen p85
4-5 Old Bond Street, W1S 4PD (7355 0088, www.alexandermcqueen.com).
Designer Chains

Algerian Coffee Stores p259
52 Old Compton Street, W1V 6PB (7437 2480, www.algcoffee.co.uk).
Drink

Alice & Astrid p107
30 Artesian Road, W2 5DD (7985 0888, www.aliceandastrid.com).
Lingerie, Swimwear & Erotica

Allens of Mayfair p244
117 Mount Street, W1K 3LA (7499 5831, www.allensofmayfair.co.uk).
Food

All Saints p76
57-59 Long Acre, WC2E 9JL (7836 0801, www.allsaints.co.uk).
High Street

Ally Capellino p128
9 Calvert Avenue, E2 7JP (7613 3073, www.allycapellino.co.uk).
Jewellery & Accessories

American Apparel p76
2-4 Carnaby Street, W1F 9PB (7734 4477, www.americanapparel.net).
High Street

Angela Flanders p146
96 Columbia Road, E2 7QB (7739 7555, www.angelaflanders-perfumer.com).
Perfumeries & Herbalists

Angel Flowers p185
60 Upper Street, N1 0NY (7704 6312, www.angel-flowers.co.uk).
Gardens & Flowers

Angels p221
119 Shaftesbury Avenue, WC2H 8AE (7836 5678, www.fancydress.com).
Crafts, Hobbies & Parties

Annie's Vintage Clothes p98
12 Camden Passage, N1 8ED (7359 0796).
Vintage & Secondhand

Anthropologie p35
158 Regent Street, W1B 5SW (7529 9800, www.anthropologie.co.uk).
Concept Stores & Lifestyle Boutiques

Antique Trader at Millinery Works p175
85-87 Southegate Road, N1 3JS (7359 2019, www.millineryworks.co.uk).
Vintage Furniture & Homewares

Any Amount of Books p195
56 Charing Cross Road, WC2H 0QA (7836 3697, www.any amountofbooks.com).
Books

Apartment C p107
70 Marylebone High Street, W1U 5JL (7935 1854, www.apartment-c.com).
Lingerie, Swimwear & Erotica

Aperture Photographic p212
44 Museum Street, WC1A 1LY (7242 8681, www.apertureuk.com).
Electronics & Photography

Apple Centre p208
78 New Oxford Street, WC1A 1HB (7692 6810, www.squaregroup.co.uk).
Electronics & Photography

Apple Store p208
235 Regent Street, W1B 2EL (7153 9000, www.apple.com).
Electronics & Photography

Apple Store
Westfield London, Ariel Way, W12 7GF (8433 4600).
Branch

Apple Store
Brent Cross, Upper West Mall, NW4 3FP (8359 1050).
Branch

A-Z Index

Aquascutum p85
100 Regent Street,
W1B 5SR (7675 8200,
www.aquascutum.co.uk).
Designer Chains

Aram p159
110 Drury Lane,
WC2B 5SG (7557
7557, www.aram.co.uk.
Furniture & Homewares

Aravore Babies p265
31 Park Road, N8
8TE (8347 5752,
www.aravore-babies.com).
Babies & Children

arckiv p153
Arch 67 Stables
Market, NW1 8AH
(07790 102204,
www.arckiv.net).
Eyewear

Aria p160
Barnsbury Hall,
Barnsbury Street,
N1 1PN (7704 1999,
www.ariashop.co.uk).
Furniture & Homewares

Arthur Beale p237
194 Shaftesbury Avenue,
WC2H 8JP (7836 9034).
Sport & Fitness

L'Artisan du Chocolat p246
89 Lower Sloane Street,
SW1W 8DA (7824 8365,
www.artisanduchocolat.
com). Food

L'Artisan du Chocolat
81 Westbourne Grove,
W2 4UL (0845 270 6996).
Branch

L'Artisan Parfumeur p146
17 Cale Street, SW3 3QR
(7352 4196, www.artisan
parfumeur.com).
Perfumeries & Herbalists

Artwords p192
65A Rivington Street,
EC2A 3QQ (7729 2000,
www.artwords.co.uk).
Books

Artworlds Bookshop
20-22 Broadway Market,
E8 4QJ (7923 7507).
Branch

Ask p208
248 Tottenham Court
Road, W1T 7QZ

(7637 0353,
www.askdirect.co.uk).
Electronics & Photography

Aston Matthews p171
141-147A Essex Road, N1
2SN (7226 7220, www.
astonmatthews.co.uk).
Furniture & Homewares

**Atelier Abigail
Ahern** p160
137 Upper Street, N1
1QP (7354 8181, www.
atelierabigailahern.com).
Furniture & Homewares

**Atlantic Electronis Ltd
(branch of Westend DJ)**
970 North Circular Road,
NW2 7JR (8208 6988).
Branch

Atlantis Bookshop p192
49A Museum Street, WC1A
1LY (7405 2120, www.
theatlantisbookshop.com).
Books

Atlantis European p214
Britannia House, 68-80
Hanbury Street, E1 5JL
(7377 8855, www.
atlantisart.co.uk).
Crafts, Hobbies & Parties

Aubin & Wills p35
64-66 Redchurch Street,
E2 7DP (3487 0066,
www.aubinandwills.com).
Concept Stores &
Lifestyle Boutiques

Audio Gold p210
308-310 Park Road,
N8 8LA (8341 9007,
www.audiogold.co.uk).
Electronics & Photography

Austique p66
330 King's Road,
SW3 5UR (7376 4555,
www.austique.co.uk).
Indie Boutiques

B

BM Soho p206
25 D'Arblay Street,
W1F 8EJ (7437 0478,
www.bm-soho.com).
CDs & Records

B&B Italia p161
250 Brompton Road,
SW3 2AS (7591 8111,

www.bebitalia.com).
Furniture & Homewares

b Store p56
24A Savile Row,
W1S 3PR (7734 6846,
www.bstorelondon.com).
Indie Boutiques

Banana Republic p76
224 Regent Street,
W1B 3BR (7758 3550,
www.bananarepublic.eu).
High Street

Banana Republic
Brent Cross Shopping
Centre, Hendon, NW4
3FP (8203 1397).
Branch

Banana Republic
132 Long Acre, WC2E
9AA (7836 9567).
Branch

Bang Bang p98
21 Goodge Street,
W1T 2PJ (7631 4191).
Vintage & Secondhand

Bang Bang
9 Berwick Street, W1F
0PJ (7494 2042). Branch

**Barbican Chimes
Music Shop** p225
Silk Street, EC2Y
8DD (7588 9242,
www.chimesmusic.com).
Musical Instruments

Bass Gallery p225
142 Royal College Street,
NW1 0TA (7267 5458,
www.thebassgallery.com).
Musical Instruments

Bates the Hatter p131
73 Jermyn Street,
SW1Y 6JD (7734 2722,
www.bates-hats.co.uk).
Jewellery & Accessories

Bead Shop p216
21A Tower Street,
WC2H 9NS (7240 0931,
www.beadworks.co.uk).
Crafts, Hobbies & Parties

Beatrix Ong p119
8 Newburgh Street,
W1F 7RJ (7287 2724,
www.beatrixong.com).
Shoes

Becca p141
91A Pelham Street, SW7
2NJ (7225 2501,

www.beccacosmetics.com).
Health & Beauty

Bedales p256
5 Bedale Street,
SE1 9AL (7403 8853,
www.bedalestreet.com).
Drink

Bedales
55 Leadenhall Market,
EC3V 1LT (7929 3536).
Branch

Bedales
12 Market Street,
E1 6DT (7375 1926).
Branch

Ben Day p131
18 Hanbury Street,
E1 6QR (7247 9977,
www.benday.co.uk).
Jewellery & Accessories

Ben Day
3 Lonsdale Road,
W11 2BY (3417 3873).
Branch

**Benjamin Pollock's
Toy Shop** p267
44 The Market, Covent
Garden, WC2E 8RF (7379
7866, www.pollocks-
coventgarden.co.uk).
Babies & Children

Ben Southgate p176
4 The Courtyard,
Ezra Street, E2 7RH
(07905 960792,
www.bsouthgate.co.uk).
Vintage Furniture
& Homewares

Berganza p133
88-90 Hatton Garden
(entrace in Greville Street),
EC1N 8PN (7404 2336,
www.berganza.com).
Jewellery & Accessories

Bermondsey 167 p37
167 Bermondsey Street,
SE1 3UW (7407 3137,
www.bermondsey167.com).
Concept Stores &
Lifestyle Boutiques

Bernard J Shapero p196
32 St George Street,
W1S 2EA (7493 0876,
www.shapero.com). Books

Bernstock Spiers p131
234 Brick Lane,
E2 7EB (7739 7385,

www.bernstockspiers.com).
Jewellery & Accessories
Berry Bros & Rudd   p256
3 St James's Street,
SW1A 1EG (7396 9600,
www.bbr.com). Drink
**Berwick Street
Cloth Shop   p217**
14 Berwick Street,
W1F 0PP (7287 2881,
www.theberwickstreet
clothshop.com).
Crafts, Hobbies & Parties
**Berwick Street
Market   p48**
Berwick Street,
Rupert Street, W1.
Markets
Beyond Retro   p98
110-112 Cheshire Street,
E2 6EJ (7729 9001,
www.beyondretro.com).
Vintage & Secondhand
Beyond Retro
58-59 Great Marlborough
Street, W1F 7JY (7434
1406). Branch
Beyond the Valley   p37
2 Newburgh Street, W1F
7RD (7437 7338, www.
beyondthevalley.com).
Concept Stores
& Lifestyle Boutiques
Bikefix   p232
48 Lamb's Conduit
Street, WC1N 3LJ 97405
1218, www.bikefix.co.uk).
Sport & Fitness
Biondi   p109
55B Old Church Street,
SW3 5BS (7349 1111,
www.biondicouture.com).
Lingerie, Swimwear
& Erotica
Birgit Israel   p176
301 Fulham Road,
SW10 9QH (7376 7255,
www.birgitisrael.com).
Vintage Furniture &
Homewares
Black Truffle   p119
4 Broadway Market,
E8 4QJ (7923 9450,
www.blacktruffle.com).
Shoes
Black Truffle
52 Warren Street,
W1T 5NJ (7388 4547).
Branch
**Blade Rubber
Stamps   p222**
12 Bury Place, WC1A
2JL (7831 4123,
www.bladerubber.co.uk).
Crafts, Hobbies & Parties
Bloch   p237
35 Drury Lane,
WC2B 5RH (7836 4777,
www.blochworld.com).
Sports & Fitness
**Bloch & Angell
Antiques   p175**
22 Church Street,
NW8 8EP (7723 6575,
www.angellantiques.com).
Vintage Furniture
& Homewares
Bloomsbury Flowers   p185
29 Great Queen Street,
WC2B 5BB (7242 2840,
www.bloomsburyflowers.
co.uk). Gardens & Flowers
**Blossom Mother
& Child   p117**
164 Walton Street,
SW3 2JL (0845 262
7500, www.blossom
motherandchild.com).
Maternity & Unusual Sizes
Blossom Mother & Child
69 Marylebone High Street,
W1U 5JJ (7486 6089).
Branch
Blue Daisy   p264
13 South End Road,
NW3 2PT (7681 4144,
www.blue-daisy.com).
Babies & Children
Blue Daisy
190 West End Lane,
NW6 1SG (7435 3100).
Branch
Bob & Blossom   p262
140 Columbia Road,
E2 7RG (7739 4737, www.
bobandblossom.com).
Babies & Children
Bobbin Bicycles   p232
397 St John Street,
EC1V 4LD (7837 3370).
Sport & Fitness
Bodas   p107
38B Ledbury Road,
W11 2AB (7229 4464,
www.bodas.co.uk).
Lingerie, Swimwear
& Erotica
Bodas
43 Brushfield Street,
E1 6AA (7655 0958).
Branch
Bookmarks   p192
1 Bloomsbury Street,
WC1B 3QE (7637 1848,
www.bookmarks.uk.com).
Books
Books for Cooks   p192
4 Blenheim Crescent,
W11 1NN (7221 1992,
www.booksforcooks.com).
Books
Born   p263
168 Stoke Newington
Church Street, N16
0JL (7249 5069,
www.borndirect.com).
Babies & Children
Borough Market   p46
Southwark Street,
SE1 1TL (7407
1002,www.borough
market.org.uk).
Markets
Borovick Fabrics   p217
16 Berwick Street, W1F
0HP (7437 2180, www.
borovickfabricsltd.co.uk).
Crafts, Hobbies & Parties
Bread & Honey   p56
205 Whitecross Street,
EC1Y 8QP (7253 4455,
www.backin10minutes.
com). Indie Boutiques
Breathless   p110
131 King's Cross Road,
WC1X 9BJ (7278 1666,
www.breathless.uk.com).
Lingerie, Swimwear
& Erotica
Brick Lane Bikes   p232
118 Bethnal Green Road,
E2 6DG (7033 9053.
www.bricklanebikes.co.uk).
Sport & Fitness
Brick Lane Market   p49
Brick Lane (north of
railway bridge), Cygnet
Street, Sclater Street, E1;
Bacon Street, Cheshire
Street, E2 (7364 1717).
Markets
**Brick Lane Thrift Store
(branch of East End
Thrift Store)**
68 Sclater Street,
E1 6HR (7739 0242).
Branch
**Bridgewood
& Neitzert   p229**
164 Stoke Newington
Church Street, N16
0JU (7249 9398,
www.londonviolins.com).
Musical Instruments
Brill   p201
27 Exmouth Market, EC1R
4QL (7833 9757, www.
clerkenwellmusic.co.uk).
CDs & Records
British Boot Company p121
5 Kentish Town Road,
NW1 8NH (7485 8505,
www.britboot.co.uk).
Shoes
Brixton Cycles   p232
145 Stockwell Road,
SW9 9TN (7733 6055,
www.brixtoncycles.co.uk).
Sport & Fitness
Brixton Market   p51
Electric Avenue, Pope's
Road, Brixton Station
Road, SW9 (7926 2530,
www.brixtonmarket.net).
Markets
Broadway Bookshop p189
6 Broadway Market,
E8 4QJ (7241 1626,
www.broadwaybook
shophackney.com).
Books
Broadway Market   p49
Broadway Market,
E8 4PH (www.broadway
market.co.uk).
Markets
Browns   p56
23-27 South Molton Street,
W1K 5RD (7514 0000,
www.brownsfashion.com).
Indie Boutiques
Browns
6C Sloane Street, Chelsea,
SW1X 9LE (7514 0040).
Branch
Browns Bride
11-12 Hinde Street, W1U
3BE (7514 0056). Branch

A-Z Index

Browns Focus (branch of Browns)
38-39 South Molton Street, W1K 5RD (7514 0000). Branch

Browns Labels for Less (branch of Browns)
50 South Molton Street, W1K 5RD (7514 0000). Branch

Browns Shoes
59 Brook Street, W1K 4HS (7514 0000). Branch

Brunswick p28
Hunter Street, Bernard Street & Marchmont Street, WC1N 1BS (7833 6066, www.brunswick.co.uk). Shopping Centre & Arcades

Buffy's Beads p216
Unit 2.3, Kingly Court, W1B 5PW (7494 2323, www.buffysbeads.com). Crafts, Hobbies & Parties

Buggies & Bikes p262
23 Broadway Market, E8 4PH (7241 5382, www.buggiesandbikes.net). Babis & Children

Burberry p85
21-23 New Bond Street, W1S 2RE (3367 3000, www.burberry.com). Designer Chains

Burberry
157-167 Regent Street, W1B 4PH (3367 3000). Branch

Burberry
2 Brompton Road, SW1X 7PB (3367 3000). Branch

Burberry
199 Westbourne Grove, W11 2SB (3367 3000). Branch

Burberry
Westfield Shopping Centre, W12 7GB (3367 3000). Branch

Butler & Wilson p98
189 Fulham Road, SW3 6JN (7352 8255, www.butlerandwilson.co.uk). Vintage & Secondhand

Butler & Wilson
20 South Molton Street, W1K 5QY (7409 2955). Branch

Button Lady p218
12 Heath Street, NW3 6TE (7435 5412, www.buttonladyhampstead.co.uk). Crafts, Hobbies & Parties

Button Queen p218
76 Marylebone Lane, W1U 2PR (7935 1505, www.thebuttonqueen.co.uk). Crafts, Hobbies & Parties

C

C Lidgate p244
110 Holland Park Avenue, W11 4UA (7727 8243, www.lidgates.com). Food

Cabbages & Frocks p46
St Marylebone Parish Church Grounds, Marylebone High Street, W1 (7794 1636, www.cabbagesandfrocks.co.uk). Markets

Camden Coffee Shop p259
11 Delancey Street, NW1 7NL (7387 4080). Drink

Camden Market p46
192-200 Camden High Street, junction with Buck Street, NW1 (7267 3417, www.camdenmarkets.org). Markets

Camera City p212
16 Little Russell Street, WC1A 2HL (7813 2100, www.cameracity.co.uk). Electronics & Photography

Caramel Baby & Child p265
77 Ledbury Road, W11 2AG (7727 0906, www.caramel-shop.co.uk). Babies & Children

Caramel Baby & Child
259 Pavillion Road, SW1X 0BP (7730 2564). Branch

Caramel Baby & Child
291 Brompton Road, SW3 2DY (7589 7001). Branch

Caravan p167
3 Redchurch Street, EC2 7DJ (7033 3532, www.caravanstyle.com). Furniture & Homewares

Cardinal Place p28
Victoria street, SW1E 5JH (www.cardinalplace.co.uk). Shopping Centres & Arcades

Casa Mexico p167
1 Winkley Street, E2 6PY (7739 9349, www.casamexico.co.uk). Furniture & Homewares

Cass Art p214
66-67 Colebrook Row, N1 8AB (7354 2999, www.cassart.co.uk). Crafts, Hobbies & Parties

Cass Art
13 Charing Cross Road, WC2H 0EP (7930 9940). Branch

Cass Art
24 Berwick Street, W1F 8RD (7287 8504). Branch

Cass Art
220 Kensington High Street, W8 7RG (7937 6506). Branch

Cath Kidston p37
28-32 Shelton Street, WC2H 9JE (7836 4803, www.cathkidston.co.uk). Concept Stores & Lifestyle Boutiques

Celia Birtwell p167
71 Westbourne Park Road, W2 5QH (7221 0877, www.celiabirtwell.com). Furniture & Homewares

Chandler Guitars p225
300-302 Sandycombe Road, Kew, Surrey TW9 3NG (8940 5874, www.chandlerguitars.co.uk). Musical Instruments

Chappell of Bond Street p225
152-160 Wardour Street, W1F 8YA (7432 4400, www.chappellofbondstreet.co.uk). Musical Instruments

Chegworth Farm Shop p248
221 Kensington Church Street, W8 7LX (7229 3016, www.chegworthvalley.com). Food

Chesney's p175
194-202 Battersea Park Road, SW11 4ND (7627 1410, www.chesneys.co.uk). Vintage Furniture & Homewares

Chesney's
734-736 Hollway Road, N19 3JF (7561 8280). Branch

Chinalife p148
101-105 Camden High Street, NW1 7JN (7388 5783, www.acumedic.com). Perfumeries & Herbalists

Chris Kerr p97
52 Berwick Street, W1F 8SL (7437 3727, www.chriskerr.com). Tailoring & Bespoke

Christian Louboutin p121
23 Motcomb Street, SW1X 8LB (7245 6510, www.christianlouboutin.fr). Shoes

Christian Louboutin
17 Mount Street, W1K 2RJ (7491 0033). Branch

Cinch p56
5 Newburgh Street, W1F 7RB (7287 4941, www.eu.levi.com). Indie Boutiques

Classic Camera p212
2 Pied Bull Yard, off Bury Place, WC1A 2JR (7831 0777, www.theclassiccamera.com). Electronics & Photography

Clifton Nurseries p183
5A Clifton Villas, W9 9PH (7289 6851, www.clifton.co.uk). Gardens & Flowers

Cloth House p217
47 Berwick Street, W1F 8SJ (7437 5155, www.clothhouse.com). Crafts, Hobbies & Parties

Cloth House
98 Berwick Street, W1F 0QJ (7287 1555). Branch

Time Out London's Best Shops **273**

A-Z INDEX

Cloud Cuckoo Land p98
6 Charlton Place,
Camden Passage,
N1 8AJ (7354 3141).
Vintage & Secondhand

Cochinechine p69
74 Heath Street,
NW3 1DN (7435 9377,
www.cochinechine.com).
Indie Boutiques

Coco de Mer p110
23 Monmouth Street,
WC2H 9DD (7836 8882,
www.coco-de-mer.co.uk).
Lingerie, Swimwear
& Erotica

Coco de Mer
108 Draycott Avenue,
SW3 3AE (7584 7615).
Branch

Columbia Road Market p50
Columbia Road, E2
(7364 1717). Markets

Comet Miniatures p221
44-48 Lavendar Hill,
SW11 5RH (7228 3702, www.comet-miniatures.com).
Crafts, Hobbies & Parties

Comfort Station p128
22 Cheshire Street, E2
6EH (7033 9099, www.comfortstation.co.uk).
Jewellery & Accessories

Compendia p221
10 Greenwich Market,
SE10 9HZ (8293 6616,
www.compendia.co.uk).
Crafts, Hobbies & Parties

Condor Cycles p232
49-53 Gray's Inn Road,
WC1X 8PP (7629 6820,
www.condorcycles.com).
Sport & Fitness

Conran Shop p161
Michelin House, 81
Fulham Road, SW3
6RD (7589 7401,
www.conran.co.uk).
Furniture & Homewares

Conran Shop
55 Marylebone High Street,
W1U 5HS (7723 2223).
Branch

Contemporary Applied Arts p168
2 Percy Street, W1T
1DD (7436 2344,
www.caa.org.uk).
Furniture & Homewares

Core One p175
The Gas Works, 2 Michael
Road, SW6 2AD (7371
5700, www.coreone
antiques.com). Vintage
Furniture & Homewares

COS p77
222 Regent Street,
W1B 5BD (7478 0400,
www.cosstores.com).
High Street

COS
124-126 Kensington
High Street, W8 7RL
(7361 1050). Branch

COS
130-131 Long Acre, WC2E
9AA (7632 4190). Branch

COS
Westfield Shopping Centre,
W12 7GB (8600 3310).
Branch

Cosmetics à la Carte p142
19B Motcomb Street, SW1X
8LB (7235 0596, www.
cosmeticsalacarte.com).
Health & Beauty

Couverture & the Garbstore p39
188 Kensington Park
Road, W11 2ES (7229
2178, www.couverture.
co.uk, ww.garbstore.com).
Concept Stores &
Lifestyle Boutiques

Covent Garden Market p28
Between King Street &
Henrietta Street, WC2E
8RF (0870 780 5001,
www.coventgardenmarket.
co.uk). Shopping Centres
& Arcades

Cox & Power p133
35C Marylebone High
Street, W1U 4QA
(7935 3530,
www.coxandpower.com).
Jewellery & Accessories

CP Hart p172
Arch 213, Newnham
Terrace, Hercules Road,
SE1 7DR (7902 5250,
www.cphart.co.uk).
Furniture & Homewares

CP Hart
103-105 Regents Park
Road, NW1 8UR (7586
9856). Branch

Cutler & Gross p153
16 Knightsbridge Green,
SW1X 7QL (7581 2250,
www.cutlerandgross.com).
Eyewear

Cutler & Gross Vintage
7 Knightsbridge Green,
SW1X 7QL (7590 9995).
Branch

Czech & Speake p172
39C Jermyn Street,
SW1Y 6DN (7439 0216,
www.czechspeake.com).
Furniture & Homewares

D

DR Harris p150
29 St James' Street,
SW1A 1Hb (7930 3915,
www.drharris.co.uk).
Perfumeries & Herbalists

D&A Binder p176
34 Church Street,
NW8 8EP (7723 0542,
www.dandabinder.co.uk).
Vintage Furniture
& Homewares

D&A Binder
101 Holloway Road,
N7 8LT (7609 6306).
Branch

Darkroom p39
52 Lamb's Conduit Street,
WC1N 3LL (7831 7244,
www.darkroomlondon.com).
Concept Stores &
Lifestyle Boutiques

Daunt Books p190
83-84 Marylebone
High Street, W1U 4QW
(7224 2295, www.
dauntbooks.co.uk).
Books

Daunt Books
51 South End Road,
NW3 2QB (7794 8206).
Branch

Daunt Books
193 Haverstpck Hill, NW3
4QL (7794 4006). Branch

Daunt Books
112-114 Holland Park
Avenue, W11 4UA
(7727 7022), Branch

Daunt Books
158-164 Fulham Road,
SW10 9PR (7373 4997).
Branch

Davenports Magic Shop p222
7 Charing Cross
Underground Shopping
Arcade, WC2N 4HZ (7836
0408, www.davenports
magic.co.uk). Crafts,
Hobbies & Parties

Daylesford Organic p248
44B Pimlico Road, SW1W
8LP (7881 8060, www.
daylesfordorganic.com).
Food

Daylesford Organic
208-212 Westbourne
Grove, W11 2RH (7313
8050). Branch

Daylesford Organic
30 Pimlico Road,
SW1W 8LJ (7730 2943).
Branch

Decathlon p236
Canada Water Retail
Park, Surrey Quays Road,
SE16 2XU (7394 2000,
www.decathlon.co.uk).
Sport & Fitness

Dege & Skinner p96
10 Savile Row, W1S
3PF (7287 2941, www.
dege-skinner.co.uk).
Tailoring & Bespoke

De Gustibus p243
53 Blandford Street, W1U
7HL (7486 6608, www.
degustibus.co.uk).
Food

De Gustibus
53-55 Carter Lane, EC4V
5AE (7236 0056). Branch

De Gustibus
4 Southwark Street, SE1
1TQ (7407 3625). Branch

De Parma p178
The Gas Works, 2 Michael
Road, SW6 2AN (7736
3384, www.deparma.com).
Vintage Furniture
& Homewares

A-Z Index

De Parma
247 Fulham Road, SW3 6HY (7352 2414). Branch

Designers Guild p161
267-271 (store) & 275-277 (showroom) King's Road, SW3 5EN (7351 5775, www.designersguild.com). Furniture & Homewares

Diane von Furstenberg (branch of Matches)
83 Ledbury Road, W11 2AJ (7221 1120). Branch

Diverse p56
294 Upper Street, N1 2TU (7359 8877, www.diverseclothing.com). Indie Boutiques

Divertimenti p168
227-229 Brompton Road, SW3 2EP (7581 8065, www.divertimenti.co.uk). Furniture & Homewares

Divertimenti
33-34 Marylebone High Street, W1U 4PT (7935 0689). Branch

Dog & Wardrobe p178
Unit 3B RegentStudios, 8 Andrew's Road, E8 4QN (07855 958741, www.thedogandwardrobe.com). Vintage Furniture & Homewares

Dolly Diamond p101
51 Pembridge Road, W11 3HG (7792 2479, www.dollydiamond.com). Vintage & Secondhand

Dover Street Market p39
17-18 Dover Street, W1S 4LT (7518 0680, www.doverstreetmarket.com). Concept Stores & Lifestyle Boutiques

Dragons of Walton Street p264
23 Walton Street, SW3 2HX (7589 3795, www.dragonsofwaltonstreet.com). Babies & Children

Dress Circle p207
57-59 Monmouth Street, WC2H 9DG (7240 2227, www.dresscircle.co.uk). CDs & Records

Duke of Uke p227
22 Hanbury Street, E1 6QR (7247 7924, www.dukeofyuke.co.uk). Musical Instruments

E

Earth Natural Foods p249
200 Kentish Town Road, NW5 2AE (7482 2211, www.earthnaturalfoods.co.uk). Food

East End Thrift Store p101
Unit 1A, Watermans Building, Assembly Passage, E1 4UT (7423 9700, www.theeastendthriftstore.com). Vintage & Secondhand

ec one p133
41 Exmouth Market, EC1R 4QL (7713 6185, www.econe.co.uk). Jewellery & Accessories

ec one
56 Ledbury Road, W11 2AJ (7243 8811). Branch

Eco p163
213 Chiswick High Road, W4 2DW (8995 7611, www.eco-age.com). Furniture & Homewares

Electrum Gallery p134
21 South Molton Street, W1K 5QZ (7629 6325, www.electrumgallery.co.uk). Jewellery & Accessories

Elias & Grace p117
158 Regent's Park Road, NW1 8XN (7449 0574, www.eliasandgrace.com). Maternity & Unusual Sizes

Ella Doran Design p168
46 Cheshire Street, E2 6EH (7613 0782, www.elladoran.co.uk). Furniture & Homewares

Ellis Brigham p236
Tower House, 3-11 Southampton Street, WC2E 7HA (7395 1010, www.ellis-brigham.com). Sport & Fitness

Ellis Brigham
Unit 2003, Westfield Shopping Centre, W12 7GF (8222 6300). Branch

Ellis Brigham
178 Kensington High Street, W8 7RG (7937 6889). Branch

Emma Hope p121
53 Sloane Square, SW1 8AX (7259 9566, www.emmahope.co.uk). Shoes

Emma Hope
207 Westbourne Grove, W11 2SF (7313 7490). Branch

Emma Hope
Westfield Shopping Centre, Ariel Way, W12 7GFF (3249 1010). Branch

Equa p69
28 Camden Passage, N1 8ED (7359 0955, www.equaclothing.com). Indie Boutiques

Expectations p113
75 Great Eastern Street, EC2A 3RY (7739 0292, www.expectations.co.uk). Lingerie, Swimwear & Erotica

Eye Company p155
159 Wardour Street, W1F 8WH (7434 0988, www.eye-company.co.uk). Eyewear

Eye Contacts p155
10 Chalk Farm Road, NW1 8AG (7482 1701, www.eyecontactscamden.co.uk). Eyewear

F

Fabrications p220
7 Broadway Market, E8 4PH (7275 8043, www.fabrications1.co.uk). Crafts, Hobbies & Parties

The Facade p181
99 Lisson Grove, NW1 6UP (7258 2017, www.thefacade.co.uk). Vintage Furniture & Homewares

Family Tree p41
53 Exmouth Market, EC1R 4QL (7278 1084, www.familytreeshop.co.uk). Concept Stores & Lifestyle Boutiques

Fandango p181
2 Cross Street, N1 2BL (7226 1777, www.thefandangointeriors.co.uk). Vintage Furniture & Homewares

Farmacia Santa Maria Novella p150
117 Walton Street, SW3 2HP (7460 6600). Perfumeries & Herbalists

Farmacia Santa Maria Novella
1 Piccadilly Arcade, SW1Y 6NH (7493 1975). Branch

Fettered Pleasures p113
90 Holloway Road, N7 8JG (7619 9333, www.fetteredpleasures.com). Lingerie, Swimwear & Erotica

Flashback p201
50 Essex Road, N1 8LR (7354 9356, www.flashback.co.uk). CDs & Records

Floral Hall p175
Corner of Crouch Hill & Haringey Park, N8 9DX (8348 7309, www.floralhallantiques.co.uk). Vintage Furniture & Homewares

Folk p59
49 Lamb's Conduit Street, WC1N 3NG (7404 6458, www.folkclothing.com). Indie Boutiques

Folk
11 Drey walk, E1 6QL (7375 2844). Branch

Foote's p229
10 Golden Square, W1F 9JA (7734 1822, www.footesmusic.com). Musical Instruments

Forbidden Planet p192
179 Shaftesbury Avenue, WC2H 8JR (7420 3666, www.forbiddenplanet.com). Books

Fortnum & Mason p21
181 Picadilly, W1A 1ER (7734 8040,

www.fortnumandmason.com). Department Stores

Foyles p190
113-119 Charing Cross Road, WC2H 0EB (7437 5660, www.foyles.co.uk). Books

Foyles
Southbank Centre, Riverside, SE1 8XX (7440 3212). Branch

Foyles
St Pancras International, Euston Road, N1C 4QL (3206 2650). Branch

Foyles
Westfield, W12 7GE (3206 2656). Branch

Freed of London p237
94 St Martin's Lane, WC2N 4AT (7240 0432, www.freedoflondon.com). Sports & Fitness

French Connection p77
396 Oxford Street, W1C 1JX (7629 7766, www.frenchconnection.com). High Street

French House p175
41-43 Parsons Green Lane, SW6 4HH (7371 7573, www.thefrenchhouse.co.uk). Vintage Furniture & Homewares

French's Dairy p134
13 Rugby Street, WC1N 3QT (7404 7070, www.frenchsdairy.com). Jewellery & Accessories

French's Dairy
3 Chichester Rents, WC2A 1EG (7242 4555). Branch

Fresh p139
92 Marylebone High Street, W1U 4RD (7486 4100, www.fresh.com). Health & Beauty

La Fromagerie p245
2-6 Moxton Street, W1U 4EW (7935 0341, www.lafromagerie.co.uk). Food

La Fromagerie
30 Highbury Park, N5 2AA (7359 7440). Branch

G

G Baldwin & Co p150
171-173 Walworth Road, SE17 1RW (7703 5550, www.baldwins.co.uk). Perfumeries & Herbalists

G Smith & Sons p223
74 Charing Cross Road, WC2H 0BG (7836 7422, www.smithandshervs.com). Crafts, Hobbies & Parties

Gallery 1930 p182
18 Church Street, NW8 8EP (7723 1555, www.susiecooperceramics.com). Vintage Furniture & Homewares

Ganesha p41
3-4 Gabriel's Wharf, 56 Upper Ground, SE1 9PP (7928 3444, www.ganesha.co.uk). Concept Stores & Lifestyle Boutiques

Ganesha
38 King Street, WC2E 8JT (7240 8068). Branch

Gay's the Word p192
66 Marchmont Street, WC1N 1AB (7278 7654, www.gaystheword.co.uk). Books

Geoffrey Drayton p163
85 Hampstead Road, NW1 2PL (7387 5840, www.geoffreydrayton.com). Furniture & Homewares

Georgina Goodman p121
44 Old Bond Street, W1S 4GB (7493 7673, www.georginagoodman.com). Shoes

Gerry's p256
74 Old Compton Street, W1D 4UW (7734 4215, www.gerrys.uk.com). Drink

Giacobazzi's p252
150 Fleet Road, NW3 2QX (7267 7222, www.giacobazzis.co.uk). Food

Gieves & Hawkes p97
1 Savile Row, W1S 3JR (7434 2001, www.gievesandhawkes.com). Tailoring & Bespoke

Ginger Pig p244
99 Lauriston Road, E9 7HJ (8986 6911, www.thegingerpig.co.uk). Food

Ginger Pig
Borough Market, SE1 1TL (7403 4721). Branch

Ginger Pig
8-10 Moxon Street, W1U 4EW (7935 7788). Branch

Ginger Pig
27 Lower Marsh, SE1 7RG (7921 2975). Branch

Ginkgo Garden Centre p183
Railway arches, Ravenscourt Avenue, off King Street, W6 0SL (8563 7112, www.ginkgogardens.co.uk). Gardens & Flowers

The Girl Can't Help It p101
Alfie's Antique Market, 13-25 Church Street, NW8 8DT (7724 8984, www.thegirlcanthelpit.com). Vintage & Secondhand

Goldsboro p196
7 Cecil Court, WC2N 4EZ (7497 9230, www.goldsborobooks.com). Books

Goodhood p59
41 Coronet Street, N1 6HD (7729 3600, www.goodhood.co.uk). Indie Boutiques

Gosh! p194
39 Great Russell Street, WC1B 3NZ (7636 1011, www.goshlondon.com). Books

Grace & Favour p41
35 North Cross Road, SE22 9ET (8693 4400). Concept Stores & Lifestyle Boutiques

Grahams p210
Unit 1, Canonbury Yard, 190A New North Road, N1 7BS (7226 5500, www.grahams.co.uk). Electronics & Photography

Gramex p205
25 Lower Marsh, SE1 7RJ (7401 3830). CDs & Records

Grant & Cutler p194
55-57 Great Marlborough Street, W1F 7AY (7734 2012, www.grantandcutler.com). Books

Green & Fay p163
137-139 Essex Road, N1 1QP (7704 0455, www.greenandfay.net). Furniture & Homewares

Green & Stone p214
259 King's Road, SW3 5EL (7352 0837, www.greenandstone.com). Crafts, Hobbies & Parties

Green Valley p252
36-37 Upper Berkeley Street, W1H 5QF (7402 7385). Food

Greenwich Market p50
Off College Approach, SE10 (8269 5096, www.greenwichmarket.net). Markets

H

H&M p77
261-271 Regent Street, W1B 2ES 97493 4004, www.hm.com). High Street

Hamleys p268
188-196 Regent Street, W1B 5BT (0871 704 1977, www.hamleys.com). Babies & Children

Harold Moores Records p205
2 Great Marlborough Street, W1F 7HQ (7437 1576, www.hmrecords.co.uk). CDs & Records

Harrods p22
87-135 Brompton Road, SW1X 7XL (7730 1234, www.harrods.com). Department Stores

Harvey Nichols p23
109-125 Knightsbridge, SW1X 7RJ (7235 5000, www.harveynichols.com).

A-Z Index

Department Stores
Hatchards p191
187 Piccadilly, W1J
9LE (7439 9921,
www.hatchards.co.uk).
Books
Heal's p163
196 Tottenham Court
Road, W1T 7LQ (7636
1666, www.heals.co.uk).
Furniture & Homewares
Heal's
234 King's Road, SW3
5UA (7349 8411). Branch
Heal's
49-51 Eden Street,
KT1 1BW (8614 5900)
Branch
Heidi Klein p109
174 Westbourne Grove,
W11 2RW (7243 5665,
www.heidiklein.com).
Lingerie, Swimwear &
Erotica
Heidi Klein
257 Pavillion Road,
SW1 0PB (7259 9418).
Branch
Henry Poole & Co p96
15 Saville Row, W1S
3PJ (7734 5985,
www.henrypoole.com).
Tailoring & Bespoke
Henry Sotheran p197
2-5 Sackville Street,
W1S 3DP (7439 6151,
www.sotherans.co.uk).
Books
Hideout p66
7 Upper James Street,
W1F 9DH (7437 4929,
www.hideoutstore.com).
Indie Boutiques
High & Mighty p118
145-147 Edgware Road,
W2 2HR (7723 8754,
www.highandmighty.co.uk).
Maternity & Unusual Sizes
High & Mighty
The Plaza, 120 Oxford
Street, W1N 9DP
(7436 4861). Branch
High & Mighty
81-83 Knightsbridge,
SW1X 7RB (7752 0665).
Branch
HMV Megastore p201

150 Oxford Street,
W1D 1DJ (7631 3423,
www.hmv.com).
CDs & Records
Hobgoblin p230
24 Rathbone Place,
W1T 1JA (7323 9040,
www.hobgoblin.com).
Musical Instruments
Holly & Lil p240
103 Bermondsey Street,
SE1 3XB (3287 3024,
www.hollyandlil.co.uk).
Pets
Honest Jon's p206
278 Portobello Road,
W10 5TE (8969 9822,
www.honestjons.com).
CDs & Records
Honeyjam p268
267 Portobello Road,
W11 1LR (7243 0449,
www.honeyjam.co.uk).
Babies & Children
Honour p113
86 Lower Marsh,
SE1 7AB (7401 8219,
www.honour.co.uk).
Lingerie, Swimwear
& Erotica
Hope & Greenwood p247
20 North Cross Road, SE22
9EU (8613 1777, www.
hopeandgreenwood.co.uk).
Food
Hope & Greenwood
1 Russell Street, WC2B
5JD (7240 3314). Branch
Hortus p184
26 Blackheath Village,
SE3 9SY (8297 9439,
www.hortus-london.com).
Gardens & Flowers
Hoss Intropia p91
213 Regent Street,
W1B 4NF (7287 3569,
www.hossintropia.com).
Designer Chains
Hoss Intropia
27A Sloane Square, SW1W
8AB (7259 9072). Branch
Hoss Intropia
124 Long Acre, WC2E 9PE
(7240 4900). Branch
House of Harlot p113
90 Hollway Road,
N7 8JG (7700 1441,

www.houseofharlot.com).
Lingerie, Swimwear
& Erotica
House of Weardowney p69
11 Porchester Place,
W2 2EU (7402 8892,
www.weardowney.com).
Indie Boutiques
howies p60
42 Carnaby Street,
W1F 7DY (7287 2345,
www.howies.com).
Indie Boutiques
Hoxton Boutique p70
2 Hoxton Street,
N1 6NG (7684 2083, www.
hotxtonboutique.co.uk).
Indie Boutiques
**HQ hair &
beautystore** p142
2 New Burlington Street,
W1S 2JE (0871 220
4141, wwwhqhair.com).
Health & Beauty
HR Higgins p260
79 Duke Street,
W1K 5AS (7629 3913,
www.hrhiggins.co.uk).
Drink
Hub p60
49 & 88 Stoke
Newington Church Street,
N16 0AR (7254 4494,
www.hubshop.co.uk).
Indie Boutiques
Hurwundeki p61
98 Commercial Street,
E1 6LZ (7734 1050,
www.hurwundeki.com).
Indie Boutiques
Hurwundeki
Kingly Street, W1B 5PW
(7734 1050). Branch

I

I Camisa & Son p252
61 Old Compton Street,
W1D 6HS (7437 7610).
Food
Igloo p263
300 Upper Street,
N1 2TU (7354 7300,
www.iglookids.co.uk).
Babies & Children
Igloo
80 St Johns Wood High

Street, NW8 7SH
(7483 2332). Branch
Igloo
227 Kings Road, SW3
5EJ (7352 4572).
Branch
I Knit London p220
106 Lower Marsh,
SE1 7AB (7261 1338,
www.iknit.org.uk).
Crafts, Hobbies & Parties
Imperious Rex! p61
75 Roman Road,
E2 0QN (8981 3392,
www.imperiousrex.com).
Indie Boutiques
International Magic p222
89 Clerkenwell Road,
EC1R 5BX (7405
7324, www.international
magic.com).
Crafts, Hobbies & Parties
Interstate p66
17 Endell Street,
WC2H 9BJ (7836 0421).
Indie Boutiques
Intoxica! p203
231 Portobello Road,
W11 1LT (7229 8010,
www.intoxica.co.uk).
CDs & Records
Iris p70
97 Northcore Road,
SW11 6PL (7924 1836,
www.irisfashion.co.uk).
Indie Boutiques
Iris
73 Salisbury Road,
NW6 6NJ (7372 1777).
Branch
Iris
129 Chiswick High Road,
W4 2ED (8742 3811).
Branch

J

JJ Fox p223
19 St James's Street,
SW1A 1ES (7930 3787,
www.jjfox.co.uk).
Crafts, Hobbies & Parties
J Reid & Sons p227
184 St Ann's Road,
N15 5RP (8800 6907,
www.jreidpianos.co.uk).
Musical Instruments

A-Z INDEX

JW Beeton p61
48-50 Ledbury Road, W11 2AJ (7229 8874).
Indie Boutiques

J&M Davidson p128
97 Golborne Road, W10 5NL (7313 9532, www.jandmdavidson).
Jewellery & Accessories

Jaeger p87
200-206 Regent Street, W1R 6BN (7979 1100, www.jaeger.co.uk).
Designer Chains

James Smith & Sons p128
53 New Oxford Street, WC1A 1BL (7836 4731, www.james-smith.co.uk).
Jewellery & Accessories

Jane Packer Flowers p185
32-34 New Cavendish Street, W1G 8UE (7935 2673, www.jane-packer.co.uk).
Gardens & Flowers

Japan Centre p252
14-16 Regent Street, SW1Y 4PH (7255 8255, www.japancentre.com).
Food

Jarndyce p197
46 Great Russell Street, WC1B 3PA (7631 4220, www.jarndyce.co.uk).
Books

Jas Musicals p230
14 Chiltern Street, W1U 7PY (7935 0793, www.jas-musicals.com).
Muscial Instruments

Jeffery-West p121
16 Piccadilly Arcade, SW1Y 6NH (7499 3360, www.jeffery-west.co.uk).
Shoes

Jeffery-West
16 Cullum Street, EC3M 7JJ (7626 4699). Branch

Jenny Packham p115
75 Elizabeth Street, SW1W 9PJ (7730 2264, www.jennypackham.com).
Weddings

Jenny Packham
3a Carlos Place, Mount Street, W1K 3AN (7493 6295). Branch

Jigsaw p79
21 Long Acre, WC2E 9LD (7240 3855, www.jigsaw-online.com). High Street

Joel & Son Fabrics p218
75-83 Church Street, NW8 8EU (7724 6895, www.joelandsonfabrics.com).
Crafts, Hobbies & Parties

John & Arthur Beare p229
30 Queen Anne Street, W1G 8HX (7307 9666, www.beares.com).
Musical Instruments

John Lewis p23
300 Oxford Street, W1A 1EX (7629 7711, www.johnlewis.co.uk).
Department Stores

John Lewis
Wood Street, Kingston upon Thames, Surrey KT1 1TE (8547 3000). Branch

John Lewis
Brent Cross Shopping Centre, NW4 3FL (8202 6535). Branch

John Lobb p126
9 St James's Street, SW1A 1EF (7930 3664, www.johnlobbltd.co.uk).
Shoes

John Sandoe p191
10 Blacklands Terrace, SW3 2SR (7589 9473, www.johnsandoe.com).
Books

John Smedley p87
24 Brook Street, W1K 5DG (7495 2222, www.johnsmedley.com).
Designer Chains

JoJo Maman Bébé p117
68 Northcote Road, SW11 6QL (7228 0322, www.jojomamanbebe.co.uk).
Maternity & Unusual Sizes

Judy Green's Garden Store p184
11 Flask Walk, NW3 1HJ (7435 3832).
Gardens & Flowers

K

KJ's Laundry p70
74 Marylebone Lane, W1U 2PW (7486 7855, www.kjslaundry.com).
Indie Boutiques

Kabiri p134
37 Marylebone High Street, W1U 4QE (7224 1808, www.kabiri.co.uk).
Jewellery & Accessories

Kabiri
18 The Market, The Piazza, WC2E 8RB (7240 1055).
Branch

Kate Kanzier p122
67-69 Leather Lane, EC1N 7TJ (7242 7232, www.katekanzier.com).
Shoes

Kazmattaz p127
39 Hoxton Square, N1 6NN (7739 4133, www.kazmattaz.com).
Shoes

Kensington Chimes Music (branch of Barbican Chimes Music Shop)
9 Harrington Road, SW7 3ES (7589 9054).
Branch

Kiehl's p141
29 Monmouth Street, WC2H 9DD (7240 2411, www.kiehls.com).
Health & Beauty

Kiehl's
20 Northcote Road, SW11 1NX (7350 2997).
Branch

Kiehl's
186a King's Road, SW3 5XP (7751 5950). Branch

Kiehl's
Units 14-15 Royal Exchange, EC3V 3LP (7283 6661). Branch

Kingly Court p29
Carnaby Street, opposite Broadwick Street, W1B 5PW (7333 8118, www.carnaby.co.uk).
Shopping Centres & Arcades

King's Aquatic & Reptile World p240
26 Camden High Street, NW1 0JH (7387 5553, www.kingsreptileworld.co.uk). Pets

Kingsley Photographic p213
93 Tottenham Court Road, W1T 4HL (7436 8700, www.kingsleyphoto.co.uk).
Electronics & Photography

Kirk Originals p155
29 Floral Street, WC2E 9DP (7240 5055, www.kirkoriginals.com).
Eyewear

Kirt Holmes p134
16 Camden Passage, N1 8ED (7226 1080, www.kirtholmes.com).
Jewellery & Accessories

Kleins p218
5 Noel Street, W1F 8GD (7437 6162, www.kleins.co.uk).
Crafts, Hobbies & Parties

Koenig Books p194
80 Charing Cross Road, WC2H 0BF (7240 8190, www.koenigbooks.co.uk).
Books

Koenig Books
Serpentine Gallery, Kensington Gardens, W2 3XA (7706 4907).
Branch

Koenig Books
Whitechapel Gallery Bookshop (managed by Koenig Books), 77-82 Whitechapel High Street, E1 7QX (7522 7897).
Branch

Kokon To Zai p63
86 Golborne Road, W10 5PS (8960 3736, www.kokontozai.co.uk).
Indie Boutiques

Kokon To Zai
57 Greek Street, W1D 3DX (7434 1316).
Branch

Konditor & Cook p243
22 Cornwall Road, SE1 8TW (7261 0456, www.konditorandcook.com).
Food

Kurt Geiger p122
198 Regent Street, W1B 5TP (3238 0044, www.kurtgeiger.com).
Shoes

L

L Cornelissen & Son p215
105 great Russell Street,
WC1B 3RY (7636 1045,
www.cornelissen.com).
Crafts, Hobbies & Parties

LCB Surf Store p237
121 Bethnal Green Road,
E2 7DG (7739 3839,
www.lcbsurfstore.com).
Sport & Fitness

LCB Surf Store
23 Chalk Farm Road,
NW1 8AG (7482 6089).
Branch

Le Labo p146
28A Devonshire Street,
W1G 6PS (3441 1535,
www.lelabofragrances.
com). Perfumeries
& Herbalists

Labour & Wait p168
18 Cheshire Street,
E2 6EH (7729 6253,
www.labourandwait.co.uk).
Furniture & Homewares

Labour of Love p73
193 Upper Street,
N1 1RQ (7354 9333,
www.labour-of-love.co.uk).
Indie Boutiques

**Lacquer Chest &
Lacquer Chest Too** p176
71 & 75 Kensington
Church Street, W8
4BG (7937 1306,
www.lacquerchest.com).
Vintage Furniture
& Homewares

Laden Showroom p73
103 Brick Lane,
E1 6SE 97247 2431,
www.laden.co.uk).
Indie Boutiques

Lara Bohinc p134
149F Sloane Steet,
SW1X 9BZ (7730 8194,
www.larabohinc107.co.uk).
Jewellery & Accessories

LASSco p176
Brunswick House,
30 Wandsworth Road,
SW8 2LG (7394 2100,
www.lassco.co.uk).
Vintage Furniture
& Homewares

Laura J p122
114 Islington High Street,
N1 8EG (7226 4005,
www.laurajlondon.com).
Shoes

Lea & Sandeman p256
170 Fulham Road, SW10
9PR (7244 0522, www.
londonfinewine.co.uk).
Drink

Lea & Sandeman
167 Chiswick High Road,
W4 2DR (8995 7355).
Branch

Lea & Sandeman
211 Kensington Church
Street, W8 7LX (7221
1982). Branch

Lea & Sandeman
51 High Street, SW13
9LN (8878 8643).
Branch

Leather Lane p48
Leather Lane, between
Greville Street & Clerkenwell
Road, EC4 (www.leather
lanemarket.co.uk).
Markets

Leila's p249
15-17 Calvert Avenue,
E2 7JP (7229 9789).
Food

Lemon Balm p151
151 Parkway, NW1
7AH (7267 3334, www.
lemonbalmonline.com).
Perfumeries & Herbalists

Lesley Craze Gallery p134
33-35A Clerkenwell
Green, EC1R 0DU
(7608 0393, www.
lesleycrazegallery.co.uk).
Jewellery & Accessories

Lewis Leathers p63
3-5 Whitfield Street,
W1T 2SA (7998 3385,
www.machine-a.com).
Indie Boutiques

Liberation p113
49 Shelton Street,
WC2H 9HE (7836 5894,
www.libidex.com).
Lingerie, Swimwear
& Erotica

Liberty p25
Regent Street, W1B
5AH (7734 1234,

www.liberty.co.uk).
Department Stores

Lifestyle Bazaar p163
11a Kingsland Road,
E2 8AA (7739 9427,
www.lifestylebazaar.com).
Furniture & Homewares

Limelight Movie Art p168
313 King's Road, SW3
5EP (7751 5584, www.
limelightmovieart.com).
Furniture & Homewares

Lina Stores p254
18 Brewer Street,
W1R 3FS (7437 6482).
Food

Lisboa p254
54 Golborne Road,
W10 5NR (8969 1586).
Food

**Lisboa Pâtisserie
(branch of Lisboa)**
6 World's End Place,
SW10 0HE (7376 3639).
Branch

Liz Earle Skincare p141
38-39 Duke of york
Square, King's Road,
SW3 4LY (7730 9191,
www.lizearle.com).
Health & Beauty

**Lomography Gallery
Store** p213
3 Newburgh Street,
W1F 7RE (7434 1466,
www.lomography.com).
Electronics & Photography

**London Graphic
Centre** p215
16-18 Shelton Street,
WC2H 9JL (7759 4500,
www.londongraphics.co.uk).
Crafts, Hobbies & Parties

London Graphic Centre
13 Tottenham Street,
W1T 2AH (7637 2199).
Branch

London Graphic Centre
86 Goswell Road, EC1V
7DB (7253 1000). Branch

**London Guitar Studio/
El Mundo Flamenco** p227
62 Duke Street, W1K 6JT
(7493 0033, www.london
guitarstudio.com, www.
elmundoflamenco.co.uk).
Musical Instruments

**London Review
Bookshop** p191
14 Bury Place,
WC1A 2JL (7269 9030,
www.lrbshop.co.uk). Books

Long Tall Sally p118
21-25 Chiltern Street,
W1U 7PH (7487 3370,
www.longtallsally.com).
Maternity & Unusual Sizes

Loop p220
15 Camden Passage,
N1 8EA (7288 1160,
www.loopknitting.com).
Crafts, Hobbies & Parties

Lost in Beauty p142
117 Regent's Park Road,
NW1 8UR (7586 4411,
www.lostinbeauty.com).
Health & Beauty

**Lost 'n' Found
Vinatge Clothing** p101
25 Stables Market,
Chalk Farm Road, NW1
8AH (7482 2848).
Vintage & Secondhand

Louis Vuitton Maison p88
17-20 New Bond Street,
W1S 2UE (7399 3856,
www.lousivuitton.com).
Designer Chains

Lower Marsh p48
Lower Marsh, from
Westminster Bridge Road
to Baylis Road, SE1
(7926 2530, www.lower-
marsh.co.uk). Markets

Lucas Bond p41
45 Bedford Hill,
SW12 9EY (8675 9300,
www.lucasbond.com).
Concept Stores & Lifestyle
Boutiques

Luella's Boudoir p115
33 Church Road,
SW19 5DQ (8879 7744,
www.luellasboudoir.co.uk).
Weddings

Lulu Guiness p128
3 Ellis Street,
SW1X 9AL (7823 4828,
www.luluguiness.com).
Jewellery & Accessories

Luna & Curious p41
198 Brick Lane, E1 6SA
(7033 4411, www.luna
andcurious.com).

Concept Stores &
Lifestyle Boutiques

M

**MDC Music
& Movies** p205
Unit 3, Level 1, Festival
Riverside, Royal Festival
Hall, South Bank, SE1 8XX
(7620 0198, www.mdc
musicandmovies.co.uk).
CDs & Records

**MW Classic
Cameras** p213
Unit 3K, Leroy House,
436 Essex Road,
N1 3QP (7354 3767,
www.mwclassic.com).
Electronics & Photography

**MacCulloch
& Wallis** p218
25-26 Dering Street,
W1S 1AT (7629 0311,
www.macculloch-
wallis.co.uk). Crafts,
Hobbies & Parties

Magma p194
117-119 Clerkenwell
Road, EC1R 5BY
(7242 9503, www.
magmabooks.com).
Books

Magma
8 Earlham Street, WC2H
9RY (7240 8498). Branch

Magma Product Store
16 Earlhan Street, WC2H
9LN (7240 7571). Branch

La Maison p176
107-108 Shoreditch
High Street, E1 6JN
(7729 9646, www.
lamaisonlondon.com).
Vintage Furniture
& Homewares

La Maison des Roses p186
48 Webbs Road, SW11
6SF (7228 5700, www.
maison-des-roses.com).
Gardens & Flowers

Mallon & Taub p155
35D Marylebone High
Street, W1U 4QB
(7935 8200, www.
mallonandtaub.com).
Eyewear

Manolo Blahnik p123
49-51 Old Church Street,
SW3 5BS (7352 3863,
www.manoloblahnik.com).
Shoes

Maplin p208
166-168 Queensway,
W2 6LY (7229 9301,
www.maplin.co.uk).
Electronics & Photography

Marc by Marc Jacobs p88
56 South Audley Street,
W1K 2RR (7408 7050,
www.marcjacobs.com).
Designer Chains

**Marc Jacobs (branch of
Marc by Marc Jacobs)**
24-25 Mount Street,
W1K 2RR (7399 1690).
Branch

Marchpane p197
16 Cecil Court,
WC2N 4HE (7836 8661,
www.marchpane.com).
Books

Margaret Howell p88
34 Wigmore Street,
W1U 2RS (7009 9009,
www.margarethowell.co.uk).
Designer Chains

Margaret Howell
111 Fulham Road, SW3
6RL (7591 2255). Branch

Margaret Howell
1 The Green, Richmond,
TW9 1LZ (8948 5005).
Branch

Markson Pianos p227
8 Chester Court,
Albany Street, NW1
4BU (7935 8682,
www.marksonpianos.com).
Musical Instruments

Matches p63
60-64 Ledbury Road,
W11 2AJ (7221 0255,
www.matchesfashion.com).
Indie Boutiques

**Matches Spy
(branch of Matches)**
85 Ledbury Road, W11
2AJ (7221 7334). Branch

McQueens p186
70-72 Old Street,
EC1V 9AN (7251 5505,
www.mcqueens.co.uk).
Gardens & Flowers

Melrose & Morgan p249
42 Gloucester Avenue,
NW1 8JD (7722 0011,
www.melroseandmorgan.
com). Food

**Merchant Archive
Boutique** p101
320 Kilburn Lane, W9
3EF (8969 6470, www.
merchantarchive.com).
Vintage & Secondhand

Michel Guillon p155
35 Duke of York Square,
SW3 4LY (7730 2142,
www.michelguillon.com).
Eyewear

Micro Anvika p208
6-17 Tottenham Court
Road, W1T 6BH
(7467 6090, www.
microanvika.com).
Electronics & Photography

Micro Anvika
53-54 Tottenham Court
Road, W1T 2EJ (7467
2030). Branch

Micro Anvika
245 Tottenham Court
Road, W1T 7QT (7467
6080). Branch

Micro Anvika
13 Chenies Street, WC1E
7EY (7467 7085). Branch

**Microworld (branch
of Westend DJ)**
256 Tottenham Court
Road, W1T 7RD (7631
1935). Branch

Miller Harris p146
21 Bruton Street,
W1J 6QD (7629 7750,
www.millerharris.com).
Perfumeries & Herbalists

Milroy's of Soho p259
3 Greek Street,
W1D 4NX (7437 9311,
www.milroys.co.uk). Drink

Mimi p131
40 Cheshire Street, E2
6EH (7729 6699,
www.mimiberry.com).
Jewellery & Accessories

Mint p163
2 North Terrace,
SW3 2BA (7225 2228,
www.mintshop.co.uk).
Furniture & Homewares

**Monmouth Coffee
House** p260
27 Monmouth Street,
WC2H 9EU (7379 3516,
www.monmouthcoffee.
co.uk). Drink

Monmouth Coffee House
2 Park Street, SE1 9AB
(7940 9960). Branch

Morgan-Davies p116
62 Cross Street,
N1 2BA (7354 3414,
www.morgananddavies
london.co.uk). Weddings

Mosquito Bikes p224
123 Essex Road,
N1 2SN (7226 8765,
www.mosquito-bikes.co.uk).
Sport & Fitness

**Mount Street Printers
& Stationers** p223
4 Mount Street,
W1k 3LW (7409 0303,
www.mountstreetprinters.
com). Crafts, Hobbies
& Parties

Mr Start (branch of Start)
40 Rivington Street EC2A
3LX (7729 6272). Branch

Muji p41
37-78 Long Acre,
WC2E 9JT (7379
0820, www.muji.co.uk).
Concept Stores
& Lifestyle Boutiques

Mulberry p89
41-42 New Bond Street,
W1S 2RY (7491 3900,
www.mulberry.com).
Designer Chains

Mungo & Maud p240
79 Elizabeth Street,
SW1W 9PJ (7467 0820,
www.mungoandmaud.com).
Pets

Mutz Nutz p240
221 Westbourne Park
Road, W11 1EA (7243
3333, www.themutznutz.
com). Pets

Myla p108
74 Duke of York
Square, King's Road,
SW3 4LY (7730 0700,
www.myla.com).
Lingerie, Swimwear
& Erotica

N

Natural Mat Company p264
99 Talbot Road, W11 2AP (7985 0474, www.naturalmat.co.uk). Babies & Children

Neal's Yard Dairy p246
17 Shorts Gardens, WC2H 9UP (7240 5700, www.nealsyarddairy.co.uk). Food

Neal's Yard Dairy
6 Park Street, SE1 9AB (7367 0799). Branch

Neal's Yard Remedies p141
15 Neal's Yard, WC2H 9DP (7379 7222, www.nealsyardremedies.com). Health & Beauty

Nelsons p151
73 Duke Street, W1K 5BY (7629 3118, www.nelsonspharmacy.com). Perfumeries & Herbalists

Nicholas Camera Company p213
15 Camden High Street, NW1 7JE (7916 7251, www.nicholascamera.com). Electronics & Photography

Nigel Hall p91
18 Floral Street, WC2H 9DS (7379 3600, www.nigelhallmenswear.co.uk). Designer Chains

Nigel Hall
15 Floral Street, WC2E 9DH (7836 7922). Branch

Nigel Hall
106A Upper Street, N1 1QN (7704 3173). Branch

Nigel Hall
75-77 Brushfield Street, E1 6AA (7377 0317). Branch

Nigel Hall
42-44 Broadwick Street, W1F 7AE (7494 1999). Branch

Nigel Williams p197
25 Cecil Court, WC2N 4EZ (7836 7757, www.nigelwilliams.com). Books

Nike Town p237
236 Oxford Street, W1W 8LG (7612 0800, www.nike.com). Sports & Fitness

9 London by Emily Evans p118
8 Hollywood Road, SW10 9HY (7352 7600, www.emilyevansboutique.com). Maternity & Unusual Sizes

1948 p127
Arches 477-478 Bateman's Row, EC2A 3HH (7729 7688, www.nike.com). Shoes

no-one p63
1 Kingsland Road, E2 8AA (7613 5314, www.no-one.co.uk). Indie Boutiques

Northcote Road Market p51
Northcote Road, SW11. Markets

O

Oasis p79
12-14 Argyll Street, W1F 7NT 97434 1799, www.oasis-stores.com). High Street

Odabash p109
48B Ledbury Road, W11 2AJ (7229 4299, www.odabash.com). Lingerie, Swimwear & Erotica

Oh Baby London p266
162 Brick Lane, E1 6RU (7247 4949, www.ohbabylondon.com). Babies & Children

Old Curiosity Shop p123
13-14 Portsmouth Street, WC2A 2ES (7405 9891, www.curiosityuk.com). Shoes

Old Hat p101
66 Fulham High Street, SW6 3LQ (7610 6558). Vintage & Secondhand

Olga Stores p254
30 Penton Street, N1 9PS (7837 5467). Food

Olive Loves Alfie p266
84 Stoke Newington Church Street, N16 0AP (7241 4212, www.olivelovesalfie.co.uk). Babies & Children

Oliver Bonas p42
137 Northcote Road, SW11 6PX (7223 5223, www.oliverbonas.com). Concept Stores & Lifestyle Boutiques

Oliver Sweeney p123
5 Conduit Street, W1S 2XD (7491 9126, www.oliversweeney.com). Shoes

Oliver Sweeney
133 Middlesex Street, E1 7JF (7626 4466). Branch

One of a Kind p103
259 Portobello Road, W11 1LR (7792 5853, www.1kind.com). Vintage & Secondhand

One Small Step One Giant Leap p266
3 Blenheim Crescent, W11 2EE (7243 0535, www.onesmallsteponegiantleap.com). Babies & Children

123 Boutique p42
123 Bethnal Green Road, E2 7DG (www.123bethnalgreenroad.co.uk). Concept Stores & Lifestyle Boutiques

On the Beat p203
22 Hanway Street, W1T 1UQ (7637 8934). CDs & Records

Opera Opera p156
98 Long Acre, WC2E 9NR (7836 9246, www.operaopera.net). Eyewear

The Other Side of the Pillow p127
61 Wilton Way, E8 1BQ (07988 870508). Shoes

Oranges & Lemons p210
61-63 Webb's Road, SW11 6RX (7924 2040, www.oandlhifi.co.uk). Electronics & Photography

Origin Modernism p182
25 Camen Passage, N1 8EA (7704 1326, www.originmodernism.co.uk). Vintage Furniture & Homewares

Orla Kiely p92
31-33 Monmouth Street, WC2H 9DD (7240 4022, www.orlakiely.com). Designer Chains

Ormonde Jayne p146
12 The Royal Arcade, 28 Old Bond Street, W1S 4SL (7499 1100, www.ormondejayne.com). Perfumeries & Herbalists

Ortigia p141
55 Sloane Square, SW1W 8AX (7730 2826, www.ortigia-srl.com). Health & Beauty

Ortigia
23 Marylebone High Street, W1U 4PF (7487 4684). Branch

Out on the Floor p203
10 Inverness Street, NW1 7HJ (7485 9958). CDs & Records

Owl Bookshop p191
209 Kentish Town Road, NW5 2JU (7485 7793). Books

P

Pak's p142
25-27 & 31 Stroud Green Road, N4 3ES (7263 2088, www.pakscosmetics.com). Health & Beauty

Palette London p103
21 Canonbury Lane, N1 2AS (7288 7428, www.palette-london.com). Vintage & Secondhand

Paperchase p223
213-215 Tottenham Court Road, W1T 7PS (7467 6200, www.paperchase.co.uk). Crafts, Hobbies & Parties

Party Party p222
9-13 Ridley Road,

E8 2NP (7254 5168).
Crafts, Hobbies & Parties
Party Party
206 Kilburn High Road,
NW6 4JH (7624 4295).
Branch
Paul & Joe p92
134 Sloane Street,
SW1X 9AX (7243 5510,
ww.paulandjoe.com).
Designer Chains
Paul & Joe Homme
33 Floral Street, WC2
E9DJ (7836 3388).
Branch
**Paul A Young Fine
Chocolates** p247
33 Camden Passage,
N1 8EA (7424 5750,
www.payoung.net).
Food
**Paul A Young
Fine Chocolates**
20 Royal Exchange,
EC3V 3LP (7929 7007).
Branch
Paul Smith p89
Westbourne House,
120 & 122 Kensington
Park Road, W11 2EP
(7727 3553, www.
paulsmith.co.uk).
Designer Chains
Paxton & Whitfield p246
93 Jermyn Street,
SW1Y 6JE (7930 0259,
www.paxtonandwhitfield.
co.uk). Food
Peanut Vendor p182
133 Newington Green
Road, N1 4RA 97226
5727, www.thepeanut
vendor.co.uk). Vintage
Furniture & Homewares
Persephone Books p195
59 Lamb's Conduit
Street, WC1N 3NB (7242
9292, www.persephone
books.co.uk). Books
Persepolis p255
28-30 Peckham High
Street, SE15 5DT
(7639 8007). Food
**Peter Jones (branch
of John Lewis)**
Sloane Square, SW1W 8EL
(7730 3434). Branch

Petersham Nurseries p183
Church Lane, off
Petersham Road,
Petersham, Richmond,
Surrey TW10 7AG (8940
5230, www.petersham
nurseries.com).
Gardens & Flowers
Pistol Panties p109
75 Westbourne Park Road,
W2 5QH (7229 5286,
www.pistolpanties.com).
Lingerie, Swimwear
& Erotica
**Petit Aimé (branch
of Aimé)**
34 Ledbury Road, W11
2AB (7221 3123). Branch
**Petticoat Lane
Market** p48
Middlesex Street, Goulston
Street, New Goulston
Street, Toynbee Street,
Wentworth Street, Bell
Lane, Cobb Street, Leyden
Street, Strype Street, E1
(7364 1717). Markets
Philip Treacy p131
69 Elizabeth Street,
SW1W 9PJ (7730 3992,
www.philiptreacy.co.uk).
Jewellery & Accessories
Phonica p206
51 Poland Street, W1F
7LZ (7025 6070, www.
phonicarecords.co.uk).
CDs & Records
Plain English p172
41 Hoxton Square, N1
6PB (7613 0022, www.
plainenglishdesign.co.uk).
Furniture & Homewares
Planet Bazaar p182
Arch 86, The Stables
Market, Chalk Farm Road,
NW1 8AH (7485 6000,
www.theplanetbazaar.
co.uk). Vintage Furniture
& Homewares
Playin' Games p221
33 Museum Street,
WC1A 1JR (7287 3080).
Crafts, Hobbies & Parties
Playlounge p221
19 Beak Street,
W1F 9RP (7287 7073,
www.playlounge.co.uk).

Crafts, Hobbies & Parties
Poilâne p244
46 Elizabeth Street,
SW1W 9PA (7808 4910,
www.poilane.fr). Food
**Portobello Road
Market** p46
Portobello Road, W10
& W11 (www.portobello
road.co.uk). Markets
Postcard Teas p260
9 Dering Street,
W1S 1AG (7629 3654,
www.postcardteas.com).
Drink
Poste Mistress p125
61-63 Monmouth street,
WC2H 9EP (7379 4040,
www.office.co.uk/poste
mistress). Shoes
Potassium p42
2 Seymour Place, W1H
7NA (7723 7800, www.
potassiumstore.co.uk).
Concept Stores
& Lifestyle Boutiques
Preen p63
5 Portobello Green,
281 Portobello Road,
W10 5TZ (8968 1542,
www.preen.eu).
Indie Boutiques
**Preposterous
Presents** p222
262 Upper Street, N1
2UQ (7226 4166, www.
preposterouspresents.
co.uk). Crafts, Hobbies
& Parties
Press p74
3 Erskine Road, NW3
3AJ (7449 0081, www.
pressprimrosehill.com).
Indie Boutiques
Prestat p247
14 Princes Arcade,
SW1Y 6DS (7629 4838,
www.prestat.co.uk).
Food
Prick Your Finger p221
260 Globe Road,
E2 0JD (8981 2560,
www.prickyourfinger.com).
Crafts, Hobbies & Parties
Primark p80
499-517 Oxford Street,
W1K 7DA (7495 0420,

www.primark.co.uk).
High Street
Primrose Hill Pets p240
132 Regent's Park Road,
NW1 8XL (7483 2023,
www.primrosehillpets.
co.uk). Pets
Puppet Planet p268
787 Wandsworth Road
(corner of the Chase),
SW8 3JQ (7627 0111,
mobile 07900 975276,
www.puppetplanet.co.uk).
Babies & Children
**Pure Groove
Records** p206
6-7 West Smithfield,
EC1A 9JX (7778 9278,
www.puregroove.co.uk).
CDs & Records

Q

**Quinto/
Francis Edwards** p198
72 Charing Cross Road,
WC2H 0BE (7379 7669).
Books

R

R García & Sons p255
248-250 Portobello Road,
W11 1LL (7221 6119).
Food
Ray Man p230
54 Chalk Farm Road,
NW1 8AN 97692 6261,
www.raymaneastern
music.co.uk).
Musical Instruments
Real Ale Shop p259
371 Richmond Road,
Twickenham, Middx
TW1 2EF (8892 3710,
www.realale.com).
Drink
Reiss p80
Kent House, 14-17 Market
Place, W1H 7AJ (7637
91121, www.reiss.co.uk).
High Street
Relax Garden p74
40 Kingsland Road,
E2 8DA (7033 1881,
www.relaxgarden.com).
Indie Boutiques

A-Z Index

Relax Garden
Unit 18, Portobello Green Arcade, WT 5TZ (8968 0496). Branch
Rellik p104
8 Golborne Road, W10 5NW (8962 0089, www.relliklondon.co.uk). Vintage & Secondhand
Revival Records p203
30 Berwick Street, W1F 8RH (7437 4271, www.revivalrecords.uk.com). CDs & Records
Ridley Road Market p51
Ridley Road, off Kingsland High Street, E8 (www.ridleyroad.co.uk). Markets
Rigby & Peller p109
22A Conduit Street, W1S 2XT (7491 2200, www.rigbyandpeller.com). Lingerie, Swimwear & Erotica
Roberson p256
348 Kensington High Street, W14 8NS (7371 2121, www.robersonwinemerchant.co.uk). Drink
Rococo p248
5 Motcomb Street, SW1X 8JU (7245 0993, www.rococochocolates.com). Food
Rococo
321 King's Road, SW3 5EP (7352 5857). Branch
Rococo
45 Marylebone High Street, W1U 5HG (7935 7780). Branch
Rokit p104
42 Shelton Street, WC2 9HZ (7836 6547, www.rokit.co.uk). Vintage & Secondhand
Rokit
101 Brick Lane, E1 6SE (7375 3864). Branch
Rokit
107 Brick Lane, E1 6SE (7247 3777). Branch
Rokit
225 High Street, NW1 7BU (7267 3046). Branch

Rough Trade East p201
Dray Walk, Old Truman Brewery, 91 Brick Lane, E1 6QL (7392 7788, www.roughtrade.com). CDs & Records
Rough Trade West
130 Talbot Road, W11 1JA (7229 8541). Branch
Rub a Dub Dub p265
15 Park Road, N8 8TE (8342 9898). Babies & Children
Rug Company p168
124 Holland Park Avenue, W11 4UE (7229 5148, www.therugcompany.info). Furniture & Homewares
Run & Become p238
42 Palmer Street, SW1W 0PH (7222 1314, www.runandbecome.com). Sport & Fitness
Ryantown p171
126 Columbia Road, E2 7RG (7613 1510, www.misterrob.co.uk). Furniture & Homewares

S

SCP p164
135-139 Curtain Road, EC2A 3BX (7739 1869, www.scp.co.uk). Furniture & Homewares
SCP
87-93 Westbourne Grove, W2 4UL (7229 3612). Branch
The Sampler p256
266 Upper Street, N1 2UQ (7226 9500, www.thesampler.co.uk). Drink
Sandys p245
56 King Street, Twickenham, Middx W1 3SH (8892 5788, www.sandysfish.net). Food
Sargent & Co p234
74 Mountgrave Road, N5 2LT (7359 7642, www.sargentandco.com). Sport & Fitness

Sasti p267
8 Portobello Green Arcade, 281 Portobello Road, W10 5TZ (8960 1125, www.sasti.co.uk). Babies & Children
Scarlet & Violet p186
76 Chamberlayne Road, NW10 3JJ (8969 9446, www.scarletandviolet.com). Gardens & Flowers
Screenface p142
48 Monmouth Street, WC2H 9EP (7836 3955, www.screenface.com). Health & Beauty
Screenface
20 Powis Terrace, Westbourne Park Road, W11 1JH (7221 8289). Branch
Sefton p65
271 Upper Street, N1 2UQ (7226 9822, www.seftonfashion.com). Indie Boutiques
Sefton (menswear)
196 Upper Street, N1 1RQ (7226 7076). Branch
Selfridges p27
400 Oxford Street, W1A 1AB (0800 123 400, www.selfridges.com). Department Stores
Les Senteurs p148
71 Elizabeth Street, SW1 9PJ (7730 2322, www.lessenteurs.com). Perfumeries & Herbalists
Sh! p114
57 Hoxton Square, N1 6PD (7613 5458, www.sh-womenstore.com). Lingerie, Swimwear & Erotica
Shelf p45
40 Cheshire Street, E2 6EH (7739 9444, www.helpyourshelf.co.uk). Concept Stores & Lifestyle Boutiques
Shepherds Bookbinders p215
76 Southeampton Row, WC1B 4AR (7831 1151, www.bookbinding.co.uk). Crafts, Hobbies & Parties

Shepherds Bookbinders
76 Rochester Row (The Bindery), SW1P 1JU (7233 6766). Branch
Shepherds Bookbinders
46 Curzon Street, W1J 7UH (7495 8580). Branch
Shepherd's Bush Market p52
East side of railway viaduct, between Uxbridge Road & Goldhawk Road, W12 (8749 3042, www.shepherdsbushmarket.co.uk). Markets
Shop at Bluebird p45
350 King's Road, SW3 5UU (7351 3873, www.theshopatbluebird.com). Concept Stores & Lifestyle Boutiques
Showgirls p114
64 Holloway Road, N7 8JL (7697 9072, www.showgirlslatex boutique.com). Lingerie, Swimwear & Erotica
Simon Finch Rare Books p198
26 Brook Street, W1K 5DQ (7499 0974, www.simonfinch.com). Books
Sister Ray p201
34-35 Berwick Street, W1F 8RP (7734 3297, www.sisterray.co.uk). CDs & Records
Sixty6 p74
4 Blenheim Terrace, NW8 0EB (7372 6100). Branch
Size? p127
37A Neal Street, WC2H 9PR (7836 1404, www.size.co.uk). Shoes
Size?
33-34 Carnaby Street, W1V 1PA (7287 4016). Branch
Size?
200 Portobello Road, W11 1LB (7792 8494). Branch

A-Z INDEX

Skandium p164
247 Brompton Road,
SW3 2EP (7584 2066,
www.skandium.com).
Furniture & Homewares
Skandium
86 Marylebone High Street,
W1U 4Q (7935 2077).
Branch
Skoob p198
Unit 66, The Brunswick,
WC1N 1AE (7278 8760,
www.skoob.com).
Books
Slam City Skates p238
16 Neal's Yard,
WC2H 9DP (7240 0928,
www.slamcity.com).
Sport & Fitness
Slam City Skates
43 Carnaby Street,
W1F 7EA (7287 9548).
Branch
Smug p45
13 Camden Passage,
N1 8EA (7354 0253,
www.ifeelsmug.com).
Concept Stores &
Lifestyle Boutiques
Soccer Scene p238
56-57 Carnaby Street,
W1F 9QF (7439 0778,
www.soccerscene.co.uk).
Sport & Fitness
Soccer Scene
156 Oxford Street,
W1D 1ND (7436 6499).
Branch
Something… p45
58 Lamb's Conduit
Street, WC1N 3LW
(7430 1516, www.
something-shop.com).
Concept Stores
& Lifestyle Boutiques
**Sounds of the
Universe** p207
7 Broadwick Street,
W1F 0DA (7734 3430,
www.soundsoftheuniverse.
com). CDs & Records
Soup Dragon p263
27 Topsfield Parade,
Tottenham Lane, N8
8PT (8348 0224, www.
soup-dragon.co.uk).
Babies & Children

Soup Dragon
106 Lordship Lane,
SE22 8HF (8693 5575).
Branch
Southall Market p51
The Cattle Market, High
Street, opposite North
Road, Southall, Middx
UB1 3DG. Markets
Space EC1 p45
25 Exmouth Market,
EC1R 4QL (7837 1344).
Concept Stores &
Lifestyle Boutiques
Space NK p144
8-10 Broadwick Street,
W1F 8HW (7287 2667,
www.spacenk.com).
Health & Beauty
Spex in the City p156
1 Shorts Gardens,
WC2H 9AT (7240 0243,
www.spexinthecity.com).
Eyewear
Spitalfields Market p46
Commercial Street,
between Lamb Street
& Brushfield Street,
E1 (7247 8556, www.
visitspitalfields.com).
Markets
Squint p164
178 Shoreditch High
Street, E1 6HU (7739
9275, www.squint
limited.com).
Furniture & Homewares
Stanfords p195
12-14 Long Acre,
WC2E 9LP (7836 1321,
www.stanfords.co.uk).
Books
Start p65
42-44 Great Rivington
Street, EC2A 3BN
(7729 3334, www.
start-london.com).
Indie Boutiques
Start (menswear)
59 Rivington Street,
EC2A 3QQ (7739 3636).
Branch
Stella McCartney p93
30 Bruton Street,
W1J 6QR (7518 3100,
www.stellamccartney.com).
Designer Chains

Steve Hatt p245
88-90 Essex Road, N1
8LU (7226 3693). Food
SuitSupply p97
9 Vigo Street,
W1S 3HH (7851 2961,
www.suitsupply.com).
Tailoring & Bespoke
Sunday (Up)Market p49
91 Brick Lane, Old Truman
Brewery (entrances on
Brick Lane & Hanbury
Street), E1 6QL (7770
6028, www.sunday
upmarket.co.uk).
Markets

T

T Fox & Co p131
118 London Wall,
EC2Y 5JA (7628
1868, www.tfox.co.uk).
Jewellery & Accessories
TW Howarth p229
31-35 Chiltern Street,
W1U 7PN (7935 2407,
www.howarth.uk.com).
Musical Instruments
Tatty Devine p136
236 Brick Lane,
E2 7EB (7739 9191,
www.tattydevine.com).
Jewellery & Accessories
Tatty Devine
44 Monmouth Street,
WC2H 9EP (7836 2685).
Branch
Teamwork p213
41-42 Foley Street,
W1W 7JN (7323 6455,
www.teamworkphoto.com).
Electronics & Photography
**Temperley London
Bridal Room** p116
6-10 Colville Mews,
Lonsdale Road, W11
2DA (7229 7857, www.
temperleylondon.com).
Weddings
Terra Plana p125
64 Neal Street,
WC2H 9PQ (7379 5959,
www.terraplana.com).
Shoes
Terra Plana
124 Bermondsey Street,

SE1 3TX (7407 3758).
Branch
Terra Plana
32 Brushfield Street, E1
6AT (7426 2158). Branch
Terra Plana
155 Kensington High
Street, W8 6SU (7937
9405). Branch
Their Nibs p267
214 Kensington Park
Road, W11 1NR (7221
4263, www.theirnibs.com).
Babies & Children
Their Nibs
79 Chamberlayne Road,
NW10 3ND (8964 8444).
Branch
Themes & Variations p182
231 Westbourne Grove,
W11 2SE (7727 5531),
www.themesandvariations.
com). Vintage Furniture
& Homewares
36 Opticians p156
36 Beauchamp Place,
SW3 1NU (7581 6336,
www.36opticians.co.uk).
Eyewear
Three Threads p65
47-49 Charlotte Street,
EC2A 3QT (7749 0503,
www.thethreethreads.
com). Indie Boutiques
Tobias & the Angel p164
68 White Hart Lane,
SW13 0PZ (8878
8902, www.tobias
andtheangel.com).
Furniture & Homewares
Tokyo Fixed p234
4 Peter Street,
W1F 0AD (7734 1885,
www.tokyofixedgear.com).
Sport & Fitness
Topman p80
214 Oxford Street,
W1W 8LG (0844 848
7487, www.topman.com).
High Street
Topshop p81
214 Oxford Street,
W1W 8LG (0844 848
7487, www.topshop.com).
High Street
Tracey Neuls p126
29 Marylebone Lane,

A-Z Index

W1U 2NQ (7935 0039, www.tn29.com). Shoes
Travel Bookshop p195
13-15 Blenheim Crescent, W11 2EE (7229 5260, www.thetravelbookshop.com). Books
Travis & Emery p198
17 Cecil Court, WC2N 4EZ (7240 2129, www.travis-and-emery.com). Books
Treacle p171
110-112 Columbia Road, E2 7RG (7729 0538, www.treacleworld.com). Furniture & Homewares
Trotters p263
34 King's Road, SW3 4UD (7259 9620, www.trotters.co.uk). Babies & Children
Trotters
127 Kensington High Street, W8 5SF (7937 9373). Branch
Trotters
86 Northcote Road, SW11 6QN (7585 0572). Branch
Trotters
84 Turnham Green Terrace, W4 1QN (8742 1195). Branch
Turkish Food Centre p255
89 Ridley Road, E8 2NH (7254 6754, www.tfcsupermerkets.com). Food
Twentytwentyone p164
274 Upper Street, N1 2UA (7288 1996, www.twentytwentyone.com). Furniture & Homewares
Twentytwentyone
18C River Street, EC1R 1XN (7837 1900). Branch
Two Columbia Road p182
2 Columbia Road, E2 7NN (7729 9933, www.twocolumbiaroad.com). Vintage Furniture & Homewares

U

Umbrella Music p225
Unit 6, Eastgate Business Park, 10 Argall Way, E10 7PG (0845 500 2323, www.umbrellamusic.co.uk). Musical Instruments
Uniqlo p83
311 Oxford Street, W1C 2HP 97290 7701, www.uniqlo.com). High Street
Unpackaged p250
42 Amwell Street, EC1R 1XT (7713 8368, www.beunpackaged.com). Food
Unto This Last p167
230 Brick Lane, E2 7EB (7613 0882, www.untothislast.co.uk). Furniture & Homewares
Unto This Last
Arch 72, Queens Circus, SW8 4NE (7720 6558). Branch
Urban Outfitters p83
200 Oxford Street, W1D 1NU (7907 0815, www.urbanoutfitters.co.uk). High Street
Urban Outfitters
42-56 Earlham Street, WC2H 9LJ (7759 6390). Branch
Urban Outfitters
36-38 Kensington High Street, W8 4PF (7761 1001). Branch

V

VV Rouleaux p220
102 Marylebone Lane, W1U 2QD (7224 5179, www.vvrouleaux.com). Crafts, Hobbies & Parties
VV Rouleaux
54 Sloane Square, WS1W 8AX (7730 3125). Branch
Victoria Park Books p268
174 Victoria Park Road, E9 7HD (8986 1124, www.victoriaparkbooks.co.uk). Babies & Children
Vinyl Junkies p207
94 Berwick Street, W1F 0QF (7439 2923, www.vinyl-junkies.com). CDs & Records
Vivienne Westwood p91
44 Conduit Street, W1S 2YL (7439 1109, www.viviennewestwood.com). Designer Chains
Vivienne Westwood
6 Davies Street, W1Y 1LJ (7629 3757). Branch

W

W Sitch & Co p171
48 Berwick Street, W1F 8JD (7437 3776, www.wsitch.co.uk). Furniture & Homewares
Walthamstow Market p51
Walthamstow High Street, E17 (8496 3000). Markets
Water Monopoly p172
16-18 Lonsdale Road, NW6 6RD (7624 2636, www.watermonopoly.com). Furniture & Homewares
Wawa p167
3 Ezra Street, E2 7RH (7729 6768, www.wawa.co.uk). Furniture & Homewares
Westend DJ p227
10-12 Hanway Street, W1T 1UB (7637 3293, www.westenddj.com). Musical Instruments
Westfield London p29
Westfield London, W12 7SL (3371 2300, www.westfield.com/london). Shopping Centres & Arcades
What Katie Did p109
26 Portobello Green, 281 Portobello Road, W10 5TZ (0845 430 8943, www.whatkatiedid.com). Lingerie, Swimwear & Erotica
Whitecross Street Food Market p48
Whitecross Weekly Food Market, Whitecross Street, EC1 (7378 0422, www.whitecrossstreet.co.uk). Markets
Whistles p83
12 St Christopher's Place, W1U 1NH (7487 4484, www.whistles.co.uk). High Street
Whiteleys p34
151 Queenswater, W2 4YN (7229 8844, www.whiteleys.com). Shopping Centres & Arcades
Wholesome p66
47 Rivington Street, EC2A 3QB (7729 2899, www.wholesomelondon.com). Indie Boutiques
Wigmore Sports p237
39 Wigmore Street, W1U 1QQ (7486 7761, www.wigmoresports.com). Sport & Fitness
Wild at Heart p186
Turquoise Island, 222 Westbourne Grove, W11 2RH (7727 3095, www.wildatheart.com). Gardens & Flowers
Wild at Heart
54 Pimlico Road, SW1W 8LP (3145 0441). Branch
Wild Guitars p227
393 Archway Road, N6 4ER (8340 7766, www.wildguitars.com). Musical Instruments
World's End (branch of Vivienne Westwood)
430 Kings Road, SW10 0JL (7352 6551). Branch
Wright & Teague p136
35 Dover Street, W1S 4NQ (7629 2777, www.wrightandteague.com). Jewellery & Accessories

Y

YMC p65
11 Poland Street, W1F 8QA (7494 1619, www.youmustcreate.com). Indie Boutiques
York Cameras p213
18 Bury Place, WC1A 2JL (7242 7182, www.yorkcameras.co.uk). Electronics & Photography

GREEN HANDBAG,
BOUGHT WHEN I DIDN'T
GET THAT PROMOTION
BECAUSE APPARENTLY
I WASN'T
"CREATIVE ENOUGH."

"WELL,"
I TOLD MYSELF,
"THIS'LL SHOW THEM HOW
OUTSIDE
THE BOX I CAN BE.

THEY'LL SEE A NEW
ALICE BENNETT-GRANT
COME MONDAY."

AND ANYWAY,
EVERYONE'S BANGING
ON ABOUT
HOW WE SHOULD
ALL GO GREENER:
£230

* * * * * * * * * * * * * * * *

KEEPING THE RECEIPT:
PRICELESS®

MasterCard

There are some things money can't buy.
For everything else there's MasterCard.

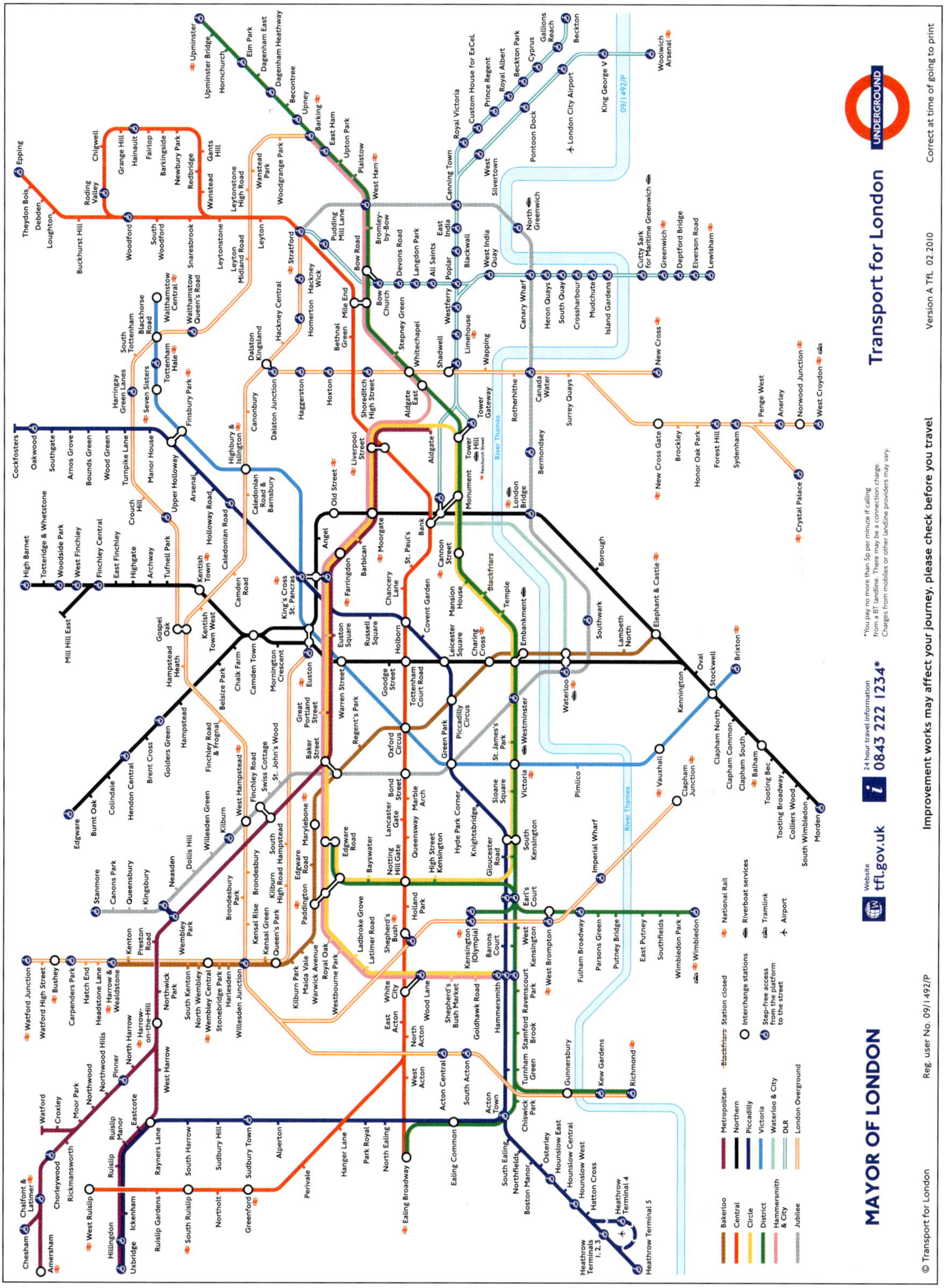

MAYOR OF LONDON
Transport for London
UNDERGROUND
Bakerloo
Central
Circle
District
Hammersmith & City
Jubilee
Metropolitan
Northern
Piccadilly
Victoria
Waterloo & City
DLR
London Overground
Blackfriars Station closed
Interchange stations
Step-free access from the platform to the street
National Rail
Riverboat services
Tramlink
Airport
Website tfl.gov.uk
24 hour travel information 0843 222 1234*
*You pay no more than 5p per minute if calling from a BT landline. There may be a connection charge. Charges from mobiles or other landline providers may vary.
Improvement works may affect your journey, please check before you travel
Version A TfL 02.2010
Correct at time of going to print
Reg. user No. 09/1492/P
© Transport for London
River Thames

Central London
Regent's Park
London Zoo
Queen Mary's Gardens
Maida Vale
Somers Town
Finsbury
Hoxton
Clerkenwell
Shoreditch
Bloomsbury
Marylebone
Fitzrovia
Paddington
Bayswater
Holborn
The City
Soho
Covent Garden
Chinatown
Mayfair
St James's
Hyde Park
The Serpentine
The Long Water
Kensington Gardens
The Round Pond
Green Park
St James's Park
Westminster
Knightsbridge
Belgravia
Kensington
South Kensington
Brompton
Earl's Court
Chelsea
West Brompton
Pimlico
South Bank
Bankside
Borough
Waterloo
Lambeth
Newington
Walworth
Kennington/Oval
Nine Elms
River Thames
Houses of Parliament
Westminster Abbey
British Museum
British Library
Science Museum
Natural History Museum
Victoria & Albert Museum
Imperial War Museum
Tate Modern
National Theatre
National Gallery
Buckingham Palace
St Paul's Cathedral
London Eye
City Hall
0.5 mile
1 km
© Copyright Time Out Group 2010